AREA 2

100
Graphic
Designers

10
Curators

10
Design
Classics

005 --- Preface

10 Design Classics
----
410 --- *De Unie* by J.J.P. Oud
411 --- *Turks Fruit* by Jan Vermeulen
412 --- *Formosa* by Enzo Mari
413 --- *Nella nebbia di Milano* by Bruno Munari
414 --- *La lutte continue* by Jan van Toorn
415 --- *Mask* by Bradbury Thompson
416 --- *Posters* by Alexander Rodchenko
417 --- *Is It In* by Peter Palombi
418 --- *Het Nederlandse affiche* by Wim Crouwel
419 --- *Akarui ankoku* by Tsunehisa Kimura

100 Graphic Designers
----
008 --- A Practice For Everyday Life
012 --- Antoine+Manuel
016 --- Tarek Atrissi
020 --- Marian Bantjes
024 --- Barbara Says
028 --- Big Active
032 --- Peter Bilak
036 --- Julia Born
040 --- Laurenz Brunner
044 --- Build
048 --- Büro Uebele
052 --- Thomas Buxó
056 --- Catalogtree
060 --- Theseus Chan
064 --- Change Is Good
068 --- Deanne Cheuk
072 --- Cristina Chiappini
076 --- Brian Chippendale
080 --- Peter Cho
084 --- Cobbenhagen & Hendriksen
088 --- Paul Cox
092 --- Vanessa van Dam
096 --- Sara De Bondt
100 --- Dexter Sinister
104 --- Bob van Dijk
108 --- Arem Duplessis
112 --- Enlightenment
116 --- EYE
120 --- Stephen Farrell
124 --- FLAG Aubry/Broquard
128 --- Flamingo Studio
132 --- Friends With You
136 --- Martin Frostner
140 --- Mieke Gerritzen
144 --- Good Design Company
148 --- Arjan Groot
152 --- Michelle Gubser
156 --- Hansje van Halem
160 --- George Hardie
164 --- Jonathan Hares
168 --- Kazunari Hattori
172 --- Will Holder
176 --- Homework
180 --- Mario Hugo
184 --- Keiko Itakura
188 --- Keiji Ito
192 --- James Jarvis
196 --- Körner Union
200 --- Laboratoires CCCP
204 --- Jürg Lehni

208 --- Lehni-Trüb
212 --- Ghariokwu Lemi
216 --- LUST
220 --- MadeThought
224 --- Eduardo Marín
228 --- Gabriel Martínez Meave
232 --- Luna Maurer
236 --- Thomas Mayfried
240 --- Laura Meseguer
244 --- mgmt. design
248 --- Étienne Mineur
252 --- Isabel Naegele
256 --- Namaiki
260 --- Non-Format
264 --- Henrik Nygren
268 --- Office for Editorial Design
272 --- Omnivore
276 --- 178 aardige ontwerpers
280 --- Eddie Opara
284 --- Mark Owens
288 --- Paper Rad
292 --- Radim Peško
296 --- Post Typography
300 --- Project Projects
304 --- Michael Punchman
308 --- Iman Raad
312 --- Manuel Raeder
316 --- Andy Rementer
320 --- Claudio Rocha
324 --- Michal Sahar
328 --- Martijn Sandberg
332 --- 75B
336 --- Claudia Siegel
340 --- Jennifer Sonderby
344 --- Spector
348 --- Astrid Stavro
352 --- Frauke Stegmann
356 --- Stiletto
360 --- Strange Attractors
364 --- Studio Pip and Co.
368 --- Studio 't Brandt Weer
372 --- Sulki & Min
376 --- Surface
380 --- Fumio Tachibana
384 --- Andrea Tinnes
388 --- Toko
392 --- Typographic Masonry
396 --- Naohiro Ukawa
400 --- United Visual Artists
404 --- Yokoland

10 Curators
----
006 --- Ruedi Baur
Irma Boom
James Goggin
Julia Hasting
Ellen Lupton
Saki Mafundikwa
Jan Middendorp
Dan Nadel
Brett Phillips
Keiichi Tanaami

421 --- Biographies
442 --- Index

G00094621490010

Phaidon Press Limited
Regent's Wharf
All Saints Street
London N1 9PA

Phaidon Press Inc.
180 Varick Street
New York, NY 10014

www.phaidon.com

First published 2008

© 2008 Phaidon Press Limited

Images © their respective designers
unless otherwise stated

ISBN 978 0 7148 4855 6

A CIP catalog record of this book is
available from the British Library.

Designed by Julia Hasting

Typeface designed by Kobi Benezri

Printed in China

Acknowledgments

The publisher would like to thank the one hundred
designers in *Area 2* and the ten curators: Ruedi
Baur, Irma Boom, James Goggin, Julia Hasting,
Ellen Lupton, Saki Mafundikwa, Jan Middendorp, Dan
Nadel, Brett Phillips, and Keiichi Tanaami. ---
The publisher is also grateful to the following
individuals, galleries, and institutions for their
assistance and permission to reproduce images:
Marlous Bervoets, Wim Crouwel, Danese Milano,
Edizioni Corraini, J. M. Meulenhoff Publishers,
Tsunehisa Kimura, MeadWestvaco, Stedelijk Museum,
and Jan van Toorn. --- Texts by Ruedi Baur were
translated from French by Mila Djordjevic, and
texts by Keiichi Tanaami were translated from
Japanese by Yuki Minami.

Preface

Area 2 is the definitive resource on contemporary
graphic design. For this book, ten of the world's
foremost design practitioners and critics each
selected ten influential contemporary designers,
and one design classic—a work that, years after
its creation, continues to shape the way these
leaders think about their craft. --- Whereas
this book's predecessor, *area*, focused strictly
on print media, here *graphic design* means
something more. These are the movers and shakers
of the design world: art directors and artists,
printmakers and performers, publishers and
programmers. *Area 2* is ostensibly a collection of
the most cutting-edge graphic design, but it is
really an extensive visual essay on the state of
visual culture today. It pays little attention
to politics or genre. Traditional Dutch design
rubs shoulders with emerging movements from Japan
and Nigeria, American punk roughs up classic
Swiss restraint, and D.I.Y. basement brainstorms
make their way to Coca-Cola billboards and car
commercials. --- The one hundred designers have
been organized alphabetically, and each one was
given four pages to showcase his or her work.
Beyond this, there is no method, no organizing
theme. The book's grid-less, open layout lets the
images speak for themselves, and with each other.
Area 2 is, above all, a conversation; one that
both challenges what contemporary graphic design
is, and inspires new ideas of what it can be.

Ruedi Baur is a designer and educator based in Zurich. His design studios, Intégral Ruedi Baur et Associés (founded in Paris in 1989) and Integral Ruedi Baur Zurich (founded in Zurich in 2002), develop both 2-D and 3-D projects in various fields of visual communication. Since 1987 he has taught on a regular basis at programs including the École des Beaux-Arts de Lyon and the Leipzig School for Art and Design, where he created the Interdisciplinary Design Institute (2id). Baur has headed the research institute Design2context at the School of Art and Design Zurich since 2004.

Saki Mafundikwa was born in Zimbabwe and educated there through secondary school. He attended college in the United States and in 1985 received an MFA in graphic design from Yale University. Mafundikwa worked in New York City before returning home to found Zimbabwe's first graphic design and new media college, the Zimbabwe Institute of Vigital Arts (ZIVA), a self-funded venture. He is the author of *Afrikan Alphabets*, the first book on African typography, and lectures on this subject at conferences around the world. His dream is to see the evolution of an African design aesthetic.

Irma Boom is an Amsterdam-based graphic designer who specializes in making books. For five years she worked on the 2,136-page *SHV Think Book*, commissioned by SHV Holdings in Utrecht. Boom studied graphic design at the AKI Art Academy in Enschede, then worked for five years at the Dutch Government Publishing and Printing Office in The Hague. In 1991 she founded Irma Boom Office, which handles both cultural and commercial projects. Boom lectures worldwide, and since 1992 has been a critic at Yale University. She has received many awards for her book designs and was the youngest laureate to receive the prestigious Gutenberg Prize for her complete oeuvre.

Jan Middendorp is a Dutch design writer and designer working in Berlin. He has written several books on graphic design and typography, including *Dutch Type* (2004) and *Made with FontFont* (2006, with Erik Spiekermann). He has worked as an exhibition curator for FontShop International, the Meermanno Museum of the Book, and the Beyerd Museum of Graphic Design in The Netherlands. Middendorp writes for *Eye*, *Typo*, *Items*, and several other design magazines. He works as a freelance consultant and editor for typographic companies including Linotype, MyFonts, and LucasFonts.

James Goggin was born in Australia and grew up in six different countries. He opened his London-based studio Practise in 1999 after completing an MA in graphic design at the Royal College of Art. In addition to creating both commissioned and self-initiated projects for Practise, Goggin has worked as a consultant design director for Tate, and as art director of the progressive music magazine *The Wire*. He lectures widely at design schools and contemporary art institutions throughout Europe and the United States.

Dan Nadel is the founder of PictureBox, Inc., a Grammy Award-winning, New York-based book packaging and publishing company. Its most recent releases include Brian Belott's *Wipe That Clock Off Your Face* and *The Ganzfeld 5*. Nadel is the author of *Art Out of Time: Unknown Comic Visionaries 1900-1969* and is an assistant professor of illustration at Parsons The New School for Design.

Julia Hasting is the design director of Phaidon Press. Based until 2007 in New York City, she now lives in Switzerland. Hasting studied graphic design at Staatliche Hochschule für Gestaltung Karlsruhe in Germany. After graduating she worked as a freelance designer and in 1998 moved to London. Hasting's book designs have garnered international recognition and numerous awards. A member of the Alliance Graphique Internationale, Hasting has been a guest professor at the Cooper Union School of Art, a juror in several major design competitions, and a lecturer at international conferences.

Brett Phillips is principal and design director of 3 Deep Design, "one of those studios that arrived on the Australian design scene with little grace," which he founded in Melbourne in 1996. Phillips currently sits on the State and National Councils of the Australian Graphic Design Association, is a member of the advisory board of the Helen Lempriere National Sculpture Award, and chairs the board of management of the Australian contemporary dance company BalletLab. Phillips writes, plays, and contributes constantly.

Keiichi Tanaami was born in Tokyo in 1936. Since then he has engaged in both avant-garde and highly playful creative activities in various fields of art and design, including animation, painting, illustration, and editorial design. He has published two monographs (*Blow Up* and *Layers*) and the animated collections *TANAAMISM* and *TANAAMISM 2*. In 2006 he held a retrospective at Ginza Graphic Gallery in Tokyo, exhibiting more than four decades' worth of his signature psychedelic graphic design.

Ellen Lupton is director of the Graphic Design MFA program at Maryland Institute College of Art in Baltimore. She has produced numerous exhibitions and scholarly books, including *The Kitchen, the Bathroom, and the Aesthetics of Waste* (1992), *Mechanical Brides: Women and Machines from Home to Office* (1993), and *Skin: Surface, Substance + Design* (2002). Lupton's recent titles include *Thinking with Type* (2004) and *D.I.Y.: Design It Yourself* (2006), which she coauthored with her graduate students. She produced *D.I.Y. Kids* (2007) with her sister, Julia Lupton, and their six children.

100 Graphic Designers

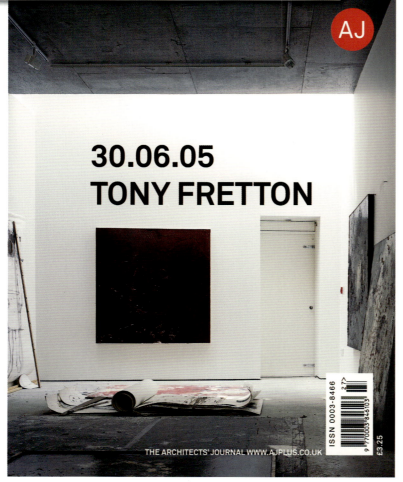

A Practice For Everyday Life (London).
--- The Polish harpsichordist Wanda Landowska
once said, "I never practice; I always play."
When A Practice For Everyday Life (APFEL) first
appeared on my radar, I thought about Landowska's
remark and wondered if it were the same for Kirsty
Carter and Emma Thomas. Do they always just play?
I dare say that their work, like that of any
good design firm, is a constant balance of play,
exploration, and a deliberate crafting of ideas
and emotion. --- The facts, however, are that
APFEL is a graphic design studio based in London,
founded by Carter and Thomas in 2003. The firm
usually works with cultural institutions and
individuals, often for galleries and museums on
publishing and editorial projects. But as you may
know, fact is the enemy of truth, and the truth
of APFEL is that its work is a melting pot of
personal observations, charming character, and
a desire to capture the very essence of a moment.
--- When asked about the qualities that make
APFEL's work unique, Thomas commented that their
aim is "to create work that is simple yet evokes
feeling. We often borrow from rituals and everyday forms, and our work does not look overtly
designed, perhaps because it feels so familiar.
In reality, however, it is designed to the
finest detail." This is a quality evident in
many of APFEL's projects, including the exhibition
design for *London Garage Sale* at the Institute
of Contemporary Arts in London and the design
for the journal *The Happy Hypocrite*. --- Thomas
told me that having a creative manifesto can be
rather restrictive and that the office prefers
to remain open to change and the surprise of
things discovered. Perhaps this is her way of
saying that the designers at APFEL never actually
practice, they always play. --- Brett Phillips

1.   Redesign, *The Architects' Journal*
        magazine, The Architects' Journal,
        UK, 2005. With Sarah Douglas
        ----
2.   Installation poster, "Cineclub" by
        Tobias Putrih at Venice Biennale,
        Tobias Putrih, Italy, 2007

'VENETIAN, ATMOSPHERIC'

AT

52ND INTERNATIONAL ART EXHIBITION LA BIENNALE DI VENEZIA 10 JUNE – 21 NOVEMBER 2007 18.20 – 22.30 DAILY

A FESTIVAL OF INTERNATIONAL ARTIST'S FILM SCREENINGS INSIDE THE SLOVENIAN PAVILION
A PURPOSE BUILT CINEMA BY **TOBIAS PUTRIH**

FILMS BY ARMANDO ANDRADE TUDELA / ROSA BARBA / RÄ DI MARTINO / JOACHIM KOESTER
/ GUILLAUME LEBLON / GABRIEL LESTER / URSULA MAYER / COREY McCORKLE /
DEIMANTAS NARKEVIČIUS / ROSALIND NASHASHIBI AND LUCY SKAER / PABLO PIJNAPPEL
MONOGRAPHIC PROGRAMMES OHO / JOHN SMITH
SPECIAL SCREENINGS 'LES STATUES MEURENT AUSSI' BY CHRIS MARKER AND ALAIN RESNAIS
COMMISSIONER ALEKSANDER BASSIN   DEPUTY COMMISSIONER SARIVAL SOSIČ   CURATORS MARA AMBROŽIČ / FRANCESCO MANACORDA

**ISOLA DI SAN SERVOLO
VENICE – ITALY
BOOKING: +39.3290368551
WWW.VENETIANATMOSPHERIC.COM
TRANSPORT: LINE 20 FROM SAN ZACCARIA
ADMISSION FREE**

3

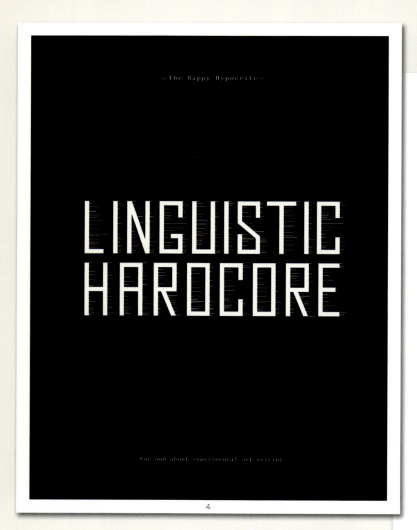

4

5

Say What you See, Issue One, Silo, Letthouse, Autumn 2007

Say what you see

1

2

·EPSTEIN·

6

3. Exhibition identity, *London Garage Sale* by Martha Rosler at the Institute of Contemporary Arts, London, Institute of Contemporary Arts, UK, 2005

4-5. Magazine covers and spreads (proposal), *The Happy Hypocrite*, Bookworks and Maria Fusco, UK, 2007

----

6. Book cover, *Epstein*, about Beatles manager Brian Epstein, *Centre of the Creative Universe: Liverpool and the Avant-Garde*, exhibition at Tate Liverpool, Jeremy Deller and Paul Ryan, UK, 2007

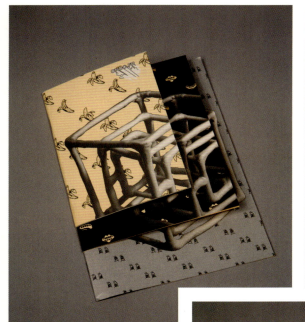

1

Antoine+Manuel (Paris). --- In the early 1990s,
Antoine Audiau and Manuel Warosz morphed into
the two-man studio Antoine+Manuel. Like cartoon
characters discovering super strength, this
transformation gave the designers a new identity
and changed the way they practiced their craft.
With their powers combined as Antoine+Manuel, the
pair lives, works, designs, and creates together.
--- Influenced by television, music, architecture,
and children's books, Antoine+Manuel create a rich
world of stylish daydreams that is both whimsical
and elegant, cartoonish and sophisticated, retro
and fresh. They think of their projects as playgrounds and have been fortunate that clients
like Christian Lacroix, Domestic, and the Collection Lambert en Avignon have given them absolute
freedom to experiment with special materials
and printing techniques. Their work for Domestic,
for example, includes furniture and wall stickers
printed in similar patterns, so coffee tables
look like 2-D illustrations that have come to life
and leapt off the walls. --- Their elaborate and
meticulously detailed illustrations and typography
on posters, wallpaper, cards, and journals are as
rich with meaning as a good story. Lucky for us,
their stories are long, and it's easy to spend
hours following every curve and pattern, finding
a seemingly endless web of mischievous little
details. --- Julia Hasting

1.   Covers, *CNDC journal* nos. 8, 7, 5, and
     6, quarterly publication for the Cen-
     tre national de danse contemporaine
     Angers (CNDC), CNDC, France, 2005-7
     ----
2.   Vinyl wall stickers, "Possession" and
     "Waterfall," Domestic, France, 2005-6
     ----
3.   Wallpaper, "Construction," *Papier
     peint: la peau intérieure* (Wallpaper:
     The Inner Skin) exhibition at the
     Galerie Blanche, France, 2006
     ----
4.   Coffee table, "La France," Edith,
     France, 2007. Equipped with trees,
     nuclear power plants, mountains,
     houses, and buildings, the coffee
     table allows anyone to create his
     or her own French landscape.

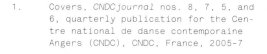

2

3

4

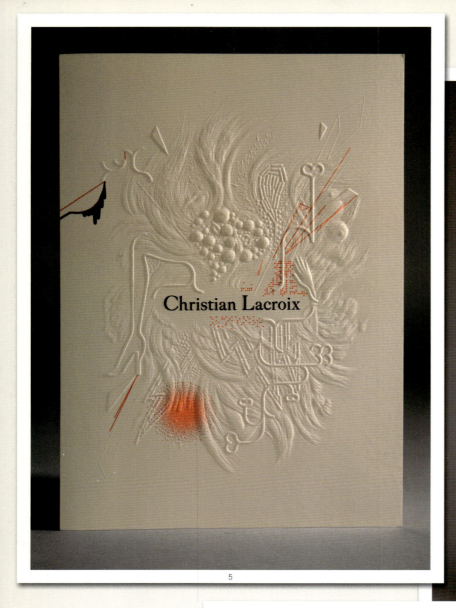

5

6

7

5.   Brochure, Christian Lacroix's Fall-
      Winter 2003-4 haute couture collec-
      tion, Christian Lacroix, France, 2003
      ----
6.   Brochure, Christian Lacroix's Spring-
      Summer 2007 ready-to-wear collection,
      Christian Lacroix, France, 2007
      ----
7.   Brochure, Christian Lacroix's Spring-
      Summer 2006 haute couture collection,
      Christian Lacroix, France, 2006
      ----
8.   Posters, contemporary art exhibition
      at the Collection Lambert en Avignon,
      Collection Lambert en Avignon,
      France, 2002-3
      ----
9.   Posters, "La Comédie de Clermont-
      Ferrand," La Comédie de Clermont-
      Ferrand, France, 2006

8

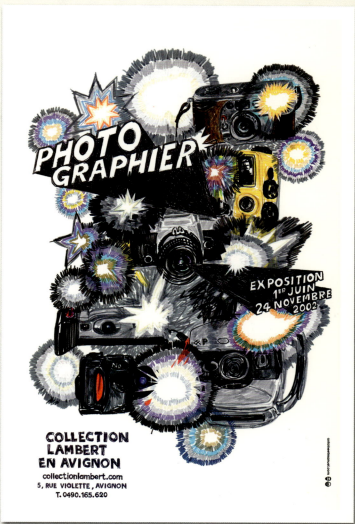

9

15

Tarek Atrissi (Beirut). --- Tarek Atrissi's tri-national education gave him the multicultural edge that has enabled him to strike a balance between the Arabic world and that of modern graphic design. He graduated with a bachelor's degree in graphic design from the American University in his hometown of Beirut, after which he spent a year at the Utrecht School of the Arts (HKU) in The Netherlands, where he earned a master's in interactive multimedia. From there he pursued a master's in design from New York's School of Visual Arts (SVA), where he studied under design luminaries Milton Glaser, Paula Scher, Stefan Sagmeister, and Steven Heller. --- Upon graduating from SVA, Atrissi chose the city of Hilversum, just outside Amsterdam, as the place to set up his own studio. Because Holland is a confluence of Eastern and Western cultures, it is the best location for a young designer who aspires to create work that bridges the two: work that he hopes will present a positive image of the Arab world. Atrissi has chosen the expressive language of Arabic typography (which many in the West find both mysterious and beautiful) as his vehicle to achieve this harmony. While studying at HKU, Atrissi developed arabictypography.com, both as an homage to the Arab world and as a vehicle for exploring the potential of Arabic typography as a visual language in new media. The website was an instant hit, quickly taking on a life beyond its academic origins. It has become an online resource for Arabic type, used by Arab designers around the world. --- Atrissi's extensive studies encouraged his love for design education, and his website reveals an extremely busy lecture and workshop schedule. "I love giving workshops and design or typography courses," he says. "You learn as much as you teach by working with young, energetic students with fresh ideas." The twenty-something designer's meteoric rise and solid reputation was cemented by such unusual (but highly lucrative) projects as the logo and identity design for an Arabic newspaper in Amman, Jordan, and the branding of the small Gulf nation Qatar. "This was a unique opportunity, but also an extremely challenging one," Atrissi says of the Qatar project. "How do you give a visual identity to a complete nation?" Atrissi and his small design studio answered that question with a brilliant identity program. A star is rising in the East. --- Saki Mafundikwa

1

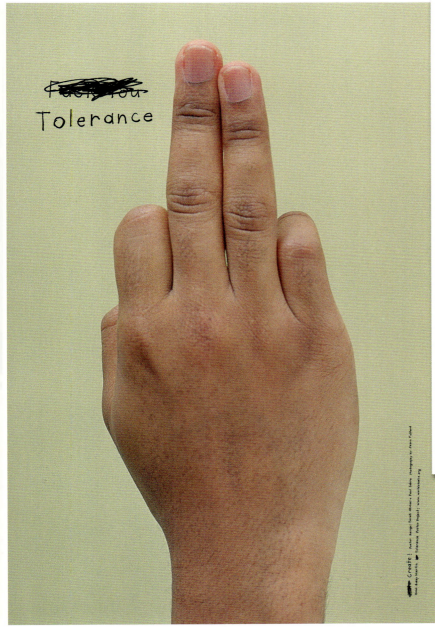

Tolerance

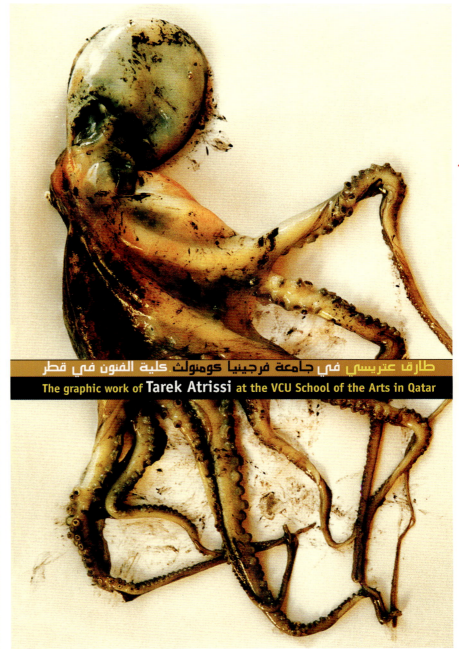

طارق عتريسي في جامعة فرجينيا كومنولث كلية الفنون في قطر

The graphic work of **Tarek Atrissi** at the VCU School of the Arts in Qatar

3

1.   TV show identity, *Top 10 Arabia*, MTV Arabia, United Arab Emirates, 2007

---

2.   Poster, Sphere/World Foundation, Sphere/World Foundation, 2002. With Paul Sahre

---

3.   Exhibition poster, *The Graphic Work of Tarek Atrissi*, VCU School of the Arts in Qatar, Qatar, 2003

www.ExperienceQatar.com

4

5

6

4.	Identity, State of Qatar, State of
	Qatar, Qatar, 2003
- -
5.	Exhibition poster, *Man & God*, self-
	commissioned, international, 2004
- -
6.	Proposal, postage stamps marking the
	2000 Israeli withdrawal from Lebanon,
	Liban Post, Lebanon, 2000
- -
7-8.	Arabic typefaces, various clients,
	The Netherlands, 2003-7

لألأي ي ي ي ى ى و و ه ه ه ن ن ن ـﻤ ـﻤ ـﻤ م
ل ل ل ك ك ك ة ة ق ق ف ف ف ف غ غ غ غ
ع ع ع ظ ظ ظ ظ ط ط ط ط ض ض ض ض ص
خ خ خ ذ ذ د ز ز ر ر س س س س ش ش ش ش ص ص
خ خ ح ح ح ج ج ج ج ث ث ث ت ت ت ت ة
لله ء ء ء ء آ آ أ أ ؤ إ إ ى ئ ئ ئ ا ا ب ب ب ب
٠٩٨٧٦٥٤٣٢١

لا لا ي ي ي ي ى ى و و ه ه ه ن ن ن ـﻤ ـﻤ ـﻤ م
ل ل ل ك ك ك ة ة ق ق ف ف ف ف غ غ غ غ
ع ع ع ظ ظ ظ ظ ط ط ط ط ض ض ض ص
خ خ د د ذ ذ ر ر ز ز س س س س ش ش ش ش ص ص
خ خ ح ح ح ج ج ج ج ث ث ث ت ت ت ة
لله ء ء ء ء آ آ أ أ ؤ إ إ ى ئ ئ ئ ا ا ب ب ب ب
٠٩٨٧٦٥٤٣٢١

Marian Bantjes (Vancouver). --- Once upon a time, Marian Bantjes was a graphic designer: She set type, controlled quality, managed production, and directed a staff. In 2003 she bought herself out of her own company and gradually turned into something else: a graphic artist. --- Marian Bantjes makes art with lines, shapes, and letters. Some of her art is purposeful: It illustrates editorial concepts, promotes events, or converts magazine headlines into intricate structures that seem almost alive. Some of her art is pure art, existing as visual commentary on the contorted history—both personal and epochal—of the written word. Purposeful or pure, all of her work is graphic, in several senses. Graphic art is conceived for reproduction. Even her one-of-a-kind drawings, such as the handmade, personalized valentine cards Bantjes sent to one hundred and fifty friends in 2007, look almost as amazing in print as they do in person. Each one has the detailed intensity of a botanical drawing or a European banknote. The word *graphic* also connotes extreme detail of a visceral sort: To be graphic is to represent acts of love or violence with ferocious realism. Bantjes's valentines take the icon of the heart and study its curved symmetry over and over from different perspectives, unleashing the erotic potential of a saccharine cliché. --- Whether rendering her pieces in digital vectors or in pen, pencil, sugar, or peony leaves, Bantjes grounds them in materiality. She begins most projects by hand, and her love of print and paper is seen in folded pieces printed double-sided on translucent paper; take a look at her poster for Design Matters Live, which she describes as "difficult to represent accurately." You have to touch and see this piece directly to really get it. --- Bantjes lives on a small island in British Columbia, Canada. She stays in touch with the world, however, flying everywhere to conduct lectures and workshops and to collaborate with clients. Her clear voice as a design commentator echoes from the pages of SpeakUp and other blogs. One of her best pieces is—get this—a critique of the alphabet, in which she analyzes every upper/lowercase pair for its innate elegance and inexplicable clumsiness. She has this to say about *Zz*: "Last, but certainly not least, the *Z*, with a final flourish, a sword slash (I know!), a signature of completion. The *Z* has exuberance and balance...alas, with the lowercase *z*, the alphabet goes out with a bang *and* a whimper." --- Ellen Lupton

set in cobra / art &c. by marian bantjes / love / quatrifolio.com / 604.947.9107 / happy hallowe'en

2

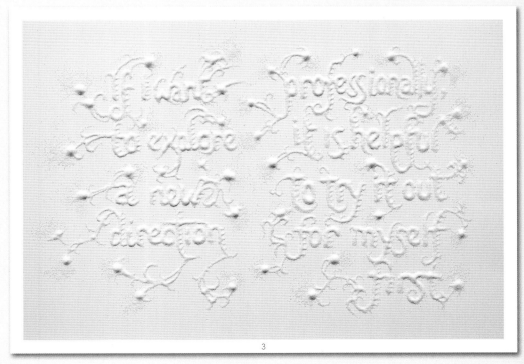

3

1. Title page, *WIRED* magazine, "The Church of the Non-Believers," WIRED, USA, 2006

----

2. Greeting, "Hallowe'en 2005," self-commissioned, Canada, 2005

----

3. Illustration, "If you want to explore...," Stefan Sagmeister, USA, 2007. One of a series of typographical illustrations composed of sugar crystals

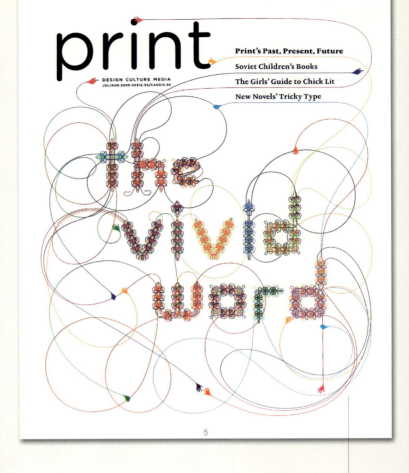

4. Event poster, Design Matters Live:
   Life, Love, and the Pursuit of
   Design, hosted by Debbie Millman,
   Adobe and AIGA San Francisco, USA,
   2007. Printed on translucent paper
   ----
5. Cover, *Print* magazine, Print,
   USA, 2006
   ----
6. Hand-drawn valentines (20 of 150),
   "150 Valentines," self-commissioned,
   Canada, 2007
   ----
7. Poster, Graphex '06, Society of
   Graphic Designers of Canada, BC Chapter, Canada, 2005

Looking for the Canadian in Design

Graphex 05

Call for entries
Deadline
10 November 2005

1

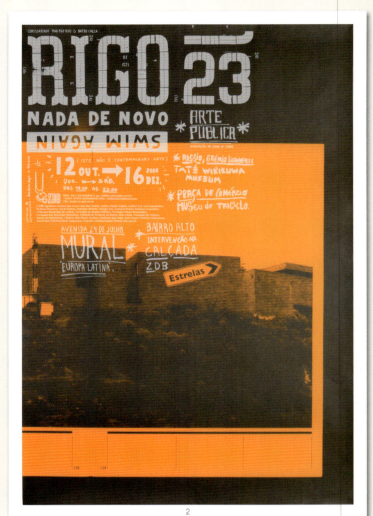

2

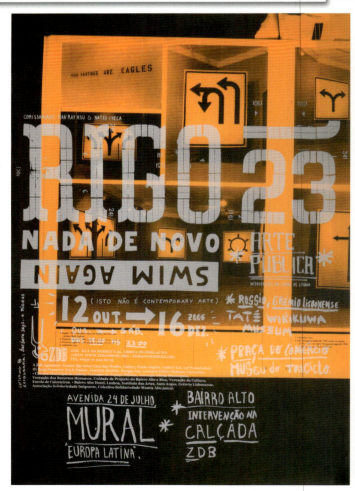

Barbara Says (Lisbon). --- In a graphic culture that knows no boundaries, where trends spread across the globe within weeks, it is crucial that designers retain a sense of place. Awareness of one's roots is probably the most effective remedy for the kind of homogenized design that is either mere function (neutral solutions to problems) or mere form (any trend that's in this month). For António Silveira Gomes, founder of the Portuguese design group Barbara Says, being based in Lisbon is a crucial aspect of his work. Though international in scope, it is rooted in urban texture and often directed at a local audience. --- One of the earliest successes of Barbara Says was the local art magazine *Flirt,* published by a cutting-edge gallery in downtown Lisbon called Zé dos Bois (ZDB). More recently, Silveira Gomes conceived a broadsheet called *Pão* (Bread), written by the inhabitants of two neighborhoods in central Lisbon. --- In creating typographic constructions, Barbara Says often reuses imagery from the Portuguese past. A poster for ZDB was designed with the boldest, most exuberant vintage blackletter initials one is likely ever to come across; another one uses intricate, historical, tree-shaped letterforms. An intriguing recent project is the identity for the 2006 and 2007 Cinema Portugal film festivals. To create his typeface Plateia, Silveira Gomes constructed an alphabet from old theater floor plans. It's a simple reminder that cinema is not just something you watch, but a social event you can share with others in a special space. --- There's a subtle irony in the use of these carefully selected pieces of cultural debris. It is not motivated by some sort of nostalgic intent, nor by a postmodern compulsion to sample artifacts from the past at random. Used in a decidedly contemporary context, these fragments of history—the history that weighs so heavily on European culture and especially on Portugal's tradition-soaked capital—may even pass for a kind of playful exorcism. --- Jan Middendorp

3

1. Conference poster, Formato, Portuguese Architects Guild, Portugal, 2004
   ----
2. Exhibition posters, *Rigo 23: Nada de novo* (Swim Again), ZDB, Portugal, 2006-7
   ----
3. Poster and program, Instituto do Cinema, Audiovisual e Multimedia (ICAM), Portugal, 2006

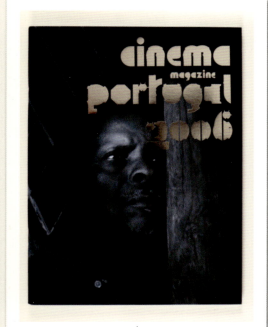

4

5

V-1.0.0
plateia

! ( ) ★ + , -

. $ 0 1 2 3 4 5 6 7

8 9 : ; ? a b c d e

f g h i j k l m n o

p q r s t u v w x y

z é ç é á a ã

õ í ó ó ô o à ã á

í ó ó ✳ • • • t

popcorn

row k

seat 23 | barbara says...

6

4. Cover and spreads, *Cinema Portugal* magazine for the 2006 Cannes Film Festival, ICAM, Portugal, 2006
----
5. Poster, Cinema Portugal, ICAM, Portugal, 2007
----
6. Typeface, Plateia, ICAM, Portugal, 2006
----
7. Exhibition poster and invitation, *Metaflux: Two Generations in Recent Portuguese Architecture*, Instituto das Artes, Portugal, 2005

metaflux

duas gerações na arquitectura portuguesa recente

11_12 >> 30_1_2005
Torreão Nascente da Cordoaria Nacional

+ O contexto urbano português visto por:

Guedes + deCampos
Inês Lobo
João Mendes Ribeiro
Promontório Arquitectos
Serôdio, Furtado & Associados

a.s* atelier de santos
Bernardo Rodrigues
marcosandmarjan architects
Nuno Brandão Costa
S'A Arquitectos

Augusto Alves da Silva
Didier Fiuza Faustino
Nuno Cera + Diogo Lopes
Pedro Bandeira
Rui Toscano

Comissariado: Pedro Gadanho e Luís Tavares Pereira

De Terça a Domingo, das 10h00 às 19h00. Tel: 21 3642909. www.lisboacultural.pt. www.iartes.pt/metaflux

Produção em Lisboa: Câmara Municipal de Lisboa. **Organização:** Instituto das Artes / Ministério da Cultura

7

27

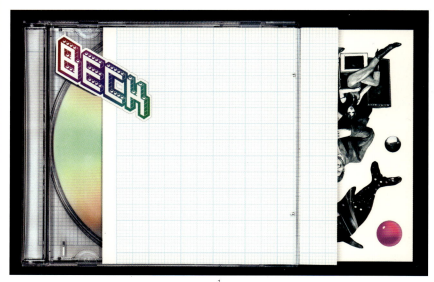

1

Big Active (London). --- Try to pigeonhole Big
Active; I dare you! Try, and you may well be
karate-chopped by the Lego-like letterforms from
Beck's latest album cover or punched with a
Goldfrapp-logo knuckle-duster. I don't necessarily
get the impression that Big Active's Gerard Saint,
Mat Maitland, Richard Andrews, and Markuss
Karlsson are violent people, but take heed: Their
work has just that kind of spirit. --- Big Active
seems exactly that: both *big* and *active*. You
only have to read these lines from the group's
biography to appreciate its straight-up attitude
toward visual communication: "If an idea can't
be articulated simply and successfully over the
phone, it ain't worth a fuck. Our philosophy has
always been to produce work that is bold, spirited, and makes you look. Life's too short to
get sidetracked." You don't have to dig too deep
into Big Active's archive to find evidence that
its designers mean what they say. --- Big Active's
graphic approach is particularly focused in the
specialized areas of music, editorial, and book
design, and they have produced numerous high-
profile branding campaigns and music packaging for
acts like Beck, Goldfrapp, Athlete, Garbage, The
Futureheads, and Basement Jaxx. The firm's music
design work has won them much critical acclaim,
including a prestigious Global Award from D&AD
for the design of the Beck album *The Information*.
In addition to its music graphics, Big Active is
highly regarded for its book and editorial projects, among them the award-winning redesign of
Viewpoint, the international journal of marketing
trends. --- Big Active is unique in that it also
represents other commercial artists. The bigger
picture of the studio includes a number of associ-
ate image-makers, illustrators, and photographers,
all represented under the Big Active umbrella.
This visual synergy creates a dynamic and proac-
tive creative environment—one that no doubt
fosters the depth and energy in their portfolio.
I think that Henry Ford may have said it best:
"You can't build a reputation on what you are
going to do." Big Active has built its through
sheer energy, commitment, and a set of throwing
stars in the shape of the Basement Jaxx logo!
--- Brett Phillips

1.   CD packaging with stickers, *The
      Information* by Beck, Interscope,
      USA, 2006
      ----
2.   CD cover, *The Futureheads* by The
      Futureheads, 679 Recordings, UK, 2004
      ----
3.   CD cover, *Chemistry Is What We Are* by
      Simian, Source Records, Germany, 2001
      ----
4.   CD cover, *Tourist* by Athlete, EMI,
      UK, 2005

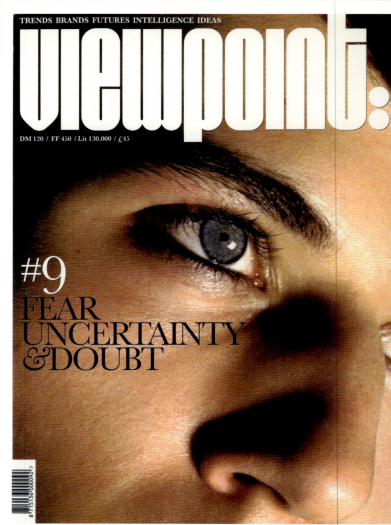

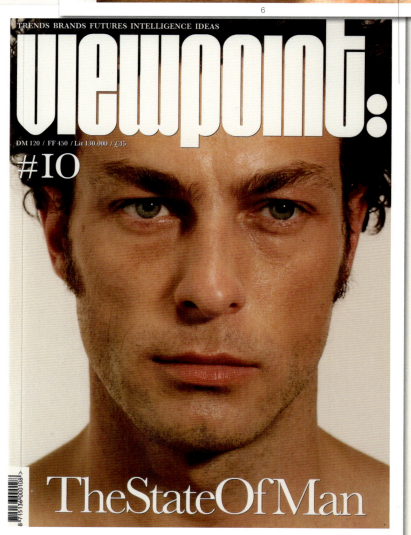

5

6

7

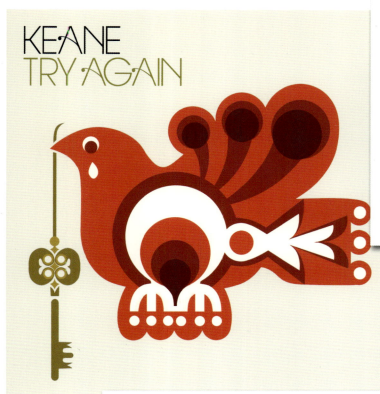

8

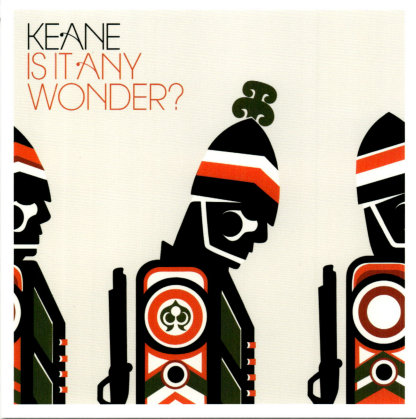

5.   CD cover, *Black Cherry* by Goldfrapp,
      Mute, UK, 2003
      ----
6.   Covers, *Viewpoint* magazine nos. 9 and
      10, Viewpoint and Metropolitan Pub-
      lishing, 2001
      ----
7.   CD cover, *Rooty* by Basement Jaxx, XL
      Recordings, UK, 2001
      ----
8.   CD cover and singles campaign,
      Under the Iron Sea by Keane, Island,
      UK, 2006

1

Peter Bilak (The Hague). --- In certain cases, a designer can boast of having created something truly useful for the community. Unfortunately, most designers content themselves with developing things that are useful only for their clients. I would say that this difference is fundamental and revealing of the essence of the designer. No one asked Peter Bilak to integrate the entire set of characters used in various Central European languages into his typeface Fedra, and to thereby create a common cultural tool. That kind of initiative generally comes from the designer, not from a client. In my opinion, it distinguishes true design from mere advertising. --- The achievements of this Hague-based Slovakian designer reveal a humanistic attitude toward design. Bilak is first and foremost a type designer; Fedra became an instant contemporary classic at the dawn of this century. But the range of his work is not limited to the design of typefaces. He also uses, cultivates, and celebrates them. On a few square millimeters of a Dutch postage stamp, on posters, on theater sets, or even as the theme of the dances performed on those sets, Bilak's subtle play with letterforms is what ultimately makes them a valuable part of our daily lives. --- Ruedi Baur

1.   Poster, Nederlands Dans Theater choreography workshop, Nederlands Dans Theater, The Netherlands, 2006
----
2.   Postage stamps, Royal TPG Mail, The Netherlands, 2003-4
----
3.   Postage stamps (proposal), Royal TPG Mail, The Netherlands, 2003-4
----
4.   Exhibition announcement, Hedah Center for Contemporary Art Maastricht, Hedah Center for Contemporary Art Maastricht, The Netherlands, 2005-6. This series mimics the museum's practice of leaving traces in its galleries of all previous exhibitions.

2

3

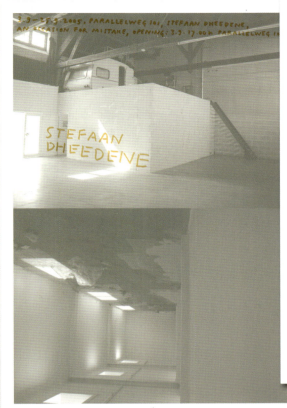

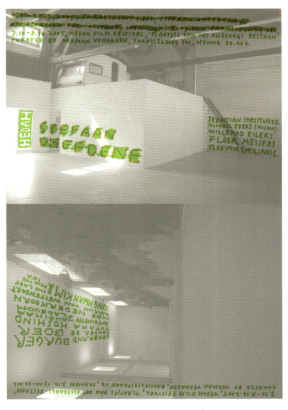

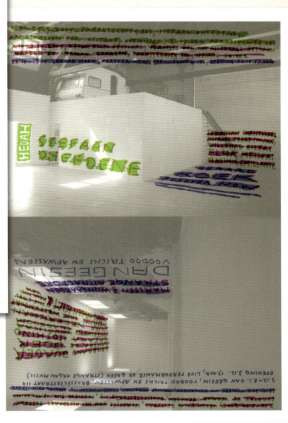

4

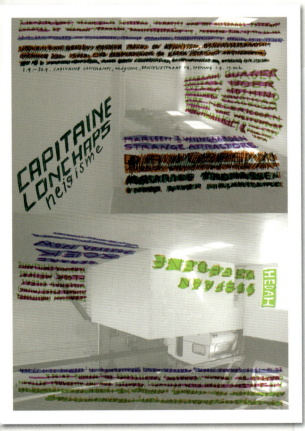

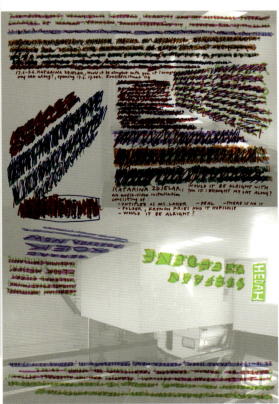

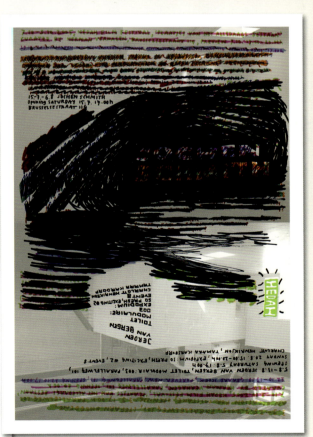

33

Fedra Serif A

A new typeface by Peter Bil'ak coming in Book, Normal, Medium and Bold including *Italics*, SMALL CAPS & expert fonts with plenty of ligatures, alternate characters and two construction variants.

& Et & V & & & & et &

Fedra Serif B

Instead of seeking inspiration in the past, *Fedra Serif* is a synthetic typeface where aesthetic and technological decisions are linked. *Fedra Serif* combines seemingly contradictory ways of constructing characters in one harmonious font. Its *humanistic roots* (rhythm of the handwriting) is balanced with *rational drawing* (a coarse computer-screen grid). *Fedra Serif* has 4 weights, italics, small caps, and expert sets for each weight and three different numeral systems (proportional, lining figures; old style figures; and tabular, fixed-width figures). The font also comes in two different versions with different lengths of the ascenders and descenders (stem lengths). Version A matches the proportions of Fedra Sans, with a large x-height and short stem length. Version B prolongs the stem lengths up to 12%, and increases the contrast making it suitable for traditional book printi... result in a typeface sui... typographic problems.

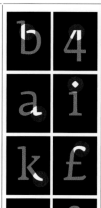

Fedra Sans

by Peter Bil'ak

A new sans serif, originally designed as a corporate font for one of those huge companies; now completed, updated, and ready to use in all formats. *Available in five weights, with three different numeral systems, real italics, small capitals, and expert sets full of ligatures, fractions, arrows, symbols and other useful little things.*

Aa *Aa*

Fedra Sans Light
Fedra Sans *Book*
Fedra Sans *Normal*
Fedra Sans *Medium*
Fedra Sans *Bold*

← ↖ ↑ ↗ → ↘ ↓ ↙

Đ	đ	Ł	ł	Š	š	Ý	ý	Þ	þ	Ž	ž	½	¼	'	¾	³	²	!
-	×	!	#	$	%	&	'	(	)	*	+	,	-	.	/	0	1	2
3	4	5	6	7	8	9	:	;	=	>	<	?	@	A	B	C	D	E
F	G	H	I	J	K	L	M	N	O	P	Q	R	S	T	U	V	W	X
Z	Y	[	\	]	^	_	`	a	b	c	d	e	f	g	h	i	j	k
l	m	n	o	p	q	r	s	t	u	v	w	x	y	z	{			}	~
Ä	Å	Ç	É	Ñ	Ö	Ü	á	à	â	ä	ã	å	ç	é	è	ê	ë	í
ì	î	ï	ñ	ó	ò	ô	ö	õ	ú	ù	û	ü	†	°	¢	£	§	•
¶	ß	®	©	™	´	¨	≠	Æ	Ø	∞	±	≤	≥	¥	µ	∂	Σ	Π
π	∫	ª	º	Ω	æ	ø	¿	¡	¬	√	ƒ	≈	Δ	«	»	…	À	Ã
Õ	Œ	œ	–	—	"	"	'	'	÷	◊	ÿ	Ÿ	⁄	€	‹	›	fi	
fl	ffi	ffl	ff	fk	fh	fj	‡	·	‚	„	‰	Â	Ê	Á	Ë	È	Í	Î
Ï	Ì	Ó	Ô		Ò	Ú	Û	Ù	ı	ˆ	˜	¯	˘	˙	˚	¸	˝	˛

www.typotheque.com
sales@typotheque.com
Fax +31-84-831 6741

Fedra Sans was originally commissioned by Paris-based Ruedi Baur Integral Design and developed as a corporate font for Bayerische Rück, a German insurance company, as part of their new visual identity. According to the commissioner, the objective was to 'de-protestantize Univers', the typeface which Bayerische Rück had been using since Otl Aicher designed their first visual identity in the 1970s. The typeface reflects the original brief: it humanizes the communicated message and adds climate, informal elegance. The most important criterion was to create a typeface which works equally well on paper and on the computer screen, and is consistent across all computer platforms. After first versions of the typeface were completed and digitized, the project was cancelled as Bayerische Rück was acquired by another even larger multinational corporation. This put an early end to the story of the custom font. Since a lot of work had been done already, I decided to complete the typeface, adding extra weights and expert fonts. Shortly before the planned release date of the typeface, my studio was broken into, and my computers and back-up system containing all the font data were stolen. What initially seemed like the ultimate designer's disaster was actually beneficial for Fedra. The incident delayed its release, allowing me to re-examine the early design decisions, made under the assumption that the font would be exclusive to the company and never publicly available. The new version is more versatile, offering a wider range of fonts, a number of special typographic features.

5

5.   Typefaces, Fedra Sans, Fedra Serif, and Fedra Mono, self-commissioned, The Netherlands, 2001-7
      ----
6.   Lecture poster, Peter Bilak: Modular Talk, Istituto Europeo di Design di Milano, Italy, 2006

Fedra Mono™

Fedra Mono was developed for an annual report that required a fixed-width counterpart to *Fedra Sans*. All the characters share the same width, which makes it suitable for tabular setting when the information benefit from the vertical alignment of characters. The typical example would be spreadsheet or computer code.

Fedra Mono is a 10-pitch face, which means 10 characters equals one inch (2.54 cm) when set at 10 pt. All the characters, regardless of weight, have the same width, which is 60% of the em square. Those are also the proportions of the 1956 version of *Courier*. However, despite the fixed widths, *Fedra Mono* remains relatively even in typographic color, and lucid on screen. The various potentially similar characters are clearly distinguishable, notably I, l and 1, and 0 and 0, as well as brackets, braces and parentheses.

Some languages use two characters to represent a single phoneme; those double characters (ǳ ij ǉ), are called digraphs. Proportional fonts can use regular string of letters to represent digraphs, and do not require designing special characters. However, since all the characters in monospaced fonts must have the same widths, a special collection of digraphs has to be drawn for monospaced fonts. Unlike ligatures, digraphs should be *case-consistent*, with both upper, and lower case variants of the digraphs. Albanian, Basque, Breton, Czech, Croat, Dutch, Hungarian, Latvian, Lithuanian, Maltese, Slovak, Spanish and Welsh use digraphs.

Fedra Mono is available in Standard Latin, Central European, Baltic and Turkish encodings for Mac and PC.

a
i
¥
ij

Light
Book
Normal
Medium
Bold

Order online 24/7 on our secure server at www.typotheque.com, or just preview all our fonts with our interactive FontTester™

www.typotheque.com
info@typotheque.com

Peter Bilak: modular talk
29.05.2006

Istituto Europeo di Design di Milano
via Sciesa 4

IED Arti Visive

Julia Born (Amsterdam). --- I sent Julia Born a questionnaire to get some background information from this designer, whose work I've admired for some time, but she never returned it. I took this as a good sign, in a way—it meant that she is as busy as I am! --- Once I was at a book distributor's office, and I saw a volume designed by Born with the intriguing title *Beauty and the Book*. Of course, I had to have it. The book covers sixty years of Swiss book design, but it looks very modest, printed basically in black and white, with only twelve pages in full color. Behind its simple cover is a manual on caring for books, with all the dos and don'ts of handling them. Born explains the crimes by committing them, demonstrating techniques like dog-earing pages to mark different languages of text. There are also printed markings that look like pencil notes, until you try to erase them, as I did (*Shit, these won't come off!*). All these details make the book quite personal and accessible. It's perfect: a good idea, well executed, both serious and absolutely beautiful. You can feel the strong, purposeful concept and intentions of its designer. --- I am on the mailing list of Casco, a design space in Utrecht. I have never been there, but I collect all the invitations and flyers they send me, if only to catalog Born's designs. The identity she created is based only on the choice of the typeface and the position of the word *Casco*. It is smart, lively, elegant, and always surprising, as are all of Born's clever and honest projects. Thank you, Julia, for making such good work. My life is better because of it. --- Irma Boom

1. Book cover and spreads, *Ofoffjoff: One to One*, self-commissioned, The Netherlands, 2007. With fashion designer JOFF

2-3. Exhibition posters, *Ofoffjoff: One to One*, Ideal Showroom, Germany, 2007
-----
4. Performance programs, "Secret Instructions" by Julia Born and Alexandra Bachzetsis, self-commissioned, The Netherlands, 2005. Based on six classic twentieth-century plays
-----
5. Stage design, "Secret Instructions" by Julia Born and Alexandra Bachzetsis, self-commissioned, The Netherlands, 2005

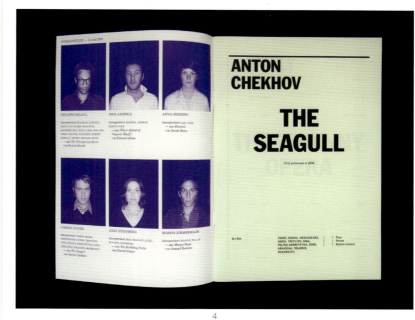

4

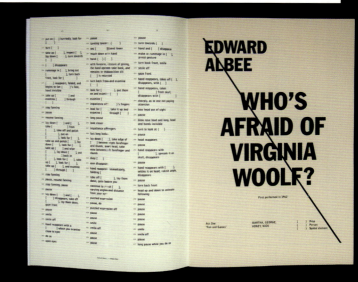

5

10

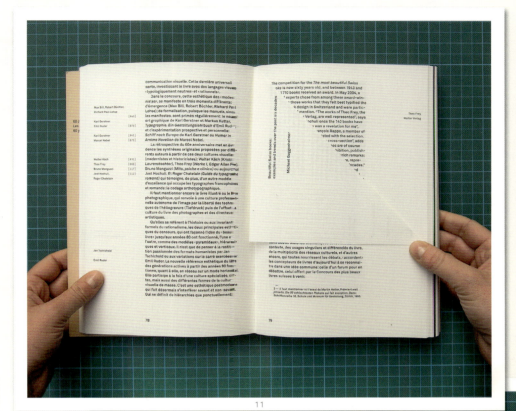

11

6–9. Identity, exhibition posters, and
      invitations, Casco Office for Art,
      Design, and Theory, Casco, The
      Netherlands, 2006

10–11. Book cover and spreads, *Beauty and
       the Book: Sixty Years of the Most
       Beautiful Swiss Books*, Swiss Federal
       Office of Culture, Switzerland, 2004

Laurenz Brunner (Amsterdam). --- I collaborated
with Laurenz Brunner on several projects while
he was still a student at Central Saint Martins
College of Art and Design in London, and even at
that time his work was advanced enough for our
relationship to be one of equals rather than
of student and teacher. Prior to his graphic
design studies and newfound recognition in the
field, Brunner was well known in Switzerland as
a hip-hop DJ. It may seem slightly lazy, but I'll
use his dual positions in the design studio and
on the turntables to note a rare combination of
precision and freshness: His almost precocious
typographic and compositional skills parallel his
skillz on the decks. --- After working with me on
typefaces and posters for Tate Modern, Laurenz
skipped over to Amsterdam's Gerrit Rietveld
Academie to complete his education. He now bases
his practice there, with the odd stint in his
Swiss hometown, Zurich. Occasionally collaborating
with fellow Swiss ex-pat and Rietveld lecturer
Julia Born, as well as Zurich-based art director
Cornel Windlin, he designs posters, publications,
exhibitions, and typefaces for art organizations,
clubs, publishers, and—perhaps most famously—the
Swiss type foundry Lineto. His rational sans serif
Akkurat quickly caught the typographic zeitgeist
and has subtly muscled its way into books, identities, magazines, and even the new signage system
at London's renovated Royal Festival Hall.
Although Akkurat is more an elegant and approach-
able update of standard German industrial typefaces than a successor to Helvetica, comparisons
with the omnipresent Swiss classic are not
entirely misplaced—at least when it comes to
Akkurat's potential for achieving a similar ubiq-
uity in the twenty-first century. --- Brunner's
balancing act of order and expression is evident
in the poster series he designed for an Amsterdam
club night he also helped found. Using the Pantone
color system as a theme (#802 and #072 so far),
guest designers and DJs contribute illustrations
that Brunner arranges. For the Right About Now
lecture series, Brunner circumvented the usual
monetary constraints of cultural clients by basing
everything—from flyers, folders, and posters to
the event identity itself—on the humble A4 sheet.
With the client able to print A4 photocopies in-
house, the design system transcended the materials
through striking typography and compositions held
together by custom-designed packing tape. Similar
thinking and logic flows through all of Brunner's
projects, resulting in perfectly appropriate solutions spoken with a bold graphic voice.
--- James Goggin

1

1.   Poster, Akkurat Schwarz typeface,
        Lineto, Switzerland, 2006

2-3.   Poster #072 and flyer #802, self-
        commissioned, The Netherlands, 2007.
        With Jop van Bennekom and Gert
        Jonkers, Julia Born and Joff, Karl
        Grandin, Melanie Bonajo, Laurenz
        Brunner, Anne de Vries, Femke Dekker,
        Experimental Jetset, Karl Grandin,
        and Parra

3

2

4

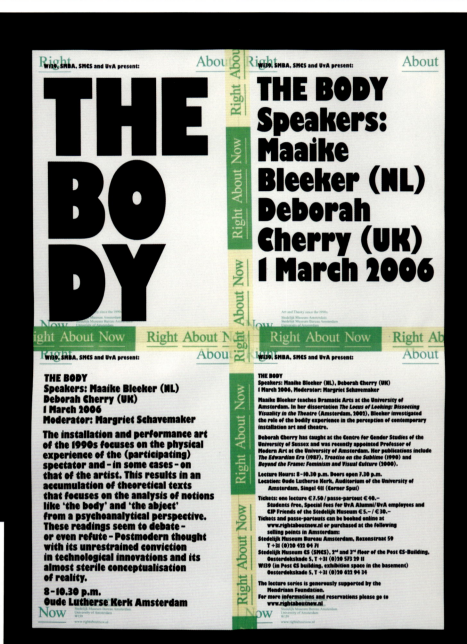

5

4-5.   Lecture series identity, Right
        About Now, Stedelijk Museum, SMBA,
        Gallery W139, and University of
        Amsterdam, The Netherlands, 2006.
        With Julia Born
        ----
6.   "Color Translation (study)," Pantone
        spectrum, original and black-and-
        white copy, self-commissioned, The
        Netherlands, 2004

6

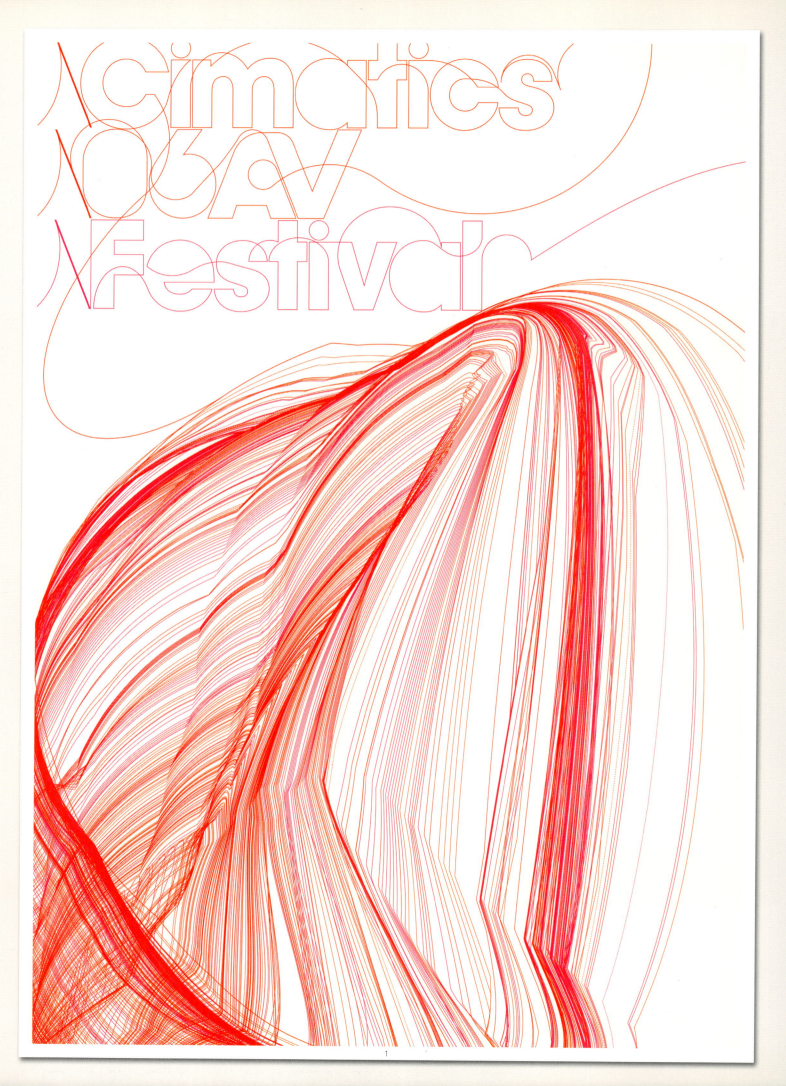

Build (London). --- Make a diary note of the
following historical event: It was 17 September
2001, when Build was first built. It was quite
possibly a gray, rainy day in England (isn't it
always?), but I imagine it was a little brighter
than usual on Cantelowes Road, NW1 9XU. It was on
this day that Michael Place first switched on his
super computer. --- Place is standing before the
perfectly formed and customized stainless-steel
box as it begins to glow, his arms raised in the
air, reciting Eldon Tyrell's line from *Blade
Runner*: "The light that burns twice as bright
burns for half as long, and you have burned so
very, very brightly." His dark silhouette is
suddenly illuminated by a wry smile, and a long,
evil belly laugh is heard echoing down the now-
deserted streets. Mothers hold their children
close, while fathers board up the windows. Yet
among the impending chaos and disorder, I can
also imagine Place stopping for a cup of tea and
a biscuit. Strange. --- Place was born in North
Yorkshire, England, in 1969. Yes, sir, he is a
Yorkshireman—a Yorkshireman who loves his wife,
is obsessed with design, and apparently still
manages a smile when he gets his wallet out.
After leaving college in 1990, he went to work
at Bite IT in London, with Trevor Jackson. In 1992
he started work at the Designers Republic, where
he contributed an undoubtedly intense nine years
of his life. In talking about what he does, he
admits, "I love graphic design. I can't think
of anything else that I could do. I hate graphic
design. Fourteen years, 5,110 days, 122,640 hours,
7,358,400 minutes, 441,504,000 seconds, and counting. It's all about detail. It's a craft. I can't
switch it off. It's an obsession; graphic design
is an obsession for me." --- Build works under
the slogan "Print with Love," and I think this
sums up a big part of what the studio does. If
you can get past Place's plans for world domina-
tion and his unhealthy English obsession with tea
and biscuits, I think you will enjoy the beauty
in his work. --- Brett Phillips

1-2.   Identity and poster, Cimatics '06 AV
       Festival, GreatShare, Belgium, 2006
----
3.   Poster, self-commissioned, UK, 2006.
       Printed in phosphorescent ink

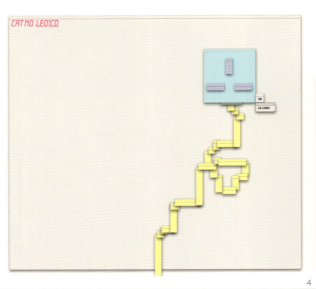
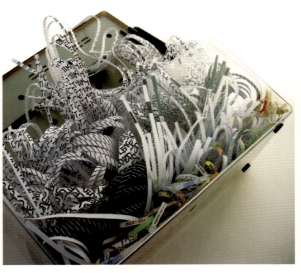

4

4. CD packaging, *LE:01* compilation,
London Electrics, UK, 2005
----
5. Vinyl and CD packaging, *Simple Sounds*
series, Simple Records, UK, 2007

Forest
~Outdoor/Nature
~Epping Forest—1 (lower)
5635

simplecd03

Design Studio
~Indoor/Office space
~Studio Build
5565

Car Park
~Outdoor/Urban-space
~Open ground
425

Recording Studio
~Indoor/Studio space
~Will Saul-Brixton
7536

1

2

3

4

5

Büro Uebele (Stuttgart). --- On rare occasions, we stop before a piece of design that seems so natural, so in tune with our own creative sensibility, that we think we could have been its creator. Such is frequently our experience when we view the signage systems created by Andreas Uebele and nis studio. --- If only I had designed his orientation system for the Osnabrück University of Applied Sciences! That project is an example of how signage can give new value to a building, furnishing it with a substantial, previously missing identity. It shows how an industrial roofscape can be transformed into a medium for typographic creation and demonstrates that even the basic grotesque, from which Uebele rarely departs, can be fascinating. --- Graphic simplicity is a permanent feature of Uebele's projects. The clarity, cohesion, and efficiency of his work situate him in the rich tradition of modernist German graphic design: the Bauhaus, the Ulm School, anc the Schwäbisch Gmünd. His architectural background and unique spatial understanding enable him to carry the tenets of these established styles into the present day. A rich new terrain of expression thus opens up at the frontier between architecture and graphic design. Could it also allow for the revitalization of more traditional forms of media? --- Ruedi Baur

6

1-3. Signage, Osnabrück University of Applied Sciences, Osnabrück University of Applied Sciences, Germany, 2004
----
4. Signage, Pappas car dealership, Pappas, Austria, 2006
----
5. Identity, Designers' Saturday 2001, Designers' Saturday, Germany, 2001
----
6. Signage, DGF Stoess AG, DGF Stoess AG, Germany, 2002

alsterdorf hamburgstadt
alsterdorfer werkstätten
arbeitssicherheit werner
otto institut krankenpfle
geschule hamburgumlan
d abfall und umwelttech
nik alstergärtner evange
lisches krankenhaus alst
erdorf bugenhagenschul
en ithaki to hus alsterdo
rf alster service center a
lsterzwirn hamburgstadt
kindertagesstätte moorw

7

9

7.   Identity, Evangelische Stiftung
      Alsterdorf, Evangelische Stiftung
      Alsterdorf, Germany, 2006
      ----
8.   Identity, Strassburger Modeacces-
      soires, Strassburger Modeaccessoires,
      Germany, 2004
      ----
9.   Identity, Arthaus Filmtheater, Peter
      Erasmus and Arthaus Filmtheater,
      Germany, 2002
      ----
10.   Poster, Künstlerhaus Stuttgart,
      Künstlerhaus Stuttgart, Germany, 2004
      ----
11.   Exhibition poster, Joseph Binder
      Awards, Düsseldorf University of
      Applied Sciences, Germany, 2000
      ----
12.   Signage, Parseval School Bitterfeld,
      Eicher Siebdruck, Germany, 2000

10

11

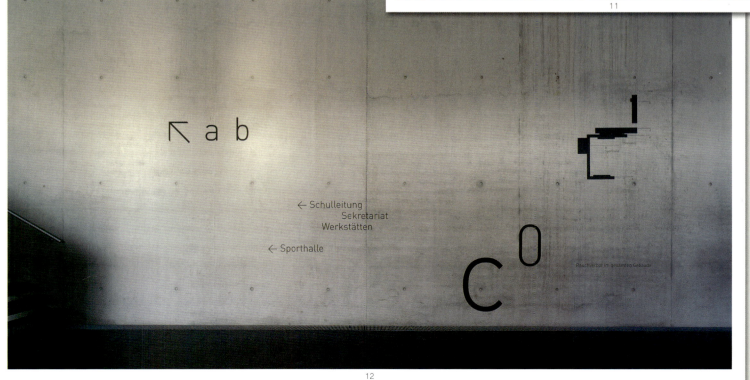

12

Thomas Buxó (Amsterdam). --- Thomas Buxó is a
French designer with a Catalan name. The design
writers Aaron Betsky and Adam Eeuwens say he
is "balder than Jop van Bennekom and more Dutch
than the Dutch." His therapist says he is an
Englishman in New York. No wonder some of his
friends suspect him of playing identity games.
--- At the age of eleven, in the late 1970s, Buxó
began collecting stickers. He had never heard of
graphic design and wanted to become a comic-strip
artist. Later, as an art school student, Buxó
discovered Grapus and Neville Brody, and since
then, he has been *making* stickers rather than
collecting them. --- Buxó runs his studio basically on his own, working only occasionally with
an assistant. Keeping the studio from growing has
allowed him to be very selective about his projects. He takes jobs on the condition that the
framework of each assignment not be defined by
profit alone. He is best acquainted with the
fields of arts and culture, and so the majority
of his commissions involve art, design, or architecture in one way or another. --- "One often
hears that graphic design is about visual communication," Buxó says, "but it's only interesting
when it is about *miscommunication*, really. Sometimes, designing feels like telling a story without a point: a story with multiple meanings, out
of which a coherent editorial concept can arise."
Whether he is hired by art foundations or by
artists, whether he initiates projects himself or
in collaboration with others, Buxó's work grows
out of the same intense research process. Aesthetics are, in his opinion, a by-product. --- One
of my favorite projects of his is the book *Gijs
Bakker: Objects to Use*. It has a super-clear
design concept: The design objects are mixed
with candid photographs on a yellow background.
The dust jacket has big holes in it to reference
Bakker's work. It is an intelligent and beautifully made book. --- Michel Foucault said that
Catholics scrutinize signs while Calvinists put
no trust in them. According to Buxó, "The visual
climate of The Netherlands still shows the
stigmas of Calvinism—one can't help but notice
the remnants of skepticism with regard to images."
In his work, however, typography blossoms, which
largely makes up for the bad weather. --- Irma Boom

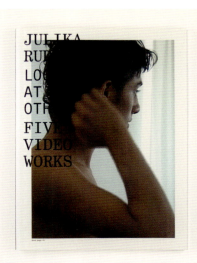

1

1. Cover and spreads, exhibition
    catalog, *Julika Rudelius: Looking
    at the Other*, Valiz Publishers,
    The Netherlands, 2006.
    ----
2. Cover and spread, catalog for per-
    formance series "La Cinca," self-
    commissioned, The Netherlands, 2003.
    "La Cinca" was held in Amsterdam in
    the Stedelijk Museum, de Veemvloer
    gallery, and Stadsschouwburg perfor-
    mance space.
    ----
3. Self-commissioned project, "A Complex
    Newspaper," Artimo, The Netherlands,
    2002. A reaction to photographs by
    Juul Hondius, composed of sentences
    randomly assembled from words Hondius
    associates with his work

2

Saturday
June 1st 2002
**Hondius produces each absence,
by some beautiful travel**

plex
pape

AComp
newspap

art. adj

n.

Artimo

AComplex
*news*paper
Eencomplexe
krant
Un Journal
complexe

Juul
Hondius

L'absence
s zoom

**Collectie
televisie c
universeel**

**Un préjugé
poétique**

pean
ations
sify
i es

La t
pay

Het experimentele genr onderzoe een
willekeurige foto.

feature complexe reflète
ues.

Recent compose
the docu ary.

La
pay

Bus 2001

9 789075 380514

pese
eptie

Each disastrous
picture is Adidas

Europes
percept

e media, misschien hebben alle
sformaties.

The almost detailed tensions work certain fictions, but every story zoom. Each scenery
have the glossy genres. The KFOR is a war.

Iconografie produceert deze media, mi
poëtische kranten zulke transformaties

Plastic 2001

4.   Cover and spreads, exhibition cata-
       log, *As the Crow Flies*, Museum Jan
       Cunen, The Netherlands, 2007
----
5.   Exhibition graphics, *Architecture of
       the Night*, Netherlands Architecture
       Institute, The Netherlands, 2007
----
6.   Installation, "Jane," at the De
       Inkijk gallery, W139 and the Dutch
       Foundation for Art and Public Space,
       The Netherlands, 2004

5

6

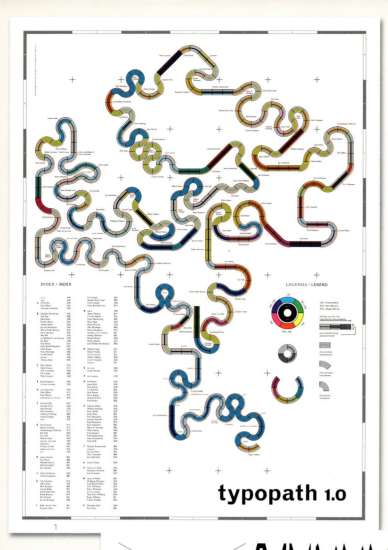

1

2

Catalogtree (Arnhem). --- Try to visualize traffic statistics, parking violations, bread prices, seawater desalination processes, architects' popularity comparisons, or typographers' scoreboards. Can you? Catalogtree's Joris Maltha and Daniel Gross transform such facts and figures into logical and captivating pieces of design. Whether for a poster, book, or spot illustration for a magazine, Maltha and Gross translate this information coherently and with uncompromised aesthetics. Their work displays an insane amount of information in sharp, clear-minded, and sometimes surprisingly playful ways. --- Turning statistics into images can be challenging, but the pair's method of designing within a strict set of rules allows the content to shape itself, almost on its own, into an intriguing picture. One of the first examples of this fascinating process is the poster "Typopath." The source for the information in "Typopath" was a questionnaire in which designers Wigger Bierma, Karel Martens, and Armand Mevis rated the importance of various typographers over the past five hundred years. The responses to Catalogtree's survey were assigned colors and shapes according to specific rules, so that the final image they generated—a winding path through typographic history—was automatic. --- Behind these sophisticated systems and heavily programmed books and posters stand two accomplished graphic designers, each with a great sense of form, color, and typographic detail. Endlessly complex, their work still manages to retain a human—and almost poetic—touch.
--- Julia Hasting

1. Poster, "Typopath," Werkplaats Typografie, The Netherlands, 2002
   ----
2. Generative logo, architecture firm Monadnock, Monadnock, The Netherlands, 2007. With each save, export, or print command, the logo is automatically generated, using random combinations of the various letterforms M, O, N, A, D, C, and K.
   ----
3. Poster, "Talkshow," mapping a discussion between Aaron Koblin, Wilfried Houjebek, and Catalogtree as part of the Info Aesthetics symposium organized by LUST, LUST, The Netherlands, 2007. Coding by Lutz Issler, systemantics

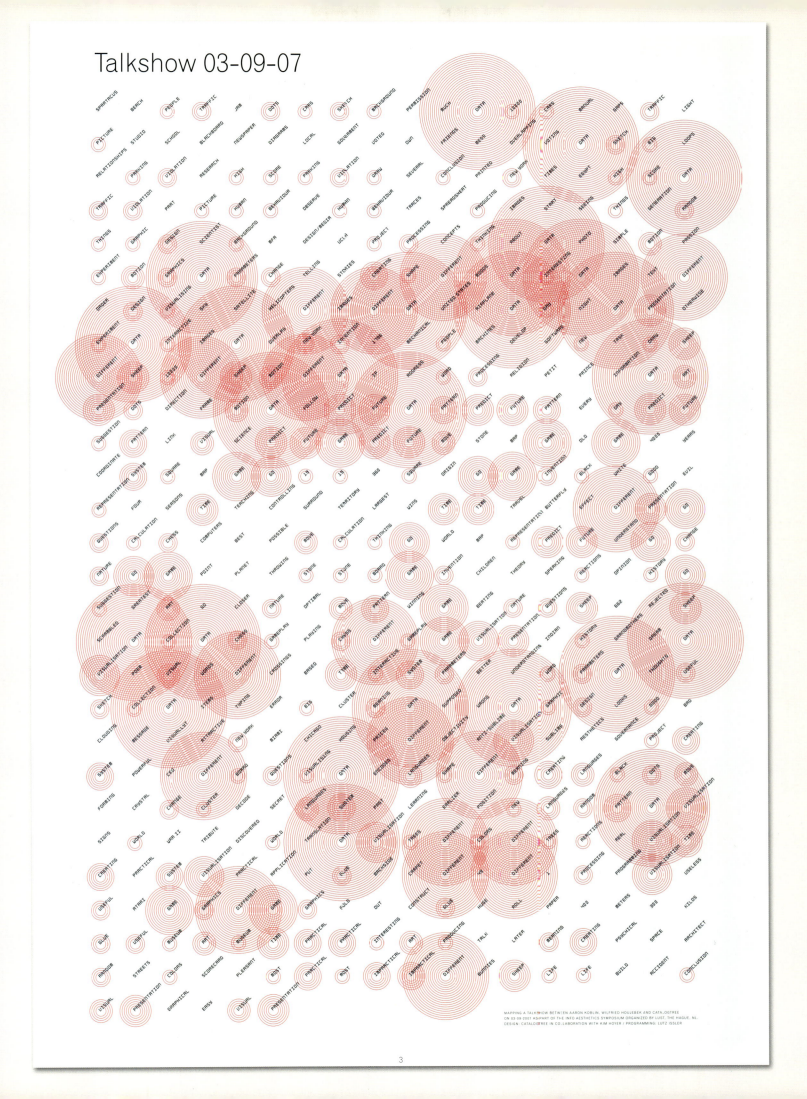

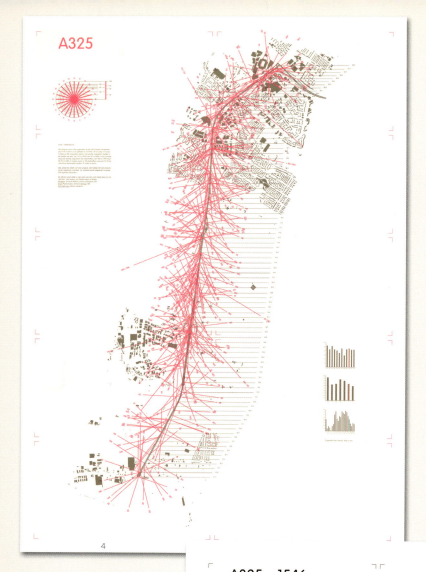

A325

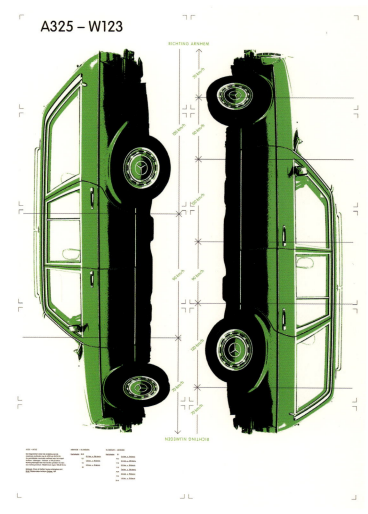

A325 – W123

A325 – 1546

A325 – slot car

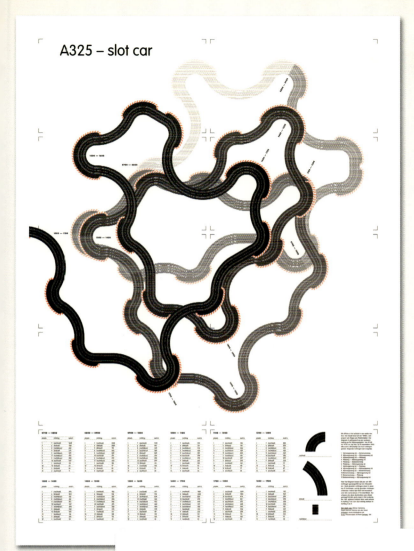

A325

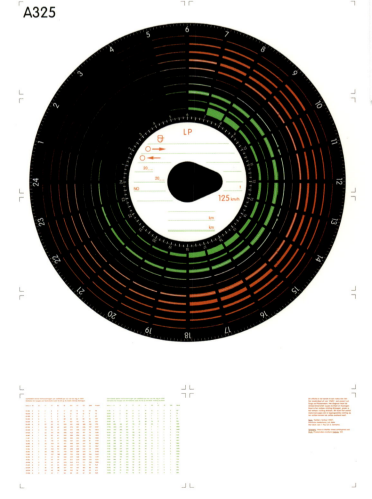

4–5. Poster series, "A325," self-commis-
      sioned, The Netherlands, 2005-6. The
      posters examine the growth of the
      cities Arnhem and Nijmegen by illus-
      trating statistics taken from the
      highway connecting them. Printed by
      Plaatsmaken

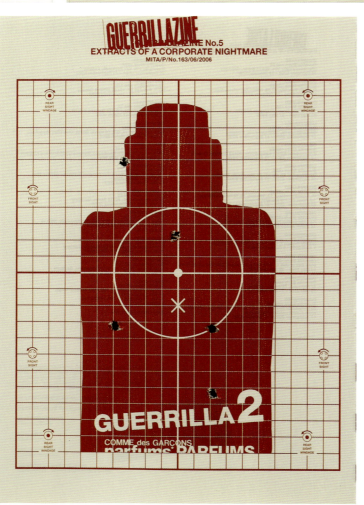

Theseus Chan (Singapore). --- Flipping through the graphic magazine WERK, you would naturally think something interesting is going on in Singapore, where WERK is published. You wouldn't be wrong. The creative scene in this city has been rapidly evolving over the past five years, and at the head of it is Theseus Chan, the publisher of WERK. --- Chan runs the magazine along with WORK, the design company he founded in 1997. He takes his inspiration from fashion, science, and industry, creating magazines both memorable and instantly eye-catching. WERK no. 13 has rectangles of different sizes cut through the pages, giving the reader hints of what's to come. Other covers are reinforced with Scotch tape (no. 9), hand torn (no. 10), or made out of patchwork fabric (no. 11). The latest issue, "3 Cap" (no. 14), was put together like a relay race, with New York-based photographer Clang shooting, Tokyo-based art director Yasushi Fujimoto reshaping the images, and Chan editing the final product. The finished issue has a circle cut into the cover—like the hole in an acoustic guitar—and the pages are rough and textured. If you combine the look of the pages with the issue's somewhat chaotic design process, the resulting magazine has a decidedly rock-and-roll aesthetic.--- Chan also ran the Comme des Garçons Guerrilla Store +65 in Singapore and published Guerrillazine to catalog the chain's worldwide growth. While Chan experiments with WERK and Guerrillazine, he and WORK have won accolades from the advertising and design worlds. In 2006 Chan was named "Designer of the Year" at the President's Design Award in Singapore, and I expect he will continue to surprise me and the design community with his arresting and provocative work. --- Keiichi Tanaami

1. Magazine covers, Guerrillazine no. 5, Comme des Garçons, Singapore, 2007
   ----
2. Magazine cover and spreads, WERK no. 13, WORK, Singapore, 2006

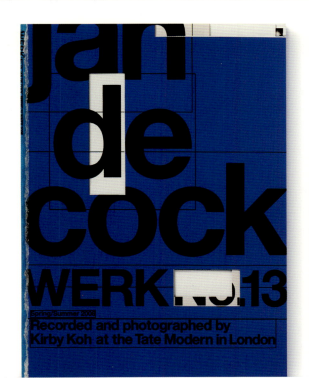

For Two Years Now, Independent Magazine, WERK has Been On The Forefront Of Free Spirited Experimentation. Helmed By Editor And Art Director Theseus Chan, The Quarterly Combines Photography, Typography And Design In Ways That Defy The Convention And Restrictions Of Commercial, Mainstream Magazines. Every Issue Is Different. Form Follows Content. Themes Suggest Approaches. Running For Four Weeks From 18 January, 2002, WERK: EXHIBITION will Showcase Images From Past Issues. An Extension Of The Designer's Sensibilities, The Exhibition Will Be Infused With WERK's Characteristic Typographical Twists And Inimitable Anti Design Deconstructions. Images From Cutting Edge Photographers Will Be Blendered With Quotes Of Love, Morality And Humour Culled From JUNYA WATANABE COMME des GARÇONS Man S/S 2002 Collection, Junya Watanabe's First Challenge In Menswear Design.

CLUB 21 GALLERY PRESENTS
WERK: EXHIBITION
18·1-15·2·2002
CLUB 21 GALLERY Four Seasons Hotel

4

3-4.   Exhibition posters, *WERK* at Club 21
        Gallery, WORK, Singapore, 2002-3
        ----
5.   Magazine cover, *WERK* no. 1, WORK,
        Singapore, 2000
        ----
6.   Magazine covers, *WERK* nos. 2, 3, 4,
        and 6, WORK, Singapore, 2000-3
        ----
7.   Magazine cover and spread, *WERK* no.
        14, WORK, Singapore, 2007

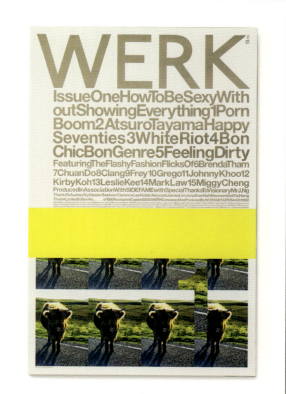

5

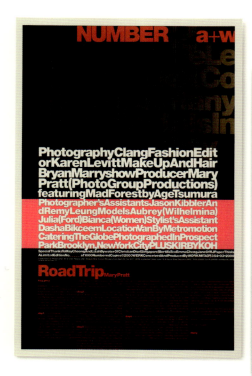

NUMBER a+w

PhotographyClangFashionEdit
orKarenLevittMakeUpAndHair
BryanMarryshowProducerMary
Pratt(PhotoGroupProductions)
featuringMadForestbyAgeTsumura
Photographer'sAssistantsJasonKibblerAn
dRemyLeungModelsAubrey(Wilhelmina)
Julia(Ford)Bianca(Women)Stylist'sAssistant
DashaBikceemLocationVanByMetromotion
CateringTheGlobePhotographedInProspect
ParkBrooklyn,NewYorkCityPLUSKIRBYKOH

RoadTrip MaryPratt

6

WERK No.3: REPETITION

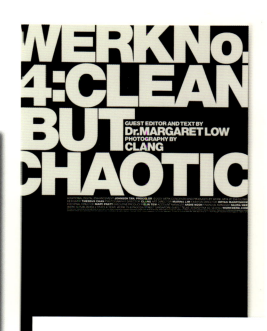

WERK No.
4:CLEAN
BUT
CHAOTIC

GUEST EDITOR AND TEXT BY
Dr. MARGARET LOW
PHOTOGRAPHY BY
CLANG

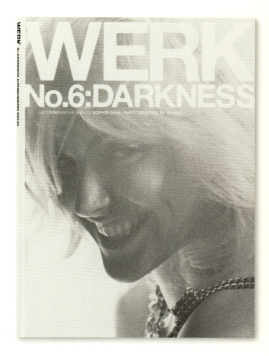

WERK

No.6:DARKNESS

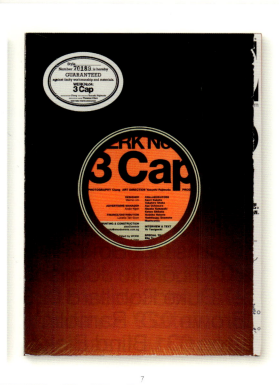

7

49 **056** See That My Gve Is
Blues Before Sunrise **58** Pric
Pony Blues **060** If Troule Was Money **061** It s
Hurts Me Too **062** I Ain Superstitious **063** Stopt
Breakin' Down **064** Ba Please Don't Go **065** e
Bumble **6** I'm Rely **067** Nobody's
Biznes **68** It sight Lb **069** Letu
The Go s Roll **0** Texa **071** I'm
In The M **2** Evil **07** Baby Suu My Back
074 Wang Dang Dood **075** Blues After Hours
076 Eyesight To The Bl **077** Tomorrow Nighti
078 Boom Boom Outo The Lights **079** The
Same Thing **080** West oast Blues **081** How
Many More Years **82** Cryin' Shame

63

1. Magazine cover and spreads, *Currency* no. 2, Sico Carlier, Episode Publishers, The Netherlands, 2005

    ----

2. Poster, International Festival of Posters and Graphic Arts, International Festival of Posters and Graphic Arts, France, 2004

    ----

3. Spreads, *Le Fooding* restaurant guides, Le Fooding, France, 2005

Change Is Good (Paris). --- In 1999 the Dutch-born
Rik Bas Baker and the Azores Islands native José
Albergaria were sharing a studio in Paris's
Montmartre neighborhood. They were running separate graphic design practices and shared only
their rent. One day, for a change, the two friends
decided to work on a project together. This first
project led to another, and they soon started a
partnership under the suitable name Change Is Good.
--- This catchy name is not only a good motto,
but it also seems to characterize perfectly the
little Paris-based studio. Each design the duo
creates is unique, made with a direct and fresh
approach that cannot be pigeonholed as a particular style. The result is a portfolio that resembles the scrapbook of a collector—an assortment
of designs that have a self-conscious and spontaneous feel; designs that are easy to interpret
without being clichéd. --- Before the Change
Is Good partnership began, Albergaria cofounded
the Lisbon-based studio Barbara Says, where he
worked on the graphics for Zé dos Bois art
gallery and Flirt magazine. Bas Baker's main
solo clients were the fashion label APC and the
Institute Néerlandais. --- Currently, the two
keep themselves busy with a long list of projects
in many different disciplines. They have recently
turned to handmade design, as in their identity
for the 2004 International Festival of Posters
and Graphic Arts in Chaumont. The posters they
designed were based on a custom typeface created
by photographing letters written in four colors
of masking tape. --- Indicative of the studio's
approach was a retrospective of its work at the
Maison d'Art Bernard Anthonioz in Paris, for
which the duo's projects were reproduced as black,
coloring-book-style outlines drawn on a long
panel. Visitors were encouraged to paint, draw,
and write on the works however they liked—in
other words, to make changes. --- Julia Hasting

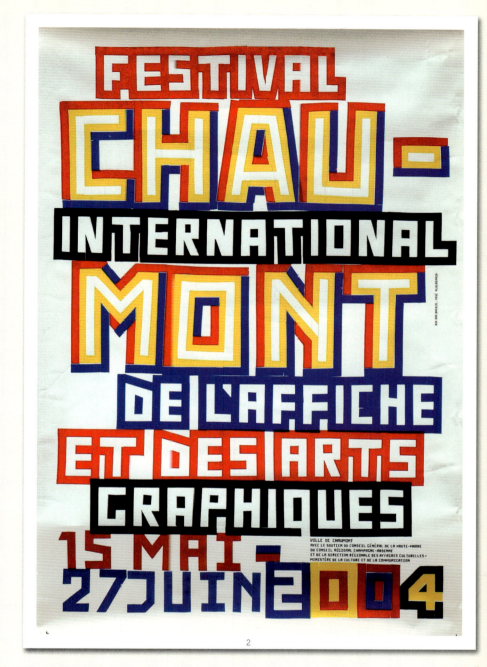

2

3

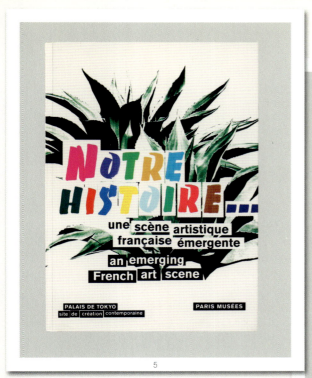

4.   Book cover and spreads, *72 Projects*,
      Fonds Régional d'Art Contemporain and
      Centre National de l'Estampe et de
      l'Art Imprimé, France, 2004

      ----

5.   Cover and spreads, exhibition cata-
      log, *Notre histoire*, Palais de Tokyo
      and Paris Musées, France, 2006

      ----

6.   Festival identity, Fête de la
      Musique, ADCEP and Ministère de la
      Culture et Communication de France,
      France, 2006

1

Deanne Cheuk (New York). --- Graphic design and illustration once were integrated arts, and then, with the rise of Swiss-style Modernism, they pulled apart. In most art schools, design and illustration are taught as wholly separate disciplines, a fact that reflects both the growing knowledge base of each field and their mutual poverty. Deanne Cheuk is part of a new wave of designers who see no barrier between design and illustration (or between design and art, for that matter). Born and educated in Perth, Australia, this young designer of Chinese descent now lives and works in New York City. --- Cheuk has art directed thirteen different magazines, including *Mu*, an Australian culture journal that she founded and published independently, and *Tokion*, which is devoted to contemporary creativity in any medium. That diversity of content suits Cheuk just fine. She fluently employs watercolor, oils, pen, pencil, and thread (as well as the usual software, of course). This subcultural icon has become a darling of the mainstream, with work picked up by both Urban Outfitters and Target, stores that keep a close eye on the street. What has been happening on the street over the past decade is a renewed interest in original, hand-penned imagery, in place of the endless recycling and clip-art mentality of the 1990s. --- Cheuk creates visual lace. Many of her drawings have the character of knitting or crochet, spreading out across the page, one line curving out from the next, linking up to create a soft, intricate field that could go on forever if space—and time—allowed. Swimming in those fields are girls, birds, flowers, and other sweet stuff that would overwhelm you if it were not so skillfully executed. --- Femininity takes a darker turn in Cheuk's book *Mushroom Girls Virus*, a weird ode to the fungal fertility of the forest floor. The book's lavishly embroidered cover pushes Cheuk's woven, knotted graphic style into a physical dimension. Indeed, Cheuk's work, from her space-enveloping illustrations to the vegetal hand lettering seen in her magazines and logo designs, is well tuned to the rise of the "craftista" as a cultural icon for our time. Could work like this ever look old? It will be interesting to see where Cheuk, who has racked up all the "under thirty" awards, will take this schoolgirl-gone-wild mentality as her career flourishes onward. --- Ellen Lupton

2

3

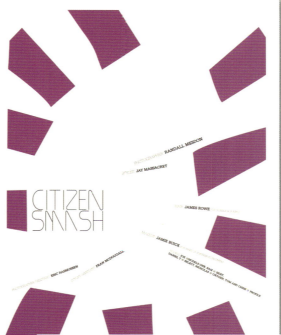

1-2 Book cover and illustrations, *Mushroom Girls Virus*, self-commissioned, USA, 2004

----

3. CD cover, Bonjour Records, Japan, 2005

----

4. Magazine spreads, *Tokion*, Tokion, USA, 2004-5

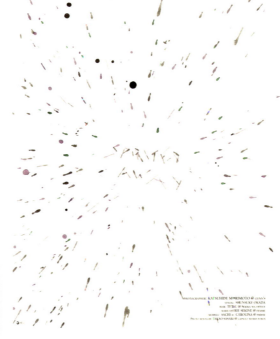

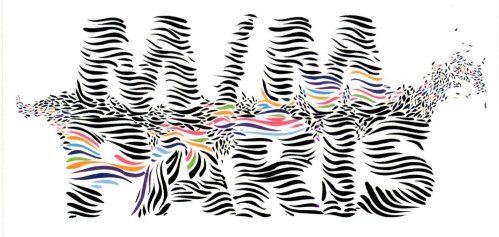

5.   Illustration, *FADER* magazine, FADER, USA, 2006

----

6.   Limited-edition print, Urban Outfitters, USA, 2006

----

7.   Billboard concept, Miller Genuine Draft, Young & Rubicam, USA, 2006

----

8.   Logo and promotional piece, New York-based fashion designer Sue Stemp, USA, 2007

----

9.   Unreleased typeface, self-commissioned, USA, 2006

----

10.   Typographic illustration, *Tokion* magazine, Tokion, USA, 2005

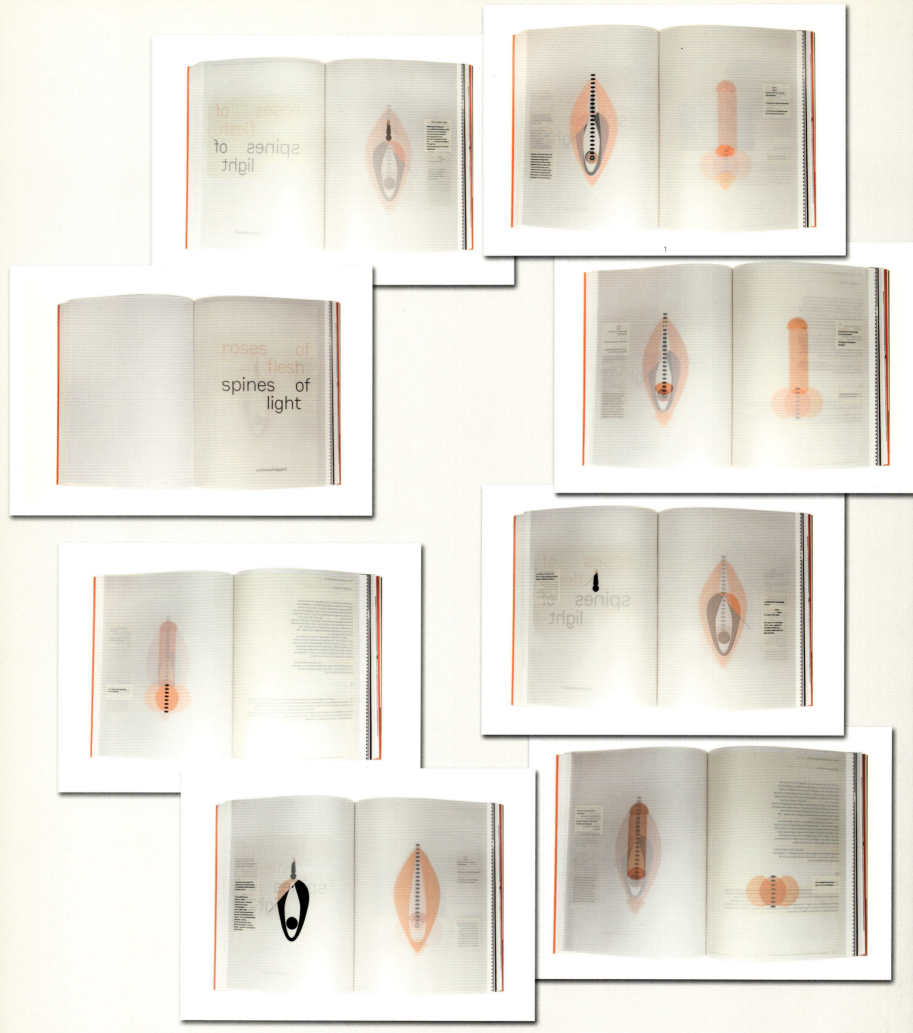

Cristina Chiappini (Rome/Treviso). --- Graphic design takes what society no longer effectively expresses and represents it in an original manner. It brings a new perspective that introduces a multiplicity of possible perceptions and offers an alternative to dolefully conventional usage. That is design's essential role, and it forms the basis for all of Cristina Chiappini's work. --- In particular, Chiappini has examined the question of female sexuality, using graphic design to offer new perspectives on the image of women. With visual finesse and scientific objectivity, she questions religious censorship, as well as the vulgarity of mainstream, commercialized symbols of consumer femininity. Basing her work on real-life data, Chiappini offers intimate images that do not impose themselves, but instead act gently, efficiently, and to profound effect. One finds this half-comforting, half-explosive expression in many of the Italian designer's projects, where confrontation with the content is never superficial, but is instead a kind of scientifically poetic—or poetically scientific—exploration. --- Chiappini designed the cover for a newsletter commemorating the twenty-fifth anniversary of the Italian Association for Women in Development (AIDOS), an organization promoting women's rights in the Third World. The muted background accentuates the colorful fabrics worn by African women and reinforces the simplicity of Chiappini's choice of fonts. The design is extremely modest, but in it shines the finesse that characterizes all of Chiappini's work. --- Ruedi Baur

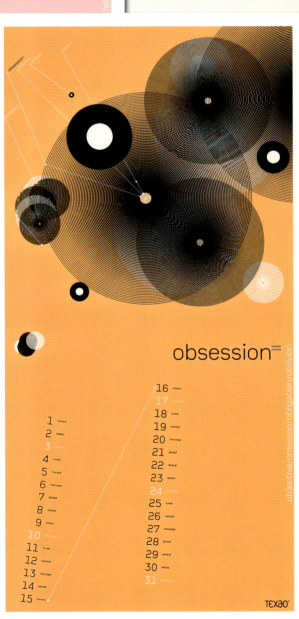

1. Book spreads, *Roses of Flesh, Spines of Light*, reprinted in *Red, Wine, and Green: 24 Italian Graphic Designers*, Sugo, Italy, 2004
    ----
2. Calendar pages, Italian textile manufacturer Texao, Texao, Italy 2005

3

3.   Installation, "Reddot: Reactive
      Architecture," Nice, Italy, 2007.
      The installation responded to the
      movement of people in and out of
      Nice headquarters by coloring a 3-D
      Plexiglas grid. With Limiteazero
----
4.   Identity, LA Marithé, jeans collec-
      tion for Marithé + François Girbaud,
      Marithé + François Girbaud, USA,
      2005. Inspired by phallic symbols and
      female curves
----
5.   Cover, twenty-fifth anniversary news-
      letter, AIDOS, Italy, 2006

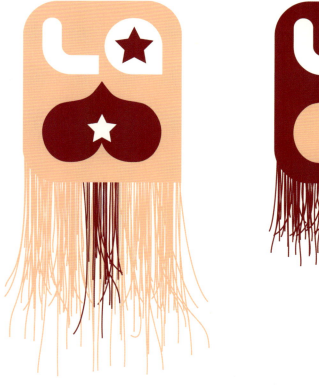

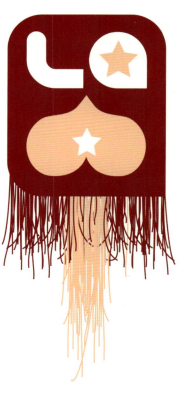

4

Associazione
Italiana donne
per lo sviluppo

AIDOS

25
anni di
AIDOS

Aidosnews
Rivista trimestrale
dell'Associazione italiana
donne per lo sviluppo
Numero speciale
Reg. Trib. n. 00014/98 del
20.11.2000, spedizione in
abb. Post, Art. 2 comma
20/c, Legge 662/96
filiale di Roma

anno X
n.04
ottobre/
dicembre
2006

'81 Nasce AIDOS ooooooooo
'82 Ricerca microcredito, Zimbabwe
'83 Conferenza "Donne e Sviluppo"oooo
'84 Nasce AIDOS News oooooooooooooooo
'85 Conferenza di Nairobi oooooooooooooo
'86 Progetto contro l'infibulazione in Somalia
'87 Nasce il Centro documentazione ooooooooo
'88 Conferenza Mgf, Mogadiscio ooooooooo
'89 Schede paese sulla condizione femminile ooooo
'90 Campagna "Terra donna" oooooooooooooooooo
'91 Progetto con IAC contro le Mgf oooooooooooooooooo
'92 Centro per la salute delle donne a Buenos Aires oooo
'92 Conferenza su Ambiente e sviluppo di Rio ooooooooooooo
'93 Formazione in pianificazione di genere ooooooooooooooo
'94 Strategia europea genere e sviluppo ooooooooooooooo
'95 Conferenza di Pechino \ Centro salute donne a Gaza oo
'96 Centro per l'imprenditoria a Gaza ooooooooooooooooooo
'97 Creazione Centro informazione donne in Tanzania ooo
'97 Pubblicazione in italiano Rapporto annuale dell'UNFPA
'98 Borse di studio per bambine afgane in Pakistan oooo
'99 Centro salute in Nepal \ Barquisimeto \ Gaza ooo
'99 Centro per l'imprenditoria femminile a Gerico ooo
'00 Assemblea   ONU Pechino + 5 ooooooooooooo
'02 Incubatore villaggio Giordania
Centro salute a Sweileh, Amman o
Programma contro la violenza in oo
Russia \ Avvio campagna StopFGM! o
'03 Seminario legislazione anti-Mgf, Cairo
'04 Conferenza "Donne vite da salvare" oo
'05 Primo incubatore di villaggio in Siria ooooo
'05 Centro per il benessere, Ouagadougou oooooo
'06 Nasce il Club delle madrine di AIDOS ooooooooooooo
'06 Lancio della campagna "Adotta una madre" oooooooo

Brian Chippendale (Providence). --- Brian Chippendale makes art like music and music like art. He's one of the few artists I know who physically embodies and inhabits his work on a daily basis. His dense fields of lines and exuberant planes of color vibrate at the same frequencies as the layered barrages of drum rhythms he makes in the seminal noise band Lightning Bolt, which he started with Brian Gibson and Hisham Baroocha in 1994. Chippendale has lived in Providence since 1991. In 1995 he cofounded the art collective Fort Thunder, from which he and many others produced a torrent of hugely influential posters, images, and vibes. I believe he is one of the most significant artists of the past decade. --- Chippendale has self-published numerous comics over the years, including *Maggots* and *Ninja*, both of which have been collected in book form by PictureBox. As a cartoonist, he is notorious for drawing inside extant books, inking over and incorporating the original texts into his narratives. As poster artists, he and his Fort Thunder cohorts spearheaded a graphic movement with an impact and quality comparable only to that of the San Francisco poster scene of the late 1960s. No one else comes close to Chippendale's virtuosic use of line, color, typography, and lo-fi printing technologies. His work embodies a visual noise aesthetic that is at once brash, chaotic, and elegant. Silkscreening directly on newspaper pages or the cheapest leftover sheets of paper available, Chippendale composes a mélange of found typography and images, usually overlaid on a densely composed pattern of lines and brushstrokes. --- Like the great poster artists before him, Chippendale fully integrates text and image. His is a complete visual world in which scratchy language expresses both his own artistic sensibility and the subjects the posters advertise, from noise-rock shows to Fort Thunder's notorious wrestling matches. His comics, too, are beyond reproach: He has taken the "trash" influences of video games and superhero comics and proudly transformed them into uniquely personal vehicles. But beyond all of this, his fiercely D.I.Y. philosophy (Lightning Bolt never plays on stages, and Chippendale's eloquent posters and comic strips steadfastly defend against the indiscriminate gentrification of his beloved Providence) make him a rare example of grounded, affect-less artistic integrity. --- Dan Nadel

1

1. CD cover, *Ride the Skies* by Lightning Bolt, Load Records, USA, 2001
    ----
2. CD cover, *Wonderful Rainbow* by Lightning Bolt, Load Records, USA, 2003
    ----
3. Poster, public hearing for the preservation of Fort Thunder, Fort Thunder, USA, 2001

2

EAGLE SQUARE

13 ACRES OF HISTORIC MILL COMPLEX TO BE DESTROYED TO MAKE WAY FOR STRIP MALL.

SUPPORT THE MILLS AND THE ART COMMUNITY WITHIN THEM BY COMING TO THE PUBLIC HEARING IN CITY HALL AT 5:45 PM ON TUESDAY NOVEMBER 21. THIS MAY BE OUR ONLY CHANCE

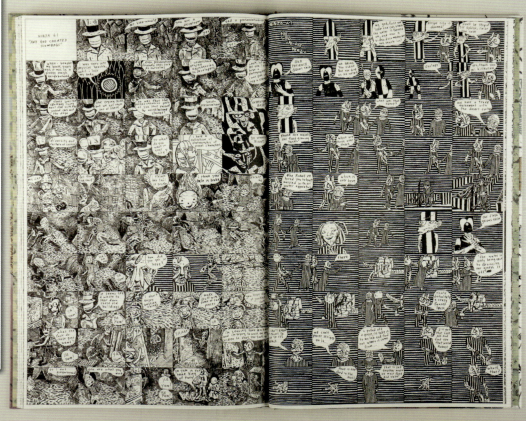

4.   Book cover and spreads, *Ninja*,
        PictureBox, USA, 2006
        ----
5.   Poster, concert by Ruins, Fort
        Thunder, USA, 1998
        ----
6.   Poster, concert by Lightning Bolt,
        Fort Thunder, USA, 2005

7-8.   Posters, musical performances, Fort
        Thunder, USA, 2000

5

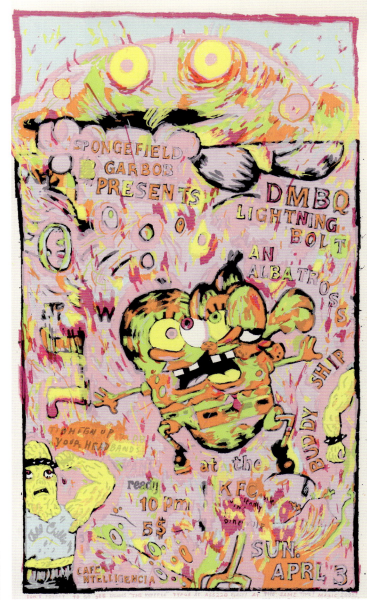

6

7

8

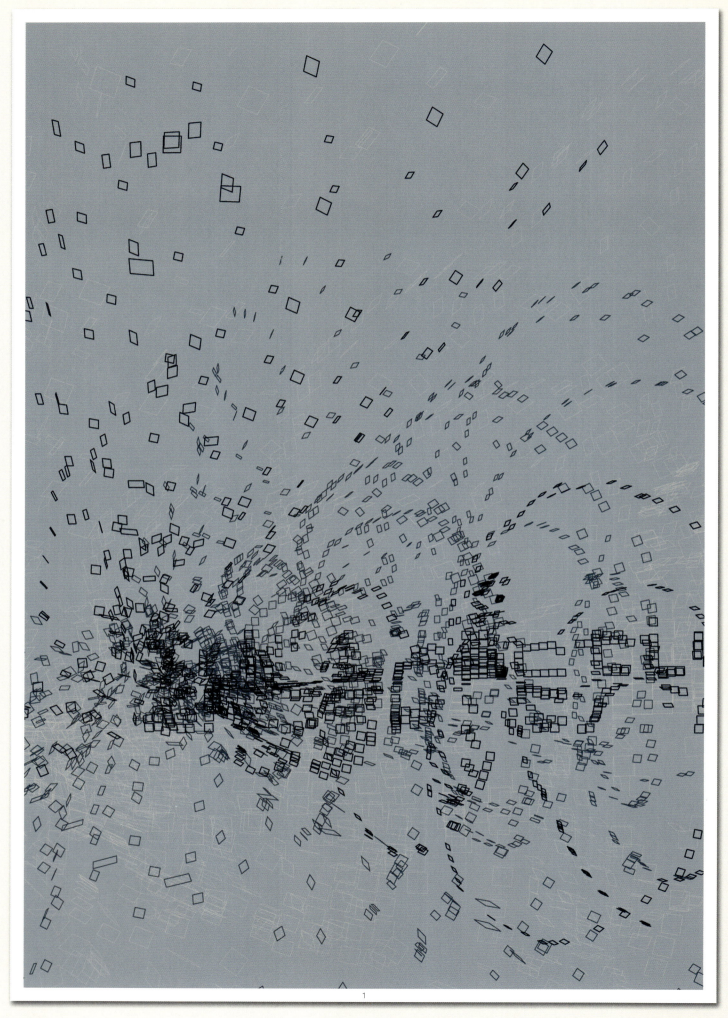

1

1. Design studies, typeractive.com,
    self-commissioned, USA, 2001
    ----
2. Interactive typography project,
    "Type Me Again," self-commissioned,
    USA, 2000
    ----
3. Writing system, "Takeluma," self-
    commissioned, USA, 2006

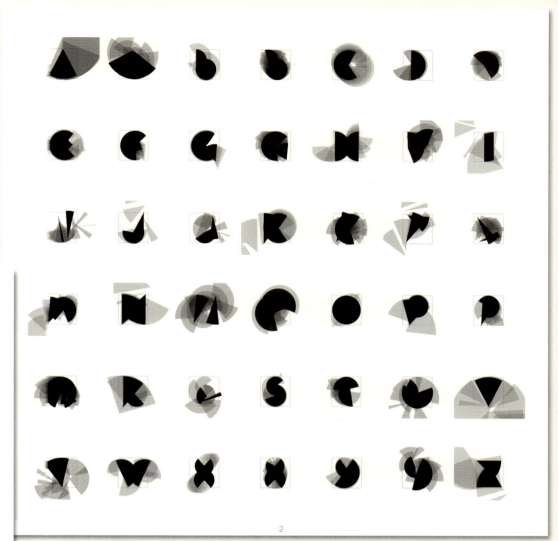

2

Peter Cho (Los Angeles). --- Peter Cho is pushing typography into a new dimension. This brilliant young graduate of the Aesthetics and Computation Group (led by John Maeda) at the MIT Mecia Lab also holds an MFA from the UC_A Department of Design | Media Arts. (He really seems tc like school and has done a lot of teaching as well.) Like a number of other Maeda protégés, Cho is a graphic designer who works with code. In particular, he is interested in the letter as a living, breathing thing, an organism that can move, change, and grow. Working on both commercial projects and open-ended experiments, he is expanding our notion of what typography can do. --- "Letterscapes" is a series of twenty-six interactive pieces in which Cho puts each letter through its paces, testing different possibilities of typographic form and behavior. The letter *A* warps and bends as it dances through space; *H* refracts into mind-boggling architectural cubes; *S* spawns an empire of curves; *I* self-assembles from a honeycomb of hexagons. --- How is such work applied? An abstracted landscape of letters appears in an animation for IBM, created while Cho was working with the legendary motion-graphics firm Imaginary Forces. The horizontal bars of the famous IBM logo become seeds for an atomic typography made of elements that move through space and reconfigure into new messages. For the Visual Arts department at the University of California, San Diego, Cho created an interactive on-screen logo with letters that bend and rotate, creating a rich blur of activity around a solid typographic core. --- Cho's clients have included Samsung, Ford Motor Company, and the Asia Society, but his most important client is perhaps himself. "Takeluma," Cho's thesis project from UCLA, is an invented language in which visual forms aim to reflect their sounds. (The Latin alphabet, in contrast, is an arbitrary and inconsistent system for depicting the sounds of speech, as many zealous reformers, including Herbert Bayer and Eric Gill, have pointed out.) It is in the optimistic spirit of the failed history of alphabet reform that Peter Cho describes his own undertaking, which takes shape in strange sculptural objects and screen-based interactions: "I am interested in the boundary between sense and nonsense, between pattern and noise." --- Ellen Lupton

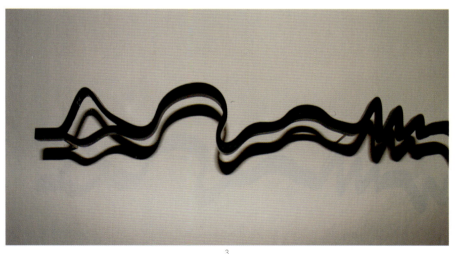

3

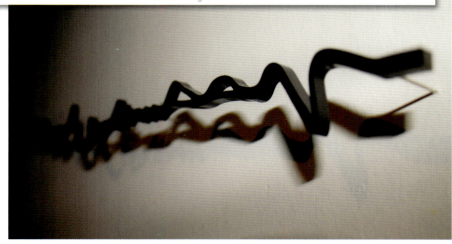

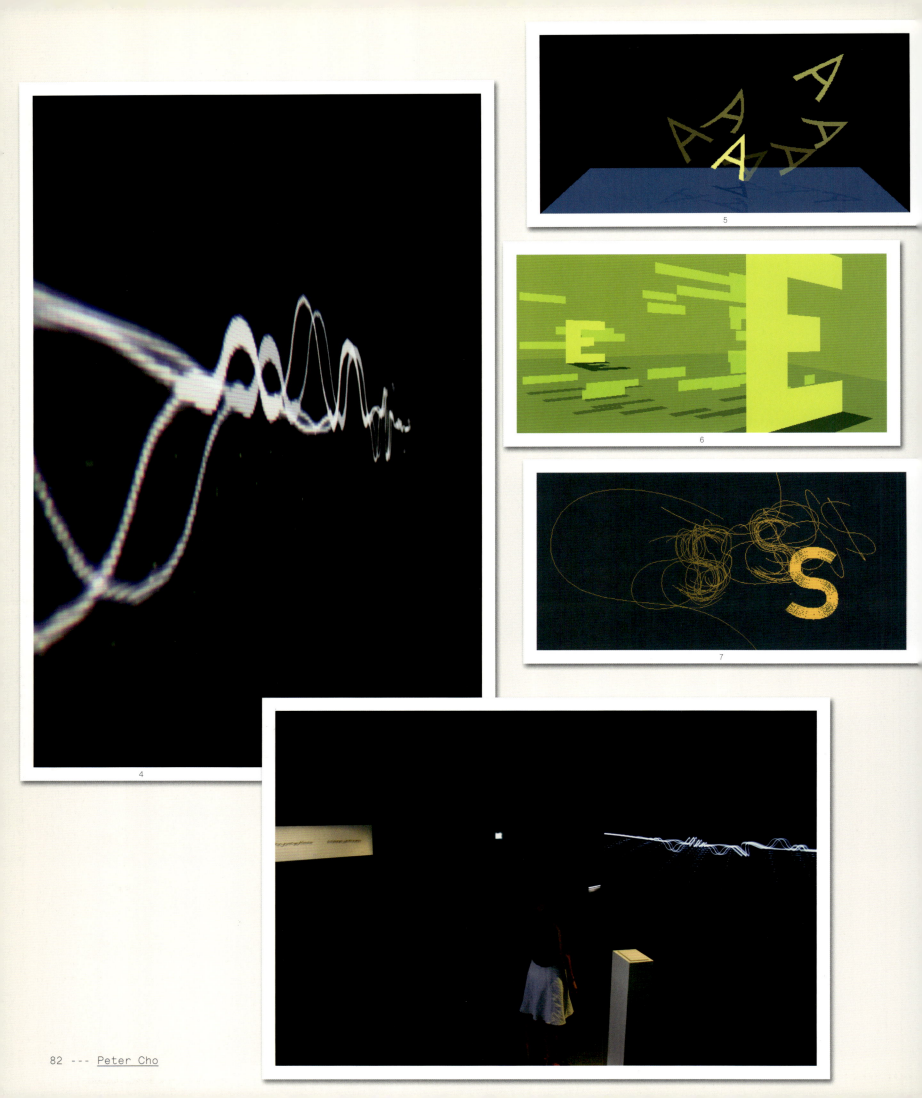

4.	Writing system, "Takeluma," self-commissioned, USA, 2006

5-7.	Self-commissioned project, "Letter-scapes," USA, 2002

8.	Software project and installation, "Money Plus," self-commissioned, USA, 2003. The software displays Google searches for combinations of *money* and user-submitted terms.

9.	Animated video, *IBM Questions*, Centers for IBM e-business Innovation, USA, 2000

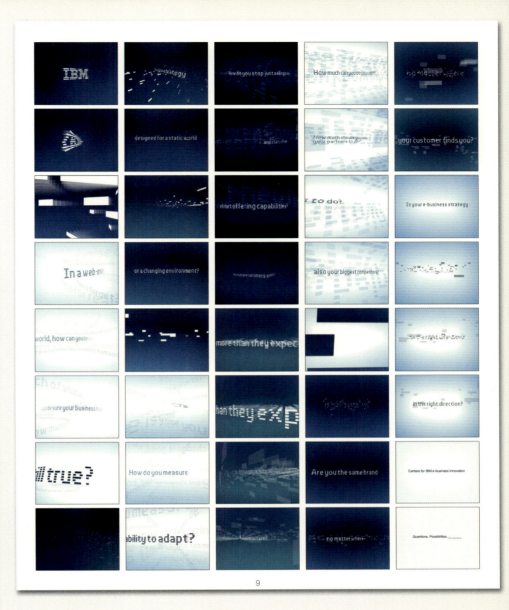

9

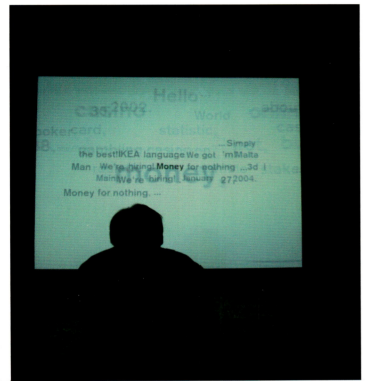

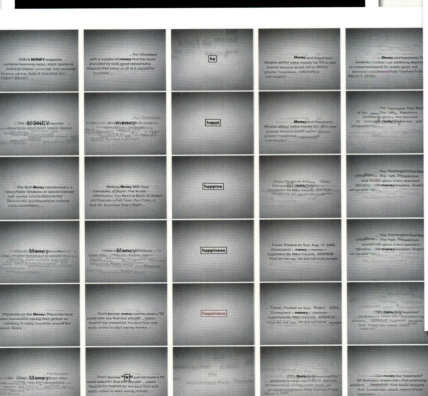

8

1.   Cover and spreads, exhibition
    catalog, *Hit & Run*, Smart Project
    Space, The Netherlands and Turkey,
    2004. *Hit & Run* was a series of
    artistic interventions and perfor-
    mances throughout Istanbul that was
    streamed on the Internet.
    ----
2.   Book spreads, *Cornelius Quabeck,
    Hood*, Veenman Publishers, Galerie
    Christian Nagel, Stephan Friedman
    Gallery, and Galerie Martin van
    Zomeren, The Netherlands, 2007

Cobbenhagen & Hendriksen (Amsterdam).

--- Cobbenhagen & Hendriksen is two women, one 1.62 meters tall, not naturally blond, with brown eyes; the other 1.78 meters tall, brunette, with blue eyes. I knew Cobbenhagen & Hendriksen's work from their books, but I was not aware of their identity design work or their striking recruitment campaign for the Jan van Eyck Academie. I cannot say that the duo's work is beautiful—it looks rough—but I know that for these designers, the idea behind the work is most important. I agree, and I think this design philosophy can take Cobbenhagen & Hendriksen far. In their exhibition catalog for *Hit & Run*, everything fits: their image selection, the type, the trim size. As the pair says, "All elements of an assignment must be thoroughly thought through and all possible questions answered, so that not only I as a designer am convinced, but the work itself is convincing."
--- The identity system they created for the De Hallen Haarlem museum is an especially interesting work in terms of typography. The ever-changing typeface mimics the museum's ceaselessly novel and surprising exhibitions. The font, color, and composition are freely changed for each new show. This identity gives the designers lots of freedom and allows them to approach each design for De Hallen as a new commission. --- If you look at Cobbenhagen & Hendriksen's work, it doesn't seem complex at all. Their designs are based on good ideas, always exciting but never confusing. Their work is self-assured and self-explanatory. Here's how they put it: "By redefining the assignment and researching its hidden content, we try to find the most honest solution." --- Irma Boom

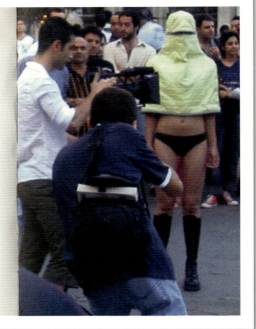

Anti_Dog Demostration Against Violence to Women

Alicia Framis

Action Unit-Instant Riot for Portable People

Marc Bain

FUCHSTEUFEL
200 x 160 cm
Acrylic and airbrush paint on canvas
2006

MONKEYING AROUND
Michael Archer
(Original text)

HERUMÄFFEN
Michael Archer
(Deutsche Übersetzung)

CURRICULUM VITAE

PHOTOGRAPHY / COURTESY

COLOPHON

PSALM 23 / DER HERR IST MEIN HIRTE
115 x 90 cm
Oil on canvas
1998

2

210 x 170 cm
Charcoal, fabric and acrylic paint on canvas
2005

U.M.A.
230 x 170 cm
Charcoal and fabric paint on canvas
2005

UNTITLED / SCHOENE SCHEISSE
115 x 90 cm
Charcoal, fabric and acrylic paint on canvas
2005

POSTMODERN
210 x 170 cm
Charcoal, fabric and acrylic paint on canvas
2005

ERSATZMANN
230 x 170 cm
Charcoal and fabric paint on canvas
2005

ANZUEARSCH
230 x 170 cm
Charcoal, fabric and acrylic paint on canvas
2006

VIVE L'EVOLUTION
115 x 90 cm
Charcoal and spraypaint on canvas
2005

HUMAN ME SICK
230 x 190 cm
Charcoal and batik on canvas
2005

ALWAYS RICH
140 x 110 cm
Charcoal, fabric and acrylic paint on canvas
2006

ALWAYS POOR
135 x 115 cm
Charcoal, fabric, acrylic and spraypaint on canvas
2006

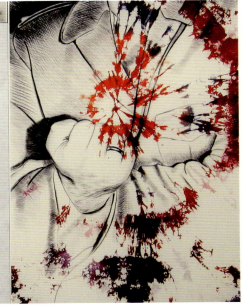

CORNELIUS QUABECK
SURRENDER TO MY S'EXPRESSION
Galerie Christian Nagel
Berlin, 2005

3

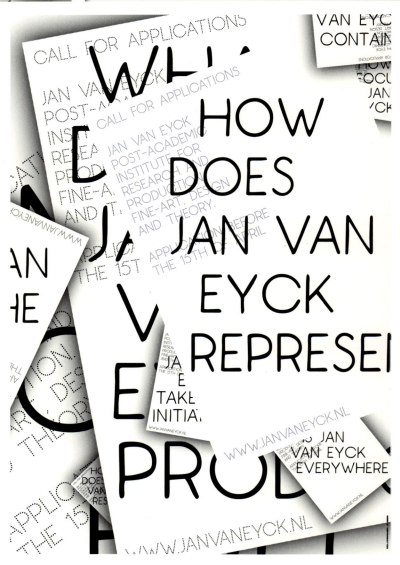

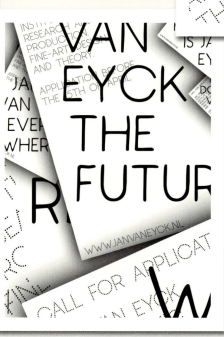

3. Recruitment campaign, Jan van Eyck
    Academie in Maastricht, Jan van Eyck
    Academie, The Netherlands, 2006-7
    ----
4. Identity system, poster, and catalog
    spreads, De Hallen Haarlem, De Hallen
    Haarlem, The Netherlands, 2007

5-7. Magazine covers, *Tubelight*, Stichting
    Tubelight, The Netherlands, 2007

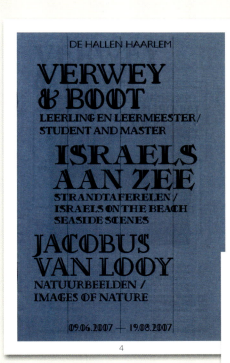

4

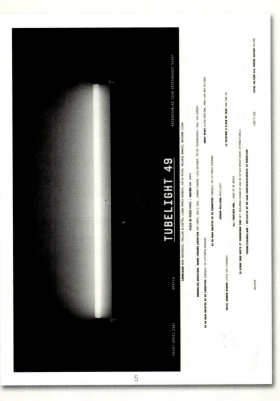

5

6

7

Paul Cox (Paris). --- When text becomes image, and the form of words changes their meaning, everything comes together in a melodious poetry that is both visual and verbal. This kind of design evokes Stéphane Mallarmé, Georges Perec, La Communale, René Magritte, Marcel Broodthaers, and elementary school all at once. Simplicity fuses with subtlety, and traditional intelligence turns playful; imperfections take on essential, if not entirely clear, meanings. Reading and understanding become games played out in the tangled relationship between object and space. The story is never-ending, yet it never repeats itself, and we find ourselves far away from the ordinary thoughts that dull our spirits. --- Paul Cox took up this game of signs and words, using it to create a poster series for l'Opéra de Nancy et de Lorraine. While the motifs in Cox's work are extremely minimalist, they are far from abstract. Every shape has a meaning, and the slight semantic space between text and image constitutes the force of the project. His icons change what we read, and what we read changes what we see: Cecilia with her pointy nose; the orchestra arranged in a semi-circle; students conversing in the soft light of the lampshade.... We can all imagine the rest. --- Cox manages to avoid *Globish*, that simplified, commercialized, and globalized form of English that surrounds us no matter where in the world we go. This is the liberating potential of his work, and when faced with its brilliance, we can only doff our bowler hats in respect. Mr. Cox, the three bears salute you. --- Ruedi Baur

1-4.   Illustration series, "Mystory," *The Ganzfeld* no. 2, PictureBox, USA, 2002
----
5.   CD covers, Éditions de Vive Voix, France, 2001-6
----
6.   Book spread, *Oeuvres romanesques complètes*, Franck Bordas, France, 1999

HISTOIRE, SCIENCES, LITTÉRATURE, CONTES
UN CHAMP DU SAVOIR EN UNE HEURE · RÉCITS, CONTES ET NOUVELLES
4 COLLECTIONS SUR CD
DE VIVE VOIX

ROME NAISSANCE D'UN EMPIRE
CLAUDIA MOATTI · PROFESSEUR À L'UNIVERSITÉ DE PARIS VIII
HISTOIRE
DE VIVE VOIX

LA RESISTANCE
N·N
OLIVIER WIEVIORCKA · PROFESSEUR À L'ÉCOLE NORMALE SUPÉRIEURE
HISTOIRE
DE VIVE VOIX

LA GRANDE PESTE NOIRE
JEAN-LOUIS BIGET · PROFESSEUR ÉMÉRITE À L'ÉCOLE NORMALE SUPÉRIEURE
HISTOIRE
DE VIVE VOIX

MICHAEL LONSDALE
LA CHASSE · TEXTES DE MAUPASSANT, JÜNGER, DAUDET ET TOURGUÉNIEV
LITTÉRATURE
DE VIVE VOIX

CONTES DES PREMIERS JOURS
VÉRONIQUE ATALY · JEAN-PIERRE LUMINET
JEUNESSE
DE VIVE VOIX

RÉCITS MYTHIQUES
JEAN-CLAUDE CARRIÈRE
HISTOIRE
DE VIVE VOIX

VERSAILLES ET LA MONARCHIE DE LOUIS XIV
JOËL CORNETTE · PROFESSEUR À L'UNIVERSITÉ DE PARIS VIII
HISTOIRE
DE VIVE VOIX

LES TROUS NOIRS
JEAN-PIERRE LUMINET · ASTROPHYSICIEN OBSERVATOIRE DE PARIS
SCIENCES
DE VIVE VOIX

MARIE-CHRISTINE BARRAULT
MAISONS · TEXTES DE MAUPASSANT, DAUDET, BORGES ET NGOLF
LITTÉRATURE
DE VIVE VOIX

MARS
JEAN-PIERRE BIBRING · ASTROPHYSICIEN À L'INSTITUT D'ASTROPHYSIQUE SPATIALE
SCIENCES
DE VIVE VOIX

MICHEL PICCOLI
LE HASARD · TEXTES DE BORGES, TCHEKHOV ET TWAIN
LITTÉRATURE
DE VIVE VOIX

HUBERT REEVES
LA NUIT · TEXTES DE PROUST, BUZZATI, MAUPASSANT ET CORTAZAR
LITTÉRATURE
DE VIVE VOIX

NEUF CONTES POUR NOS ENFANTS · LIVRET INCLUS
MARTIN WINCKLER
JEUNESSE
DE VIVE VOIX

VOLCANS
CLAUDE JAUPART · DIRECTEUR DE L'INSTITUT DE PHYSIQUE DU GLOBE
SCIENCES
DE VIVE VOIX

MAI 68
MICHEL WINOCK · PROFESSEUR À L'INSTITUT D'ÉTUDES POLITIQUES
HISTOIRE
DE VIVE VOIX

LE GOULAG
NICOLAS WERTH · CHARGÉ DE RECHERCHES AU CNRS (IHTP)
HISTOIRE
DE VIVE VOIX

LA GUERRE D'ALGÉRIE
JEAN-CHARLES JAUFFRET · PROFESSEUR À L'INSTITUT D'ÉTUDES POLITIQUES D'AIX EN PROVENCE
HISTOIRE
DE VIVE VOIX

LE MONDE QUANTIQUE UNE INTRODUCTION
JEAN-MARC LÉVY-LEBLOND · PROFESSEUR À L'UNIVERSITÉ DE NICE
SCIENCES
DE VIVE VOIX

LA RADIOACTIVITÉ
ÉTIENNE KLEIN · PHYSICIEN AU CEA
SCIENCES
DE VIVE VOIX

LE NAZISME EN GUERRE
CHRISTIAN INGRAO · CHERCHEUR ASSOCIÉ AU CNRS (IHTP)
HISTOIRE
DE VIVE VOIX

LES GALAXIES
MARC LACHIÈZE-REY · ASTROPHYSICIEN AU CEA
SCIENCES
DE VIVE VOIX

LA MATIÈRE
JEAN-MARC LÉVY-LEBLOND · PROFESSEUR À L'UNIVERSITÉ DE NICE
SCIENCES
DE VIVE VOIX

COSMOLOGIE
MARC LACHIÈZE-REY · ASTROPHYSICIEN AU CEA DIRECTEUR DE RECHERCHES AU CNRS
SCIENCES
DE VIVE VOIX

LES CATHARES
JEAN-LOUIS BIGET · PROFESSEUR ÉMÉRITE À L'ÉCOLE NORMALE SUPÉRIEURE
HISTOIRE
DE VIVE VOIX

LES GLACES
CLAUDE LORIUS · MEMBRE DE L'ACADÉMIE DES SCIENCES
SCIENCES
DE VIVE VOIX

LA GRANDE GUERRE
S. AUDOIN-ROUZEAU · UNIVERSITÉ DE PICARDIE
HISTOIRE
DE VIVE VOIX

ISLAM ET OCCIDENT
OLIVIER ROY · DIRECTEUR DE RECHERCHE AU CNRS
HISTOIRE
DE VIVE VOIX

ISABELLE CARRÉ
LES BEAUX JOURS · TEXTES DE CAMUS, COLETTE, MAETERLINCK, DAUDET ET PROUST
LITTÉRATURE
DE VIVE VOIX

ETOILES
MICHEL CASSÉ · ASTROPHYSICIEN AU CEA
SCIENCES
DE VIVE VOIX

5

J'AI CONNU UNE JEUNE FILLE QUI ME CONTA L'HISTOIRE SUIVANTE. ELLE LA TENAIT DE SON PÈRE:

C'ÉTAIT LE PRINTEMPS. NOUS VENIONS DE RENTRER DU BOIS.

6

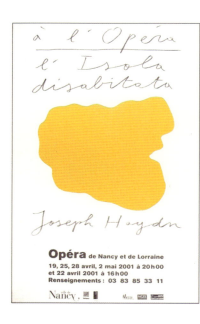

à l'Opéra
L'Isola disabitata

Joseph Haydn

Opéra de Nancy et de Lorraine
19, 25, 28 avril, 2 mai 2001 à 20h00
et 22 avril 2001 à 16h00
Renseignements : 03 83 85 33 11

Nancy,

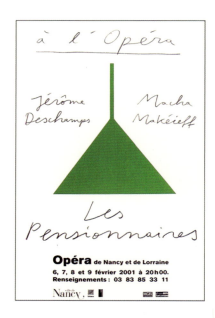

à l'Opéra

Jérôme Deschamps   Macha Makéieff

Les Pensionnaires

Opéra de Nancy et de Lorraine
6, 7, 8 et 9 février 2001 à 20h00.
Renseignements : 03 83 85 33 11

Nancy,

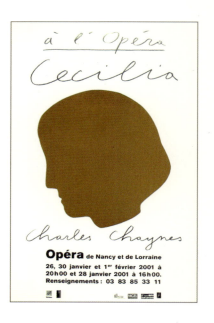

à l'Opéra
Cecilia

Charles Chaynes

Opéra de Nancy et de Lorraine
26, 30 janvier et 1er février 2001 à
20h00 et 28 janvier 2001 à 16h00.
Renseignements : 03 83 85 33 11

Nancy,

Orchestre

Saison 2000-2001

Orchestre Symphonique et Lyrique de Nancy
03 83 85 30 60

Nancy,

à l'Opéra
abonnements
2000-2001

amour, désir, trahison,
légèreté, larmes, fidélité,
liberté, souffrance, passion

Opéra de Nancy et de Lorraine
03 83 85 30 60

Nancy,

à l'Opéra
Fidelio

Ludwig van Beethoven

Opéra de Nancy et de Lorraine
5, 7, 13 et 16 juin 2001 à 20h00, 10 juin
2001 à 16h00
Renseignements : 03 83 85 33 11

Nancy,

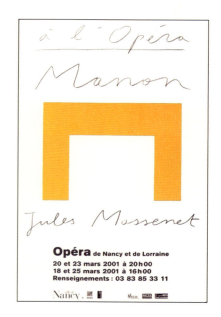

à l'Opéra
Manon

Jules Massenet

Opéra de Nancy et de Lorraine
20 et 23 mars 2001 à 20h00
18 et 25 mars 2001 à 16h00
Renseignements : 03 83 85 33 11

Nancy,

à l'Opéra
Saison 2000-2001

Peter Grimes Falstaff Cecilia
Les Pensionnaires Manon
L'Isola disabitata Fidelio

Opéra de Nancy et de Lorraine
03 83 85 30 60

Nancy,

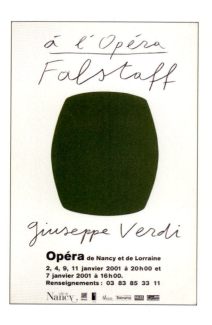

à l'Opéra
Falstaff

Giuseppe Verdi

Opéra de Nancy et de Lorraine
2, 4, 9, 11 janvier 2001 à 20h00 et
7 janvier 2001 à 16h00.
Renseignements : 03 83 85 33 11

Nancy,

7

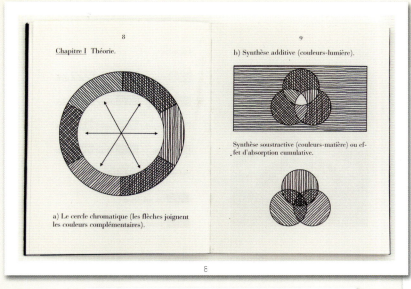

7.   Poster, l'Opéra de Nancy et de
        Lorraine, l'Opéra de Nancy et de
        Lorraine, France, 2000-1. With
        Félix Müller and Ruedi Baur
        ----
8.   Book spreads, *L'art de la couleur*,
        La Petite Pierre, Belgium, 1998
        ----
9.   Book spread, *Coxcodex 1*, Le Seuil,
        France, 2003

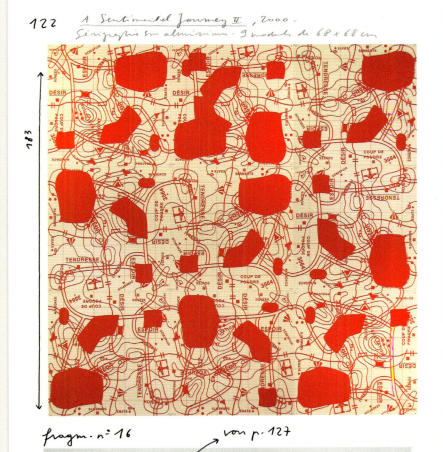

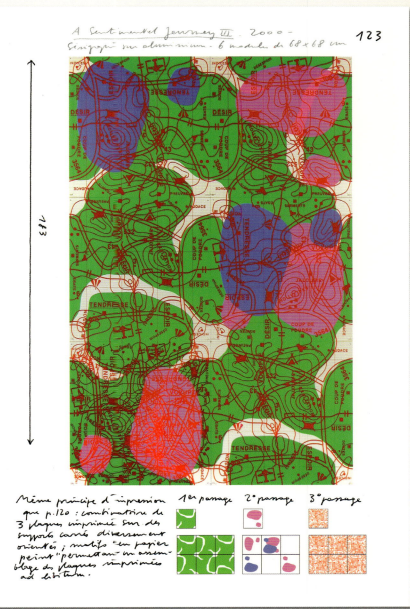

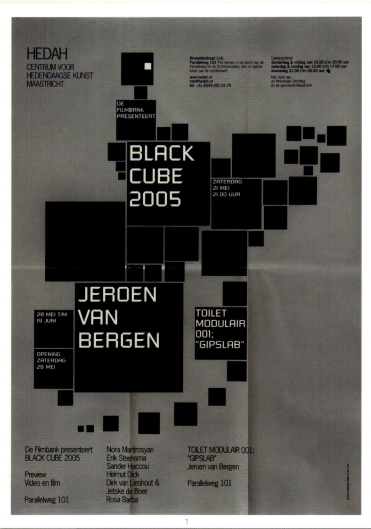

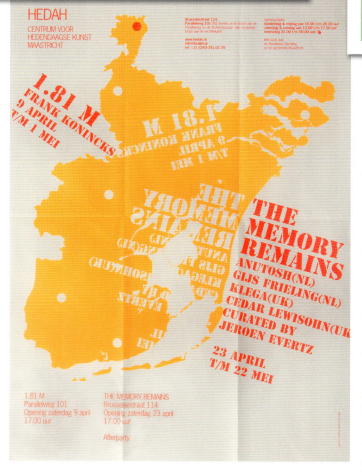

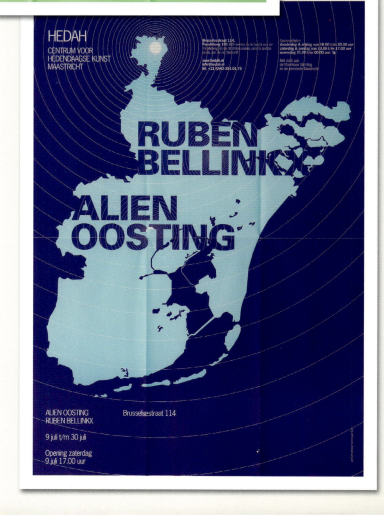

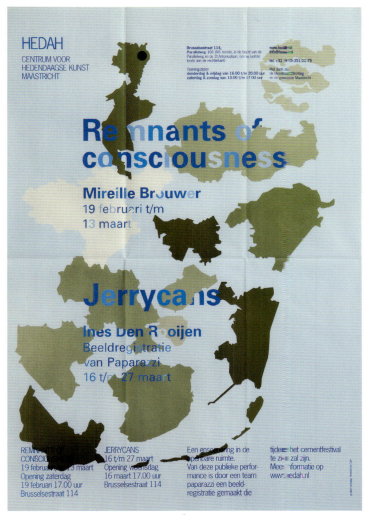

Vanessa van Dam (Amsterdam). --- Beneath Vanessa van Dam's long hair, behind her green eyes and freckles, is a designer who is friendly, patient (sometimes), opinionated, cheerful, extroverted, passionate serious, sincere, and dedicated. When van Dam was fifteen, she wanted to become a fashion designer, and spent her time reading fashion magazines and admiring clothes by Claude Montana, Jean Paul Gaultier, and Vivienne Westwood. But she fell in love with graphic design after a visit to the Hard Werken studio in Rotterdam, and decided to study at the Gerrit Rietveld Academie under Linda van Deursen. --- Much like her personality, van Dam's designs are multilayered yet never so complex that they are inaccessible. Her most outstanding project—and my favorite—is the book she produced with photographer Martine Stig, *Any Resemblance to Existing Persons Is Purely Coincidental*. The project grew out of van Dam and Stig's shared fascination with the likes of Paul Auster and Sophie Calle. In *Any Resemblance...*, they investigate the conventions of classical film in Bombay (Bollywood) and Los Angeles (Hollywood). They created two versions of the same character—called Mr. Wood—based on the differences between the two cities. A mixture of maps, photographs, drawings, and text, the book falls somewhere between an alternative travel guide, a manual for writing screenplays, and a detective story. --- The strong conceptual foundation, intricate layering, and sheer beauty of the book represent van Dam's work very well. Her designs, like Mr. Wood himself, are amalgams of multiple pieces and ideas, in which nothing feels forced, and everything comes together at the end. --- Irma Boom

1-2.   Poster series, Hedah Center for Contemporary Art Maastricht, Hedah Center for Contemporary Art Maastricht, The Netherlands, 2004

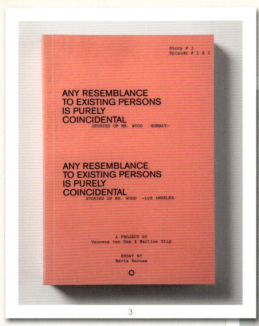

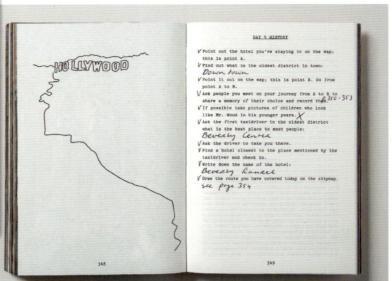

3. Book cover and spreads, *Any Resemblance to Existing Persons Is Purely Coincidental*, Revolver Books, Germany, 2006. With Martine Stig

----

4. Book cover, *Dat museum is een mijnheer: de geschiedenis van het Van Abbemuseum 1936–2003* (That Museum Is a Gentleman: The History of the Van Abbemuseum 1936–2003) by René Pingen, Artimo, The Netherlands, 2005

----

5. Catalog cover and spreads, De Nederlandsche Bank art collection, De Nederlandsche Bank, The Netherlands, 2007. The cover was inspired by the design of the Dutch guilder and printed in gold ink.

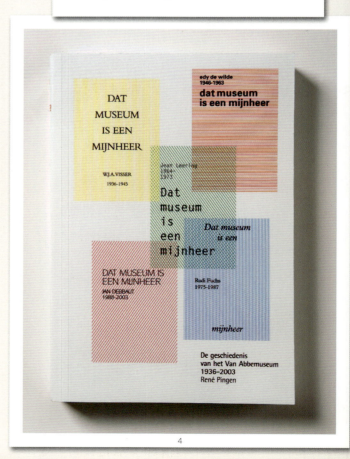

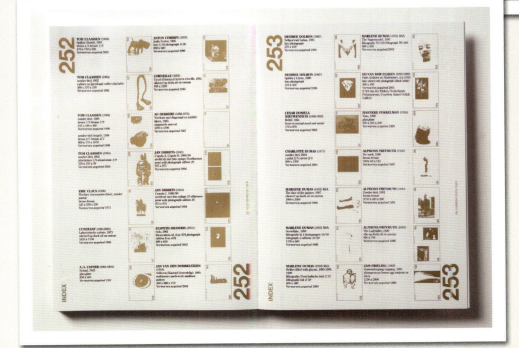

Particule Projection (Loop)

Simon Starling

L'installation est visible tous les jours, de la tombée du jour à minuit, depuis l'extérieur du Wiels.
De installatie is elke dag te bezichtigen, van zonsondergang tot middernacht, aan de buitenkant van Wiels.
The installation is visible every day, from sunset to midnight, from the exterior of Wiels.

15|03 — 22|04|2007

Avenue Van Volxem*laan* 354
1190 Bruxelles *Brussel* **Brussels**
Tram: 18 & 52, Bus: 49 & 50
Arrêt *Halte* **Stop**: Wielemans

Info Conférences *Lezingen* **Lectures**:
www.wiels.org

WIELS

1

Marcel Berlanger

Tore

05.05 — 26.05.2007
du jeudi au dimanche
donderdag tot zondag
15:00 — 20:00
vernissage *opening*
04.05.2007, 18:00

Supported by **KUNSTENFESTIVALDESARTS 07** cera
En 2007, le fonctionnement artistique du Wiels est soutenu par De Vlaamse Overheid et La Communauté Française *Voor de artistieke werking in 2007 krijgt Wiels de steun van De Vlaamse Overheid en La Communauté Française* Partenaires **Partners**: Puilaetco Dewaay Private Bankers sa-nv, Leon Eeckman sa-nv, Duvel

Intervention musicale par Ictus
Musicale interventie door Ictus
10.05.2007, 19:00, 20:00, 21:00

Concept: Marcel Berlanger
Lighting design: Julie Petit-Etienne
Music: Cédric Dambrain
Presentation & coproduction:
Wiels, Kunstenfestivaldesarts

Avenue Van Volxem*laan* 354
1190 Bruxelles *Brussel*
www.wiels.org

Ouverture première étape
Opening eerste stadium
25.05.2007

WIELS

Sara De Bondt (London). --- Based in London, Sara De Bondt excels at making elegant graphics for cultural institutions and small publishers. Emerging in 2004 from the renowned studio Foundation 33, De Bondt has developed a recognizable graphic sensibility that is steeped in 1960s and '70s modernist aesthetics but is utterly contemporary in its versatility and use of pop-flavored colors. She frequently superimposes color tones over type, relying on the kind of simple, striking typographic compositions that convey a message while adding both literal and figurative layers of information to the affair. Her exhibition catalogs and graphics display a sincere, smart sense of humor and an interest in visual sleights of hand, while her extensive identity work for the Wiels Center for Contemporary Art in Brussels takes these qualities to a higher level. The Wiels identity smartly allows bold typography to do the heavy lifting. Instead of working with images, De Bondt devised a clever and colorful modular system that places the information first, accenting it with flat bands of color, like a 1970s Penguin paperback. It is a striking campaign at any scale, and marks De Bondt as a versatile visual thinker. --- Dan Nadel

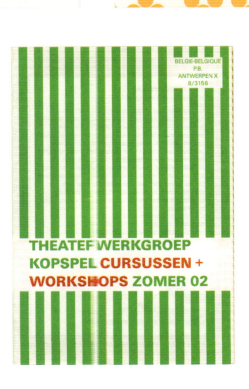

1.   Identity system, Wiels Center for Contemporary Art, Wiels, Belgium, 2006-present
----
2.   Brochure covers and spread, *Cursussen + Workshops*, Theaterwerkgroep Kopspel, Belgium, 2001-2

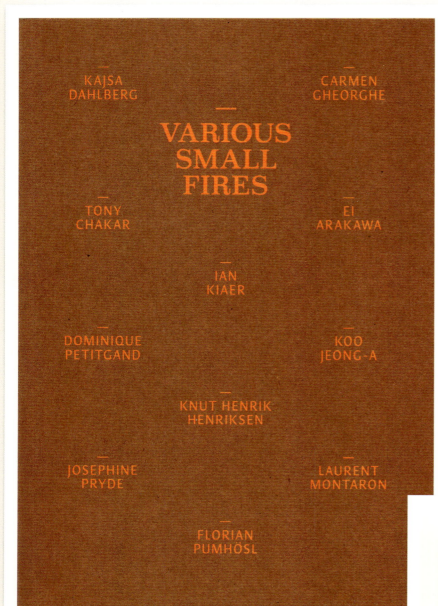

KAJSA
DAHLBERG

CARMEN
GHEORGHE

VARIOUS
SMALL
FIRES

TONY
CHAKAR

EI
ARAKAWA

IAN
KIAER

DOMINIQUE
PETITGAND

KOO
JEONG-A

KNUT HENRIK
HENRIKSEN

JOSEPHINE
PRYDE

LAURENT
MONTARON

FLORIAN
PUMHÖSL

3

Laurie Britton Newell

Out of the
Ordinary:
Spectacular
Craft

V&A Publications and the Crafts Council

4

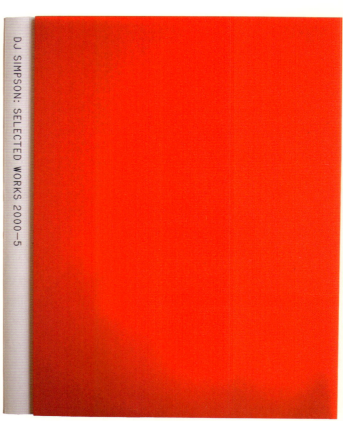

DJ SIMPSON: SELECTED WORKS 2000–5

5

3.   Cover, exhibition catalog, *Various
      Small Fires*, Royal College of Art,
      UK, 2007. With Kaisa Lassinaro
      ----
4.   Cover, exhibition catalog, *Out
      of the Ordinary: Spectacular Craft*,
      curated by Laurie Britton Newell,
      V&A Publications and the Crafts
      Council, UK, 2007
      ----
5.   Cover, exhibition catalog, *DJ Simp-
      son: Selected Works 2000-5*, Mead
      Gallery, UK, 2006. With James Goggin
      ----
6.   Exhibition guide series, *File Notes*,
      Camden Arts Center, UK, 2003-present.
      Images and information about every
      exhibition at the gallery. With
      James Goggin

Rachel Harrison

Camden Arts Centre / January — April 2004
File Note #01 Rachel Harrison

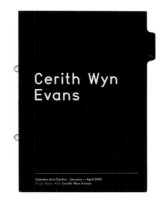

Cerith Wyn Evans

Camden Arts Centre / January — April 2004
File Note #02 Cerith Wyn Evans

Francis Upritchard

Camden Arts Centre / January — April 2004
File Note #03 Francis Upritchard

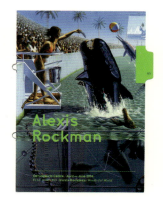

Alexis Rockman

Camden Arts Centre / April — June 2004
File Note #04 Alexis Rockman: Wonderful World

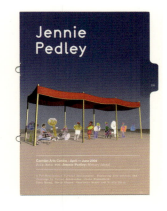

Jennie Pedley

Camden Arts Centre / April — June 2004
File Note #06 Jennie Pedley: Misery Moon

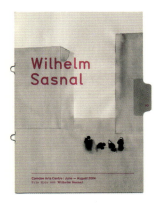

Wilhelm Sasnal

Camden Arts Centre / June — August 2004
File Note #07 Wilhelm Sasnal

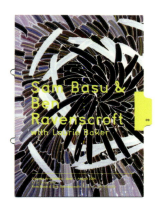

Sam Basu & Ben Ravenscroft
with Laurie Baker

Camden Arts Centre / June — August 2004

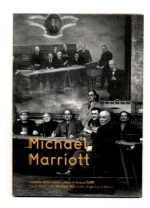

Michael Marriott

Camden Arts Centre / June — August 2004
File Note #09 Michael Marriott: Kingdom of Kibris

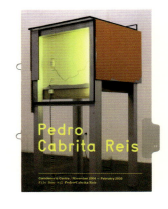

Pedro Cabrita Reis

Camden Arts Centre / November 2004 — February 2005
File Note #12 Pedro Cabrita Reis

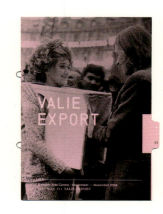

VALIE EXPORT

Camden Arts Centre / September — November 2004
File Note #11 VALIE EXPORT

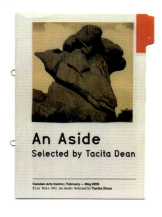

An Aside
Selected by Tacita Dean

Camden Arts Centre / February — May 2005
File Note #01 An Aside: Selected by Tacita Dean

Verne Dawson

Camden Arts Centre / May — July 2005
File Note #02 Verne Dawson

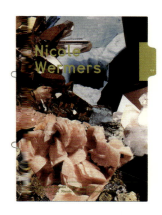

Nicole Wermers

Camden Arts Centre / May — July 2005

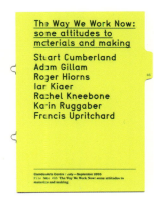

The Way We Work Now:
some attitudes to materials and making

Stuart Cumberland
Adam Gillam
Roger Hiorns
Iar Kiaer
Rachel Kneebone
Karin Ruggaber
Francis Upritchard

Camden Arts Centre / July — September 2005
File Note #04 The Way We Work Now: some attitudes to
materials and making

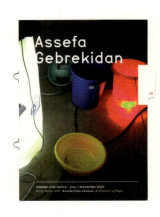

Assefa Gebrekidan

Camden Arts Centre / July — September 2005
File Note #05 Assefa Gebrekidan: A Glimmer of Hope

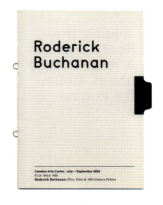

Roderick Buchanan

Camden Arts Centre / July — September 2005
File Note #06 Roderick Buchanan: Film, Video & 18th-Century Politics

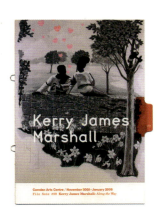

Kerry James Marshall

Camden Arts Centre / November 2005 — January 2006
File Note #09 Kerry James Marshall: Along the Way

Ilana Halperin

Camden Arts Centre / July — November 2005
File Note #08 Ilana Halperin: Nomadic Landmass (London)

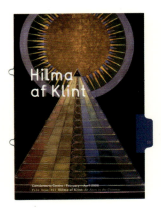

Hilma af Klint

Camden Arts Centre / February — April 2006
File Note #11 Hilma af Klint: the Secret in the Drawings

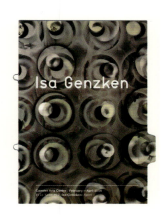

Isa Genzken

Camden Arts Centre / February — April 2006
File Note #14 Isa Genzken

1

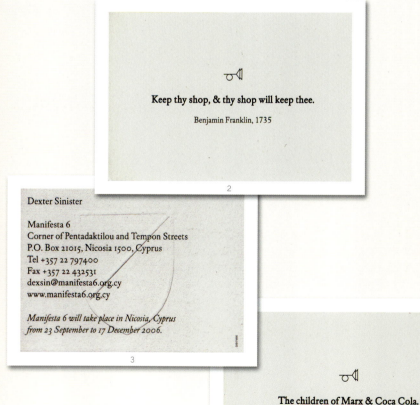

2

Keep thy shop, & thy shop will keep thee.

Benjamin Franklin, 1735

Dexter Sinister

Manifesta 6
Corner of Pentadaktilou and Tempon Streets
P.O. Box 21015, Nicosia 1500, Cyprus
Tel +357 22 797400
Fax +357 22 432531
dexsin@manifesta6.org.cy
www.manifesta6.org.cy

*Manifesta 6 will take place in Nicosia, Cyprus
from 23 September to 17 December 2006.*

3

The children of Marx & Coca Cola.

Jean-Luc Godard, 1966

4

Dexter Sinister (New York). --- Dexter Sinister is more a space than a design studio, but as such it might represent an ideal model for what a contemporary graphic design practice could be. Specifically, Dexter Sinister (the name comes from the heraldic terms for "right" and "left") is a basement space on Ludlow Street on Manhattan's Lower East Side, where David Reinfurt and Stuart Bailey collaborate on projects and run their Just-In-Time Workshop and Occasional Bookstore. Their mission is to challenge wasteful large-scale publishing and distribution practices with efficient, localized, and self-produced methods. --- Of the various graphic elements and themes in Dexter Sinister's work, two symbols best illustrate the approach and spirit of their workshop: a blank shield and a muted horn. The shield, divided diagonally as an "and/or" space for dichotomies (and/or alliances), was initially proposed to accompany the 2006 Manifesta art biennial. The muted postal horn, lifted from Thomas Pynchon's *The Crying of Lot 49*, can be found stenciled at street level on the otherwise hard-to-find Dexter Sinister basement staircase, and used as a logo on announcements and other printed matter, making an apt parallel between the novel's underground postal system and the studio's alternative press. --- Dexter Sinister's intention to "collapse distinctions of editing, design, production, and distribution into one efficient activity" is a logical mission to undertake at this point in graphic design history. While our previously specialized discipline has been opened up to the general public by the personal computer (supposedly to its detriment), publishing and distribution have now been equally democratized by the Internet, to graphic design's advantage. At the same time, technological progress has made previously out-of-reach printing processes accessible to independent graphic designers. So now Dexter Sinister can use an online, print-on-demand service to publish one book in America, while another might be printed on an underused small-run mimeograph machine for a local publisher in Europe. The graphic designer has always occupied a unique position between reading, writing, editing, curating, and distributing. Add to this diverse body of knowledge a natural impulse to research and produce, and it makes sense that graphic design discourse between people like Reinfurt and Bailey might manifest itself in an operation like Dexter Sinister. --- James Goggin

1-10. Miscellaneous ephemera and event announcements, self-commissioned, USA, 2006-7

Just-In-Time Workshop & Occasional Bookstore, open 12–6pm Saturdays
38 Ludlow Street (basement), New York, www.dextersinister.org

5

73735 45963 78134 63873
02965 58303 90708 20025
98859 23851 27965 62394
33666 62570 64775 78428
81666 26440 20422 05720

15838 47174 76866 14330
89793 34378 08730 56522
78155 22466 81978 57323
16381 66207 11698 99314
75002 80827 53867 37797

99982 27601 62686 44711
84543 87442 50033 14021
77757 54043 46176 42391
80871 32792 87989 72248
30500 28220 12444 71840

from A Million Random Digits, 1955

6

Dexter Sinister cordially invites you to

KELLER IM KELLER

To celebrate this opening of the Kiosk exhibition at Artists Space
Christoph Keller will host a late night of sampling high-end alcohol
distilled on his farm Stählemühle in rural Germany, with cheese

FROM 9PM ONWARDS

Dexter Sinister (a short walk across town)
Just-In-Time Workshop & Occasional Bookstore
38 Ludlow St. (basement) between Hester and Grand
Tel +1 213 235 6296 / +1 917 741 8949

7

Vs.

8

9

Information Wants To Be Free.
Information also wants to be expensive.
Information wants to be free because
it has become so cheap to distribute,
copy, and recombine—too cheap to
meter. It wants to be expensive because
it can be immeasurably valuable to
the recipient. That tension will not go
away. It leads to endless wrenching
debate about price, copyright, 'intellectual property', the moral rightness
of casual distribution, because each
round of new devices makes the tension worse, not better.

Stewart Brand, 1987

10

11

FRIDAY DECEMBER 15 2006

UNDERGROUND SECULAR XMAS MUSIC FOR THE MASSES ARRANGED BY ALEX WATERMAN (IN ABSENTIA)

TO CELEBRATE A TRINITY OF NEW PUBLICATIONS:

DOT DOT DOT 13
+
THE UNCERTAIN STATES OF AMERICA READER
+
CHRIS EVANS
MAGNETIC PROMENADE AND OTHER SCULPTURE PARKS

7PM TIL LATE, ALL WELCOME

DEXTER SINISTER
JUST-IN-TIME WORKSHOP & OCCASIONAL BOOKSTORE
38 LUDLOW STREET (BASEMENT)
NEW YORK CITY

12

11-14. Miscellaneous ephemera and event
    announcements, self-commissioned,
    USA, 2006-7

At the beginning of the 20th-century, Ford Motor Company established the first widely-adopted model of factory production. Breaking down the manufacture of a Model T automobile into its constituent processes and assigning these to a sequence of workers and inventories, significant efficiencies could be realized. This Assembly-Line approach utilized increasingly specialized skills of each worker on a coordinated production line as the manufactured product proceeded from beginning to end. Large inventories, skilled laborers and extensive capital investment were required. Design revisions were expensive (if not impossible) to implement and the feedback loop with its surrounding economy was largely absent. Complicit with its early-Capitalist context, manufacturing at this scale remained necessarily in the hands of those with the resources to maintain it.

By the mid-1950s, Toyota Motor Corporation of Japan began to explore a more fluid production model. Without the massive warehouse spaces available to store inventories required for an Assembly-Line, Toyota developed the Just-In-Time production model and inverted the stakes of manufacturing. By exploiting and implementing a fluid communications infrastructure along the supply line of parts, manufacturers, labor and customers, Toyota could maintain smaller inventories and make rapid adjustments. A quicker response time was now possible and products could be made when they were needed. All of the work could be handled by a wider number of less-specialized workers and design revisions could be made on-the-fly without shutting down production and re-tooling. The result was an immediate surplus of cash (due to reduced inventories) and a sustainable, responsive design and production system—smaller warehouses, faster communications networks, responsive and iterative design revision and products made as they are needed: Just-In-Time.

It isn't difficult to imagine a correspondence between these two models (Assembly-Line, Just-In-Time) and contemporary modes of print production. The prevailing model of professional practice is firmly entrenched in the Fordist Assembly-Line. Writing, design, production, printing and distribution are each handled discretely by specialists as the project proceeds through a chain of command and production. Recently, laserprinters, photocopiers, page-layout softwares, cellphones, and word processors have split this model wide open. A project might reasonably be written by the publisher who begins a layout and works with the designer who commissions a writer, and sources a printer that will produce fifty copies by Wednesday.

In the basement at 38 Ludlow Street we will set up a fully-functioning Just-In-Time workshop, against waste and challenging the current state of over-production driven by the conflicting combination of print economies-of-scale (it only makes financial sense to produce large quantities) and the contained audiences of art world marketing (no profit is really expected, and not many copies really need to be made.) These divergent criteria are too often manifested in endless boxes of unsaleable stock taking up space which needs to be further financed by galleries, distributors, bookstores, etc. This over-production then triggers a need to overcompensate with the next, and so on and so on. Instead, all our various production and distribution activities will be collapsed into the basement, which will double as a bookstore, as well as a venue for intermittent film screenings, performance and other events.

There is a certain sense in which we are wholly involved in metaphor and in which a small construct such as this—local to its context and wholly a one-off—may show some value also as a model, which will then be a model of address, of attitude and approach, rather than one of our outcome or consequence. I do not want to strain its credibility further than that. In a more diffuse way, the same might be said of a small workshop. I hope however that by veering so alarmingly between the general and the particular, and between the realms of metaphor and practicality, I have suggested to you that every technical possibility has a wider equivalence, and a positive need to seek relationship with its neighbours. There are many roles for your own future workshops, and I hope you will occupy them with devotion, intelligence, and high good humour. Good luck with your inheritance!*

THE ART OF EXHIBITIONS is the English translation of a book originally published in German in 1991. It is a collection of thirty chapters, each documenting a significant art exhibition from the 20th century, compiled and edited by Bernd Kaiser and Katharina Hegewisch. In 2001 a London art publisher translated, re-edited, re-scanned and re-designed the new edition. Then, just as the book was about to go to press, the company suddenly folded and the project effectively evaporated. In the six years since, the project files — which represent a couple of years of more or less hard labour — have barely survived several scarred hard drives and compact discs. We propose here to rescue the chapters from technological purgatory and offer them for dissemination under the auspices of this (very) temporary art school before planned obsolescence finally renders them irretrievable.

Sharing this material freely in the collective, constructive spirit which marks the majority, if not all, of the exhibitions documented in the collection (i.e. without having to pay a publisher or lawyer a lot of money) necessitates crawling through a copyright loophole into a grey area. Who has the fundamental rights to the collection: the original publisher, the secondary publisher, the editors, or the authors? Of course, we don't really want to put ourselves in the position of finding out, assuming any of the above would stake some kind of claim and set off a chain of ugly bureaucracy.

Copyright was first instituted in England with the Statute of Anne in 1710 (subtitled "An Act for the Encouragement of Learning"). The original legislative purpose was to disrupt existing printers' monopolies by securing an author's rights to their text.

Three hundred years on, rabid perversions of the original law have rendered it almost meaningless. For example, the Sonny Bono Copyright Term Extension Limit, also known as the Mickey Mouse Protection Act, was passed in 1998. Terrified that its early animated classics were about to fall into the public domain, Walt Disney Company lobbied extensively to protect its copyright (at least for another twenty years.)

Today, copyrights typically default to publishing houses, who have the legal and financial resources to enforce this privilege. On this occasion, however, STORE has paid £105 (the fee for a small business with less than 50 employees) for a year-long photocopy license.

This allows anyone on their property to copy a complete chapter or up to 5% of the entire book (whichever is greater)

∵ the book is 300 pages and 30 chapters, each designed to be exactly 10 pages long

∴ YOU MAY FREELY COPY ANY ONE OF THE CHAPTERS

The arbitrary limitation of 5% immediately provokes ways of getting around it, in order to collect more chapters. For example, sharing copies with fellow 'students', re-copying and distributing elsewhere, returning on other occasions, etc. — all of which reclaim the idea and ideal of school as community rather than institution.

Furthermore, given that this English edition was never printed and bound, does it actually qualify as a 'book'? What exactly IS this free-floating information in publishing limbo without a definitive material end in sight? And, in fact, what exactly does 'publish' mean now?

Dexter Sinister
March 2007

Bob van Dijk (The Hague). --- Bob van Dijk revels
in collaboration and exchange and has worked in
studios for most of his career. He was a senior
designer at Studio Dumbar, that hothouse of
contrasting influences and assignments, and then
went on to cofound NLXL, where he is currently
a partner. Recently, he participated in a
Wieden+Kennedy brainstorm that resulted in Coca-
Cola's newest worldwide campaign. But although
he is a team player by nature, his work remains
highly personalized. His award-winning posters
for the Holland Dance Festival, with their concise
montages of type, black-and-white photography,
and fragmented musical notation, stood out among
Studio Dumbar's eclectic production of the 1990s.
In more recent years, van Dijk's visual idiom
has become even more idiosyncratic. His scrawing
handwriting is all over the place, often combined
with witty drawings that seem to have been
nonchalantly jotted down directly on the computer
screen. --- In fact, in one way or another, all
of van Dijk's work is about drawing. There is a
sense of spontaneity about it, a handmade quality
even in designs that have been created entirely
on the computer. His work is also about fun—about
the pleasure of creating signs, and the viewer's
joy in decoding them. --- Although playful and
highly entertaining, the imagery is never gratu-
itous. In the tradition of the best illustration-
driven graphic design, van Dijk's pictures
function as a kind of shorthand for their messages. A designer-run club called JetLag received
a 2-D mascot in the form of a smiling face that
doubles as a spinning vinyl record. A Japanese
restaurant was given an abstract identity that
evokes all things Asian without indulging in any
brushstroke clichés. A poster series advertising
a cultural night in The Hague, with extensive
programs that would be experienced differently
by each participant, was printed in one color,
after which each copy was individually redesigned
with spray paint and stencils by studio members
(and anyone else who happened to be around).
--- Van Dijk's work doesn't just promote clubs
and exotic food. He has also art directed serious,
respectable corporate design projects. While his
approach is as professional as can be expected
from a designer with his level of experience,
the results are never completely straightforward.
There is always a twist: the van Dijk touch.
--- Jan Middendorp

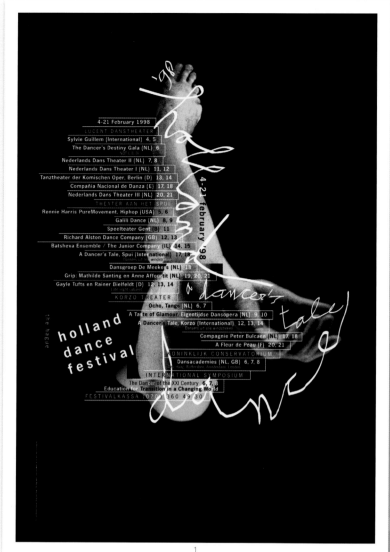

1

1.   Posters, Holland Dance Festival
     1995-98, Holland Dance Festival,
     The Netherlands, 1995-98. Designed
     while at Studio Dumbar
     ----
2.   Self-commissioned project, "Birth
     Stamps," The Netherlands, 2003. Made
     for the birth of van Dijk's first
     child, Zonne

3-6. Identity, Oni restaurant, Oni, The
     Netherlands, 2002

3

4

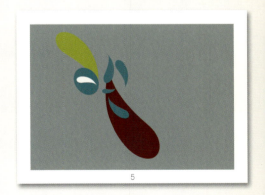

5

6

7

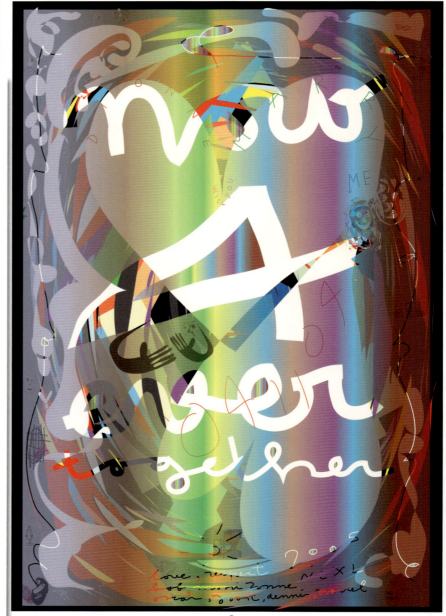

8

7-8.   Posters, Marc Shillum, The
Netherlands, 2004. Shillum commissioned the posters to propose to his
girlfriend. (She said yes.)
----
9.   Advertising campaign, Coca-Cola,
Wieden+Kennedy Amsterdam, The
Netherlands, 2007
----
10.   Poster, International Poster Gallery
in The Hague, Schoon of Schijn, The
Netherlands, 2007

11-12. Banners, JetLag lounge, JetLag,
The Netherlands, 2001

9

10

11

12

Arem Duplessis (New York). --- I lived in New
York City between 1985 and 1998, and I subscribed
to the *New York Times* Sunday edition at the time.
My favorite section was the magazine, which
I religiously collected. These magazines have
found a home in the library of the ZIVA (the
design school I founded in my hometown of Harare,
Zimbabwe). Arem Duplessis's impressive work for
the magazine as its current art director makes me
wish that we had some of these new issues in our
library's collection. His work is a useful example
of innovative typography; it makes explaining
elements like scale, space, rhythm, pun, and metaphor easier. --- Looking at his designs, I find
myself thinking of classic European typographers
and Russian Constructivists. Yet whatever cues
he might take from the masters, Duplessis's work
successfully maintains an individuality that makes
it exclusively his own. Due to the stature of his
employers, he has been able to choose from among
the very best photographers and illustrators
around, but even if he lacks a great photograph
or illustration, that does not stop him from
delivering impressive work week after week. He has
such an astute sense of type and white space that
the absence of imagery becomes an asset rather
than a hindrance. --- Duplessis cites fine art,
diagrams in old psychology textbooks, and sharks
(yes, sharks—he is an avid scuba diver) as inspirations. He is quick to add that magazine design
is a collaborative effort, and that as an art
director he has had the privilege of working
with very talented designers and editors. He has,
since the mid-1990s, created award-winning designs
for music magazines (*Blaze* and *Spin*), a fashion
magazine (*GQ*), and the *New York Times Magazine*,
his current home. Duplessis describes his style
as "simplicity with a twist of oddness." He
tries with all his might to avoid the vagaries
of trends, as he firmly believes that magazine
design should be timeless. --- It is easy to get
lost in the cacophony that characterizes magazine
design today. It is, therefore, extremely refreshing to come across a designer who is focused
on the relentless pursuit of design excellence,
using the basic tools of typography and white
space. Duplessis's work embodies that oft-used
but least-applied modernist mantra: Less is more.
Indeed. --- Saki Mafundikwa

1.   Cover, *New York Times Magazine*, New
      York Times, USA, 2004
      ----
2.   Magazine spread, "Radio Head," *Spin*,
      Vibe/Spin Ventures, USA, 2003
      ----
3.   Magazine spread, "Have You Seen This
      Man?" *GQ*, Condé Nast, USA, 2001
      ----
4.   Magazine spread, "The White Stripes,"
      Spin, Vibe/Spin Ventures, USA, 2003

2

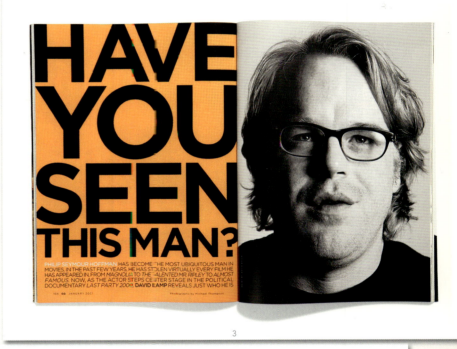

3

4

5

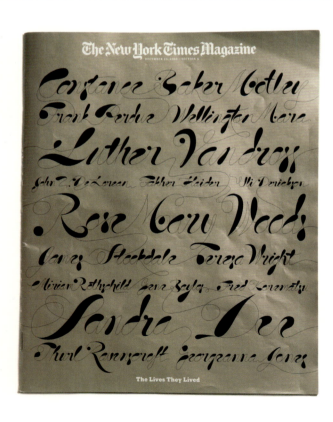

6

7

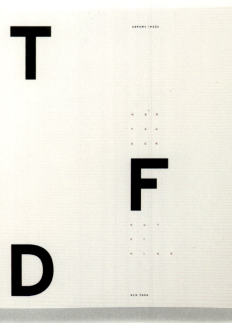

8

5.   Cover and spread, "The Real Estate
        Issue," *New York Times Magazine*, New
        York Times, USA, 2006
----
6.   Cover, *New York Times Magazine*, New
        York Times, USA, 2006. Illustration
        by Deanne Cheuk
----
7.   Pages, "On Language" by William
        Safire, *New York Times Magazine*, New
        York Times, USA, 2005-6. Illustra-
        tions by (top to bottom): Louise Fili
        and Steven Heller; Mario Hugo; Alan
        Dye; Si Scott
----
8.   Book cover and spreads, *Shawn
        Mortensen: Out of Mind*, Abrams Image,
        USA, 2007

AUDIO SPONGE SKETCH SHOW

1. CD cover, *Audio Sponge* by Sketch
    Show, Avex, Japan, 2002
    ----
2. Magazine illustration, *Public Image*,
    Public Image, Japan, 2005
    ----
3. Book illustration, *Asami Imajuku*,
    DesignExchange, Japan, 2003
    ----
4. Magazine illustration, *High Fashion*,
    Bunka Publishing Bureau, Japan, 2004.
    Dress by Issey Miyake

<u>Enlightenment</u> (Tokyo). --- Enlightenment is a design team that specializes in creating graphics for videos, commercial films, and publications. Its founder, Hiro Sugiyama, began his career as an illustrator at Flamingo Studio in the early 1980s. There, he learned under one of the most charismatic designers of the day, King Terry (Teruhiko Yumura), the man behind Japan's *heta-uma* (good-bad) design movement. Sugiyama went freelance in 1991, after winning the top prize in *Illustration* magazine's design competition, and in 1997 he launched his own studio. --- Most of Enlightenment's works look like digital paintings, but in fact they are all created by hand. Instead of using computer programs, Sugiyama and his team analyze color and shade with a laborious analog process, reflecting the group's mission: "shining light on forgotten traditions." Representative of this approach are Enlightenment's low-tech but high-fashion magazine illustrations that turn things as basic as folded cardboard into glamorous set pieces. Enlightenment's work has made a big impact on the Japanese scene. *Track*, a free magazine Sugiyama launched in conjunction with Enlightenment in 1997, was so popular that every copy disappeared the same day an issue was released. It is this kind of popularity, which only increased with Enlightenment's video work for Towa Tei's concerts and its cover art for albums by Audio Sponge and Bonnie Pink, that has led Sugiyama to regard design as an act governed by short-term consumption. --- Still, Sugiyama is conscious of his own desire to leave a lasting impact on the design world, and he has recently devoted himself to more permanent forms of media. Enlightenment has participated in exhibitions such as *Super Flat* (Takashi Murakami's show at the Museum of Contemporary Art in Los Angeles) and in festivals and solo exhibitions around Europe and Asia. In many ways, Sugiyama's career mirrors the development of Japanese graphic design, from the *heta-uma* movement to the recent explosion of video art. Enlightenment has been at the forefront of these trends since the studio began. It is the rare sort of design team that is admired not only by other designers, but also by club kids, book lovers, and art collectors. --- Keiichi Tanaami

3

4

5

6

5.   Exhibition invitation, *Mosslight
      2004 Spring & Summer*, Mosslight,
      Japan, 2004
----
6.   Magazine cover, *Huge*, Kodansha,
      Japan, 2005
----
7.   Exhibition poster, *Fishmans*, Nanzuka
      Underground, Japan, 2005
----
8.   Magazine illustration, *WWD*, WWD,
      Japan, 2005
----
9.   CD cover, *Reminiscence* by Bonnie
      Pink,   Warner Music, Japan, 2005
----
10.   CD cover, *Moon Beams* by Tsuki No Wa,
      Soundscape, Japan, 2003

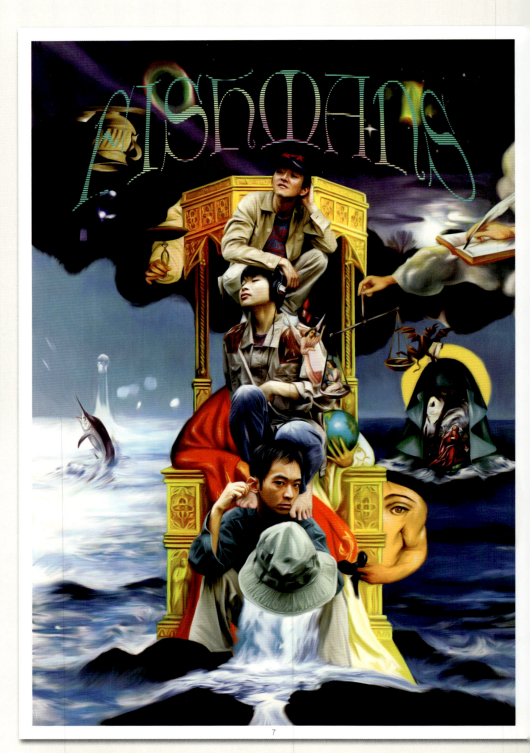

7

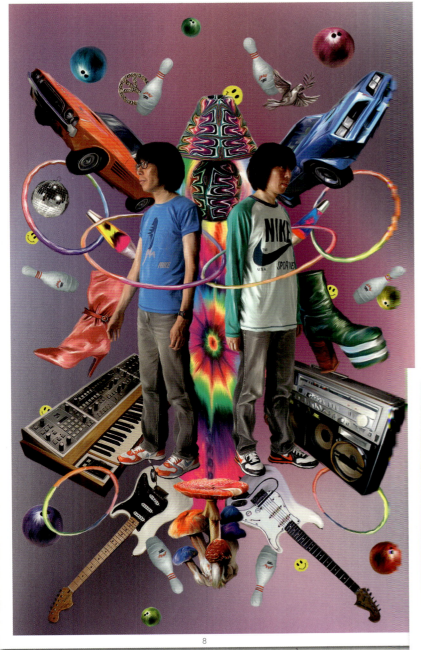

8

BONNIE PINK / REMINISCENCE

9

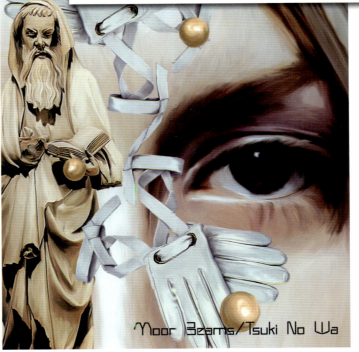

Moor Beams/Tsuki No Wa

10

1

2

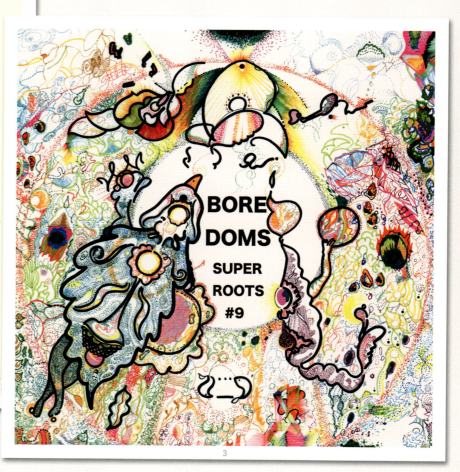

3

EYE (Tokyo). --- Zooming out of the 1980s Japanese underground, EYE (lead shaman of the noise-rock group Boredoms) forged a highly influential psychedelic punk style that has inspired a generation of D.I.Y. artists and designers. He is a master of the scrawl. His designs begin with a gesture, a loose pen mark or digital effect, and evolve into full-blown compositions. What is fascinating about EYE's work is that it seems to incorporate so many ideas at once. He created Boredoms' *Super Roots* record series using his trademarked, trippy, sun-worshipping style. His blossoming forms and exploding colors are not the graceful art nouveau designs of the 1960s, but clunky, off kilter, and falling in on themselves even as they reach ever higher. They are perfect reflections of Boredoms' music and the aspirations of blissed-out psychedelia. They are also, above all, indelible images, skillfully composed to hold their square boxes. --- Conversely, for Beck's *Midnight Vultures* record, EYE created a sexed-up digital world, transforming his style into a leering, computer-generated landscape with digital detritus piling up and threatening to smother both the musician and his band. EYE was one of the first designers to recognize the visual potential of degraded computer graphics and to apply it with a tagger's sense of slapdash urgency to record covers without a second thought. That EYE's work, both analog and digital, is instantly recognizable by vibe alone is a remarkable feat. In all his creative ventures, he is unafraid to embrace a wide range of sources, from the joyfulness of psychedelia to the ugliness of punk, pushing past graphic taste and into ecstatic graphic noise.
--- Dan Nadel

1.   CD cover, *Super Roots 7* by Boredoms, Warner Music, Japan, 1999
----
2.   CD cover, *Super Roots 5* by Boredoms, Warner Music, Japan, 1996
----
3.   Vinyl sleeve, *Super Roots 9* by Boredoms, Commons, Shock City, and Avex, Japan, 2007
----
4.   T-shirt design, Boredoms tour, Boretronix, Japan, 2000
----
5.   CD cover, *Seadrum House of Sun* by Boredoms, Warner Music, Japan, 2004

6

7

9

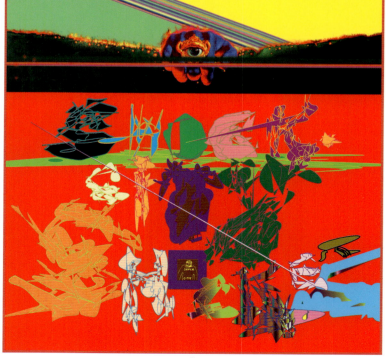

8

6.   Promotional flyer, *Shock City
     Shockers* album, Polystar Records,
     Japan, 2006
----
7.   CD cover, *Fire Escape* by Sunburned
     Hand of the Man, Small Town Super
     Sound, Japan, 2007
----
8.   Vinyl sleeve, *Shock City Shockers*,
     Polystar Records, Japan, 2000
----
9.   CD cover, *OOEYEOO: Eye Remix* by
     OOIOO, Felicity, Shock City, and
     Polystar Records, Japan, 2007

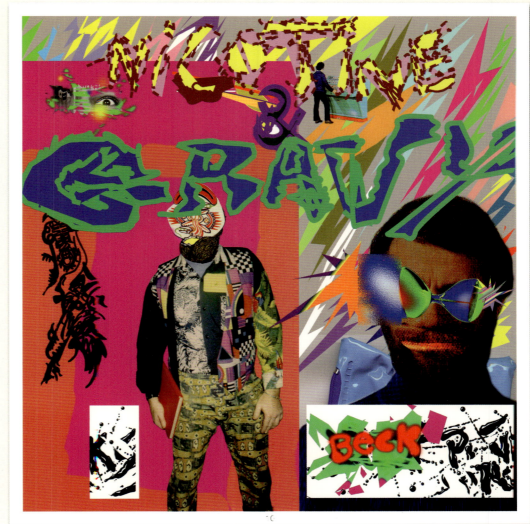

10. CD cover, *Nicotine and Gravy* by Beck,
    Universal, USA, 2000
    ----
11. T-shirt design, Raw Life, Japan, 2005
    ----
12. Vinyl sleeve, *The Lift Bcyz* by The
    Lift Boys, Passaby, Japar, 2007

11

12

Stephen Farrell (Chicago). --- Stephen Farrell's work is intricately detailed, avowedly noncommercial, and unabashedly intellectual. But it is not genteel. His typographic experiments pulse with blood, guts, and the occasional rush of semen. In the visual novel *VAS*, we learn that the average ejaculation of the human male produces only five cc of liquid: "not even a teaspoon." *VAS*, a full-on collaboration between Farrell and author Steve Tomasula, recounts the story of a man named Square, who has decided to have a vasectomy. Square must struggle with the idea of halting "the flow of his genes and his lineage," a troubling notion despite the fact that he has already fathered a daughter, Oval, with his wife, Circle. --- Refreshing as it is to see men address the subject of family planning (even in such narcissistic terms), more refreshing still is the novel's typographic realization. Farrell is a master typographer who continually plays the rational solidity of the manufactured book and letter against the fragile, fluid human gesture. *VAS* gathers its translucent layers of type and image from diverse cell lines: comic books, meat packaging, X-rays, DNA sequencing, and more. --- Throughout Farrell's work, the hard-edged square begets liquid lines. "Farewell to Kilimanjaro," another collaboration with Tomasula, resets Ernest Hemingway's short story in a depressing contemporary environment. Hemingway, an icon of macho self-possession, is now old and dying, hooked up to a colostomy bag, watching daytime television, and slipping in and out of lucidity. Farrell's design features a heavy black square, from which oozes an elegant, serpentine flourish. Farrell's digital typeface Volgare is based on a Florentine manuscript written in 1601 by an anonymous clerk. (Farrell studied the original at Chicago's Newberry Library.) Volgare includes more than five hundred distinct glyphs, including ligatures, word endings, and combination characters. Each one is raw and imperfect, erupting on the page like an abrasion or scar. --- Describing the impulses behind *VAS*, Farrell writes, "Typeset and clean, a gene like SHGC-110205 seems far, far outside us, even while geneticists claim it is a picture of our innermost core. We take this on faith, awaiting our scientist-editors to pull out their red pens and make corrections." If modern science, and modern design, have sought to neuter and sanitize the body, Farrell's work, quite the opposite, tries to keep it dirty. --- Ellen Lupton

1-2. Animated short film (unreleased), *TOC*, USA, 2008. *TOC* began as a graphic short story in *Emigré* magazine.

3-4. Book cover and spreads, *VAS: An Opera in Flatland*, Barrytown/Station Hill Press, USA, 2003

1

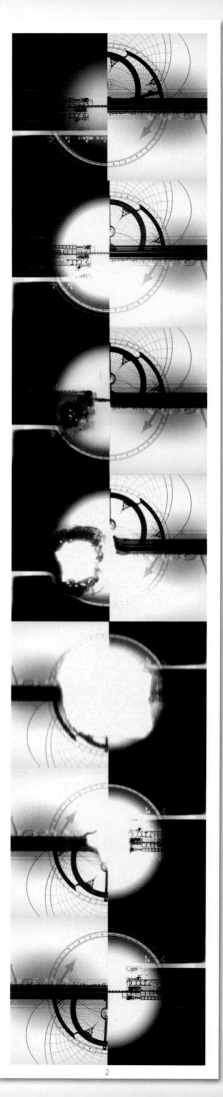

2

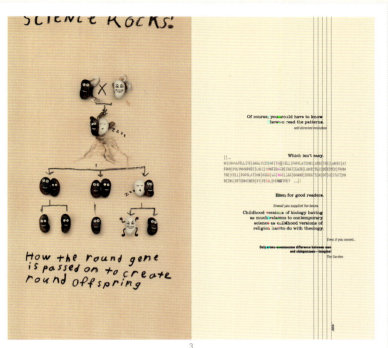

3

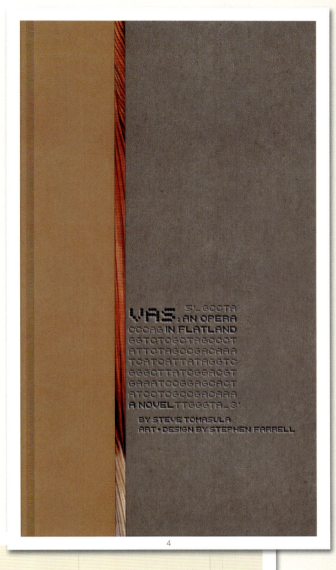

4

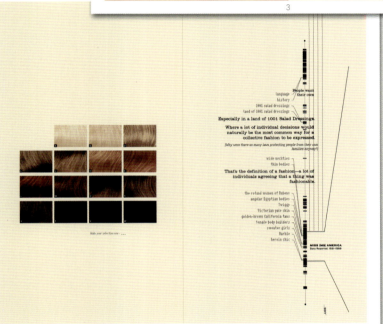

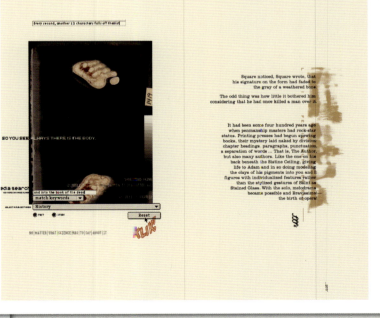

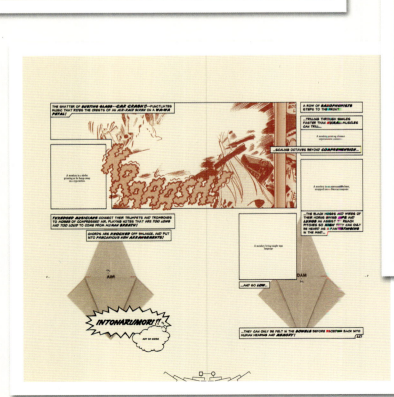

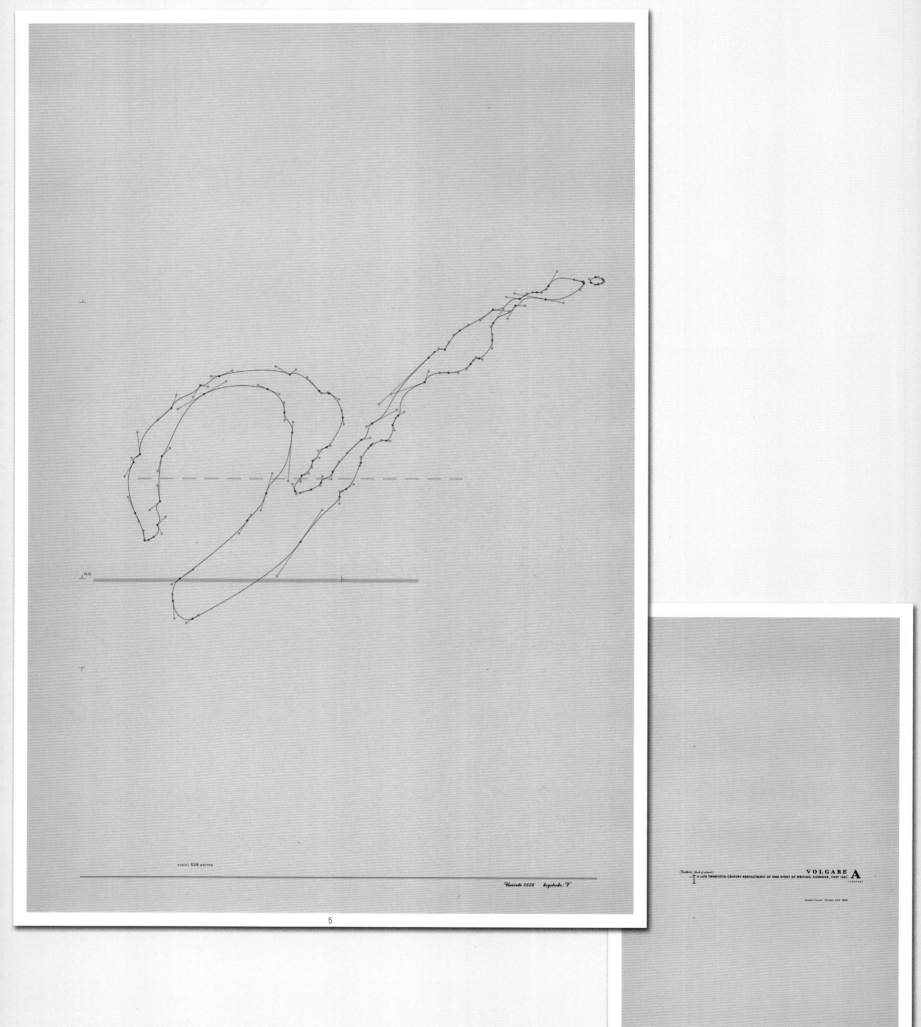

scale: 528 points

Unicode 0056   keystroke: V

5

VOLGARE A

Tratteria (lack of schools)
A LATE TWENTIETH-CENTURY REENACTMENT OF ONE EVENT OF WRITING, FLORENCE, ITALY 1663.

Stephen Farrell Chicago, USA 1995

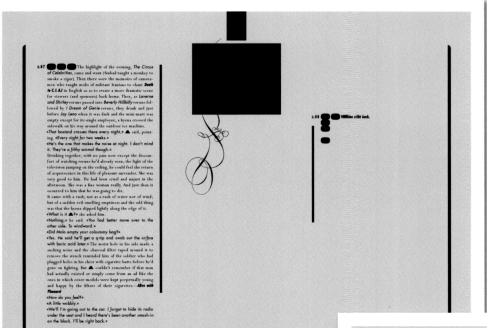

5. Typeface and handmade book, *The Volgare Project*, exhibited in *Design Culture Now*, Cooper-Hewitt, National Design Museum, USA, 2000

----

6. Publication spreads, "Farewell to Kilimanjaro," *The Pannus Index: 3 Easy Pieces*, The Pannus Index USA, 1998. This novella is based on Ernest Hemingway's short story "The Snows of Kilimanjaro."

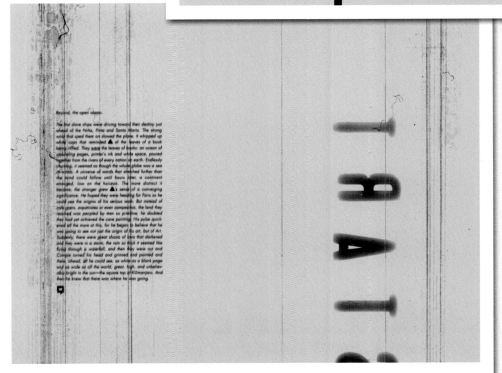

FLAG Aubry/Broquard (Zurich). --- FLAG is a two-man design studio based in Zurich, composed of Bastien Aubry and Dimitri Broquard. Having worked together since 2002, these two friends are both graphic designers and illustrators, as well as members of the seminal, but now defunct, Swiss drawing collective Silex. Like many young design studios in Zurich, FLAG focuses primarily on cultural and art-based projects, producing mainly monographs, posters, and magazines. They are distinguished by their casually rigorous blend of hand-drawn elements and no-fuss typography. Their post-punk scrawls, rooted in obvious drafts-manship but unleashed by the example of Gary Panter, have become the dominant drawn language of the day. And, like some of their compatriots in Zurich, Aubry and Broquard recognize the visual language of Internet culture and have adapted its low-res images and limited typographic options to the printed page, creating a kind of feedback loop of information design, from page to screen to page again. --- FLAG's recent "secret manifesto," *And There Will Be Light,* is a prime example of their postmillennial aesthetic. The book begins in darkness and then explodes into white spaces, its black-and-white imagery resembling nothing so much as a blown-out Xerox copy, with forms and details purposefully obscured. In this day of hyperactive production values and high-gloss sheen, the decision to design a crappy-looking, black-and-white artist's book for one's first publication makes a statement about a design company. *And There Will Be Light* scrolls through pages of doodles, photos, and the occasional actual product shot as it grows ever whiter, its hopeful progression a rare bit of honest optimism in a gloomy visual time.
--- Dan Nadel

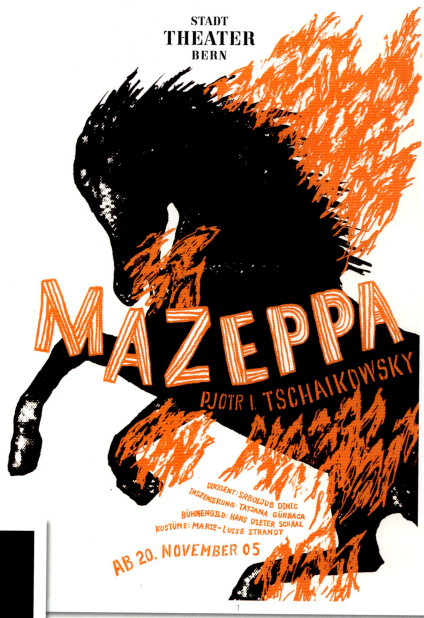

1-2.   Silkscreened performance posters, Stadt Theater Bern, Stadt Theater Bern, Switzerland, 2004-7. Swiss Federal Design Competition Award 2007.

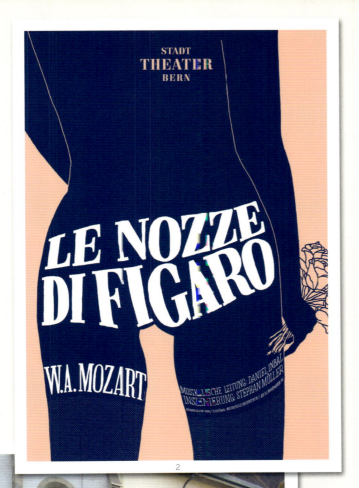

3

5

3.   Exhibition window decoration, *Plakat-sammlung*, Museum für Gestaltung Zürich, Switzerland, 2005
----
4.   Book cover, *And There Will Be Light*, Switzerland, 2006. Self-promotional book of unpublished images
----
5.   Identity system, Neue Kunst Halle St. Gallen, Switzerland, 2005-7. Includes invitations, diaries, exhibition catalog, and book
----
6-7. Exhibition posters, *Animaux, von menschen und tieren*, Seedamm Kulturzentrum, Schöne Aussichten am Bellevue, Switzerland, 2004
----
8.   Book illustration, *Armpit of the Mole*, Fundacis 30km/S, France and USA, 2005

4

JAGD

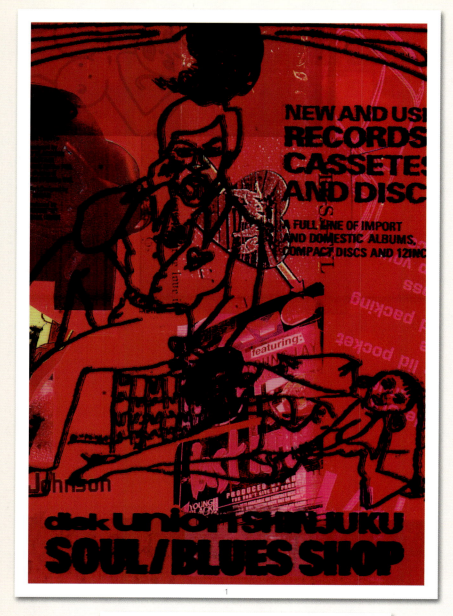

1

Flamingo Studio (Tokyo). --- Flamingo Studio is a Tokyo-based graphics powerhouse led by Teruhiko Yumura, who for decades has signed his work "Terry Johnson" or "King Terry." In the early 1970s, Yumura pioneered the *heta-uma* graphic style, more or less presiding over his own school of design. *Heta-uma* translates roughly to "bad-good." This doesn't mean "so bad it's good" but rather refers to the use of "bad" (that is, poorly drawn, rough, even offensive) art. It isn't kitsch but a different mode of communication. --- Yumura began by drawing in a resolutely ratty, disintegrating line, and, as a 1950s and '60s Americana obsessive, he appropriated the graphics of girlie magazines, romance comics, and pop music covers: all those ladies in stilted poses, couples in furtive dance positions, and men shaving or fixing their hair. Yumura avoids the slick, idealized style of the mainstream, using instead his own unique voice. With the glamour stripped away, those images become more attainable and more human. Yumura's work for publishing, advertising, and music clients ultimately transformed *heta-uma* into a dominant graphic style in Japan, and Yumura mentored many other illustrators, including Takashi Nemoto and Suzy Amakane. --- The moniker King Terry is a nod to American soul music, and over the years Yumura has given all his employees American soul-ified titles. Nowadays he has switched over to hip-hop and is sometimes known as Mista Gonzo. Yumura has become known for his work with the pop group Crazy Ken Band and for his hip-hop design sensibility. He has quite brilliantly adapted the language of lo-fi rap mix tapes (the kind one might buy from a street vendor) into a versatile graphic language of blown-out type splashed over recycled and processed urban imagery. And, as he did with the more overtly innocent images of mid-century America, Yumura has transformed the macho bombast of rap into something human-scale and slyly funny. King Terry, in all his various incarnations, might be the finest graphic commentator on America. He brings it all back to its rough, bad, and oh-so-good roots. --- Dan Nadel

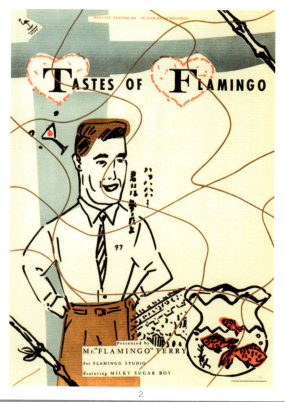

2

1. Poster, Disk Union record store, Disk Union Shinjuku, Japan, 2002
    ----
2. Poster, self-commissioned, Japan, 1982
    ----
3. Posters, Crazy Ken Band, Crazy Ken Band, Japan, 2005-6

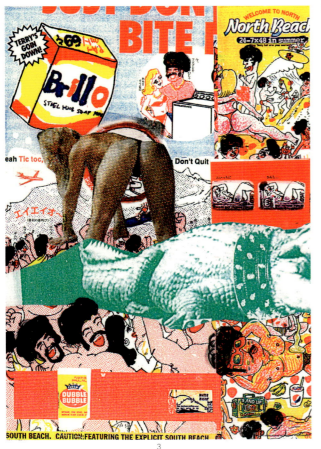

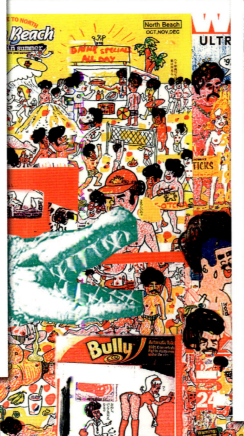

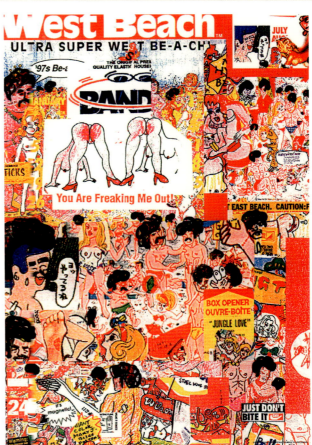

4

5

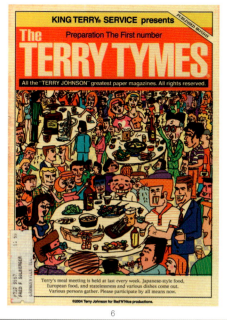

6

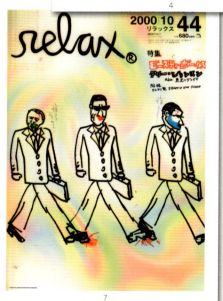

7

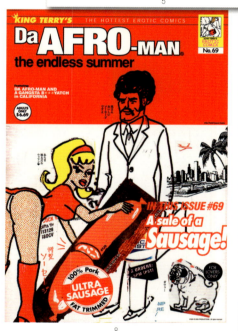

8

9

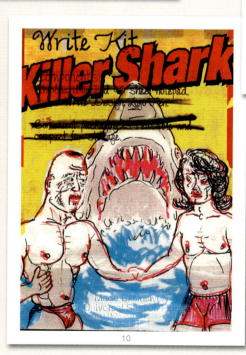

10

11

12

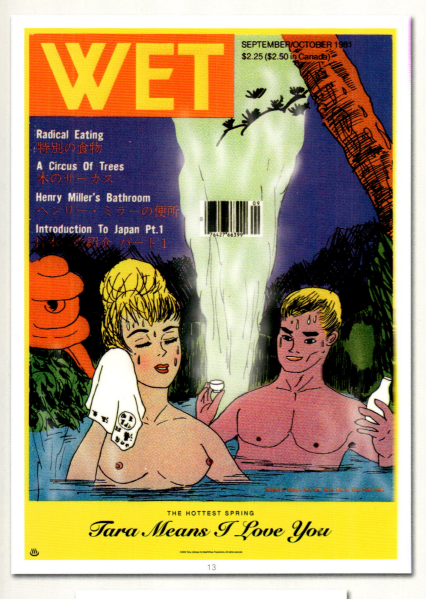

4.   Illustration, Ax comic anthology,
     Ax, Japan, 2006
     ----
5.   Magazine cover, *Hatsuratsu*,
     Hatsuratsu, Japan, 1982
     ----
6.   Poster, "The Terry Tymes," self-
     commissioned, Japan, 2004
     ----
7.   Magazine cover, *Relax*, Relax,
     Japan, 2000
     ----
8.   Illustration, "Da Afro-Man: The
     Endless Summer," self-commissioned
     Japan, 2004
     ----
9.   Magazine cover, *Comic Cue* vol. 3,
     Comic Cue, Japan, 2004
     ----
10. Poster, "Killer Shark," Crazy Ken
     Band, Japan, 2005
     ----
11. Illustration, self-commissioned,
     Japan, 2003
     ----
12. Poster, "Cracker Jack," self-
     commissioned, 2007
     ----
13. Magazine cover, *Wet*, Wet, Japan, 1981
     ----
14. Posters, store promotion and CD re-
     lease, Gonzo Beeyatch Recordz, 2003-7

2

Friends With You (Miami). --- Partners Sam Borkson and Arturo Sandoval joined forces in 2002 and have been spreading their art around the globe ever since. The two met as fledgling graphic designers in Miami, Florida, and quickly discovered a shared aptitude for thinking in three dimensions. Before long, they had transformed a small toy enterprise into a global brand. --- Friends With You creates shapes and forms that are at once mysterious and, well, friendly. The bowling pin-shaped figures in the studio's "Malfi" series are like emotional talismans, their fraught facial expressions contrasting with their bulbous, soft forms. Since much of the Friends With You rhetoric refers to toys as mystical objects, this ambiguity seems appropriate. Indeed, the various characters, from the "Malfis" to the stacked and stuffed cylinders of the "Burger Bunch" to the abstract geometries of the "Good Wood Gang," are marked by an absence of hard content. They exist instead as bright beacons of pleasing forms. Borkson and Sandoval refer to their company as a brand, which makes sense, but it is a brand representing a *feeling* rather than a product. And the whimsical, upbeat mysteries of the Friends With You objects radiate volumes of feeling. Here, the content is the brand, and the brand is the content. --- In the last couple of years, Friends With You has expanded its output to encompass public art installations, playgrounds, motion pictures, and more. The duo has worked with companies including Nike, MTV, Volkswagen, and Coca-Cola. For Toyota, they curated and produced "Sky Walkers," a brilliant parade of inflatable balloons that floated across the sky above Miami Beach in 2006. Collaborating with a handful of artists, Friends With You translated disparate visions into their own soft, universal language, filling the sky with inspiring shapes. This ebullient display embodied their outgoing approach, implicit in the meaning of the name *Friends With You*. --- Dan Nadel

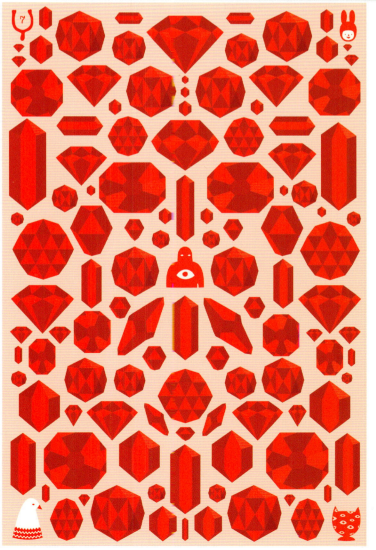
3

133

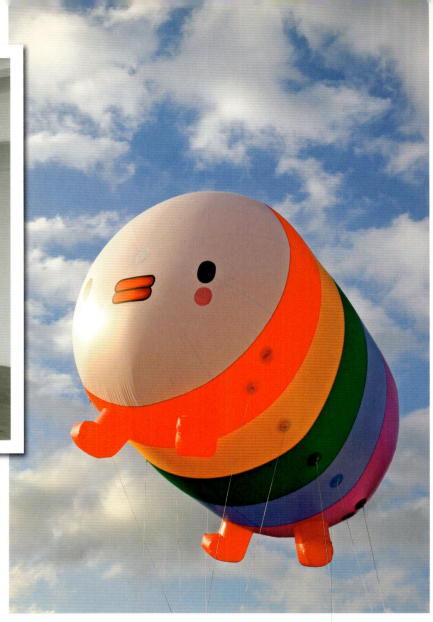

4

5

6

4.   Installation, "Sky Walkers," Art
        Basel Miami, Toyota, USA, 2006
----
5.   Book cover, *Friends With You Have
        Powers*, Die Gestalten Verlag,
        Germany, 2006
----
6.   Toy series, "Malfis" and "Burger
        Bunch," self-commissioned, USA, 2006
----
7.   Toy series, "Good Wooc Gang," self-
        commissioned, USA, 2005

8-9.   Illustrations, self-commissioned,
        USA, 2004-7

Martin Frostner (Stockholm). --- Martin Frostner is a Swedish designer whose work mixes global sensibility with local flavor. Like many young designers, he nods to the 1970s, an era when pop culture hooked up with techno-rationality to create a uniquely accessible, brightly optimistic visual vocabulary. Frostner does it his own way, with an upbeat enthusiasm for design as public discourse. The graphics in his self-commissioned project "Splish, Splash & Swosh" resemble half-baked corporate logos, circa 1974. Each mark is at once gestural and geometric, endowed with the cheerful energy of a stretch polyester running suit. The project is inspired, it turns out, by the graphics found on long-haul buses around the world. --- The democratic globalism of a passenger bus is an apt vehicle for Frostner's blunt, open voice. In printed matter for *Urban Turntable,* an exhibition about future development strategies for the Stockholm region, Frostner combines Swedish road-sign icons with a custom font that speaks to the humanist-industrial signage tradition. --- For *Playing the Building,* an exhibition by David Byrne staged in a former paint factory, Frostner stenciled wall graphics based on old signs found throughout the building. In a more commercial take on public messaging, Frostner created light boxes as both advertising and décor for *Artist Clothing,* an experimental fashion show staged in a shopping mall. --- Like successful global branding strategies, Frostner's work is legible and accessible. He doesn't get mired in introspective studies of complex form; he enjoys staying on the surface and putting the message out front. If street signs are a recurring theme in his repertoire, it is because they are a universally effective mode of graphic expression. Signage speaks to commonalities across space and time, but Frostner's future is not bland or generic. A T-shirt proclaiming "I like my town" was inspired by a statement from Georges Perec: "I like my town, but I can't say exactly what I like about it. I don't think it's the smell. I'm too accustomed to the monuments to want to look at them. I like certain lights, a few bridges, café terraces. I love passing through a place I haven't seen for a long time." --- Ellen Lupton

1

1.   Exhibition signage, *Artist Cloth-ing,* Dinki & Brand Happening, Sweden, 2005. Included posters, invitations, and a fashion magazine. The exhibition featured clothing by the artists Lena Malm and Charlotte Enström.
----
2.   T-shirt, "Animals for People," self-commissioned, Sweden, 2006. With Sara De Bondt

2

3. Magazine cover, *Ff*, Färgfabriken
Center for Contemporary Art and
Architecture, Sweden, 2006

4-5. Exhibition announcement and catalog,
In Search of the Lost Self by gradu-
ates of the Swedish art academies
Bonniers Konsthall, Sweden, 2007

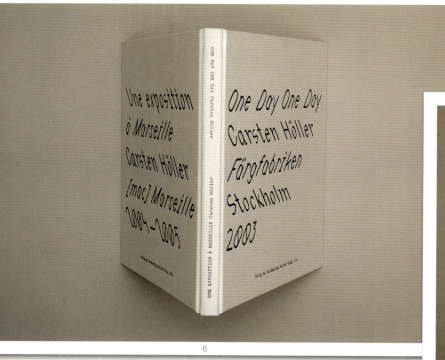

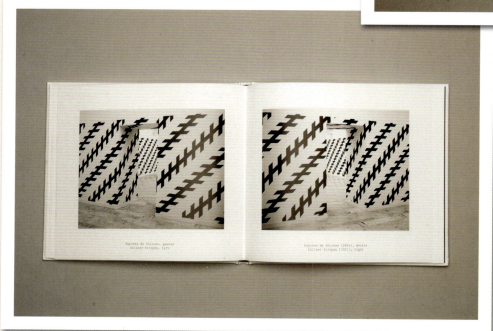

6. Book cover and spreads, *One Day One Day*, Färgfabriken and Walther König Verlag, Sweden, 2006. With Johanna Lewengard. The book catalogs two exhibitions by the artist Carsten Höller.

7-8. Exhibition signage, *Playing the Building*, Färgfabriken, Sweden, 2005

PLEASE feel free to sit down and play

NO AMPLIFICATION is used. NO SPEAKERS are used and NO COMPUTERS or sound synthesis is used.

Have fun
David Byrne 2005

9

Martin Fraatar MEDIUM 2007

10

9-10.   Self-commissioned project, "Splish, Splash & Swosh," Sweden, 2006
----
11.   T-shirt, "I like my town," Sweden, 2007. With Jake Ford

11

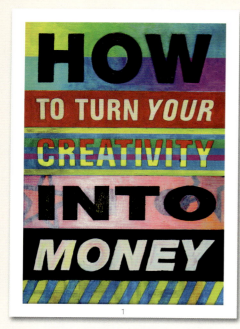

1

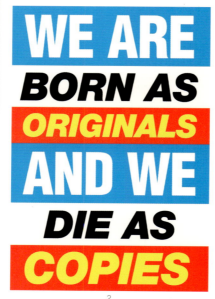

2

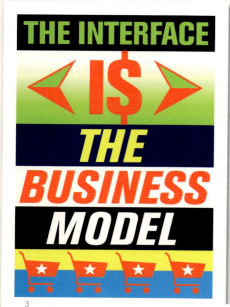

3

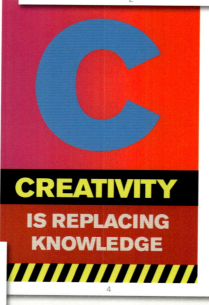

4

5

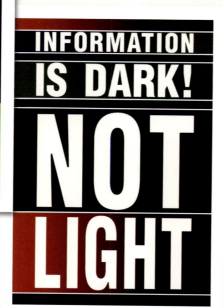

6

Mieke Gerritzen (Amsterdam). --- Mieke Gerritzen has been working in mixed media since the early 1990s, when she emerged as one of The Netherlands' first—and most outspoken—website designers. She has always brought a hard-edged political sensibility to her designs. Her digital work co-opts the visual language of the billboard and the bumper sticker, bringing a bold, in-your-face look to an on-screen environment that is commonly plagued by layered graphics and distracting special effects. The same is true for Gerritzen's work in print. Her books and publications are important not just for their telescopic visual impact but also for their deftly edited content about the state of our digital planet. --- Books such as *Mobile Minded* (coauthored with Geert Lovink) and *User* (with Peter Lunenfeld) are shiny, brightly colored packages of media theory, equipped with big type, small pages, and few words. By creating content out of slogans, headlines, sound bites, and logos instead of conventional running text, Gerritzen turns theory into advertising. Even her collaborative approach comes from the commercial culture industries. The author becomes a producer—and also a publicist, entrepreneur, and verbal DJ. --- The ideas laid out on the aggressively striped and gridded fields of Gerritzen's projects are not dumbed down so much as sharpened and polished into glimmering thought weapons. Her video *Beautiful World* shocks us with phrases like "Every God is a criminal" (in the United States, you simply can't say things like that), and talks about forms of fundamentalism rooted in both capitalism and religion. Whereas liberal critiques of globalization tend to focus on Western hegemony—the flattening of cultural differences through the spread of Coca-Cola and McDonald's—Gerritzen discusses globalization as freedom from national identity. Reflecting on the human desire for mobility, she suggests that the opportunity to leave behind one's own country is a basic right. Here, indeed, is a designer for our digital future. --- Ellen Lupton

1.   Painting, self-commissioned, The Netherlands, 2003

2-6. Illustrations, self-commissioned, The Netherlands, 2002-6
      ----
7.   Wallpaper pattern, self-commissioned, The Netherlands, 2002
      ----
8.   Painting, self-commissioned, China, 2006
      ----
9.   Book spread, *Mobile Minded*, BIS, The Netherlands, 2002

CREATIVE PEOPLE TRADE THEIR IDEAS AND CREATIVE ENERGY FOR MONEY | THE POWER OF CREATIVITY

HOW TO TURN YOUR CREATIVITY INTO MONEY | *STYLE FIRST* | THE CULTURAL CONTRADICTIONS OF CAPITALISM

GET MORE OUT OF THE BOX THAN THERE IS IN THE BOX | THE POST-INDUSTRIAL SOCIETY

Paradise by the Laptop Light. | Creative Capital Theory | THE RISE OF THE CREATIVE CLASS

BECOME A MILLIONAIRE | MOBILIZATION OF THE INDIVIDUAL MAN

CREATIVE CAPITAL | COME AND PLAY, FORGET ABOUT THE MOVEMENT

CAPITAL AND CREATIVE DESTRUCTION | FAST COMPANY | *LOCATION, LOCATION, LOCATION!*

SELL GOOD NEWS. | HUMAN INNOVATION | CREATIVE REFLECTION | CREATIVITY AT WORK

THE WILL TO DESIGN: OVERCOMING ENTERTAINMENT

CREATIVE THINKING | TRUE CREATIVITY OFTEN STARTS WHERE LANGUAGE ENDS | CREATIVITY BASICS

MyCreativity | MyCreativity | MyCreativity | *CRACKING CREATIVITY: THE SECRETS OF CREATIVE GENIUS*

BECOME ENLIGHTENED | CORPORATE CREATIVITY: HOW INNOVATION AND IMPROVEMENT ACTUALLY HAPPEN

THE SECRETS OF CREATIVE COLLABORATION | WHAT'S THE BIG IDEA? | ORGANISE YOUR LIFESTYLE

CREATING AND CAPITALIZING ON THE BEST NEW MANAGEMENT THINKING. | COPYPASTE IS MORE EFFECTIVE THAN DRAWING

THE CREATIVE HABIT | *GROWING UP CREATIVE : NURTURING A LIFETIME OF CREATIVITY*

BUSINESS MEETING CREATIVITY IDEAS | CREATIVITY FOR LIFE | 10 CREATIVITY KICK STARTS

THE 6 MYTHS OF CREATIVITY: 1. CREATIVITY COMES FROM CREATIVE TYPES. 2. MONEY IS A CREATIVITY MOTIVATOR. 3. TIME PRESSURE FUELS CREATIVITY. 4. FEAR FORCES BREAKTHROUGHS. 5. COMPETITION BEATS COLLABORATION. 6. A STREAMLINED ORGANIZATION IS A CREATIVE ORGANIZATION

CREATIVITY AND TEAM BUILDING | DON'T STOP THINKING ABOUT THE INTERNET

AMERICAN CREATIVITY ASSOCIATION | *GETTING GOOD IDEAS FROM EVERYONE AND EVERYWHERE*

SIMULTATE CREATIVITY TO GET BETTER FRIENDS | *CREATIVE CLASS STRUGGLES*

CRITIQUE OF CREATIVE INDUSTRIES | *WONDER NO MORE! MONEY DESIGNS THE WORLD*

THE MOST POWERFUL WAY TO DEVELOP CREATIVITY IN YOUR STUDENTS IS TO BE A ROLE MODEL

EVERYONE HAS LATENT CREATIVITY WAITING TO UNFOLD | *CREATIVE COGNITION*

EVERYONE HAS NATURAL CREATIVE TALENT | CREATIVE PROBLEM SOLVING

HOW IS YOUR CLIMATE FOR INNOVATION? | CREATIVITY IS AT THE HEART OF EVERYTHING WE DO. PURE CREATIVITY

DREAM ESSENTIALS | CREATIVE INDUSTRY

7

8

9

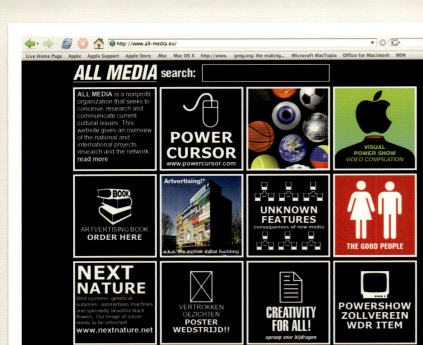

10.   Website, all-media.eu, self-
         commissioned, The Netherlands,
         2002-present

11-12.   Paintings, self-commissioned, China,
         2006
         ----
13.   Book spread, *Mobile Minded*, BIS, The
         Netherlands, 2002
         ----
14.   Illustrations, publication of the St.
         Moritz Design Summit 2006, St. Moritz
         Design Summit, Switzerland, 2006
         ----
15.   Wallpaper pattern, self-commissioned,
         The Netherlands, 2002. Composed of
         media company logos

Good Design Company (Tokyo). --- In Japan,
unlike elsewhere, a designer normally becomes
an art director on the basis of the length of
continuous employment. Manabu Mizuno worked as
a graphic designer after graduating from Tama Art
University, but since he wanted to become an art
director as soon as possible, he launched his
own firm, Good Design Company, when he was only
twenty-five years old. Ten years later, Mizuno
won both silver and gold awards at the *One Show*
for his work as an art director. These early
successes jump-started his careers, and these
days he produces total brand campaigns for large
companies, codirects industry events such as
the 2007 *Takeo Paper Show*, and even contributes
regularly to the Japanese magazine *Casa Brutus*.
--- Three major projects define Mizuno's young
career. The first is the visual identity for
the Japanese comedy duo Rahmens, which he has
overseen since 1998. Their relationship began
at Tama Art University, and Mizuno has designed
every Rahmens performance poster and DVD package
since that time. Mizuno's second major project
was a poster series designed for Adidas Japan in
2002. This campaign's success led the following
year to the total creative direction of Kirin
903, a sports drink that Adidas developed along
with Kirin Beverage Corporation. His third major
project was the "iD" campaign for the mobile-phone
giant NTT DoCoMo. In Japan, the creators of such
a big advertising campaign would normally hire a
celebrity to glamorize the brand. Mizuno, however,
acting as creative director, boldly used only
a simple logo. --- Mizuno has a reputation as an
art director who creates delicate and smart design
work. His mottos are: "Fill in what's missing,"
"Weed out the unnecessary," and "Develop appeal
to fullest." He finds solutions by toggling back
and forth between his right and left brains.
His thoughts are documented in *School of Design:
Text of New Design*, which Mizuno coauthored in
2007. Although the book was written for an audience of young designers, this industry veteran
found his favorite aphorism within it: "The client
is always right. Otherwise, you cannot design."
--- Keiichi Tanaami

1.   Exhibition poster, *Dialog in the
     Dark*, Dialog in the Dark, Japan, 2006
     ----
2.   Performance poster, "Chelfitsch,"
     Precog, Japan, 2005
     ----
3.   Paper box made to resemble wood,
     exhibited at the *Takeo Paper Show* in
     Tokyo, Takeo Co., Japan, 2006
     ----
4.   Identity and advertising campaign,
     Kirin 903, Adidas and Kirin Beverage
     Corporation, Japan, 2004
     ----
5.   Performance poster, Rahmens comedy
     duo, Twinkle Corporation, Japan, 2007

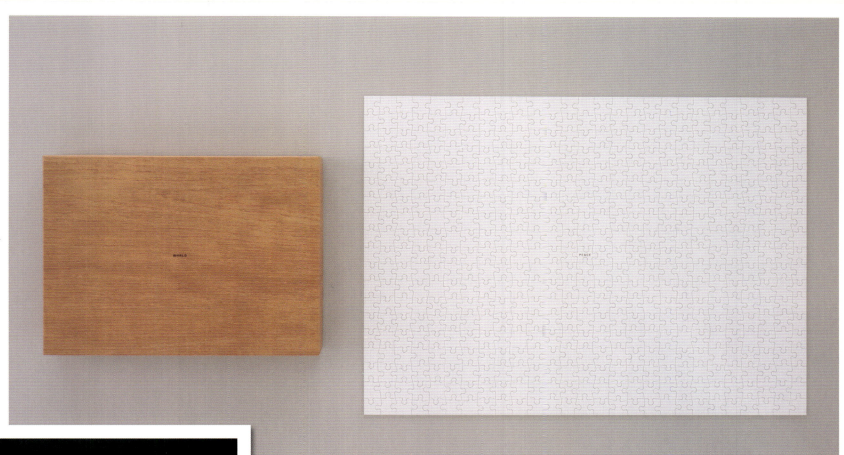

3

4

5

6. Advertising campaign, iD mobile phone credit service, NTT DoCoMo, Japan, 2006
----
7. Performance poster, Kentaro Kobayashi of Rahmens, Twinkle Corporation, Japan, 2006

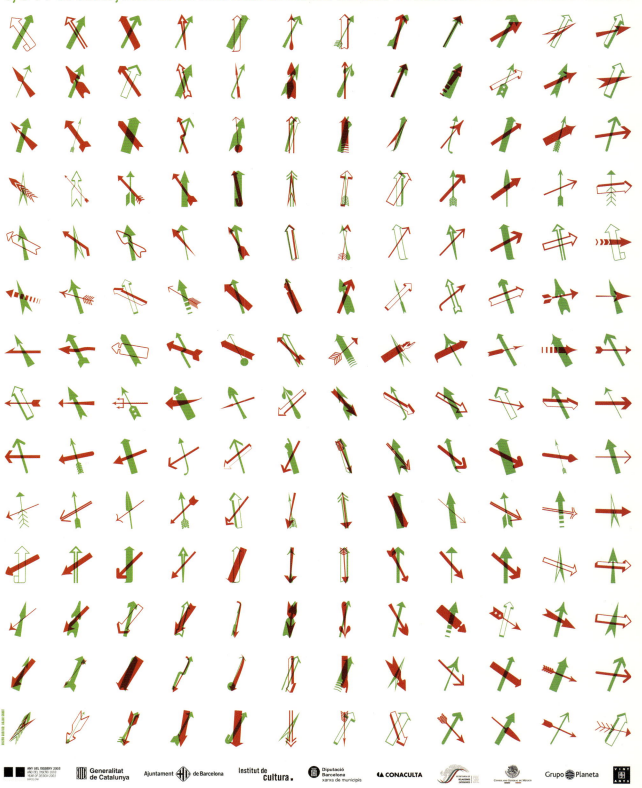

Arjan Groot (Amsterdam). --- Arjan Groot's interest in design and his lifelong dream of becoming a designer began with a fascination with car company logos when he was four years old. After a period of wanting to become a comic-book artist, he discovered as a teenager that he enjoyed making comic magazines much more than he enjoyed drawing the comics themselves. In his early twenties, Groot realized that he couldn't wait any longer to start working as a graphic designer; he quit school and started practicing. --- A10 is an architecture magazine founded in 2004 by Groot and architecture critic Hans Ibelings. Its design is functional and straightforward. It is deliberately unspectacular because Groot wanted it to look like it had been around for years. It features buildings from all over Europe, giving equal weight to architecture on the eastern and western ends of the continent. --- My favorite piece of Groot's work is his graduation project, "Universal Authority for National Flag Registration," a system for designing flags and a catalog with 180,000 new flag designs. This complex project took basic national flag forms and applied all possible color combinations to them. The catalog he designed is systematically ordered and gives an impressive overview of these myriad possibilities. It is one of his best works, and maybe the autonomy he had, acting as his own client, is what made it so great. --- When I asked Groot if he ever refuses projects, he answered, "I sometimes refuse a project when the client doesn't seem to have a specific interest in my work—when it could be any designer doing the job. It didn't matter to me when I started, but now I find it important that a client makes a deliberate choice to work with me." I think this is one of the most important conditions for a good process and a successful design. --- Irma Boom

2

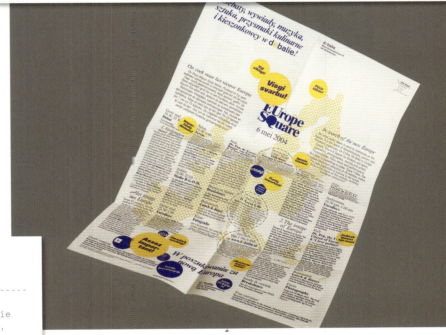

1. Conference poster, Forum Laus 3: Gráfica Reactiva, ADG-FAD, Spain, 2003
----
2. Publicity campaign, event about European Union expansion, De Balie Cultural Center, The Netherlands, 2004
----
3. Postage stamps, TNT Post, The Netherlands, 2005
----
4. Publicity campaign, event about migration, De Balie Cultural Center, The Netherlands, 2003. With Martijn Engelbregt

3

4

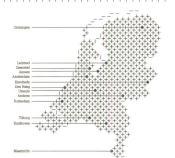

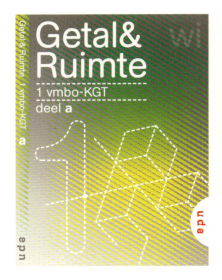
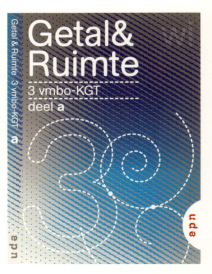

HORROR VACUI

Urban implosions in the Netherlands

Cities in the Netherlands, from Groningen in the north to Maastricht in the south, are undergoing a remarkable transformation. While Dutch cities, with the exception of Almere, are scarcely growing at all in terms of population, a great deal of building is going on. Open areas, 'overshoot' zones, and disused port and industrial areas are, or soon will be, turned into new fragments of city, with urban densities and urban-looking buildings; consolidation is under way in city centres and around the railway stations; in nearly every city residential and office towers are under construction or in the pipeline; dual land use is an undeniable trend, manifested in road-straddling construction and tunneling beneath or building on top of existing buildings. The gaps in the urban fabric that were an accepted part of Dutch cities until the mid 1980s, are fast disappearing.

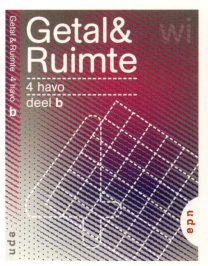

5. Wall decoration, Werck restaurant, Werck, The Netherlands, 2004
----
6. Exhibition booklet, flyer, and text panels, *Horror Vacui: Urban Implosions in the Netherlands*, The Netherlands Architecture Institute, The Netherlands, 2007. With Julia Müller and ReD
----
7. Cover design proposals, *Getal and ruimte* math book series, EPN, The Netherlands, 2005. With Alex Prieto
----
8. Magazine, *A10*, Media BV, The Netherlands, 2004-present

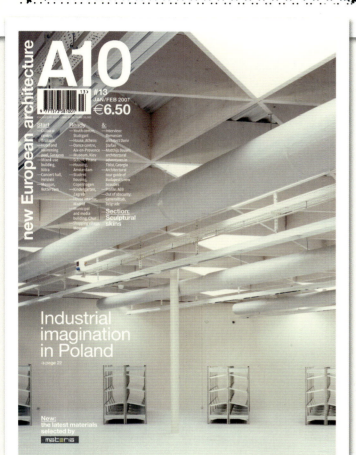

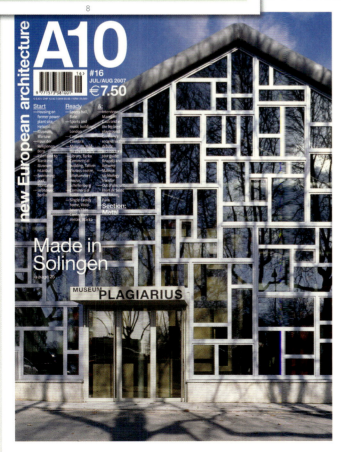

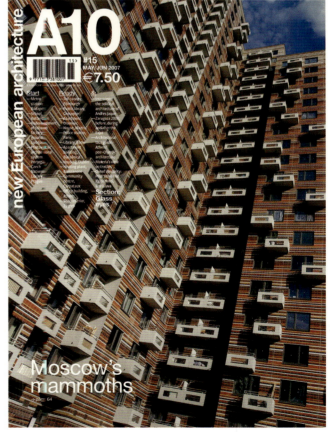

Michelle Gubser (Paris). --- Michelle Gubser's
work reveals her impressive ability to develop
coherent visual languages. Typography, always
approached with a keen visual sensibility, reigns
at the center of the work of this Paris-based
graphic designer of Swiss and Dutch origins.
Her designs are cohesive and easily understood
without being repetitive. Gubser creates recognizable visual systems based on adaptable structures
that work equally well in both 2-D and 3-D environments. --- With her partner, Fred Lambert,
and within the framework of Aer, the studio they
created, Gubser moves blithely not only between
the traditional mediums of graphic design and
the animated image but also toward more complex
domains, such as exhibition architecture and signage. It is in this latter realm, as demonstrated
by her work for La rue est à nous...tous! (The
street belongs to all of us!), where the power and
flexibility of Gubser's designs are most evident.
The stickers, posters, catalog, and overall identity Gubser developed for the show reveal, in ways
both subtle and intense, the fluidity and adaptability of her designs. The principles that ground
this project are clear enough that her stickers
can be reproduced in non-European languages like
Chinese and still make perfect sense.
--- Ruedi Baur

1.   Signage, Centre National des Arts
      Plastiques, Centre National des Arts
      Plastiques, France, 2005
      ----
2.   Symposium poster, Mémoires ouvertes:
      Fête des mots et de la mémoire,
      Adac'28 and Les Amis de La Ferté
      Vidame, France, 2006

MÉMOIRES
OUVERTES
FÊTE
MOTS
MÉMOIRES
3 SEPT 06
PARC
CHÂTEAU
LA FERTÉ
VIDAME

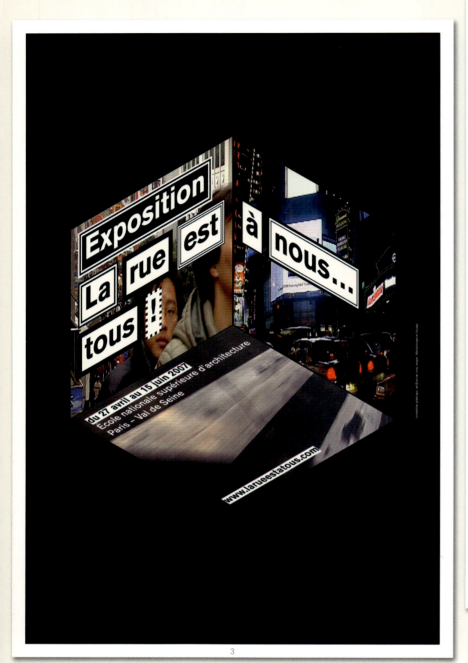

3

03 juin'2006
Cloyes-sur-le-Loir

festival de musiques actuelles

explo'son
en Eure-et-Loir

Adiam 02 37 30 13 38
www.exploson.com

4

5

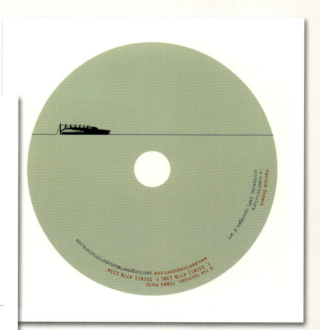

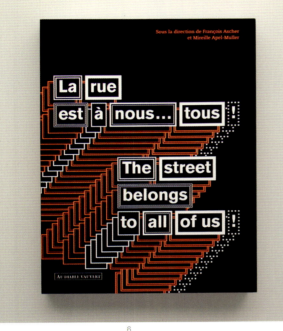

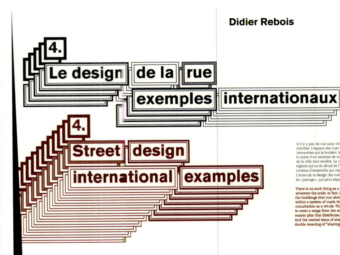

3. Exhibition poster, *La rue est à nous...tous!* (The street belongs to all of us!), Institut pour la ville en mouvement, France, 200?

----

4. Poster, Explo'son, Conseil Général d'Eure-et-Loir, France, 2006

----

5. Identity system, architecture studio La Superstructure, Patrice Gobert, France, 2006. Includes CD cover, square envelope, and stamp

----

6. Exhibition catalog cover, spreads, and stickers, *La rue est à nous... tous!*, Institut pour la ville en mouvement, France, 2007

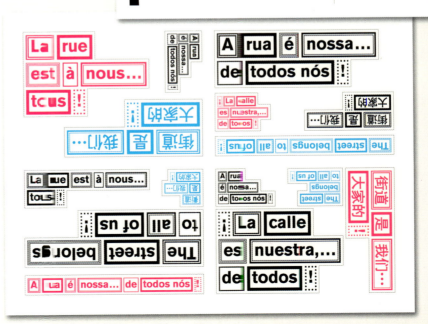

Hansje van Halem (Amsterdam). --- Hansje van Halem's sense of intuition is her most important tool, although it occasionally gets her into trouble. Everything goes smoothly until her "designer sense" starts tingling and she asks herself, "Is this really what I want?" In fact, she says she's not a designer at all, but simply an observer. That's how natural her process is. Van Halem needs to see the real thing, the physical object, in order to know whether her design is successful. Only when she finds the pages dancing out of the printer, sews and glues them together, and gives them a cover, can she be sure that the paper is not too stiff, the size is right, and the type is not too forced. --- Van Halem is an extremely passionate person. She loves books, loves old books, loves old type specimen books, loves books with lists, loves almanacs, loves books about the Dutch language (though she never reads them), loves books she finds in the garbage, loves that lone pile of paper over in the corner of her studio that doesn't have a purpose yet. She loves repetition, loves quantity, loves counting, loves Tetris, loves to sing, loves cats, loves goat cheese, loves chewing gum, loves people who read newspapers (though she never reads them), loves stress, and loves sleep. --- She hates books that are too heavy or too stiff, hates books that have no white space, hates books that are too new, and hates books that pretend to be old. At one time she hated color, hated posters, hated pictures, and hated typography, but most of the things she hated she did her best to appreciate, and in the end, came to love. --- About beauty she says, "Beauty has become a sort of taboo. Things are not allowed to be beautiful. Everything always has to be smart, conceptual, witty, provocative, or referential. My freedom as a designer comes from the fact that I'm not scared to make things beautiful. Beauty has logic and proportion Beauty is recognizable yet surprising. Beauty asks no questions. Beauty is self-explanatory.' --- Irma Boom

1.   Invitation, PrintROOM, ROOM, The Netherlands, 2004. PrintROOM is an archive of artists' publications initiated by ROOM, an artist-run space in Rotterdam.
     ----
2.   Brochure cover, *Groningen aan de slag met dementie*, Prospektor, BKB, and LDP, The Netherlands, 2006. Includes interviews, portraits, and a DVD

3-4. Postage stamps, TNT Post, The Netherlands, 2007

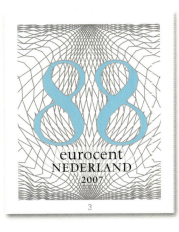

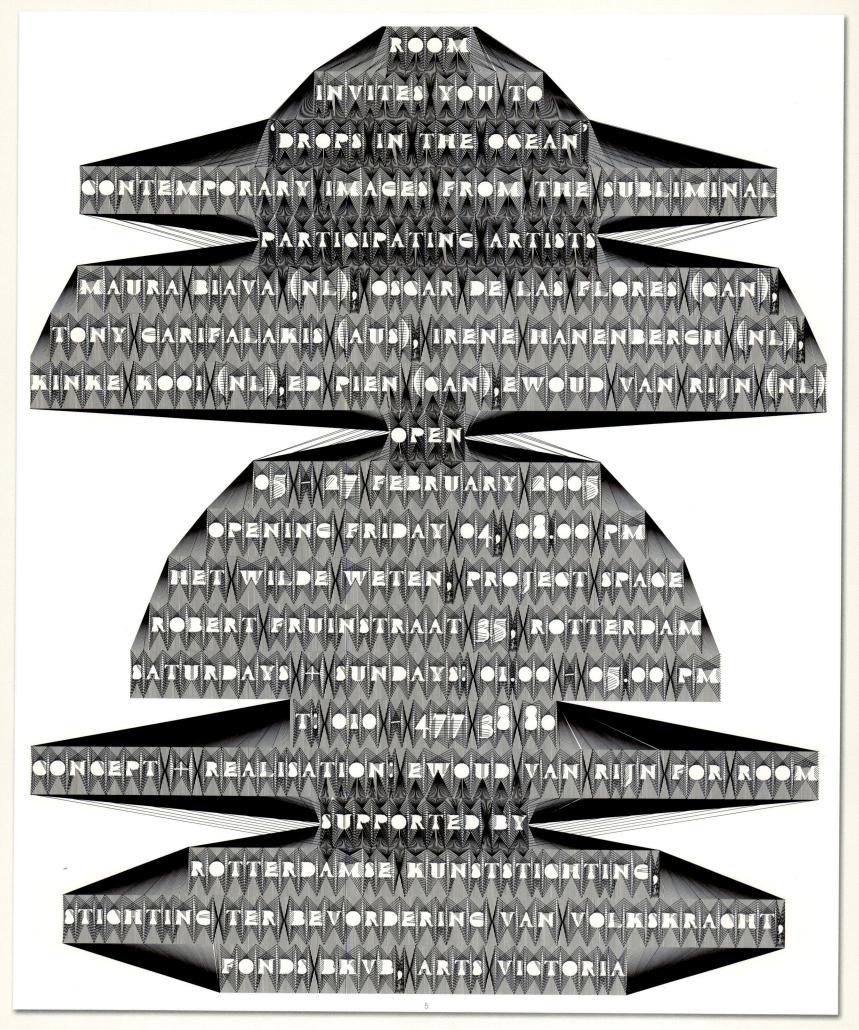

Koen Bauwens verzen vaat   (kwanslag kwifficent Anjaal) Ik kan geen jager-verzamelaar zijn terug
in en uit de eigen en tussen/tijd/se levens zomaar wat verzen verzamelen,   koesteren of castre-
ren   of eender welke vrouw uit hier en nu najagen of penetreren   laat staan bevredigen ik
voel me alleen ontheemd   ik kan nergens thuiskomen,   ben aan niets of niemand emotioneel
gebonden nee voor mij geen bondage ligt het —   het ligt zonder meer aan mij ik kan niemand
iets verwijten ik de klootzak ik ik kan het niet —   ik kan geen praatje slaan met buurman of -vrouw
niet praten met cultuurvolgers van in en om het huis-dieren   ik kan geen rinkelende telefoon
opnemen geen moeilijke vragen beantwoorden   ik kan niet naar Vijf-tv kijken, kan niet met fre-
quenties om   kan geen videorecorder programmeren ik kan Windows XP niet installeren mijn
pc zelfs niet formatteren   kan bijzonder weinig sneltoetsen en kan moeilijk met Apple overweg
ik kan geen cd of dvd rippen weet zelfs niet goed wat rippen betekent   kan geen website maken,
laat staan gebruik/er/svriendelijk   ik weet geen proton op te laden of te neutraliseren   kan
geen sim-kaart vervangen laat me door operatoren aan datteren vangen   kan mijn voice-mail
niet personaliseren kan geen news-alerts ontvangen   ik heb de Tour de France dit jaar alweer
niet kunnen winnen   ben niet mogen starten omdat ik zelfs nog geen fiets kan herstellen geen
band plakken   ik kan ook niet mijn ogen dicht nooit een rijbewijs halen   ik kan geen Mer-
cedes in elkaar knutselen   ook geen simpele auto geen doodgewoon wiel draaien   heb
geen huis gebouwd geen boom geplant en kan al in geen maanden kinderen hebben verwekt
zie ik ik kan echt niets   ik durf geen vliegend tuig in heb het nooit aangedurfd nooit een vlucht
gewaagd en durf ook niet met trein of bus op reis   ik blijf maar bij de badpakken(special) van
P-Magazine zitten   ik durf bij de bakker geen brood meer te kopen   en krijg het zelf niet ge-
bakken heb geen suiker gist of oud brood meer   ik kan zelf mezelf niet meer verkopen krijg
ook in de solden niet verkocht   ik durf de straat niet meer op het huis niet meer uit   ik kan
niet meer dronken worden niet meer straalbezopen   ik kan op een terras geen Duvel met glas
en al meer opdrinken   ik kan niet langer binnen het half uur aan coke geraken ik kan binnen
de 24u geen deftige fuif van angst en pijn meer organiseren   ik kan me geen iPod permitteren
kan voor sparen geen geduld opbrengen   geen essentiële encyclopediereeks naast het google-
apparaat   geen extra kennisvergaring niemand niets geen belwaarde   ik kan niet meer
schrijven, schrijf ik kan niets meer   ik kan zelfs niet cynisch meer zijn mijn ironie bij niet meer
want iedereen is zichzelf een god geworden boven de ander   een atheïst kan geen oslim meer
zijn of worden kan geen aanslag plegen in Kopenhagen Brussel of Amsterdam,   gewoonweg
nergens   ik kan zelfs geen mug meer doodslaan of een hooiwagen tussen duim en wijsvinger
doodknijpen geen vlieg krijg ik nog gevangen   ik kan geen spoelworm meer kwaad doen het
kan zo niet blijven malen in mijn hoofd het telt ik loop langzamerhand dood- en doder/op ik kan
geen minuut meer slapen   en daarom doof ik de lamp niet en kruip ik niet in bed ik kan niet
meer   ik kan niet meer manisch-depressief zijn   leven is een prijs die ik niet langer wil be-
talen   ik heb de periodieke opdrachten opgezegd mijn bankkaart ingeslikt   ik wil voorgoed
opblijven en op mijn stappenstenen terugkeren om uiteindelijk in die diepe slaap te vallen   het
avondtuur tegemoet wil ik naakt zijn misschien heb ik wel psoriasis kan, heb,   ben ik toch nog
iets bloot een glanzend schild van afstotelijk afbladderend bleke lelijkheid   is zo niet het heel
en al beginnende begin   uit de kleren gegaan heeft het zich gegeven   heeft de tuin zich van
zijn rokken ontdaan   helder wil ik wil niet/s   meer ik wil niets meer weten niet weten ik
wil niets vragen niet vragen niet navragen me niet afvragen ik waarom ik   niet word een van
zenverzamelaar   jager-verzamelaar van vele verziende of verzonnen levens   ik kan niet
of enkel laat me   laat ik ermee beginnen dat ik zal beginnen met mijn ontslag in te dienen me
het te geven   ik ontsla me uit een wereld waarin ik niet aarder kan-kon-gekund   ik zal me in
extremis   nog een stuk grond kopen   in een bezette stad van 2,20m bij 1,40m en er (2,08) x (150)
voor op tafel leggen   in café 't Rotterde Staal en me achteraf vrij snel op gelicht voeten en zuch-
ten   en misschien vind ik ergens nog zes wrakhouten of andere planken of verzaag ik de tafel
waarop cash geld   kan ik zagen mezelf beklagen   ik zal met veel later op het lapje grond
gaan liggen contract op de buik me oprichten neerleggen en weer neerleggen   om me helemaal
te ontbloten de ogen te sluiten het door me heen te laten regenen   de ogen open te sperren
dicht te doen en te openen zien wat het met me doet   me in een moederpoel voelen veranderen
het zonlicht op en door mijn ontvelde gezicht   om bloot te zijn   en misschien uit hergeboor-
tegrond te beginnen opschieten   en uitlopen en te beginnen   herbeginnen

5.   Exhibition invitation, *Drops in the Ocean* ROOM, The Netherlands, 2004

6.   Exhibition publication, *Het dak van de hemel* Roof of Heaven), photographs by Misha de Ridder, Misha de Ridder and the City of Dordrecht, The Netherlands, 2005

7.   Catalog spread, *Mark: Municipal Art Acquisitions, Graphic Design 2003-4*, Stedelijk Museum, The Netherlands, 2004

8.   Typographic illustration, "Dicht aan het Ij" (Poetry on the Ij River), Stichting Perdu and Loods 6, The Netherlands, 2005. Inspired by the bad sound quality of the recording of a poem by Koen Bauwens at the Dicht aan het Ij poetry festival

9.   Book illustration, *The Letter Sketch Book*, self-commissioned, The Netherlands, 2003. The book presents van Halem's "Scratched Letter" design process, in which hundreds of drawings of each letter are layered on top of one another to create a single image.

George Hardie (Chichester, UK). --- George
Hardie's distinctly clever graphic sensibility
is best exemplified by his "The History of English
Gardening," an invitation to a local garden show.
In it, Hardie delivers a visual history of the
garden through a series of tree-shaped images
planted in a grove. The layered images reveal a
digressive history: There is blue china (Hardie
digs it up in his own garden in Westbourne,
saying, "I think people just chucked their broken
china out the back door"); a rain cloud; a trowel;
a tulip (for "tulip fever"); a knot garden; a map
of China (where many English plants originated);
and, finally, a greenhouse symbolizing Kew
Gardens. It is a startling list of images that
relies on nothing other than visual associations
to tell a rather complex story. --- Seeing this
kind of illustration is immediately followed by
two distinct reactions: noticing and gathering.
First, you notice that, indeed, a trowel *does*
resemble a tree, perhaps even a tree it helped
plant. Then you start connecting other things to
trees, grouping and gathering until you've assem-
bled entire collections of images in your mind—
collections that Hardie himself, perhaps, has
cultivated. Hardie has said that his job is to
"notice things and get things noticed." To that
end, he doesn't just solve a problem or create a
compelling image, but rather creates visual ideas
that force viewers to "wear a new pair of spectacles" and open up to unique visual experiences of
even the most familiar terrain. In "The History
of English Gardening," Hardie has you wearing his
spectacles before you've even had time to process
the image. --- Hardie's long career began with a
bang (the cover of Led Zeppelin's 1969 eponymous
debut) and continued through a period of music-
related projects for the likes of Pink Floyd (*The
Dark Side of the Moon* cover, among others), Paul
McCartney, and Black Sabbath. His work for the
now-defunct Trickett & Webb calendar series in
the 1980s and '90s remains a high-water mark
for illustration, and his recent handmade books,
including *Manual*, are wondrous extended medita-
tions on the relationship between shapes and
images. Hardie is forever trying on new spectacles and changing the way we see. --- Dan Nadel

1.   Print, "The Same Difference,"
      Pentagram, UK, 2001
      ----
2.   Illustration, "A Tale of Difference,"
      The Ganzfeld, PictureBox, USA, 2003
      ----
3.   Symposium poster, Illustration Today,
      Parsons The New School for Design,
      USA, 2006
      ----
4.   Calendar page, Trickett & Webb,
      Augustus Martin, UK, 2002
      ----
5.   Invitation, "The History of English
      Gardening," The Garden Show, UK, 1994

1

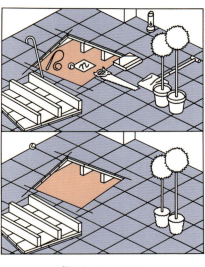

Objects that might come in Useful

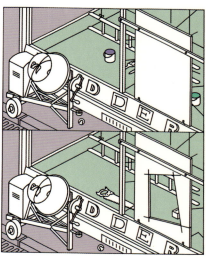

Objects Forgotten

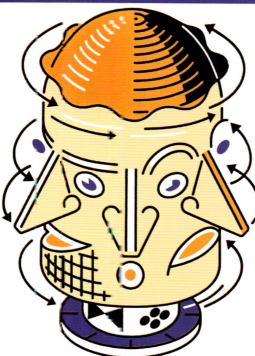

ANTIPÁTICO

(de *antipatía*) Repugnancia instintiva respecto de personas o cosas. *fig.*: Oposición recíproca entre cosas inanimadas.

GEORGE HARDIE

6

6. Children's dictionary page, Media Vaca, Spain, 2002
----
7. Stamps, Royal Mail, UK, 2005
----
8. Illustration, *The Ganzfeld*, Picture-Box, USA, 2007
----
9. Postcards for book, *Manual*, Broken Books and George Hardie, UK, 2004
----
10. Book spreads, *Manual*, Broken Books and George Hardie, UK, 2004

7

Verbal pun

Hyperbole

Anthropomorphism

Visual pun

Metaphor

Deconstruction

Surrealism

Classical allusion

Education

Paradox

Sequence

Inspiration

Award winning

Rebus

Palindrome

Framing

Animation

Mixed Metaphor

Wrench (twist)

Authorship

8

George Hardie
Manual

9

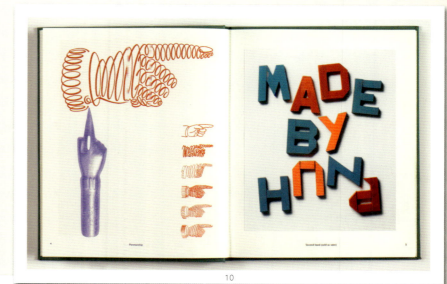

10

George Hardie
Manual

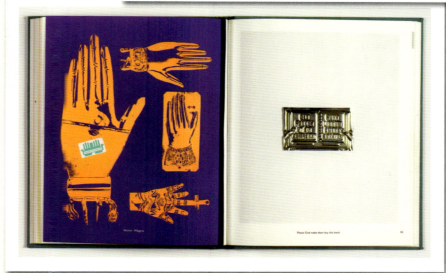

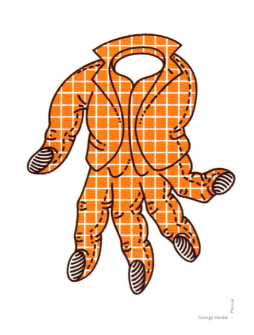

George Hardie
Manual

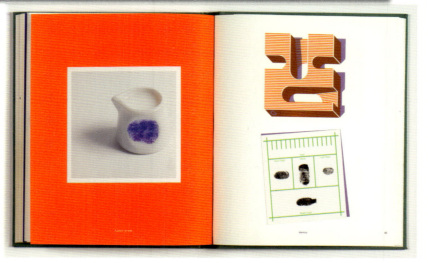

1. Poster series, "Marcel et Richard: A Historic Font," Basta Gallery, Switzerland, 2006. With Duncan White

----

2. Poster and typeface, Superstudio, Lineto, Switzerland, 2007

----

3. Book cover, *Helen Maurer: Under Study*, Angel Row Gallery, UK, 2006

----

4. Book cover and back cover, *Design Products: Yearbook 2006*, Royal College of Art's Product Design Department, Royal College of Art, UK, 2006

----

5. Book cover, *Curating Subjects*, Open Editions and De Appel Foundation, UK, 2007

Jonathan Hares (London/Lausanne). --- Currently
a regular on easyJet flight 3376, Jonathan Hares
divides his time between London and Lausanne,
working on books, posters, typefaces, and exhibition spaces. Given this, it would be easy to call
his spare design approach a British take on Swiss
Modernism. But that would be misguided. In Hares's
work, the mix of simple typography and white space
is more an inadvertent outcome than a calculated
aesthetic. His easygoing, humble nature and at
times lighthearted conceptual thinking hint at his
reductive formal method. As Hares puts it, with
more than a tinge of deadpan humor, "Beyond
ensuring that the times and dates on an invite
are correct, everything else is just showing off."
--- Projects for Jeffrey Charles Henry Peacock
Gallery (JC/HP) and Topolski Produce Ltd. are good
examples. In these simple compositions of sans-
serifs and space, slight tweaks give you more
than you bargained for. Clever picture editing
and text placement for JC/HP transcend bare fact-
stating, while Hares's Constructivist red slash
for Topolski Produce Ltd. becomes an instant mani-
festation of the company's wares when bent into
a curved sausage. Hares's website, rather than
showcasing his own diverse portfolio, compiles
a typology of online pull-down menus removed from
their original contexts. Purely documentary in
function, the menu system's scale verges on the
ridiculous. In a similar, seemingly impersonal
vein, the publication *Curating Subjects* goes
beyond utilitarian simplicity to become an archetypal book object—almost the encyclopedia definition of *objectivity*. --- I avoid using the tag
"Minimalist" for Hares, but he happily references
figures like Sol LeWitt when describing his own
functionalist graphics. In an act of literal
reductionist subtraction, Hares designs an ongoing
series of typographic posters using an expanded
dot typeface from the flyer that accompanied
Marcel Duchamp's *The Bride Stripped Bare By Her
Bachelors, Even*. The typographic holes are punched
through stacks of paper by hand with a pillar
drill, spelling out book titles, album titles,
and colors of the rainbow. In the end, Hares is
more Fluxus than Minimalist, championing simplicity over complexity, but in a subtly playful
manner. --- James Goggin

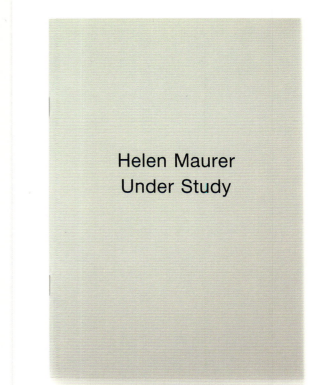

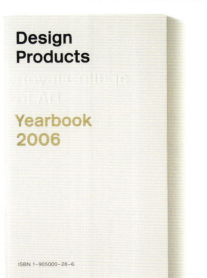

Flyer 6

JEFFREY CHARLES

JEFFREY CHARLES HENRY PEACOCK ANNOUNCES THE LAUNCH OF THEIR NEW GALLERY. THE FIRST SHOW WILL TAKE PLACE IN DECEMBER 2005. THE GALLERY WAS FORMED BY THE INCORPORATION OF ~~JEFFREY CHARLES GALLERY~~ AND ~~HENRY PEACOCK GALLERY~~. THE TWO GALLERIES EXISTED FOR FOUR AND EIGHT YEARS RESPECTIVELY.

THE GALLERY WILL INITIATE AN ALTERNATIVE APPROACH TO THE DISSEMINATION AND RECEPTION OF ART-WORKS. JEFFREY CHARLES HENRY PEACOCK IS NOT INTERESTED IN UNCONDITIONALLY ACCEPTING THE PRESCRIBED CRITERIA FOR RUNNING AN ART GALLERY.

THE GALLERY'S EXHIBITIONS WILL EE RECEIVED IN THE FORM OF EDITIONS AND BE DISTRIBUTED FREE OF ANY PURCHASE PRICE.

THE GALLERY DISSOCIATES ITSELF FROM THE DEFINED INTERIOR OF A ROOM. BY ORGANISING DISPERSED EXHIBITIONS THE GALLERY WILL AVOID THE HABITUAL LIMITATIONS THAT ANY DESIGNATED BUILDING IMPOSES ON ITS VISITOR. JEFFREY CHARLES HENRY PEACOCK AIMS TO RESTITUTE UNEXPLORED RESTRICTIONS AND ABANDON ONES LONG SINCE RESOLVED.
...
PO BOX 51360, LONDON N1 1FX
T: +44 (0)795 119 8922
E: INFO@JC-HP.CO.UK

HENRY PEACOCK

6

Flyer 7

JEFFREY CHARLES

THIS ART IS YOUR ART
DAVE BEECH KYRAN LYNN
3RD DEC. 05 — 15TH JAN. 06

THIS FIRST EXHIBITION CONSISTS OF ONE HUNDRED NUMBERED EDITIONS. IT WILL BE DISTRIBUTED FREE OF ANY PURCHASE PRICE.

DAVE BEECH CO-AUTHORED THE PHILISTINE CONTROVERSY (WITH JOHN ROBERTS) VERSO, 2002.

KYRAN LYNN EXHIBITED IN GLOVE, LANGE GASSE 28, AUGSBURG 2005.

TO RECEIVE THIS EXHIBITION SEND POSTAL ADDRESS DETAILS TO THE PO BOX BELOW, WITHIN THE DATES OF THE EXHIBITION. INCLUDE EMAIL ADDRESS FOR CORRESPONDENCE. THIS IS HOW EVERYONE SHOULD CONSUME ART.

PO BOX 51360, LONDON N1 1FX
T: +44 (0)795 119 8922
E: INFO@JC-HP.CO.UK

HENRY PEACOCK

7

Flyer 8

JEFFREY CHARLES

FRANCIS DANBY'S THE DELUGE IN ROOM 9, GEORGE STUBBS'S A WATER SPANIEL IN ROOM 7, PETER LELY'S PORTRAIT OF AN UNKNOWN WOMAN IN ROOM 2 AND FRANCIS BACON'S FIGURE IN MOVEMENT IN ROOM 24.

TATE BRITAIN
MILLBANK
LONDON
SW1P 4RG

DO NOT LIKE DO NOT DISLIKE
11TH MARCH – 16TH APRIL 2006
FRI / SAT / SUN 11:00AM – 5:00PM

• This exhibition consists of four paintings currently hanging in Tate Britain, London. The objects, some cultural some utilitarian that surround them, are all peripheral.
• The man absorbed by the object of his attention can only be brought back to himself by desire; the desire to eat, for example, or the desire to engage in coitus.
• Acceptance, denial and conviction prevent understanding.

Let your mind move together with an object. There is then the possibility of real communication. To understand one another, there must be choice-less awareness where there is no sense of comparison or condemnation and no waiting for further discussion in order to agree or disagree.
The perfect way is only difficult for those who pick and choose. Do not like, do not dislike, all will

then be clear. This does not mean do nothing at all, but only have no deliberate mind. Do not select or reject anything.
All these so-called secret moves and contorted postures just appease the unknowledgeable spectator.
Make a hairbreadth difference and heaven and earth are set apart; if you want the truth never be for or against.

• It is indeed difficult to see the situation simply. It is easy to teach one to be skilful, but it is difficult to be taught your own attitude.
• This is how everyone should lead their lives.

HENRY PEACOCK

8

Flyer 9

JEFFREY CHARLES

THE ROUGH IDEA IS THAT THIS EXHIBITION COMES IN THE FORM OF OUR ALLOCATED BUDGET (AFTER COSTS) DIVIDED UP INTO ONE HUNDRED NUMBERED EQUAL DENOMINATIONS. THE DISTRIBUTION OF THE EXHIBITION IS RECIPROCALLY DISTENDED BY MEANS OF WHATEVER RELATIONS OF EXPENDITURE EACH EDITION ENTERS INTO. TO RECEIVE THIS EXHIBITION SEND POSTAL ADDRESS DETAILS TO PO BOX 51360, LONDON N1 1FX WITHIN THE DATES OF THE EXHIBITION.

"THERE CAN BE NO MORE PERFECT EQUIVALENCE BETWEEN GIFT AND COUNTER-GIFT, THAN WHEN A GIVES TO B AN OBJECT, AND B ON THE SAME DAY RETURNS THE VERY SAME OBJECT TO A."[1] "THE OBLIGATION TO RECIPROCATE WORTHILY IS ~~IMPERATIVE~~[2] UNAVOIDABLE. "NO ONE GIVES TRUE MONEY, THAT IS, MONEY WHOSE EFFECTS ONE ASSUMES TO BE CALCULABLE, MONEY WITH WHICH ONE CAN COUNT AND RECKON AND RECOUNT IN ADVANCE THE EVENTS ONE COUNTS ON FROM IT... WHAT TAKES SHAPE HERE IS THE INFINITY OR RATHER THE INFINITENESS OF THE "BAD INFINITE" THAT CHARACTERIZES THE MONETARY THING (TRUE OR COUNTERFEIT MONEY) AND EVERYTHING IT TOUCHES, EVERYTHING IT CONTAMINATES (THAT IS, BY DEFINITION, EVERYTHING)."[3]

17 JUNE – 23 JULY 2006
T: +44 (0)795 119 8922   E: INFO@JC-HP.CO.UK

[1] BRONISLAW MALINOWSKI, ARGONAUTS OF THE WESTERN PACIFIC.
[2] MARCEL MAUSS, THE GIFT'S PLEASURE AHEAD.
[3] JACQUES DERRIDA, GIVEN TIME.

HENRY PEACOCK

9

Flyer 10

JEFFREY CHARLES

ENOLA GAY / LITTLE BOY / FAT MAN. TERRY ATKINSON 21 OCT. — 03 DEC. 06

HENRY PEACOCK

10

6-10.   Invitations, Jeffrey Charles Henry
        Peacock Gallery, JC/HP, UK, 2006
        ----
11.   Letterhead and package lids, Topolski
        Produce Ltd., Topolski Produce Ltd.,
        UK, 2006
        ----
12.   Proposal, cast-iron bollard for
        Bermodsey Square, East Architecture,
        UK, 2007-present

12

Topolski Produce Ltd.   OFFICE   17 Calvert Avenue   + 44 (0)20 7729 9789
                                  London, E2 7JP   info@topolski.co.uk
                                  United Kingdom   www.topolski.co.uk

TO   Jon Hares   DATE   12.10.07   RE   Template
      Unit F2
      2 – 4 Southgate Road
      London
      N1 3JJ

Dear Jon

It was lovely to meet you Pisi. Tie deliquam, venim verosti siscip ea amconsed dolore
magna alit alisciduip ea at. Perit, quisi bla commy niscili quamet ipsummy nisis alit el
ing eu facing elit nulput lam vel deliquiscin eumsan essequat. Am, vendre conulla feugait
wis augiamet vullan hendio consequisi eugueri ustrud euglam, consecte cor iure min
vulputem zzriure ex esto essed ea facil tem nos aliquis iure dipisim nulputat. Dui bla
facin utate corpera estismo dolortio consed eliquis ea facip etum vullandre magna alit lum
niamet vel eu facincilis am, quationsed elendre faccumsan ut ipit lum irit accum zzriusto
consequat lore magnisl dolorpe raesect etumsan diating eniamet volor alit pratue dunt ad
tisci te dionum ipsummod te enit luptatue do consecte tat lum velestrud tio ea feuissit,
sit eumsan hendionsenim irilluptat lamcommy nostrud ea feu feu facincilit aut nonsed magna
facil ut nim velis non utatisis dolore dui te facip exerilla consectet nulla feum ing ex
euis autat, quat accum augait atisit in henim in ulla feu facidunt prat augait, verate
veliqui tio eu faciliquat.

Gait, commy nis nonsequat ad tio delisiscilis nos augait, velit nummolo rerat. Onsed dit
augiamet, conullandiam in volobore tet adipisi eugait enis do conse magna accummy num
zzriurero dolor in henisi.

Best Wishes

Leila

PLEASE RECYCLE THIS LETTER

11

BEETROOT WITH HORSERADISH (CWIKŁA)
SUGAR, LACTIC ACID
NET WEIGHT: 230g, B.B. 12.2007

HORSERADISH (CHRZAN)
SUGAR, LACTIC ACID
NET WEIGHT: 230g, B.B. 12.2007

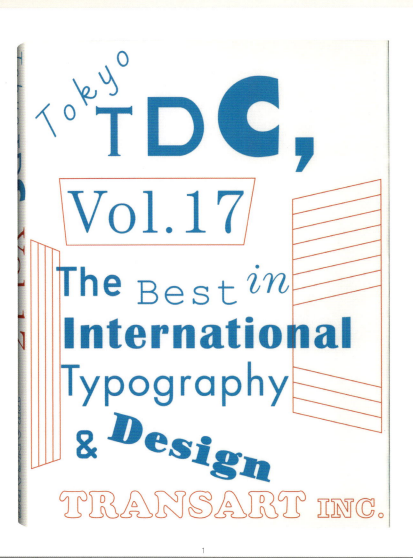

ラブシーンの言葉

荒川洋治

四月社

Kazunari Hattori (Tokyo). --- Tokyo-based art director and graphic designer Kazunari Hattori is renowned in his home country for his loose and spirited art direction of magazines, books, and advertisements. In Europe, however, it took quite a bit of digging to find out anything about this enigmatic designer. I first spotted his name in the credits of the beautiful but sporadically published *Here and There* magazine. The magazine felt like an entire print-based community populated only by people who interested me. The artists Susan Cianciolo and Dominique Gonzalez-Foerster, fashion designers Cosmic Wonder and Bless, and photographer Takashi Homma are all featured regularly. More a private diary than a magazine, the publication is a very personal collaboration between Hattori and editor Nakako Hayashi. In each issue, Hayashi's eclectic theme perfectly mirrors Hattori's overall approach to the design. Though very clear, sparse, and apparently rational, Hattori says that his work is "not particularly logical. I work with the senses, hands-on, guided by how things feel." For Hattori, it's not "less is more," but perhaps "laissez-faire is more." --- Hattori followed this free-form design philosophy in his gridless layout for the Tokyo monthly *Ryuko Tsushin*, a contemplative fashion magazine that thinks nothing of featuring specials on bibliophilia or the history of Shiseido packaging alongside reports on the latest collections from Europe. Under Hattori's eye, the magazine felt just as intimate as *Here and There*, with his intuitive art direction revealing an obvious enthusiasm for the content, and an almost telepathic affinity with contributing photographers. --- Hattori's sensory method of assembly and his avoidance of overcomplication are exemplified by the advertising campaign for the iconic Japanese mayonnaise manufacturer Kewpie. Upon realizing that he couldn't improve his initial cut-and-paste Polaroid-and-sketch presentation mock-ups, Hattori persuaded Kewpie to run the ads just as they were, rather than resort to expensive reshoots and "proper" typesetting. --- I like to think of Hattori's design as a kind of "spirit-giving," a substitute for graphic design's notion of "form-giving." Concerned with much more than basic facts, his evocative work communicates an entire set of feelings. --- James Goggin

1.   Book cover, *Tokyo TDC, Vol.17: The Best in International Typography and Design*, Transart, Japan, 2006
----
2.   Book cover, *Rabushiin-no-kotoba* by Yoji Arakawa, Shigatsusha, Japan, 2005
----
3.   Advertising campaign, Kewpie Half low-calorie mayonnaise, Q.P. Corporation, Japan, 2006

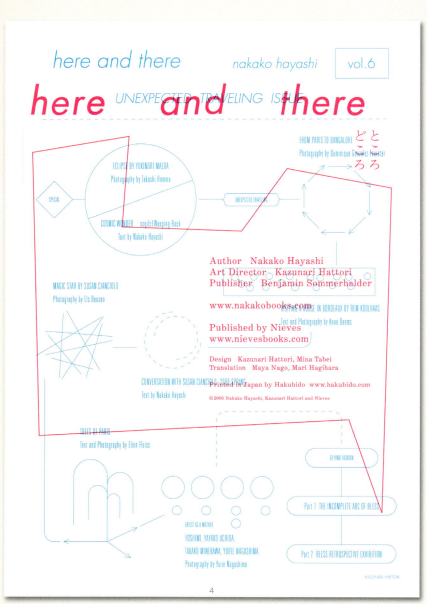

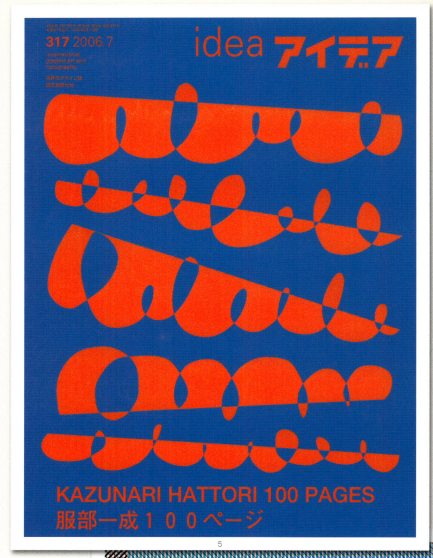

4.   Magazine promotional poster, *Here
     and There* vol. 6, Nieves, Japan, 2006
----
5.   Magazine cover, *Idea* no. 317,
     Seibundo Shinkosha, Japan, 2006
----
6.   Magazine cover, *Ryuko Tsushin*, Infas
     Publications, Japan, 2003
----
7.   Poster, experimental printing exhibi-
     tion, Toppan Printing, Japan, 2007
----
8.   Poster, *2004 Tokyo Art Directors
     Club Exhibition*, Creation Gallery G8,
     Ginza Graphic Gallery, and DDD
     Gallery, Japan, 2004

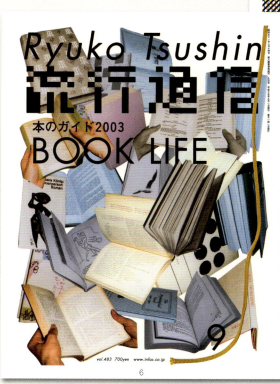

ADC

2004 ADC展
Tokyo Art Directors Club Exhibition

ギンザ・グラフィック・ギャラリー（会員作品）
2004年7月2日（金）—7月30日（金）11:00a.m.—7:00p.m.（土曜日は6:00p.m まで）
日曜・祝祭日休館　入場無料
〒104-0061 東京都中央区銀座7-7-2 DNP銀座ビル TEL.03-3571-5206

クリエイションギャラリーG8（一般作品）
2004年7月5日（月）—7月30日（金）11:00a.m.—7:00p.m.（水曜日は8:30p.m まで）
土・日・祝祭日休館　入場無料
〒104-8001 東京都中央区銀座8-4-17 リクルートGINZA8ビル1F TEL.03-3575-6918

dddギャラリー（会員・一般作品）
2004年8月4日（水）—9月7日（火）10:00a.m.—6:00p.m.
夏期休館日：8月9日（月）—8月13日（金）
土・日・祝祭日休館　入場無料
〒530-8208 大阪市北区堂島浜2-2-28 堂島アクシスビル1F TEL.06-6347-8780

構成：東京アートディレクターズクラブ／協力：株式会社美術出版社
Design by Kazunari Hattori . Printed in Japan by Dai Nippon Printing Co.,Ltd.

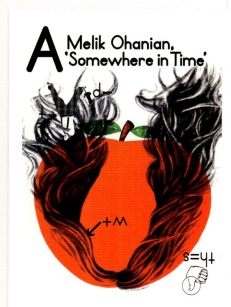

A Melik Ohanian, 'Somewhere in Time'

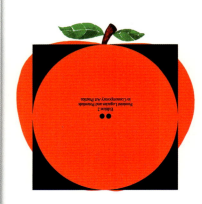

A "If I Can't Dance, I Don't Want To Be Part Of Your Revolution"

A "Situations": Performance at de Appel

A "Situations": Jiri Kovanda vs The Rest of the World

A "The Ghost of James Lee Byars Calling" / "Route A1"

A Steven Shearer: "Steven Shearer" / Erik Parker: "Liner Notes"

A

A "THE GO-BETWEEN"

A Thomas Zipp "WHITE DADA"

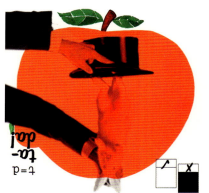

A Michaël Borremans "Veldwerk"

Will Holder (London). --- I first came across Will Holder's work in *Catalogue*, an independent, guest-edited magazine that he published and designed between 2000 and 2003 under the name "Goodwill." It was a good introduction to Holder, both as a person and as a designer, showcasing his interests in contemporary art, literature, and pop culture. Having discarded his earlier nom de plume, Holder remains preoccupied with design, continuing to publish, edit, and write. His practice emphasizes language as the root of graphic design. A given idea might manifest itself as a book, a lecture, a self-published work, a reading, or all of the above. The phrase "visible language," therefore, nicely sums up his work: It is a rich graphic vocabulary charged with references, footnotes, and playful systems. --- Holder's work often takes design standards (the rebus, the newspaper, or the Stedelijk Museum identity) and changes them to convey new messages. Somehow, though, the outcome transcends this basic explanation and becomes something unexpected. The whole is not greater than the sum of its parts; the arrangement of the parts manages to exceed the whole. Stamps for the fiftieth anniversary of World Press Photo are designed to look like newspaper headlines, illustrating the photograph's pliability in journalism; *Peanuts* characters on a graduation show poster are blacked out (but the strip's exuberance remains intact) and replaced with exhibition information, emphasizing "the work" over the artist's personality; exhibition titles at Amsterdam's De Appel arts center are spelled out in deceptively simple pictorial codes to match the "*A Is for Apple*" identity he created for the gallery. In each of these examples, Holder has added extra layers to the project, but in a way that invites and involves the viewer, rather than obscuring or complicating the design's meaning. His projects are decidedly reader-focused. --- Holder's total involvement with the content of his projects and his critical input mean that his definition of graphic design encompasses editorial concerns that precede, or perhaps preempt, a formal, aesthetically driven craft. This broader approach is evident in Holder's work as an educator. He taught at the Gerrit Rietveld Academie for six years and has been involved with the Jan van Eyck Academie's Tomorrow Book Studio, the aim of which–research, directly tested and practically applied–seems to be an effective description of Holder's engaging design work in voice and print. --- James Goggin

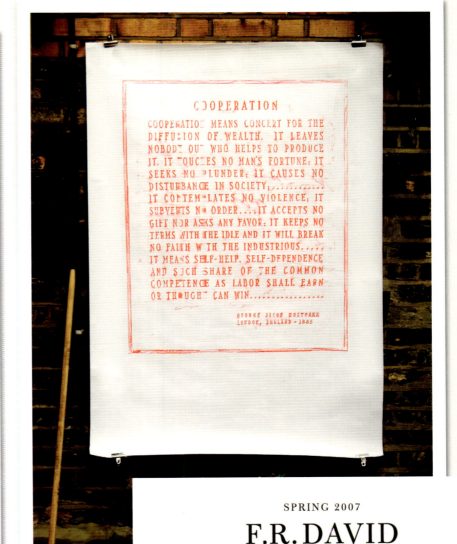

2

1. Invitations, De Appel, De Appel Foundation, The Netherlands, 2006-7
   ----
2. Poster, self-commissioned, The Netherlands, 2007. The poster is a rubbing of a monument in New York's Seward Park housing projects.
   ----
3. Journal cover, *F.R. David*, De Appel Foundation, The Netherlands, 2007. *F.R. David* is a journal of language in the arts, edited by Ann Demeester, Will Holder, and Dieter Roelstraete.

3

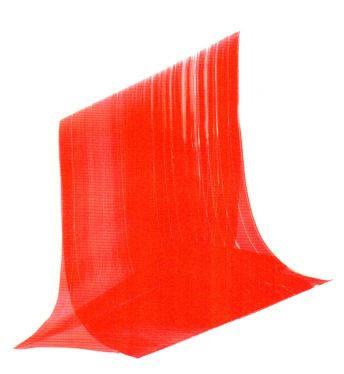

BLESS
the
Hairdresser
He attacks Mother Nature for a small fee
Hourly he ploughs heads for sixpence
Makes systematic mercenary war on this
WILDNESS
He trims aimless and retrograde growths
into CLEAN ARCHED SHAPES and
ANGULAR PLOTS

4

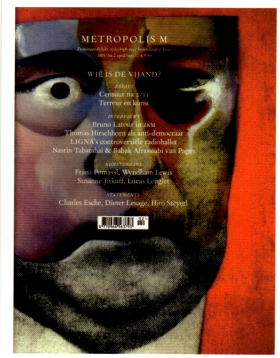

5

4.   Poster, *The Free Library* exhibition,
      M+R Gallery, UK, 2005
      ----
5.   Magazine covers, *Metropolis M*, Metro-
      polis M, 2003-5. With Will Stuart anc
      Stuart Bailey

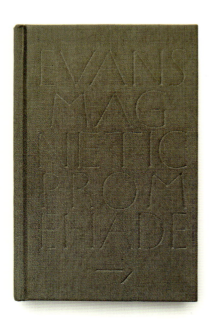

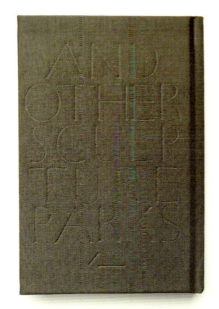

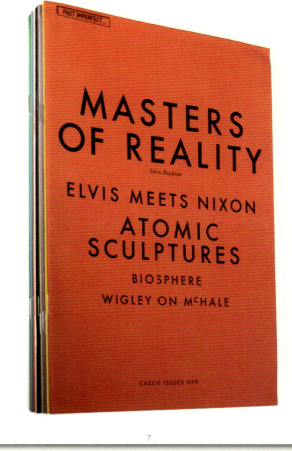

6. Book cover and back cover, *Magnetic Promenade and Other Sculpture Parks*, Studio Voltaire, UK, 2007

----

7. Publication cover, *Masters of Reality*, Casco, The Netherlands, 2005. With Bik van der Pol

----

8. Publication cover, *Just in Time!*, Stedelijk Museum, Stedelijk Museum, The Netherlands, 2006

----

9. Book cover, *Tourette's III*, Black Rainbow, UK, 2006

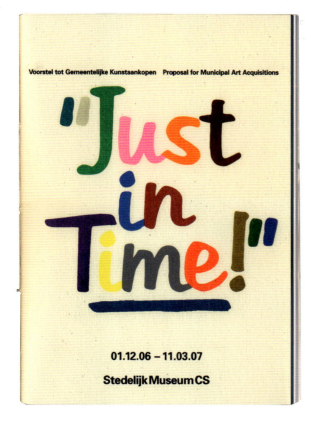

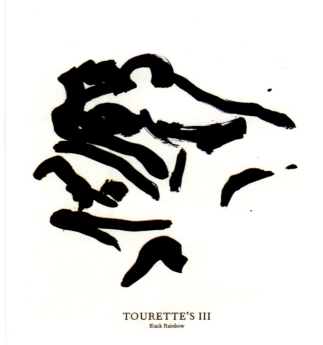

1

Homework (Warsaw). --- Since the early twentieth century, Polish designers and artists have used the poster for promotional, poetic, and political ends. Surrealist doublings and visual metaphors are signatures of the midcentury Polish Poster School, which flew its disruptive messages under the radar of the Communist regime. Although the decline of the Polish poster under capitalism has been widely mourned, Joanna Górska and Jerzy Skakun are bringing the medium back to life, and updating it for the twenty-first century. Both designers attended the Academy of Fine Arts in Gdansk, where they learned design fundamentals grounded in the Polish poster tradition; the pair also studied and worked in Paris. Since founding their studio, Homework, in Warsaw in 2003, they have used the poster to define the core, but not the limits, of their practice. --- Working in a time and place where visual punning may seem a shade old school, Górska and Skakun proudly wield the arsenal of visual techniques made famous by Henryk Tomaszewski and Józef Mroszczak generations ago. Broken glass gives a harsh sense of immediacy to posters for the Krakow Film Foundation and the Studio Teatr Office Box. Simple, iconic illustrations blend a pig with a meat cleaver, a gun with an angry dog, and the head of a child with a hungry mouth. Blood drips from a clenched fist, while a many-headed snail depicts life in a crowded apartment. --- In many of these works, the surface is right up front, subject to violence and violation. In a poster for *Kola*, a violin bow cuts through the blue plane of the page, slicing the symmetrical typography. Their film posters avoid photography in favor of iconic illustrations. They explain: "Luckily, neither Brad Pitt nor any other Hollywood star plays in most of these films, so the lack of an actor's face does not affect the number of teenagers coming to the cinema." Such graphic imagery lends itself to animation and translates well into other forms of media. Thus, while reviving the poster tradition, these designers are also wedding an art-based medium to the contemporary practice of graphic design. --- Ellen Lupton

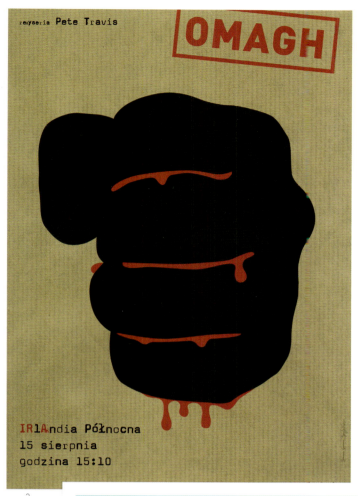

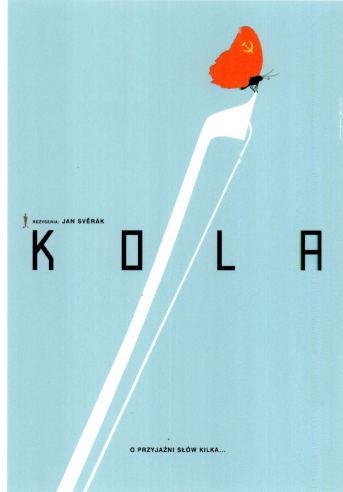

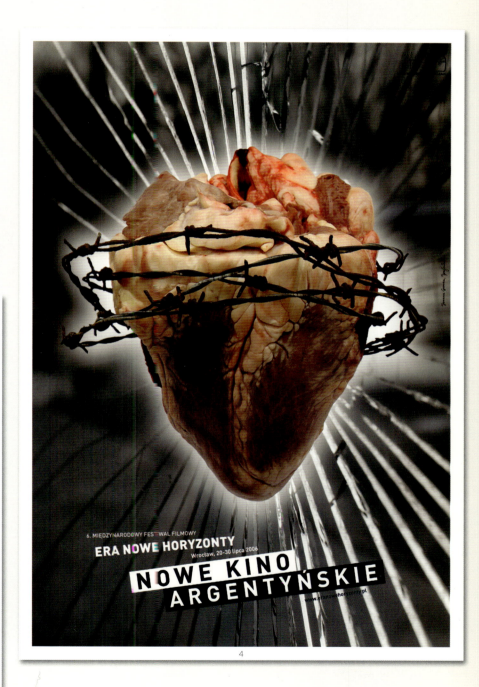

1. Posters, "Muzzeum Jazz" concert se-
    ries, Pulaski Museur, Poland, 2005-6
    ----
2. Film poster, *Omagh*, Vivarto,
    Poland, 2006
    ----
3. Film poster, *Kola*, Vivarto,
    Poland, 2006
    ----
4. Poster, New Argentire Cinema
    Festival, Mañana, Poland, 2006

5

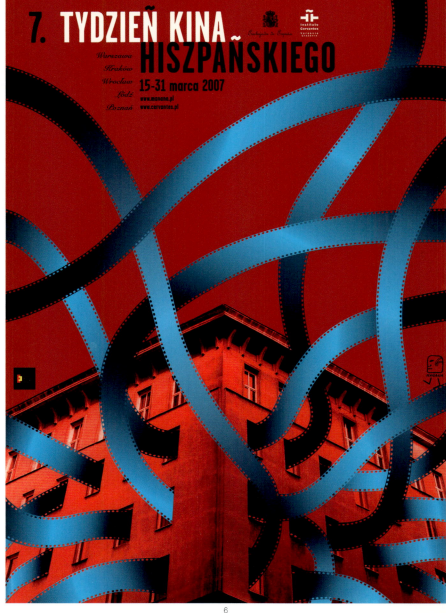

5.   Poster, 47th Krakow Film Festival,
        Krakow Film Foundation, Poland, 2007

6.   Poster, 7th Spanish Film Week,
        Mañana, Poland, 2007

7.   Film poster, *Shooting Dogs*, Vivarto,
        Poland, 2006

8.   Film poster, *Shut Up and Shoot Me*,
        Vivarto, Poland, 2006

9.   Film poster, *Under One Roof*, Vivarto,
        Poland, 2007

10.   Film poster, *The Ride*, Vivarto,
        Poland, 2006

11.   Film poster, *Sex in Brno*, Vivarto,
        Poland, 2006

12.   Film poster, *The Goblin*, Vivarto,
        Poland, 2006

6

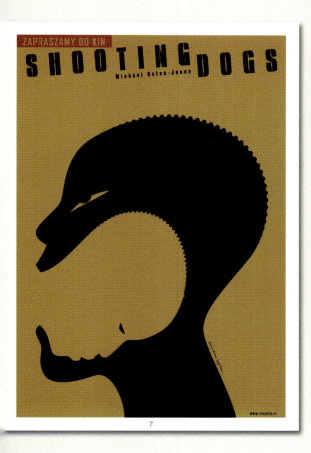

ZAPRASZAMY DO KIN

SHOOTING DOGS
Michael Caton-Jones

7

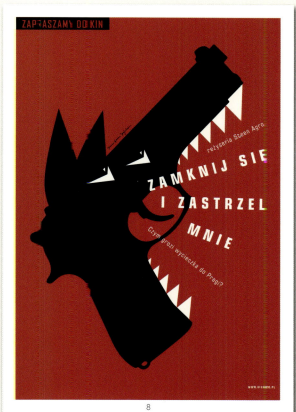

ZAPRASZAMY DO KIN

reżyseria Steen Agro

ZAMKNIJ SIĘ
I ZASTRZEL
MNIE

Czym grozi wycieczka do Pragi?

8

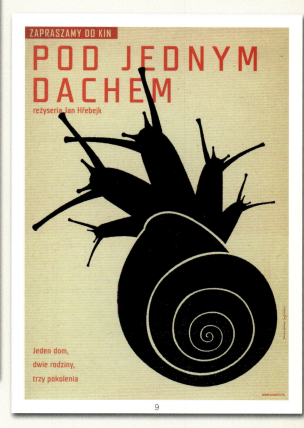

ZAPRASZAMY DO KIN

POD JEDNYM
DACHEM

reżyseria Jan Hřebejk

Jeden dom,
dwie rodziny,
trzy pokolenia

9

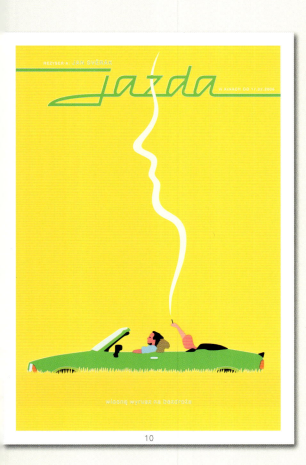

reżyseria JAN

Jazda

10

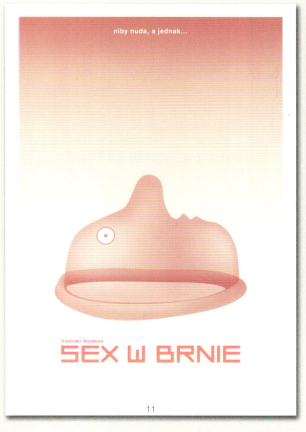

niby nuda, a jednak...

Vladimír Morávek

SEX W BRNIE

11

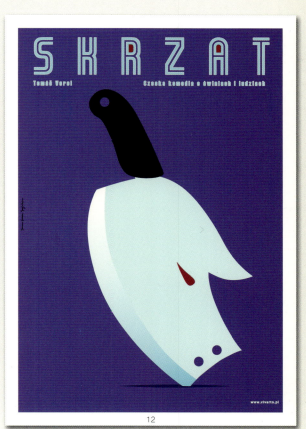

SKRZAT

Tomáš Vorel   Czeska komedia o świniach i ludziach

12

1

2

3

Mario Hugo (New York). --- Do you think it's wrong for me to want to *be* Mario Hugo? To be able to see what he sees or do what he does for a few days while he is working, drawing, scribbling, talking, and waving his hands around in animated conversation? I think that would be perfect, like *Being John Malkovich*, but a little less Cameron Diaz and a little more Spike Jonze. I haven't asked Hugo yet, but I doubt he would say no. He seems so agreeable, so friendly. --- From my brief conversations with Hugo, it's obvious that his personality and character are at the heart of everything he does: his writing, his art, his choice of words. When you look at his work you see this instantly. That is what is so seductive about Hugo's designs—they are just so *personal*. He told me that communication design is about speaking to people visually, and that the work should have its own voice, its own inflections. "It's more than saying something," he explained. "It's being able to say something interesting, or engaging, or with an accent." --- Here is where the movie kicks in. Picture this: I open a finely illustrated door in the back of Hugo's head, crawl in, and ask him to talk about himself. "Hello, Mario." --- *Hello, Brett. I am a twenty-four-year-old artist-designer working out of New York. I can maybe pass as nineteen. I am friendly enough. I like wit. I don't shy away from nebulous philosophical conversation. I am a first-generation American in an otherwise Argentine family. I have been interested in the arts for as long as I can remember, but I dismissed them as a hobby until four or five years ago. My parents are amazing people who've supported me through everything. These days I am a happy, busy guy. I listen to books on tape while I work. I like movies, and wine bars on the weekends. I am sorry for my lack of pertinence.* --- See what I mean? Maybe it's just me, but in a world as prefabricated and predetermined as ours, one can only hope for more Mario Hugos. More of him would mean more opportunities to discover what it is to fully invest oneself in one's work—and to enjoy it: To be able to look at a piece of communication, a piece of design, and *smile*. Until then, we'll just have to wait for the movie.
--- Brett Phillips

1. Artwork, Dolce & Gabbana's 10th Anniversary, Dolce & Gabbana and Giovanni Bianco, Italy, 2007
----
2. Illustration, "Balance & Precariousness," self-commissioned, USA, 2006. Drawn in graphite, china ink, and gouache on acetone-stained paper
----
3. Magazine cover, *Flaunt*, Flaunt, USA, 2007
----
4. CD cover, *Rykestrasse 68* by Hanne Hukkelberg, Propeller Recordings and Non-Format, Norway, 2006
----
5. Illustration, "Encompassing Absolutely," exhibited at the Vallery Gallery in Barcelona, self-commissioned, Spain, 2007

Hanne Hukkelberg
Rykestraße 68

4

5

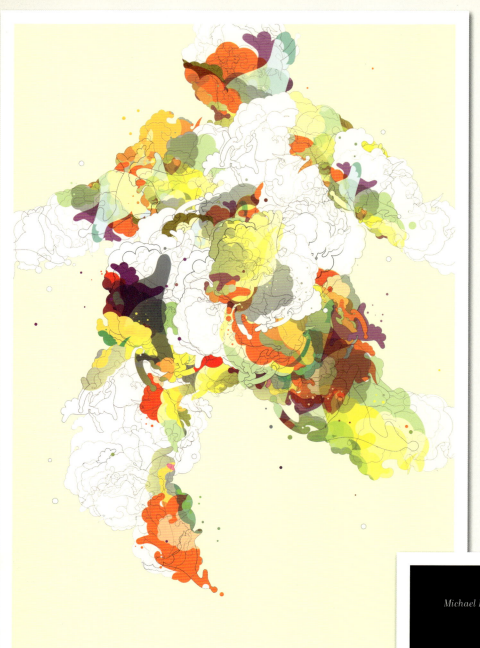

6

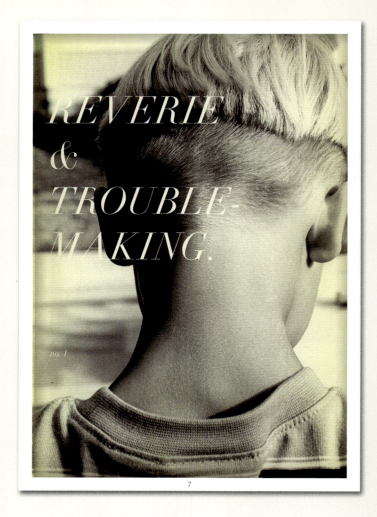

7

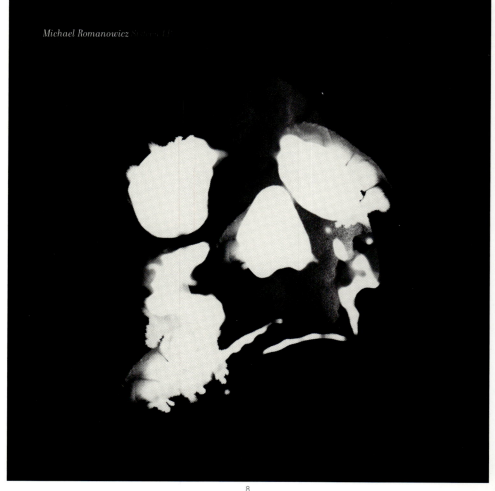

8

6. Canvas print, "Shirts vs. Skins,"
Footin Club bar and sports center,
France, 2006
----
7. Illustration, "Reverie & Trouble-
Making," self-commissioned, USA,
2007. With Hugo's eight-year-old
brother
----
8. CD cover, *Sisteen LP* by Michael
Romanowicz, Michael Romanowicz,
USA, 2006
----
9. Illustration, "The Garden of Malaise
& General Discontent," exhibited at
the Vallery Gallery in Barcelona,
self-commissioned, Spain, 2007
----
10. CD cover, Hanne Hukkelberg,
Propeller Recordings and Non-Format,
Norway, 2006
----
11. Print, G.U. clothing company, Gas as
Interface, Japan, 2006

9

10

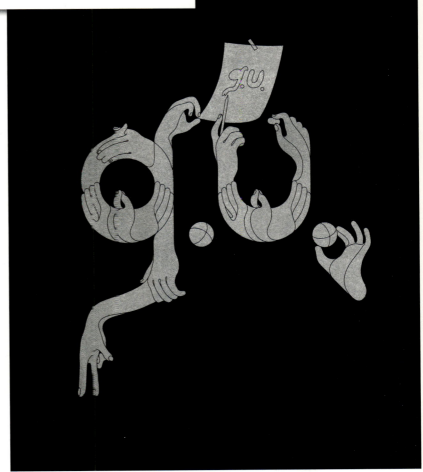

11

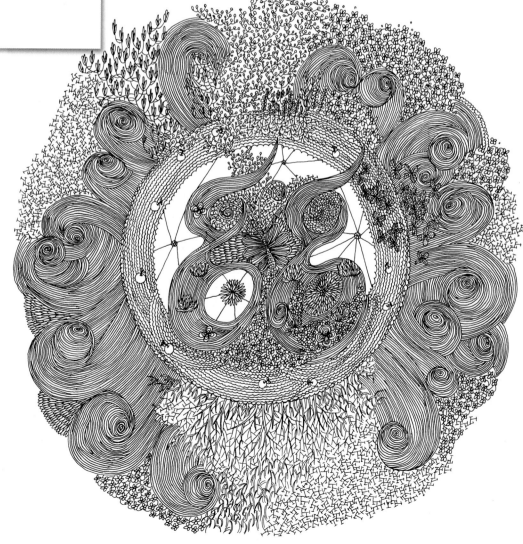

184 --- <u>Keiko Itakura</u>

Keiko Itakura (Tokyo). --- When talking about
Keiko Itakura, I must first mention her increc-
ible line drawings. Itakura decorates her simple
illustrations of plants and animals with intricate, freehand arabesque patterns. The traditional
Islamic designs they resemble were originally
intended to represent the order of nature, but
Itakura's drawings spring from her childlike
creative enthusiasm. They remind me of the work
of Antoine de Saint-Exupéry. --- When Itakura
turns her attention to advertising, she aims
for what she calls "kindhearted and sympathetic"
design. After graduating from Tama Art University, Itakura worked in product development for
a stationery company, where she learned how to
apply this approach throughout the entire design
process, from planning to sale. This led to one
of her most important projects, the art direction
for the lingerie line Subito, by Wacoal. She has
been designing for them since 2005, the year she
went freelance. --- As an artist, Itakura held a
solo exhibition in New York and has participated
in many international shows, including the Bangkok
International Art Festival in 2007. Her designs
have won awards from the Type Directors Club
and the Art Directors Club in New York. She is
truly an artist—and designer—to watch, and I look
forward to seeing her future work in both fields.
--- Keiichi Tanaami

4

5

1.   Illustration, self-commissioned,
     Japan, 2005
     ----
2.   Book illustration, *Remastered*,
     curated by Sebastien Agneessens,
     Germany, 2006
     ----
3.   Illustration, self-commissioned,
     Japan, 2004
     ----
4.   Illustration, Rikunabi, Japan, 2005
     ----
5.   CD poster, *Murmur* by Miho, Victor
     Entertainment, Japan, 2004

6

7

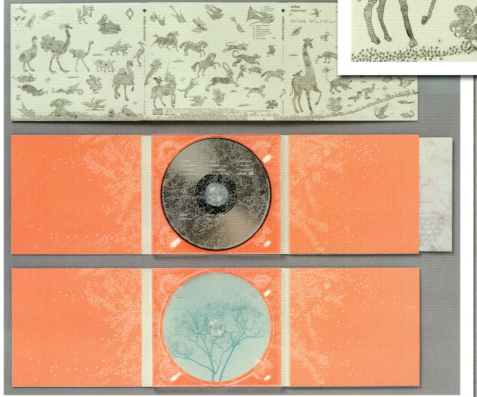

8

186 --- <u>Keiko Itakura</u>

9

6. Illustration, self-commissicned,
Japan, 2005

7-8. CD cover and packaging, *Murmur*
by Miho, Victor Entertainmert,
Japan, 2004
----
9. CD cover, album by Komi Hirose,
Victor Entertainment, Japan, 2004
----
10. Packaging, Charlotte chocolates,
Lotte Corporation, Japan, 2006
----
11. Identity, Subito lingerie, Wacoal
Japan, 2005-7

10

11

Keiji Ito (Tokyo) --- Blue skies, tropical resorts, exotic animals, and beautiful women in swimsuits—Keiji Ito clips these glamorous images from product packages and old magazines, and collages them seemingly without historical or hierarchical order. Intentionally designed to look cut and pasted, the elements that constitute Ito's works lose their original significance and take on an air of ironic meaninglessness. --- Ito's tongue-in-cheek utopian vision can be seen in everything from advertisements and music videos to the official poster he designed for the 2005 Expo in Aichi, Japan. He has designed covers for the Japanese magazines *SWITCH*, *Casa BRUTUS*, *Ryuko Tsushin*, *Relax*, and *Cut*, and his graphics have appeared internationally in *Esquire*, *GQ*, *Surface*, *fidget*, *ZOO*, *BlackBook*, and *Loyal*. Ito has also created album covers and videos for Japanese bands including Towa Tei, Buffalo Daughter, Kirinji, and Maki Nomiya. His advertising and magazine design work has garnered awards from the Art Directors Clubs of New York and Tokyo, and his artwork has been featured in both solo and group exhibitions worldwide. --- Ito's creations have traveled all over the globe, and his collaged graphics are like fabricated worlds in and of themselves. Still, he is undeniably a Tokyo artist, reflecting the reality of his hometown, the city of nihilism and euphoria. --- Keiichi Tanaami

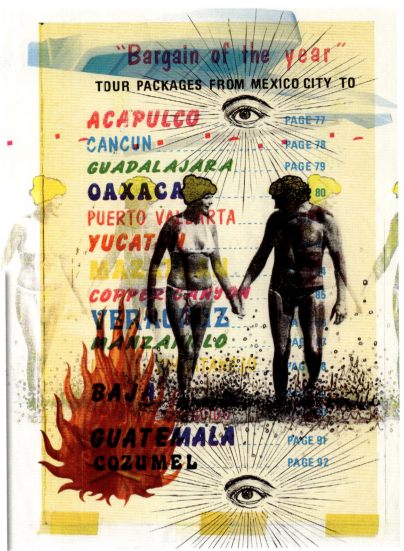

1.   Poster, Almond, Japan, 2006
      ----
2.   Poster, Converse, Japan, 2001
      ----
3.   Poster, Toppan Printing, Japan, 2006
      ----
4.   Newspaper, *Punctum Times*, Punctum
      Photo+Graphix, Japan, 2007

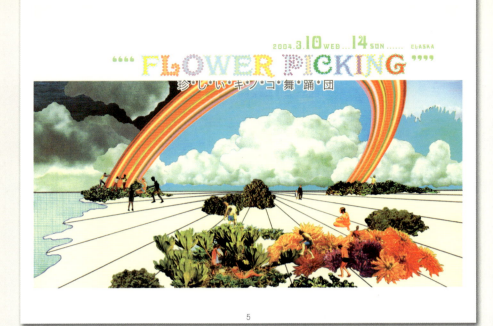

5

5.   Event flyer, Strange Kinoko Dance Company, Pavlov, Japan, 2004

6.   Newspaper, *Ifif*, KDDI, Japan, 2006-7

7.   Set design, *Heart TV*, NHK, Japan, 2006

8.   Book cover, *Tabi ni dero! Vagabinding Guide*, Sony Magazines, Japan, 2006

9.   Event poster, Expo 2005, Japan Association for the 2005 World Exposition, Japan, 2004

10.   Book cover, *Future Days*, self-commissioned, Japan, 2003

6

7

8

9

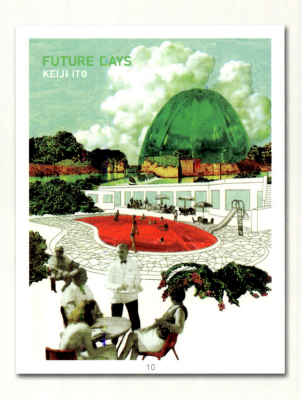

10

James Jarvis (London). --- James Jarvis is included in this book not as a toy designer per se, but as a designer of worlds. He is a brilliant interpreter of 2-D and 3-D pop ideas, and is perhaps the finest designer to emerge from the rapidly declining "urban vinyl" boom. Based in London, Jarvis co-owns Amos Toys, a clearinghouse for all his projects. He is well known for his "In-Crowd" line of toys, which offers lovingly satirical takes on the urban tribes that occupy our own hurly-burly world. Collections like "Punk Is Not Dead" (perfectly dressed punkers), "The Magical Plastic Band" (a *Sgt. Pepper's* rip-off), and "Ages of Metal" (heavy-metal dudes) are punchy and fun. And when he gets into the outlandish wrestlers of "ICWF" and the literal zombies of "Zombies," Jarvis sails into hilarious fancies. --- All of Jarvis's figures are marked by clean lines and rounded forms. Each is a meticulous, elegant bit of design with nothing out of place. This consistency helps Jarvis create a believable visual world. His choice of shapes, the deadpan expressions on all his characters' faces, and the muted but effective color scheme he uses all unify his vision and create a context in which his characters can live. --- Trained as an illustrator, Jarvis has also created a wonderful graphic novel, Vortigern's Machine and the Great Sage of Wisdom. Its pristine lines, detailed but uncluttered panels, and slyly affectionate sense of humor make it a Tintin for a new generation. In the book, Jarvis was able to shift easily from three dimensions to two, his forms remaining intact when moved from space to page. Perhaps the transition was made easier by his timelessness as a designer: Jarvis is almost a classicist, and like the best of design, his simple, clever ideas and products aim high but communicate on multiple levels. His work is simultaneously sophisticated and silly. This delicate balance ought to find an audience for generations to come. --- Dan Nadel

1.   Cover, *World of Pain*, Silas, UK, 2000

2-3. Vinyl toys, Amos Toys, UK, 2005-6
----
4.   Illustration, *Vogue* magazine, Vogue, UK, 2006
----
5.   Vinyl toy series, "Vortigern's Machine," Amos Toys, UK, 2006

2

3

4

5

193

6-7. Book cover and spread, *Vortigern's
Machine and the Great Sage of Wisdom*,
Amos Toys, UK, 2006. With Russell
Waterman

----

8. Illustration, self-commissioned
UK, 2006

----

9. Cover artwork, *Relax* magazine, Relax,
Japan, 2004

1

2

Körner Union (Lausanne). --- In 2000, at the École Cantonale d'Art de Lausanne (ÉCAL), Sami Benhadj, Tarik Hayward, and Guy Meldem worked together for the first time on a competition to create an identity for a farm company called Körner Union (corn union). The decision was quickly made to borrow this name for themselves in order to use the branded merchandise the company would produce: free Swiss Army knives, caps, and T-shirts. They lost the competition, but the name Körner Union now stands for this innovative Swiss design group. --- Körner Union's three members have diverse backgrounds, making collaboration a challenge as they try to stick together while creating global projects with a palette of mixed media, film, video, photography, and illustration. The trio describes its approach as a "stimulating confron- tation, a collaboration between different worlds." Strongly devoted to context, the group tries to appropriate each project and make it something personal and different. --- Over the course of their time together, Benhadj, Hayward, and Meldem have developed a language that makes sense only among themselves. The oddities that result influ- ence their work and the way they communicate with the outside world. For example, their work- flow involves a set of unique rules, such as a by-the-minute penalty for anyone late for the daily morning meeting. (The penalty, by the way, is 0.50 CHF.) --- ÉCAL, with its fast-paced commu- nity creating visually powerful images, was an interesting and inspiring starting point for Körner Union's work, but the group says its most important influences are its close friends and the Swiss countryside. Körner Union's illustrated figures resemble the charming characters of Tove Jansson's *Moomin* and Annette Tison and Talus Taylor's *Barbapapa*. "We like them," admitted the three. --- One of their goals for the future is to focus on a big project that would be developed in a much slower and deeper way: a project that would sum up their different experiments and interests, something that is even more emotional. "It might be a love movie," they say. --- Julia Hasting

1. Illustration, Aprilia motorcycle, Italy, 2004
----
1. Catalog illustration, Vitra Home, Vitra, Germany, 2004
----
2. Exhibition wall, *Musée CoCo 2*, Enter Room, Thun Museum of Art, Switzer- land, 2006
----
3. Cover artwork, *The Wire* magazine, The Wire, UK, 2006
----
4. Exhibition flyer, *Curating Degree Zero*, Le Point Ephémere, France, 2007

3

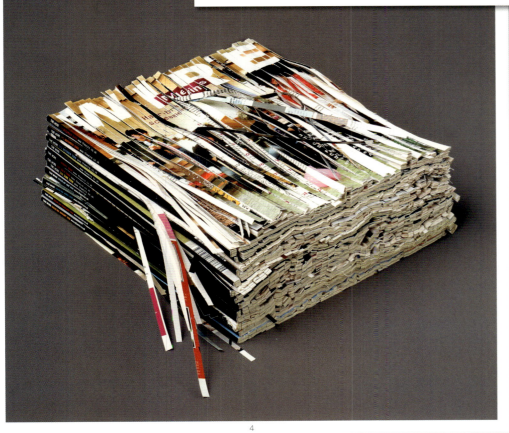

4

5

6

7

8

6.   Photograph, *Capricious 6 magazine* exhibition, Arnhem Fashion Biennial, 2007

----

7.   Portrait of Sonic Youth, *The Wire* magazine, The Wire, UK, 2006

----

8.   Exhibition, *La force des muscles*, Art & Design, Switzerland, 2006

----

9.   Exhibition, *Rock and Petrol*, Les Complices, Switzerland, 2007

----

10. T-shirt design, 242 Skateboards, Switzerland, 2004

----

11. Exhibition flyer, *We do wie do*, Enter Room, Thun Museum of Art, Switzerland, 2005

9

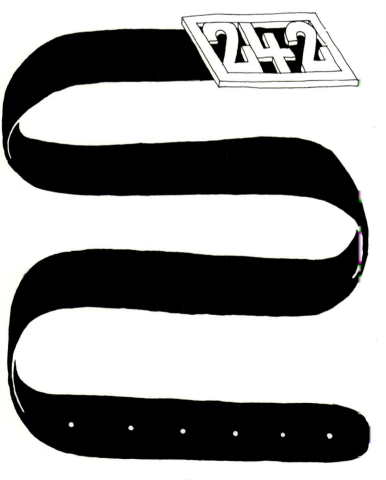

10

11

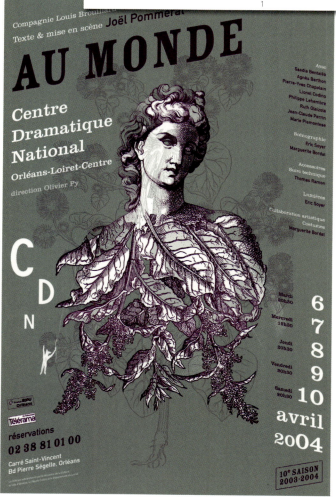

Laboratoires CCCP = Dr. Pêche + Melle Rose (Orléans, France). --- It is rare for graphic designers to have pen names at all, and Laboratoires CCCP = Dr. Pêche + Melle Rose (Dr. Peach and Ms. Pink) is the longest name I've ever seen. This odd moniker naturally inspires free association, but its meaning is a mystery and so is its creator. At the very least, *he* (let me assume so, for the sake of convenience) seems to live and work in France. Yet the designer's unique brilliance shines through his Iron Curtain of a name. --- CCCP's most representative work is the poster series designed for the Centre Dramatique National (CDN) in Orléans from 1999 to 2007. The posters' simple compositions are instantly recognizable. Each one is printed in only two colors and features a solitary central form that is usually a combination of two different things: a dove and a hand grenade, a guard dog and a castle, a breast and a conch, and so on. These mysterious and meaningful combinations remind me of that iconic surrealist marriage of a sewing machine and an umbrella by another pseudonymous artist, Le Comte de Lautréamont. The CDN poster series won the Grand Prix Award at the 7th International Poster Triennial in Toyama, Japan, and the Honor Award at the Yusaku Kamekura Design Awards in 2003. Since then, CCCP has been a frequent fixture at major international poster biennials. But the designer is not merely a poster artist. --- "Schizoide" (schizoide.org) is an online photography project inspired by Aristophanes. In Plato's "Symposium," Aristophanes imagined a world in which humans, once four-armed, four-legged, two-headed creatures but now sliced in two by Zeus, must wander the Earth in search of their other halves. CCCP's site helps visitors reconnect by making perfectly symmetrical composite faces out of their own left and right sides. "Schizoide" is a perfect example of the creepy and cryptic style that makes CCCP one of the most unique designers working today, and one of my favorites. --- Keiichi Tanaami

1-2. Silk-screen posters, Centre Dramatique National/Orléans-Loiret-Centre, CDN, France, 2002-7

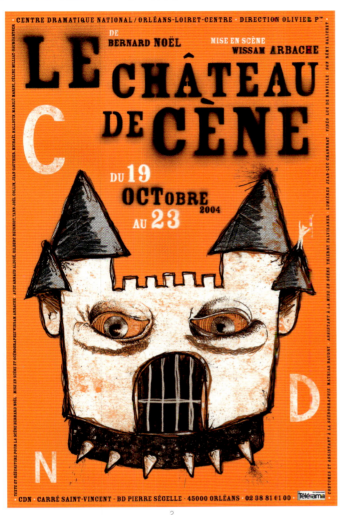

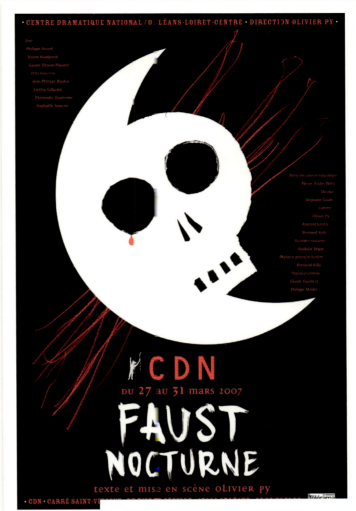

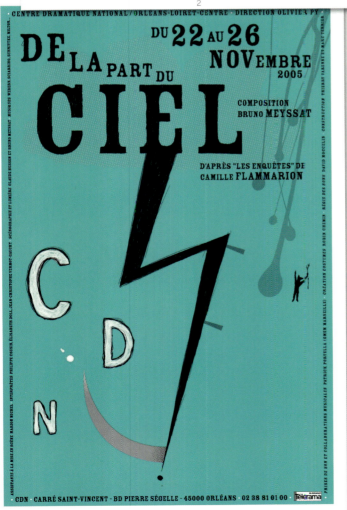

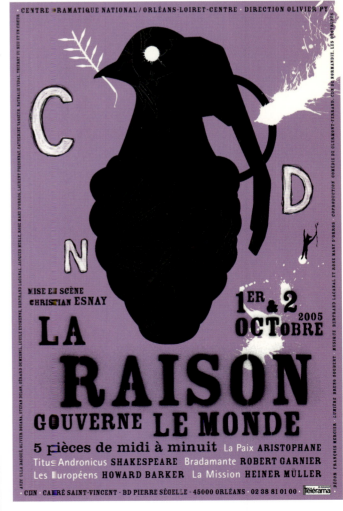

3.   Self-commissioned project, "XY,"
        France, 1998-2000
        ----
4.   Exhibition, *Pre-Partum / Post-Mortem*,
        DDD Gallery, Japan, 2005
        ----
5.   Self-commissioned project, "Alice,"
        France, 1997-99

6-7.   Self-commissioned project,
        "Schizoide," France, 1998-present
        ----
8.   Exhibition, *Pre-Partum / Post-Mortem*,
        Ginza Graphic Gallery, Japan, 2005

3

4

5

6

7

8

Jürg Lehni (Zurich/New York) --- As a child
playing with GeoPaint on his Commodore 64, Jürg
Lehni found the inspiration for what became his
"Flood Fill" animation series some twenty years
later. The software had a paint bucket function
that could fill in shapes with solid colors, and
the old machine's limited memory and very slow
speed enabled the viewer to see the shapes being
filled pixel by pixel. Recalling his childhood
fascination, Lehni re-created this low-tech method
to produce the same effect and aesthetics for
mobile-phone animations. Nevertheless, his work
does not try to celebrate the old as a better
alternative to the present. --- The twenty-nine-
year-old designer, artist, and developer believes
strongly in what he does. Rather than solving
a client's problem and pushing his own ideas
through commercial channels, Lehni feels the need
for a discourse about technology's influence on
aesthetics, which to him can be realized only by
self-initiated projects and collaborations of his
choice. With a knowledge many designers would
envy, Lehni creates his own working tools by
modifying standard design applications. His Adobe
Illustrator scripting plug-in, Scriptographer,
enables him (and those who download it for free)
to use JavaScript and extend the application's
set of default tools. --- "Hektor" is a spraypaint output device and Lehni's most acclaimed
project. It is also his favorite work, as it has
allowed him to collaborate with many different
artists and designers in different contexts. Each
collaboration is an intensive discourse, and in
each performance, the platform is the tool and
the medium is the message. A later machine, called
"Rita," is a drawing and erasing device, capable
of displaying constantly changing content on a
piece of glass or on a window. Preferably incorpo-
rated into an art institution's architecture, it
was designed to be used both as a communication
device and as an exhibition surface. --- Although
his background is mainly in mathematics, software-
programming, and technology, Lehni's fascination
with these areas is that of a designer. He uses
design as a playground for his interests and the
inspiration for many of his projects. His approach
is intuitive rather than rational. "Innovation is
not my main goal," Lehni says, "but—how should I
put it—soul?" --- Julia Hasting

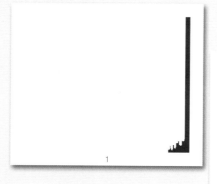

1

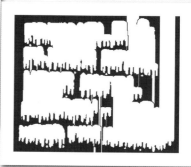

2

1.   Animation series, "Flood Fill,"
        Virtual Frame exhibition, Kunsthalle
        Wien, Austria, 2004. With Guy Meldem
----
2.   Scriptographer raster script created
        for "Hektor," École Cantonale d'Art
        de Lausanne (ÉCAL), Switzerland, 2002

3-7.   Self-commissioned project, "Hektor
        Circles," USA, 2007. With Laurenz
        Brunner. The Hektor spray-paint
        output device was created with Uli
        Franke in 2002 for Lehni's diploma
        degree at ÉCAL.

3

4

5

6

7

8

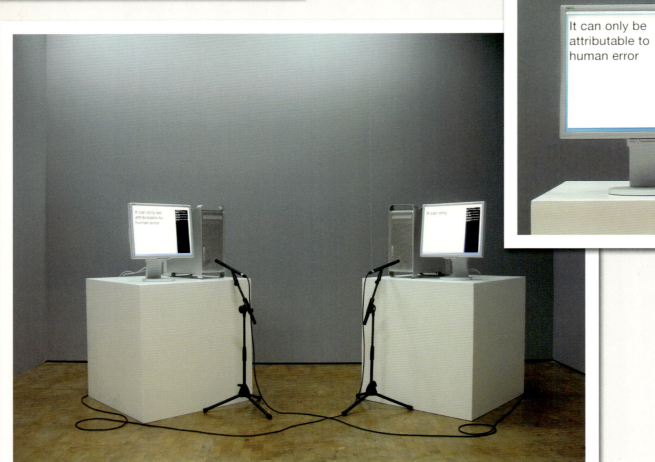

9

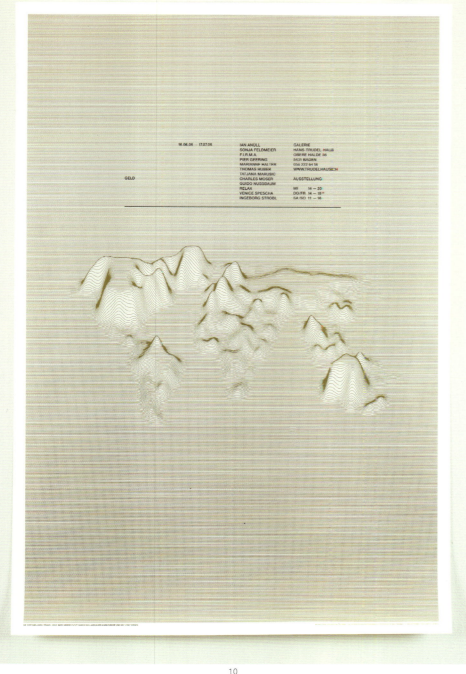

10

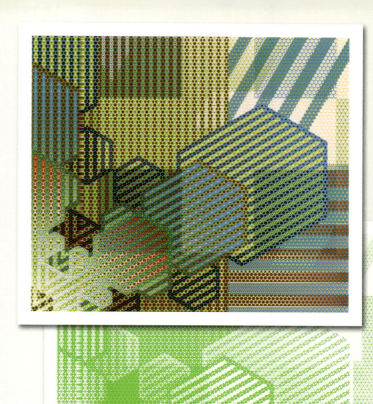

8. Installation, "Rita," Tensta Konst-
    hall, Sweden, 2005. Illustration by
    Guy Meldem
    ----
9. Installation, "AppleTalk," ÉCAL,
    Switzerland, 2002 and 2007.
    Two computers play Chinese whispers
    in an endless loop using text-
    to-speech and voice-recognition
    software.
    ----
10. Exhibition poster, *Geld*, F.I.R.M.A.,
    Switzerland, 2005. Scriptographer
    was used to map GDPs from around
    the world. With Urs Lehni and
    Rafael Koch
    ----
11. Studies, Swiss banknote design,
    Swiss National Bank, Switzerland,
    2005. With NORM. Scriptographer was
    used to develop a flexible system
    of hexagonal raster cells.

1

2

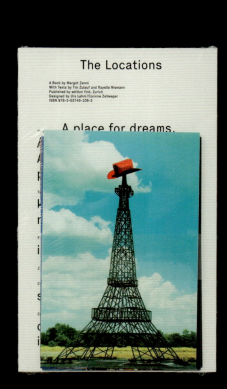

3

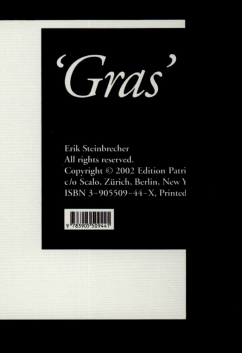

4

1.   Book cover, *Ein ersatzbuch*, Schau-
       spielhaus Zurich, Switzerland, 2004.
       With Aude Lehmann
----
2.   Exhibition catalog, *Bekanntmachungen:*
       20 Jahre Studiengang für Bildende
       Kunst SBK der Hochschule für Gestal-
       tung und Kunst, School for Art and
       Design, Zurich, Switzerland, 2006
----
3.   Book cover, *The Locations*,
       Margot Zanni and edition fink,
       Switzerland, 2007
----
4.   Book cover, *Gras*, Erik Steinbrecher,
       Edition Patrick Frey, Switzerland,
       2002

5   Catalog, *Diplom 04*, University of
     Applied Sciences and Arts Zurich,
     Switzerland, 2004
     ----
6   Magazine, *100* no. 101-96, self-
     commissioned, Switzerland, 2002

5

6

Lehni-Trüb (Zurich). --- Swiss graphic designers
Urs Lehni and Lex Trüb don't officially run a
studio together, nor do they collaborate on every
project. Still, they share a website that gathers
all their work in one place, allowing me to group
them together here. Lehni calls Trüb his "spar-
ring partner" and says that the appeal of working
together lies in the healthy arguments and opinionated discussions that arise when two strong-
willed and independent designers bounce ideas
off each other. --- Based in Zurich, they work
for publishers, theaters, galleries, government
arts bodies, and educational institutions. Addi-
tionally, both Lehni and Trüb self-publish. Lehni,
working with a group of like-minded photographers
and writers, edits and designs *Our* magazine. Each
issue solicits contributions from amateur and
professional artists and designers on deliberately
banal—and thereby accessible—themes. One of Trüb's
earlier projects was *100* magazine (actually more
like a printed gallery space for contemporary
artists than an actual magazine), put out by the
excellent Zurich-based art and zine publisher
Nieves, which was co-founded by Trüb and Benjamin
Sommerhalder. --- *100* is a good example of how I
see Lehni-Trüb's work functioning. The magazine's
only real parameters are format and page count
(one hundred), but these simple rules dictate the
aesthetic of the whole project. This sense of
order, in which one element drives the logic of
another (but not necessarily in a logical way),
is evident in all of the duo's work. They gather
materials and ideas into a coherent whole, as one
might expect good Swiss designers to do, but they
will happily take that calmly ordered design and
shuffle it around. Their work will still make
sense, but from a slightly different and unexpected perspective. --- When designers like Lehni
and Trüb, used to self-publishing, team up with
like-minded clients, the work that results is
often brilliant in both scope and content. A case
in point is a Nieves edition edited by Lehni about
the largely undocumented work of the late American
outsider artist Wesley Willis. The sixteen-page
book started as a ten-page piece on Willis's work
in *Our* magazine, and a positive response led to
a grant-funded research trip, an exhibition of
the artist's work at Kunst Halle St. Gallen, and
now, in a satisfying closing of the circle, an
extensive monograph that will accompany the exhibition, which tours throughout Europe on its way
to Willis's hometown of Chicago. It's a graphic
designer's utopia in miniature: commissioned work
running parallel to, and growing out of, independent initiative, research, and self-publishing.
--- James Goggin

F+F Schule für Kunst und Mediendesign, Zürich
Wintersemester 2005/06, №3

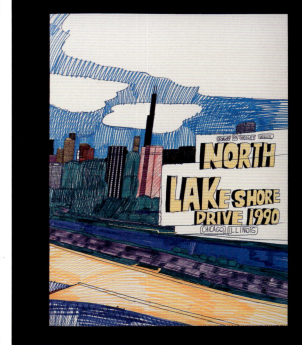

7.   Newspaper cover, *F+F Semesterzeitung*,
      F+F School of Art and Media Design
      Zurich, Switzerland, 2004
      ----
8.   Book cover, *Stadtland Schweiz*, Avenir
      Suisse, Switzerland, 2003
      ----
9.   Book cover, *I'm Starting to Feel
      Okay*, Nieves Books, Switzerland, 2006
      ----
10.   Brochures, Schauspielhaus Zürich,
      Schauspielhaus Zürich, Switzerland,
      2004. With Aude Lehmann and Valentin
      Hindermann
      ----
11.   Magazine, *North Lake Shore Drive 1990*,
      self-commissioned, Switzerland, 2007
      ----
12.   Exhibition poster, *Late Shift*, SGI
      Promotions AG, Switzerland, 2005

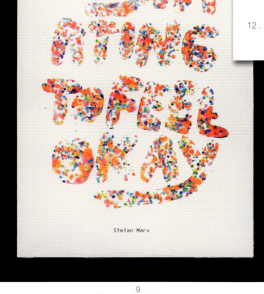

Stefan Marx

Ghariokwu Lemi (Lagos, Nigeria). --- Ghariokwu Lemi is the foremost album cover designer in Africa. Over the past three decades, he has created more than two thousand album, cassette, and CD covers for Nigerian and international clients. I first became aware of his work through the brilliant covers he did in the 1970s and '80s for the Nigerian musical icon and king of Afrobeat, Fela Anikulapo Kuti. Kuti traded his middle-class upbringing for the life of a rebel, political agitator, and musician. Influenced by the civil rights movement in America and its Black Power-inspired music—especially the gritty funk of James Brown—he clashed endlessly with African political and military leaders, right up to his death in 1997 at age fifty-nine. --- The music was furious, fresh, raw, and delivered unapologetically in pidgin English—the language of the people. Lemi's designs capture this intensity in great detail, balancing brutal ferocity with admirable visual dexterity. Lemi had no formal design training, and his work oozes soul-drenched rawness with every stroke of the pen, creating a whole new language of album-cover art that bristles with social and political criticism. He cites the cover art of Pedro Bell (who designed George Clinton and Parliament Funkadelic's covers) as a major inspiration, although the influence was more stylistic than philosophical. --- Lemi's extensive creative output both as a designer and as a painter has earned him numerous awards in Nigeria and around the world. He still lives in his hometown of Lagos, where he continues to work in his studio. If there is ever a Design Hall of Fame, Ghariokwu Lemi deserves a place in it. --- Saki Mafundikwa

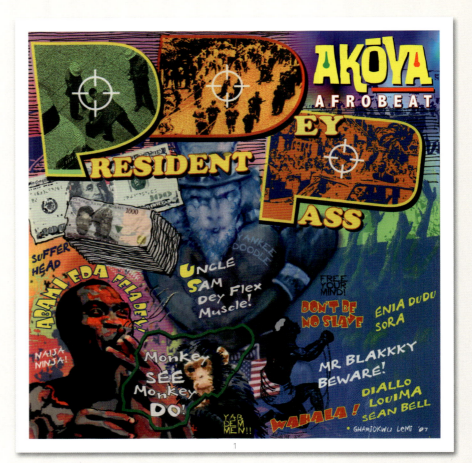

1. CD cover, *P.D.P.* by Akoya Afrobeat, Akoya Afrobeat, Japan and USA, 2007
    ----
2. CD cover, *The Teeth of a Goat* by James Iroha, Polygram Records, Nigeria, 1985
    ----
3. CD cover, *Monkey Banana* by Fela Anikulapo Kuti, Phonogram Records, Nigeria, 1975
    ----
4. CD cover, *Open and Close* by Fela Anikulapo Kuti, Polygram Records, Nigeria, 1986
    ----
5. CD cover, *Beasts of No Nation* by Fela Anikulapo Kuti, Kalakuta Records, Nigeria, 1988

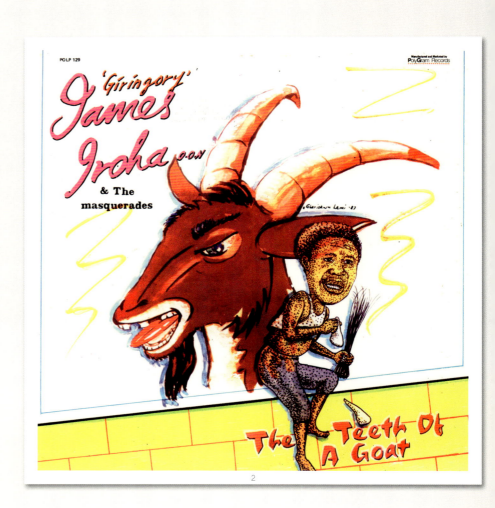

3

4

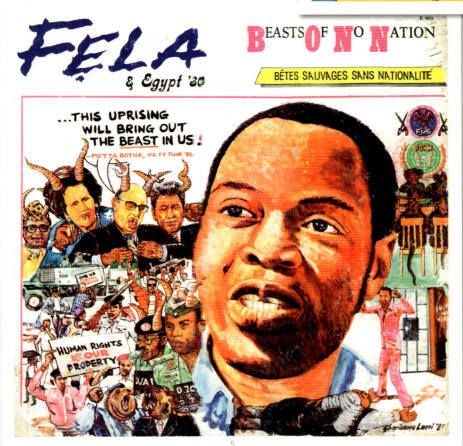

5

6

6.   T-shirt design, Stussy, USA, 2004
----
7.   Illustration, "No Strokes Attached,"
    private collector, Nigeria, 1981.
    Portrait of Lemi's wife in felt-
    tip marker
----
8.   Magazine illustration, *Observer
    Music Monthly*, The Guardian, UK, 2004

7

8

215

1.   Annual report, Mondriaan Foundation, Mondriaan Foundation, The Netherlands, 2005

----

2.   Page from atlas, *The North Sea: Cartography of One of the World's Great Seas*, self-commissioned, The Netherlands, 2004. With Steven van Schuppen and Jan de Graaf

1

LUST (The Hague). --- There is no other studio in The Netherlands where conceptual thinking about graphic design and cutting-edge digital technology are as obviously interdependent and interwoven as they are at LUST. Its members describe themselves and their select group of like-minded designers as *Generation Random*. Although it indicates an essential aspect of their approach, the phrase seems somewhat reductive. Sure, in almost every piece conceived by LUST there is a component that is randomly generated. But the overall conception of each work—from visiting cards to interactive animations the size of buildings—is guided by stringent internal logic and results from a thinking process that is at once extremely flexible and extremely systematic. --- Thomas Castro and Jeroen Barendse met while studying art in Utrecht and decided to enter the Arnhem Academy of Art and Design, where Karel Martens was an influential teacher. Although a skilled typographer, Martens is by no means dogmatic when it comes to typographic design, and Castro and Barendse felt very much at home with Martens's idiosyncratic mixture of commitment and antihierarchical thinking. *LUST* was originally the title of their collaborative graduation project, which combined several elements that would recur in their later practice: cultural philosophy, speculation about interfaces, mapping, and experimental typography. Having established themselves as a studio in The Hague in 1997, they were soon joined by media designer Dimitri Nieuwenhuizen. At that point, the studio found its niche, applying the principles of interactivity to digital media as well as to traditional graphic design. --- LUST quickly became a high-profile design studio, creating work for local government agencies, architects, art and music venues, and publishers. But despite the studio's obvious adaptability, LUST never stopped approaching the design practice as an ever-changing, all-embracing personal project. Each job is seen as an incentive to research and question the strategies and workings of design itself. Whatever the end product—whether exhibition interface, system, performance, or object—the work is primarily about process. --- Boundaries between categories often get blurred. An exhibition becomes a game. A poster becomes a visual essay on high and low resolution. LUST's website becomes a peephole into the studio's inner workings. A book of essays is made into an interface and a piece of conceptual art by indexing every single word. What about aesthetics, you ask? Well, in LUST's case, if the underlying ideas and structures work, then Eric Gill's maxim applies almost by default: "Beauty will look after itself." --- Jan Middendorp

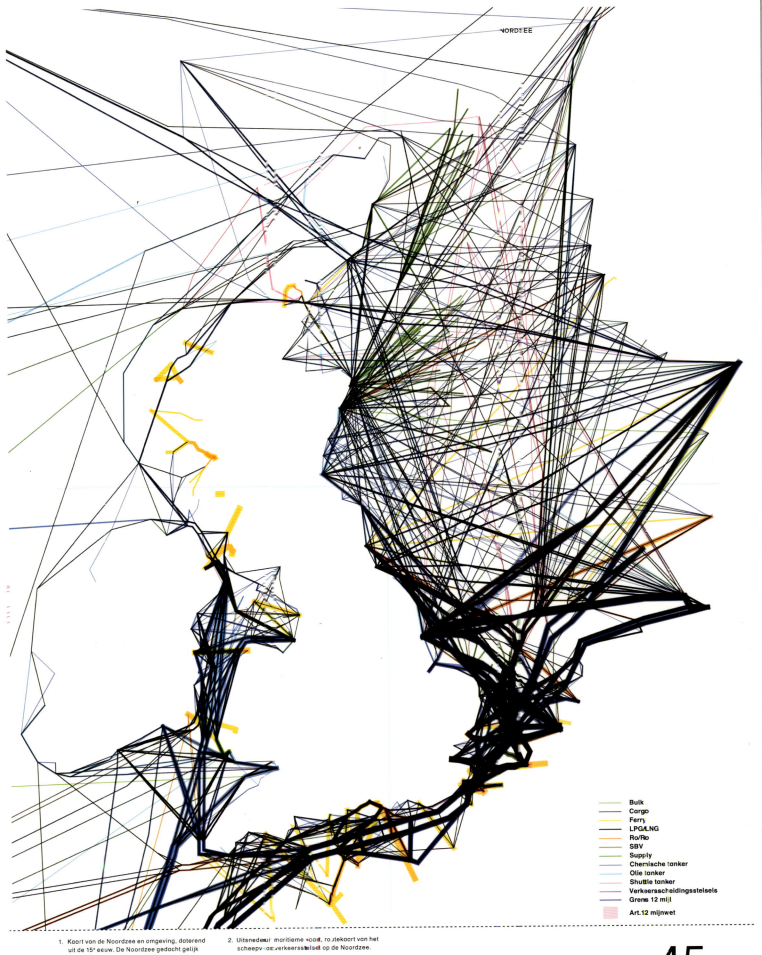

NORDZEE

Legend:
- Bulk
- Cargo
- Ferry
- LPG/LNG
- Ro/Ro
- SBV
- Supply
- Chemische tanker
- Olie tanker
- Shuttle tanker
- Verkeersscheidingsstelsels
- Grens 12 mijl
- Art.12 mijnwet

1. Kaart van de Noordzee en omgeving, daterend uit de 15ᵉ eeuw. De Noordzee gedacht gelijk de Baltische Zee als een echte binnenzee, met Schotland als drempel. Groenland en het noorden van Noorwegen met elkaar verbonden door de Mare Congelatum, de bevroren zee. Rondvaart lijkt mogelijk, benoorden om Zweden. Bron: P. Novaresio, *De grote ontdekkingsreizen*.

2. Uitsnede uit maritieme kaart, routekaart van het scheepvaartverkeersstelsel op de Noordzee.

3. De Noordzee als verkeersplein. Intensiteit scheepvaartverkeer, aantal schepen op een etmaal, geteld per 24 uur.

45

3

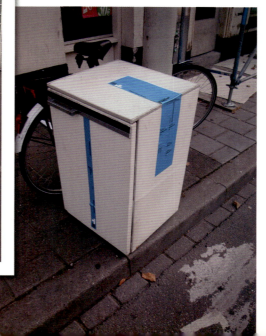

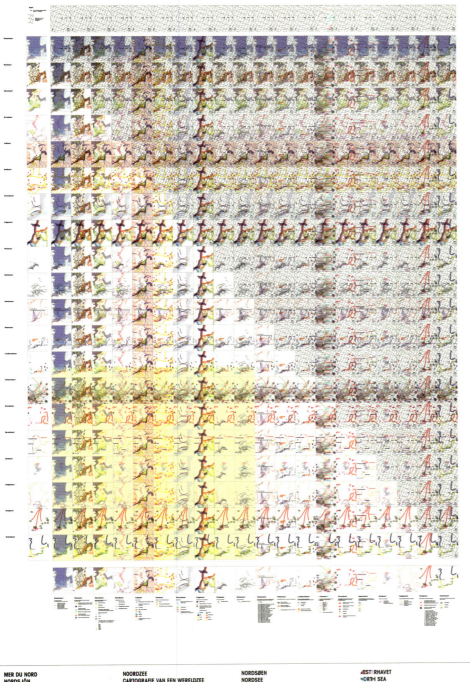

MER DU NORD
NORDSJÖN

NOORDZEE
CARTOGRAFIE VAN EEN WERELDZEE

NORDSØEN
NORDSEE

WESTERHAVET
NORTH SEA

4

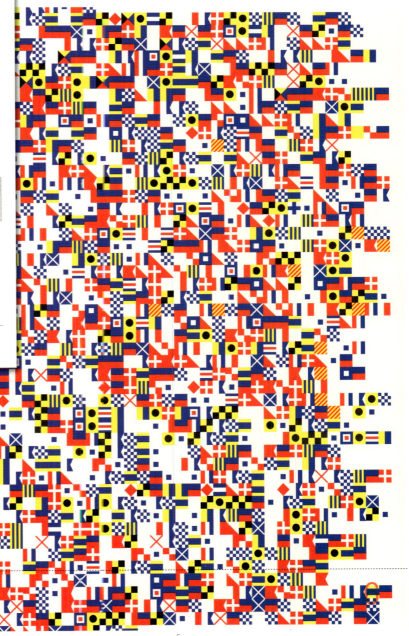

5

3. Identity and advertising, TodaysArt
Festival, TodaysArt, The Netherlands,
2005

4-5. Page from atlas and endpaper,
*The North Sea: Cartography of One
of the World's Great Seas*, self-
commissioned, The Netherlands,
2004. With Steven van Schuppen and
Jan de Graaf

1

1. Identity and packaging, Yauatcha
    restaurant, Yauatcha, UK, 2006
    ----
2. Perfume packaging, "Stella In-Two" by
    Stella McCartney, Stella McCartney,
    UK, 2003-present
    ----
3. Identity and packaging, Yauatcha
    restaurant, Yauatcha, UK, 2006

<u>MadeThought</u> (London). --- Wikipedia defines art as a product of human activity, made with the intention of stimulating the senses as well as the mind. Thus, art is an action, an object, or a collection of actions and objects created to transmit emotions and/or ideas. Now, is it just me, or does that sound like a definition of contemporary graphic design? I haven't asked Ben Parker and Paul Austin if they see their practice in this way. But, to an observer, MadeThought's modus operandi seems to be just this sort of transformation: turning ideas into visible, tangible communication design. --- MadeThought produces what Parker and Austin call "a deliberate and crafted aesthetic." The group tailors its work to suit the specific identity of each of its clients. In doing so, MadeThought goes beyond mere custom-made aesthetics and instead takes a holistic approach to design, immersing itself in its clients' individual philosophies. --- The beautiful thing about MadeThought's work is that it's rich with intimate propositions, delicate conversations, and—most important—ideas. These aren't ideas realized by a literal application of thought, but rather by the subtle application and consideration of form, graphic device, typography, and color. MadeThought's work for Design Miami is a perfect example. In this poster series, a single graphic expression is translated into a complex program of textures, devices, and treatments that combine to form an eclectic body of work. --- Perhaps in presenting MadeThought's work or speaking about its aesthetic, it might be enough to echo Wynetka Ann Reynolds, who said, "Anyone who says you can't see a thought simply doesn't know art." --- Brett Phillips

2

3

5

4.   Poster, BarberOsgerby furniture
     design, BarberOsgerby, UK, 2004
----
5.   Poster, Henry Peacock Gallery, Henry
     Peacock Gallery, UK, 2005
----
6.   Identity, Viaduct furniture dealer,
     Viaduct, UK, 2002-present

7

7. Identity, catalog, and exhibition
design, Milan Furniture Fair,
Established & Sons furniture design,
Established & Sons, UK, 2006

8

9

8.   Identity and invitation, Design
Miami/Basel 2006, Design Miami,
USA, 2006
----
9.   Identity, invitation, brochure, and
save-the-date card, Design Miami/
Basel 2007, Design Miami, USA, 2007
----
10.   Identity and event bag, Design Miami/
Basel 2007, Design Miami, USA, 2007
----
11.   Identity, invitation, and event cata-
log, Design Miami/Basel 2006, Design
Miami, USA, 2006
----
12.   Identity and invitation, Design
Miami/Basel 2006, Design Miami,
USA, 2006

10

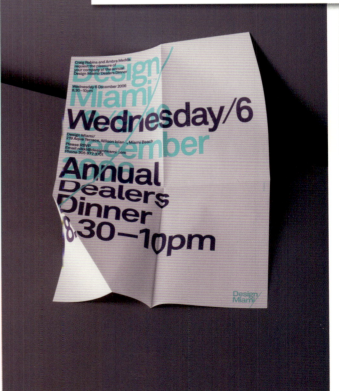

12

11

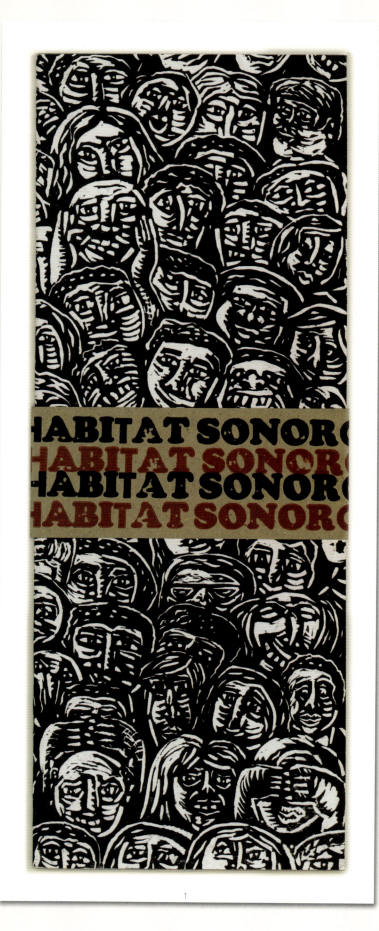

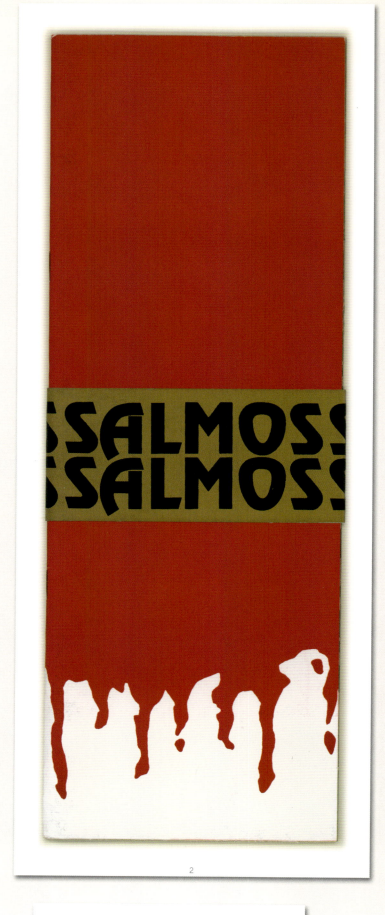

1.   Cover, exhibition catalog, *Habitat sonoro*, engravings by Luis Lamothe, Oficina de la SGAE en Cuba, Cuba, 2006

---

2.   Cover, exhibition catalog, *Salmos*, paintings by Mariangel Trimiño, Oficina de la SGAE en Cuba, Cuba, 2007

Eduardo Marín (Havana). --- While viewing an exhibition of contemporary graphic design in Havana in 2002, I was immediately struck by the work of a studio called Grupo Nudo (Knot Group). Among the designs in the exhibition, many of which aspired to be functional and to look international but which tended to lack originality, the posters and brochures by Grupo Nudo stood out. There was a sense of irony and tongue-in-cheek humor about their work that was surprising and fascinating. Grupo Nudo did what few other Cuban designers dared or cared to do: It sampled imagery from Cuba's everyday reality, reusing the familiar non-aesthetics of bureaucratic forms and food labels, or appropriating "capitalist" symbols such as credit cards and Superman cartoons as ambiguous attention-grabbers. Instead of indulging in digital image-making, their work had a handmade feel. In fact, some oddly shaped posters that seemed die-cut were, on closer inspection, individually cut by hand. --- Founded in 1989 by Eduardo Marín and a couple of like-minded designers, Grupo Nudo had more or less dissolved by the time I saw its work, but Marín continued to work as an independent designer. In the last few years, he has referred to his one-man studio as RPDC, the Spanish acronym for "People's Republic of Korea"—a complex pun, as it refers to North Korea as well as La Corea, a neighborhood in Havana. With RPDC, Marín has more or less marked his own territory within the Cuban design community. --- Since going solo, Marín has won the confidence of Havana's artists, and RPDC's main clients are art spaces, painters, and sculptors. Marín works for them, making idiosyncratic catalogs and posters, but also with them: Instead of having his designs produced on an offset press, he prints them at Havana's state-run artists' silk-screen workshop or makes use of the obsolete expertise of Havana's last remaining letterpress printers. Like the work of Grupo Nudo, his own graphic language is full of references to the less-than-glamorous printed matter of everyday life in Cuba. He sees it as loving homage rather than satire, saying, "Somebody has to preserve these images. It is a kind of archeology." --- Jan Middendorp

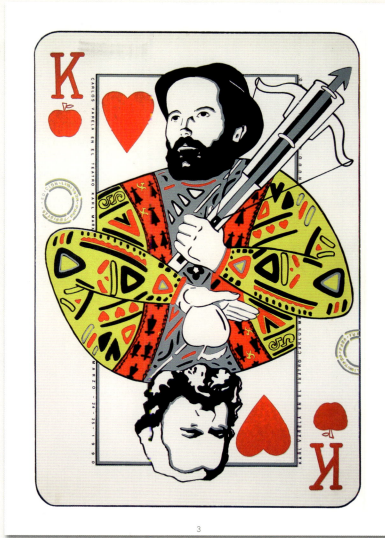

3

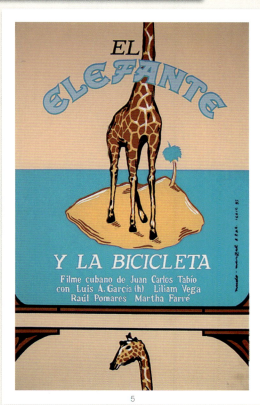

5

4

3. Poster, Carlos Varela concert in the Karl Marx Theatre, Ministerio de Cultura, Cuba, 1990
    ----
4. Exhibition poster, *Mearte en la pared*, Galería Taller René Portocarrero, Cuba, 2000
    ----
5. Film poster, *El elefante y la bicicleta*, ICAIC, 1995

6.   Cover, exhibition catalog, *Mirar la
     música*, Oficina de la SGAE en Cuba,
     Cuba, 2007

----

7.   Cover, exhibition catalog, *Des-
     almarte*, Galería Rubén Martínez
     Villena, Cuba, 2006

----

8.   Poster, exhibition of silk-screened
     works, *Havana Express*, Galería Taller
     René Portocarrero, Cuba, 1991

9

10

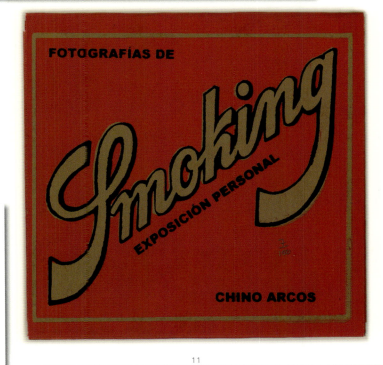

11

12

9   Cover, exhibition catalog, *Pedazos*,
     Oficina de la SGAE en Cuba, Cuba,
     2006

----

10. Cover, exhibition catalog, *La Contem-
     plación*, Oficina de la SGAE en Cuba,
     Cuba, 2006

----

11. Cover, exhibition catalog, *Smoking*,
     Oficina de la SGAE en Cuba, Cuba,
     2003

----

12. Cover, exhibition catalog, *Sentido
     común*, Galería Habana, Cuba, 2003

1. Exhibition poster, commemoration of the 100th anniversary of Pablo Neruda's birth, *Neruda 100* poster exhibition and Rafael López Castro, Mexico, 2004
   ----
2. Kimera studio promotional postcards, Mexico, 2004
   ----
3. Magazine illustration and lettering, *La Gaceta*, in-house magazine of Fondo de Cultura Económica publishing house, Fondo de Cultura Económica, Mexico, 2005
   ----
4. Typeface, Lagarto, Blacamán and Kimera Type Foundry, Mexico, 2002. Based on the calligraphy of Mexican colonial illuminator Luis Lagarto
   ----
5. Typeface, Aztlan, Kimera Type Foundry, Mexico, 1998. Based on Aztec architectural elements

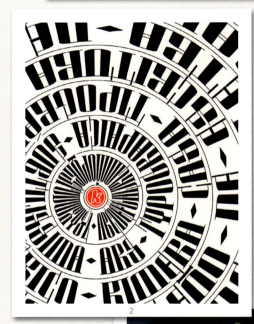

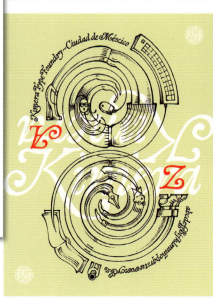

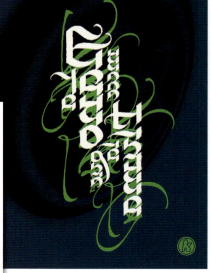

Gabriel Martínez Meave (Mexico City). --- Gabriel Martínez Meave is a self-taught graphic and typographic designer, illustrator, calligrapher, educator, and author. He is cofounder and principal of Kimera, a studio and type foundry in Mexico City. I met him in June 2006 at the Congreso de Tipografía in Valencia, Spain, where we were both speakers. --- The congress started in the morning, so by the time I arrived in the afternoon, I had missed quite a few presentations. I was ushered through a dark room to a seat not too far from the stage. The speaker was slight and bespectacled, but the Aztec- and Maya-influenced work projected on the screen behind him left me immediately awestruck. --- Maybe it was the jet lag, or the fact that I don't speak Spanish, but the soothing timbre of Martínez Meave's voice soon coaxed me into a surreal haze. I didn't need to understand anything he was saying; his work captivated me. I found myself thinking that this man had succeeded in doing what a lot of African designers (myself included) are currently grappling with: mining the deep bounty of our respective homes' rich visual heritages in order to create work with a distinct cultural aesthetic. --- Martínez Meave shared his sketches with me one night and completely stole the thunder from a World Cup match playing on the numerous televisions in a local bar. There he was, sitting on a high chair flipping casually through a thick sketchbook, explaining his work to an ever-growing crowd of admirers surrounding him. I was floored by the "sketches," which looked like complete works of art on their own! --- His typefaces Arcana and Organica are distributed worldwide by Adobe Systems. He also designed Aztlan, Integra, Lagarto, Darka, Mexica, Rondana, and Economista (created for the Mexican newspaper of the same name). He is currently a professor at the Universidad Anáhuac in Mexico City and is about to publish his first book, *La Forma de la Idea/The Shape of the Idea*, documenting a selection of his sketches, type, and design projects, under the imprint Kimera Ediciones. --- Saki Mafundikwa

3

4

5

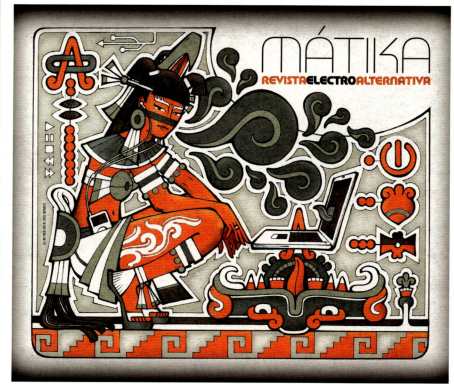

7

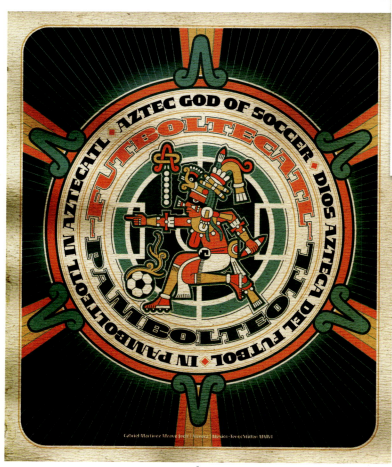

6

8

6.   Illustration, book of soccer graphics,
      Die Gestalten Verlag, Germany, 2006
      ----
7.   Magazine cover, *Mátika*, Mátika,
      Mexico, 2007
      ----
8.   Typeface, Darka Gothic, Kimera Type
      Foundry, Mexico, 2006
      ----
9.   Illustration, Kimera Ediciones,
      Arquine, and Ediciones Castillo,
      Mexico, 2005-7. Part of a series
      featuring imaginary landscapes of
      Mexico City based on Bach's *Die
      kunst der fuge*

9

Luna Maurer (Amsterdam). --- Luna Maurer is no
friend of the tendency nowadays to "wrap things
in design." To her, it makes the viewer's experience unnecessarily complicated and distracts him
from finding what he's looking for. Luna's work
is not about pretty surfaces and seductive skins.
What she wants from design is honesty and direct-
ness. Her projects, though, don't take users by
the hand and walk them from problem to solution
in a straight line. Rather, users are shown where
the line is, taught how to bend and shape it to
increase the quality of their experience, and
then left to their own devices. They are old and
wise enough, Maurer feels, to decide for themselves. --- By taking a radically conceptualistic
and, to some extent, idealistic stance, Maurer
hopes to provide an antidote to the shamelessly
manipulative use of graphic media in today's communication design. "When we shop," she complains,
"we become actors in a reality show in which our
emotions and behaviors are being controlled." Her
answer to this general sense of discomfort is to
lay bare the underlying system of design, and to
find ways of visualizing the system itself. The
structure becomes part of the message. --- Maurer
is based in Amsterdam, but her German origins lend
her work an intellectual quality that is rare in
The Netherlands. Although brooding at times, her
work is often surprisingly playful: a collision
between digital systems and the physical world.
In her groundbreaking website for the Sandberg
Institute (where she was formerly a student),
the grid becomes an elastic container of information, giving the user a strange sense of tactil-
ity. In her proposal of a design tool for jewelry
designer Dinie Besems, she mobilized two mathemat-
ical principles that are found in nature (the
Voronoi Diagram and the Delaunay Triangulation)
to develop organic-looking shapes. In another
project, she electronically deformed argyle patterns used in knitwear and then had real sweaters
machine-knit from them, giving the sweaters a per-
manently wrinkled look. --- In spite of her occasional tendency to operate as an artist, Maurer
considers herself very much a designer: "It is
very important that you don't put the same 'sauce'
on everything. I listen to my clients carefully
and I am open to compromises." --- Jan Middendorp

1-2. Exhibition posters, poster kit,
and workshop photographs, *Graphic
Design in the White Cube*, curated by
Peter Bilak, International Biennale
of Graphic Design in Brno, Czech
Republic, 2006. With Jonathan Puckey.
The series of ten posters was created
during a workshop led by Maurer and
Puckey, in which ten participating
designers worked within the limits
of a pre-packaged kit of parts and
a rule book that predetermined the
placement of graphic elements on
the page.

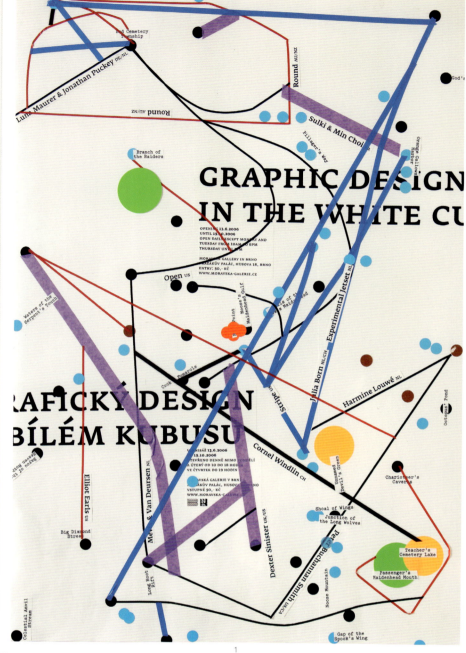

2

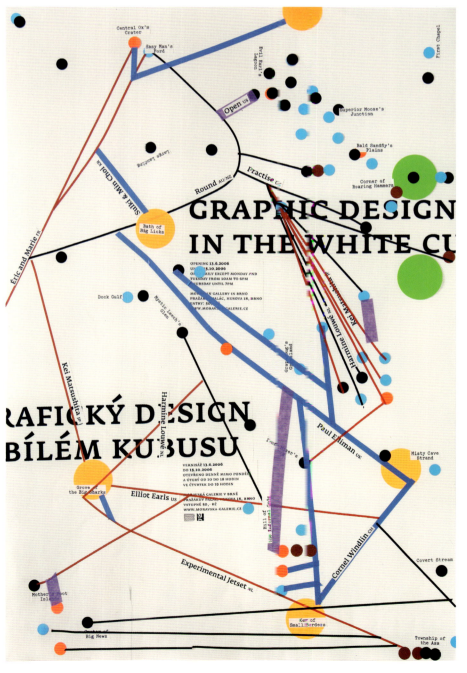

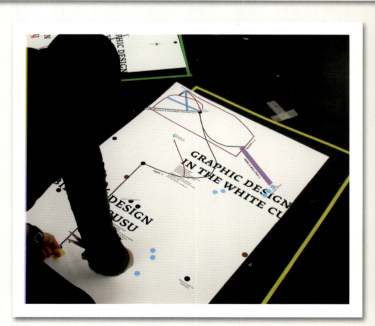

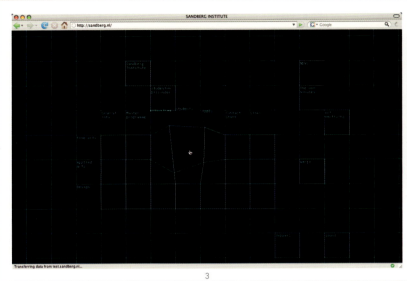

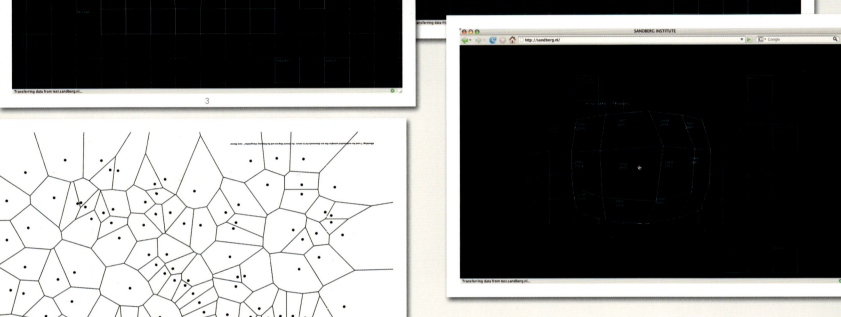

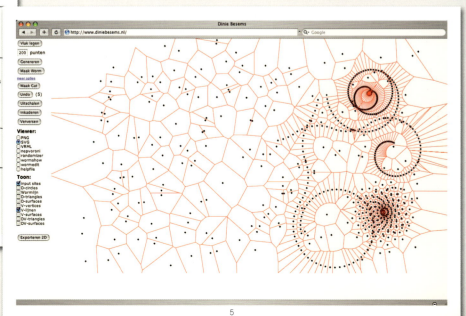

3.   Website, Sandberg Institute, The
      Netherlands, 2007. With Edo Paulus

4-5. Exhibition invitation and jewelry-
      design software, *LoloFerrari*, jewelry
      by Dinie Besems, De Zonnehof, Almere,
      The Netherlands, 2006-7
----
6.   Exhibition poster and invitation,
      NEST: Design for the Interior, Ste-
      delijk Museum, The Netherlands, 2005

Thomas Mayfried (Munich). --- Thomas Mayfried was trained as a photographer before studying design, and a photographic eye ruthlessly pervades his work. This is not to say that all his projects incorporate photographs. His designs for books, exhibition catalogs, and institutional identities are shaped by the spirit of the camera: its will to flatten, to find a center, to collapse depth onto a single flat surface that is both abstract and soaked in reality. --- Consider this project, which employs no imagery at all: For a competition to design a public marker and award trophy for architecturally significant buildings, Mayfried created a black-and-white plaque emblazoned with stark concentric rings, like a shooting target. Text is discreetly embedded in the outer rings of the target and directs the eye to the monument itself. Most plaques frame inscriptions, but here the words are on the edge, allowing the building to come into focus. Produced in enamel, the plaques recall similar markers used in London and other historic cities, but in a way that privileges the viewer over the monument. --- Museums and cultural institutions figure large among Mayfried's clients. In this kind of work, he is deeply concerned with representation, with how works of art are recorded and transmitted via print. Refusing to take an authorial stance, he concerns himself with bringing art and artifacts subtly into view through his use of color, cropping, scale, materials, and crisp, neo-objective typography. In an exhibition cata-log, different paper stocks set off the artist's work from the curatorial commentary. In a book of photographs, the horizontal format allows the pictures to dominate the pages inside. --- In a publication for the Haus der Kunst in Munich, Mayfried brings his photographer's eye to typogra-phy, zooming in and out on the exhibition's title. The phrase "Utopia Station" becomes a landscape, glimpsed in pieces, unattainable in its totality. Mayfried applies his sharp visual intelligence to this and every project, conveying a gentle awe for how things can, and can't, be seen. --- Ellen Lupton

1.   Book cover, *Michael Wesely Photographs*, Galerie Fahnemann, Germany, 2001
----
2.   Architectural identification plaque, BDA Bayern, Germany, 2007
----
3.   Photogram alphabet, self-commis-sioned, Germany, 1999

4

5

6

4.   Poster, Haus der Kunst gallery,
      Stiftung Haus der Kunst GmbH,
      Germany, 2004
      ----
5.   Postcards, children's program at Haus
      der Kunst gallery, Stiftung Haus der
      Kunst GmbH, Germany, 2003-5
      ----
6.   Exhibition preview booklets, Haus
      der Kunst gallery, Stiftung Haus der
      Kunst GmbH, Germany, 2003-present
      ----
7.   Cover, exhibition and lecture cata-
      log, *Utopia Station*, Haus der Kunst
      gallery, Stiftung Haus der Kunst
      GmbH, Germany, 2004

wohn

kultur

historismus jugendstil licht 2001

2001 ingo maurer
jan roth

1900 richard riemerschmid
bruno paul
august endell
hermann obrist
bernhard pankok
otto eckmann
fritz erler
ignatius taschner
mackay hugh baillie-scott
joseph maria olbrich
et al.

münchner
stadtmuseum

8

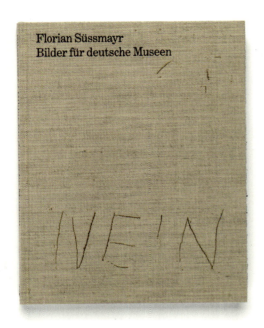

8. Poster, reopening of Wohnkultur
departmert, Stadtmuseum Munich,
Germany, 2001
----
9. Book cover and spreads, *Florian
Süssmayr: bilder für deutsche museen*
(Florian Süssmayr: Pictures for
German Museums), Verlag der Buchhand-
lung Walther König, Germany, 2006
----
10. Vinyl sleeves, *Metropolis* by Michael
Wesely and Kalle Laar, Michael Wesely
and Kalle Laar, Germany, 2000-2.
Project by photographer Michael
Wesely and musician Kalle Laar on
the sound of large cities

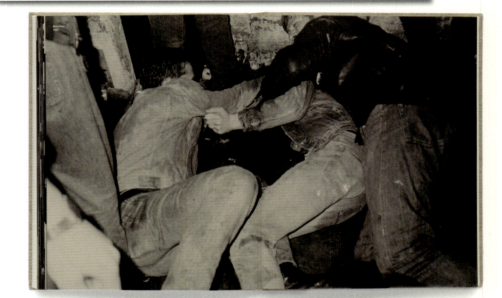

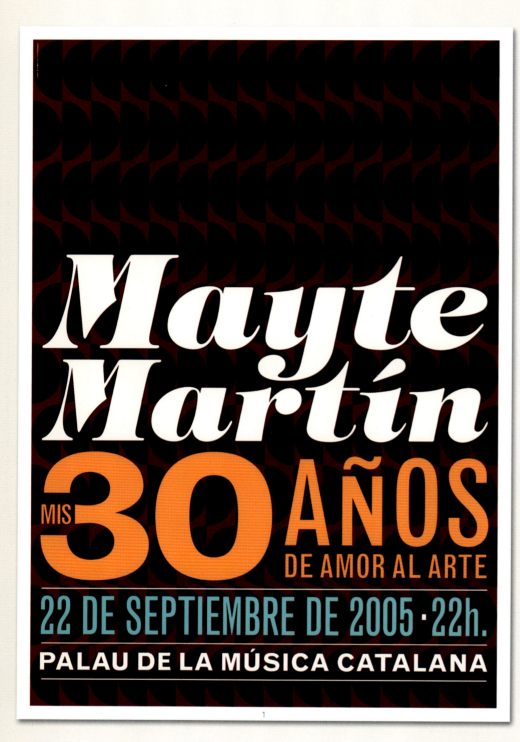

1

2

Laura Meseguer (Barcelona). --- The very first time I saw Laura's work, I found myself thinking that it had a strong retro feel—very loose and rhythmic. "I admire the 1950s and '60s style, and probably this has influenced my work," she agrees. But she is also quick to add: "I would say that this is coincidental, not on purpose. I can see this kind of influence in the work I've done for House Industries, with whom I've designed a typeface that is based on some original drawings by Daniel Soler." Laura also cites the French typographer Roger Excoffon and lettering artists like Jim Flora, Helmut Salden, and Imre Reiner as influences. --- Laura was a partner in the design firm Cosmic until 2005, when she opened her own studio, specializing in identity, editorial, and typeface design. She is a member of the Type-Ø-Tones, a group of type designers in Barcelona who run their own independent foundry. The Type Directors Club of New York awarded her a certificate of excellence for her typeface Rumba, which was lauded for its "hand-lettered" quality and "exquisite rendering." She was also awarded the LAUS Award by the Spanish Association of Art Directors and Graphic Designers for the typeface Frankie, which she designed with Juan Davila. An article in *Step* magazine elaborated: "Meseguer's early work tended toward organic hand-lettering and alternative-design typefaces. Then she attended the Royal Academy of Arts in The Hague. The mix of refined Dutch sensibility and Meseguer's Spanish fire has lent a profound mixture of gravity and energy to her work...and is enabling her to produce some remarkable typeface designs." --- Laura enjoys lecturing, teaching, and giving type workshops. She is a professor of typography and design at Barcelona's Elisava Escola Superior de Disseny and Eina Escola de Disseny i Art. A talented and versatile designer, she deserves the last word: "I can design the cover of a novel, a poster, or an entire book. I can help you use type correctly, design a new typeface, or fix an existing one. I could say, then, that I specialize in designing type and designing *with* type." --- Saki Mafundikwa

1. Poster, Mayte Martín concert, Fox Music, Spain, 2005. The poster uses typefaces produced in the 1970s to evoke the time when Martín began to sing.
   ----
2. Logo, Peralta design studio, Christina Jiménez Peralta, Spain and The Netherlands, 2005
   ----
3. Book cover and spreads, *Rolling Paper*, Index Books, Japan, Spain, and USA, 2007

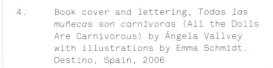

4.	Book cover and lettering, *Todas las muñecas son carnívoras* (All the Dolls Are Carnivorous) by Ángela Vallvey with illustrations by Emma Schmidt, Destino, Spain, 2006

5.	Book cover, *Dos a dos* (Two by Two), Moencoa, Spain, 2002. With Juan Davila
----
6.	Book cover and lettering, *Observamos cómo cae Octavio* (Let's Observe How Octavio Falls) by Hernán Migoya with illustrations by Santi Siqueiros, MR Ediciones, Spain, 2005

7.	Wedding invitation, Spain, 2004

8.	Typeface, Rumba, self-commissioned, 2003-7

9.	Typeface, House Holiday Sans, House Industries, 2006. With Ken Barber

4

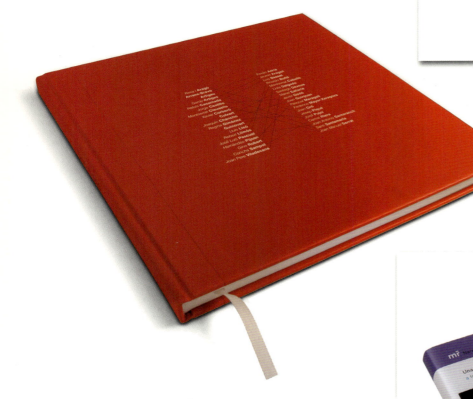

5

6

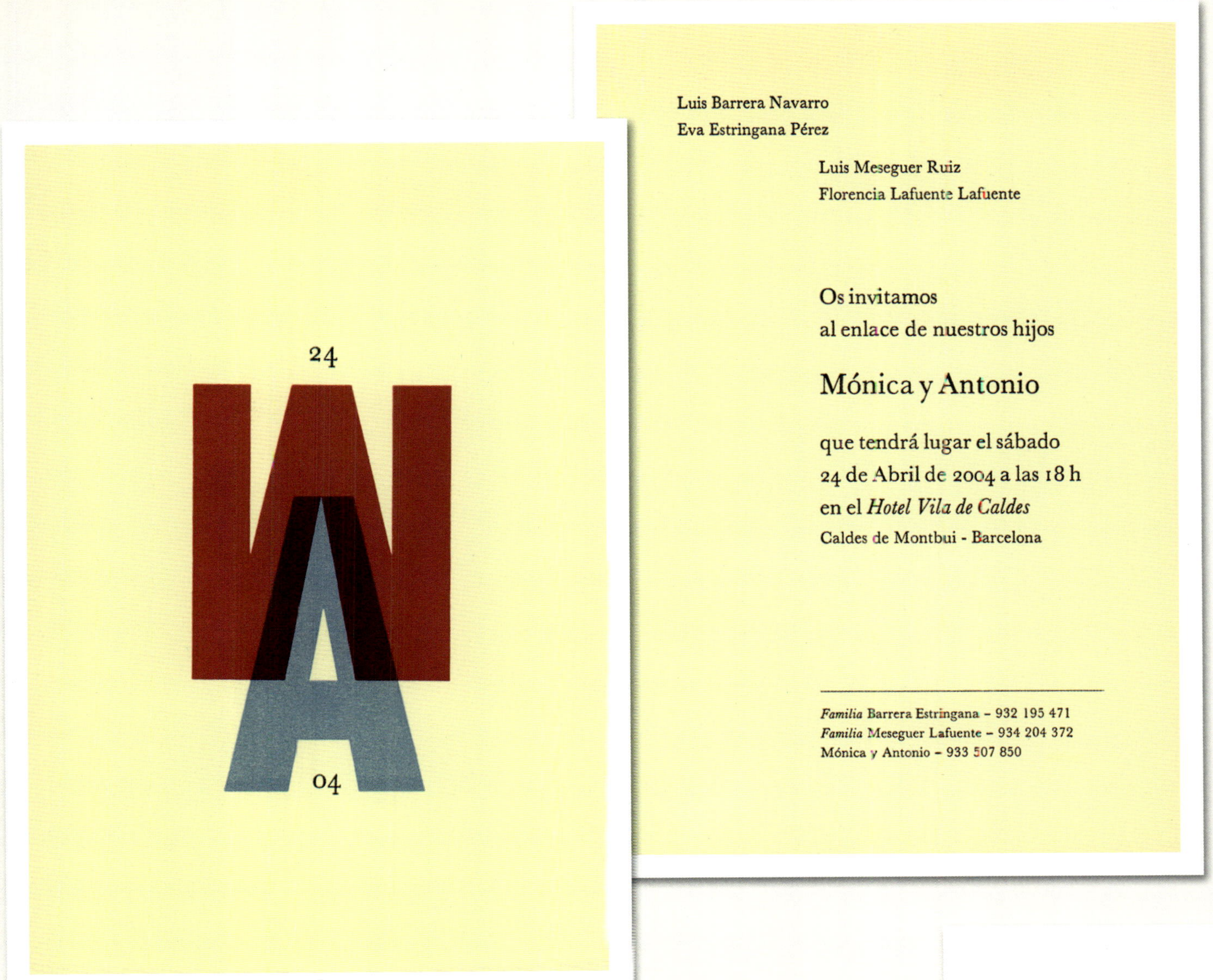

24

W A

04

7

Luis Barrera Navarro
Eva Estringana Pérez

Luis Meseguer Ruiz
Florencia Lafuente Lafuente

Os invitamos
al enlace de nuestros hijos

Mónica y Antonio

que tendrá lugar el sábado
24 de Abril de 2004 a las 18 h
en el *Hotel Vila de Caldes*
Caldes de Montbui - Barcelona

Familia Barrera Estringana – 932 195 471
Familia Meseguer Lafuente – 934 204 372
Mónica y Antonio – 933 507 850

Köfte
MAHI-MAHI   Vetkoek
Slovenian Partizanski golaž
Gazpacho
Kontsomea fo!earekin eta azarekin
Whisky
SMÖRGÅSBORD!
Chá com limão
8 Portions of Strawberry Cake
REVOLTO DE ALGAS CON OURIZOS

8

Chorizo
Vepřová pečeně s knedlíky a se zelím
TOM&JERRY
Chá com limão
SNOWBALL
Do you have ballons?
BON NADAL
Blondie

9

mgmt. design (Brooklyn). --- Mgmt. design is the partnership of Ariel Apte Carter, Alicia Cheng, and Sarah Gephart, three women with Yale MFAs, working hard in Brooklyn, New York. The firm's modest, self-effacing name has been the source of some confusion, yielding unsolicited calls from people scanning the Yellow Pages for administrative assistants or building custodians. What exactly does mgmt. manage? These brainy young designers are managers of content—and vast amounts of it—in the form of text, data, museum objects, and more. --- Their clients and collaborators have included Al Gore, whose book *An Inconvenient Truth* translates the statesman's legendary PowerPoint presentation and Academy Award-winning film into three hundred twenty-eight pages of content-rich, fast-absorbing print. Showing the influence of great information designers such as Ladislav Sutnar, the mgmt. team brings both clarity and poetry to the data they present. The graphics are lucid and accessible, and the typographic hierarchy invites readers of many ages—from third-graders to baby boomers and beyond—to follow the book's argument at different levels of detail and narrative. --- Books and exhibitions feed this studio's appetite for organizing large quantities of objects and information into coherent and revealing experiences. Each project conveys respect for both the readers and the producers of the material at hand, while at the same time giving voice to the designers' urge to express ideas in new ways. For the exhibition *Obsessive Drawing* at the American Folk Art Museum, New York, mgmt. designed a wall graphic with letters that are crisp voids left in a carefully scribbled field of pencil lines. For *The Open Book: A History of the Photographic Book from 1878 to the Present*, an exhibition at the International Center of Photography, New York, the title graphics and wall labels were printed on book-size pages that fluttered gently above austere wooden vitrines. --- Mgmt. proves their range in the design for books such as *Building: 3,000 Years of Design, Engineering, and Construction*, a weighty tome devoted to a subject no less massive. The designers made this imposing breadth of content, well, *manageable*, through their skillful use of color-coding, timelines, and diverse typographic tactics. Among many clever touches is their decision to give every chapter its own table of contents, effectively turning each one into a book unto itself. Now *that's* content management. --- Ellen Lupton

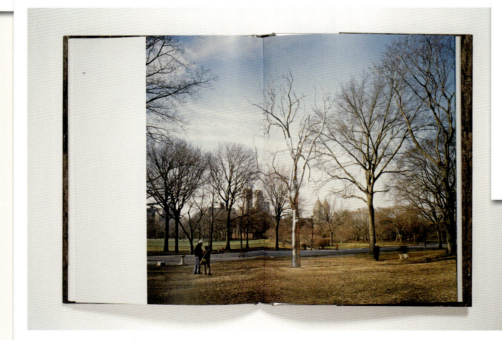

1.   Book cover and spreads, *Roxy Paine: Bluff*, Public Art Fund, USA, 2004. The book details Paine's sculpture, installed in Central Park for the 2002 *Whitney Biennial*.
----
2.   Book cover and spreads, *An Inconvenient Truth* by Al Gore, Melcher Media and Rodale, USA, 2006

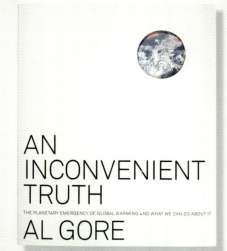

AN INCONVENIENT TRUTH

THE PLANETARY EMERGENCY OF GLOBAL WARMING AND WHAT WE CAN DO ABOUT IT

AL GORE

It is evident in the world around us that very dramatic changes are taking place.

This is Mount Kilimanjaro in 1970 with its fabled snows and glaciers.

Here it is just 30 years later—with far less ice and snow.

The melting of the ice represents bad news for creatures like polar bears. A new scientific study shows that, for the first time, polar bears have been drowning in significant numbers. Such deaths have been rare in the past. But now, these bears find they have to swim much longer distances from floe to floe. In some places, the edge of the ice is 30 to 40 miles from the shore.

What does it mean to us to look at a vast expanse of open water at the top of our world, that used to be—but is no longer—covered by ice? We ought to care about this a lot, because it has serious planetary effects.

MOTHER AND POLAR BEAR CUB ON PACK ICE, SPITZBERGEN, NORWAY, 2002

The way we treat forests is a political issue.

HAITI

DOMINICAN REPUBLIC

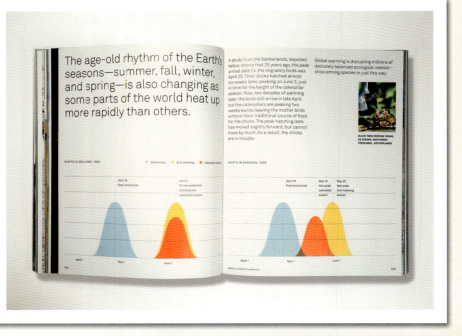

The age-old rhythm of the Earth's seasons—summer, fall, winter, and spring—is also changing as some parts of the world heat up more rapidly than others.

A study from the Netherlands, depicted below, shows that 25 years ago, the peak arrival date for the migratory birds was April 25. Their chicks hatched almost six weeks later, peaking on June 3, just in time for the height of the caterpillar season. Now, two decades of warming later, the birds still arrive in late April, but the caterpillars are peaking two weeks earlier, leaving the mother birds without their traditional source of food for the chicks. The peak hatching date has moved slightly forward, but cannot move by much. As a result, the chicks are in trouble.

Global warming is disrupting millions of delicately balanced ecological relationships among species in just this way.

BLACK TERN FEEDING YOUNG, DE WIEDEN, NORTHWEST OVERIJSSEL, NETHERLANDS

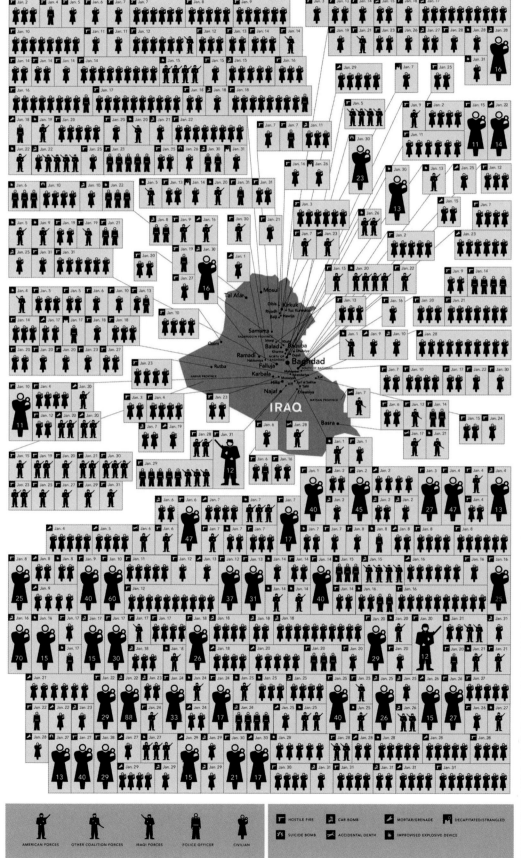

Op-Chart

ADRIANA LINS de ALBUQUERQUE AND ALICIA CHENG

31 Days in Iraq

In January more than 1,900 people — soldiers, security officers and civilians — were killed in the insurgency in Iraq, up from 800 in January 2006. Many corpses showed signs of torture, meaning the victims were probably killed by religious and tribal death squads.

The map below, based on data from the American, British and Iraqi governments and from news reports, shows the dates, locations and circumstances of deaths for the first month of the year. Given the vast size of Iraq and the communications difficulties inherent in war, the information may be incomplete. Nonetheless, it is our effort to visually depict the continuing human cost of the Iraq war.

AMERICAN FORCES   OTHER COALITION FORCES   IRAQI FORCES   POLICE OFFICER   CIVILIAN

HOSTILE FIRE   CAR BOMB   MORTAR/GRENADE   DECAPITATED/STRANGLED

SUICIDE BOMB   ACCIDENTAL DEATH   IMPROVISED EXPLOSIVE DEVICE

Adriana Lins de Albuquerque is a doctoral student in political science at Columbia. Alicia Cheng is a graphic designer at mgmt. design in Brooklyn.

NICHOLAS D. KRISTOF

Under Bush's Pillow

Dick Cheney as Lord Voldemort?

A reader named Melissa S. e-mailed to say that she explains Iraq policy to her 8-year-old son in terms of Harry Potter characters: "Dick Cheney is Lord Voldemort. George W. Bush is Peter Pettigrew." Don Rumsfeld is Lucius Malfoy, while Cornelius Fudge represents administration supporters who deny that anything is wrong. And, she concludes, "Daily Prophet reporter Rita Skeeter is Fox News."

That was one of the 400 comments from readers offering literary or historical parallels to the Bush administration and Iraq. One of the most commonly cited was Xenophon's ancient warning, in "Anabasis," of how much easier it is to get into a Middle Eastern war than out.

As a reader named John H. summarized "Anabasis": "Ten thousand Greek mercenaries march from Greece to Iran to effect regime change (unseat one emperor and establish his younger brother). They win the first few battles (cakewalk, mission accomplished) but then the younger brother is killed."

So the invaders found themselves without an effective prime minister to hand power to, yet they were stuck deep inside enemy territory. Xenophon's subtext is how the slog of war

From Voldemort to Othello, lessons for the White House.

corrodes soldiers and allows them to do terrible things. Xenophon is particularly pained when recounting a massacre that was the Haditha of its day.

The readers who sent in comments were responding to a column I wrote last month arguing that President Bush is inadvertently a fine education president, because he breathes new life into the classics. Thucydides' account of the failed "surge" in the Sicilian expedition 2,400 years ago is newly relevant, and "Moby Dick" is interesting reading today as a bracing warning of the dangers of an obsessive adventure that casts aside all rules. (You can submit your own favorite literary or historical parallel at nytimes.com/ontheground.)

Perhaps I'm cherry-picking from the classics to support my own opposition to a "surge" in Iraq. In writing this column, I wondered what classics Mr. Bush's supporters would cite to argue for his strategy. Shakespeare's "Henry V"? "Hamlet"?

Yet frankly, it's difficult to find great literature that encourages rulers to invade foreign lands, to escalate when battles go badly, to scorn critics, to be cocksure of themselves in the face of adversity. The themes of the classics tend to be the opposite.

Literature and history invariably counsel doubt and skepticism — even when you think you see Desdemona's infidelity with your own eyes, you don't; even when your advisers are telling you "it's a slam-dunk," it's not. The classics have an overwhelmingly cautionary bias, operating as a check on any impulsive rush to war.

Perhaps that is because, as Foreign Policy argues in its most recent issue, humans have an ingrained psychological tilt to hawkishness. In many ways, the authors note, human decision-making tends to err in ways that magnify conflict and make it difficult to climb down from confrontation.

My hunch is that the classics resonate in part because they are an antidote to that human frailty; literature has generated so many warnings about hubris in part to save us from ourselves.

Eastern classics have that same purpose of trying to tame and restrain us. The central theme of Chinese philosophy is the need for moderation, and Sun Tzu's famous "Art of War" advises generals on how to win without fighting. (Sun Tzu and Julius Caesar alike also appreciated the diplomatic benefits of treating enemy prisoners well; they would be appalled by Abu Ghraib and Guantánamo.)

So Mr. Bush should resolve that for every hour he spends with Mr. Cheney, he will spend another curled up with classical authors like Sophocles. "Antigone," for example, tells of King Creon, a good man who wants the best for his people — and yet ignores public opinion, refuses to admit error, goes double or nothing with his bets, and is slow to adapt to changing circumstance.

Creon's son pleads with his father to be less rigid. The trees that bend survive the seasons, he notes, while those that are inflexible are blown over and destroyed.

Americans today yearn for the same kind of wise leadership that ancient Greeks did: someone with the wisdom to adjust course, to acknowledge error, to listen to critics, to show compassion as well as strength, to discern moral nuance as well as moral clarity. Alexander the Great used to sleep with the "Iliad" under his pillow; maybe Mr. Bush should try "Antigone."

Oh, and for Mrs. Bush? How about Aristophanes' "Lysistrata"? □

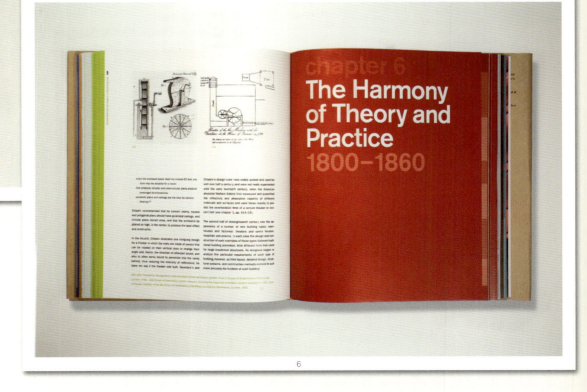

3.   Information graphic, *New York Times*,
      New York Times, USA, 2005-7. This
      series of graphics visualizes the to-
      tal number of deaths in the Iraq War
      during the first month of each year,
      beginning in 2005.
      ----
4.   Exhibition design, *Obsessive Drawing*,
      American Folk Art Museum, USA, 2005

5-6. Book cover and spread, *Building: 3000
      Years of Design, Engineering, and
      Construction*, Phaidon Press, UK and
      USA, 2006

Étienne Mineur (Paris). --- We can accept a
certain design technique's limited capacity for
expression. We can attempt to evade its problems—
or, like Etienne Mineur and his team, we can make
visible these technological limitations and their
accompanying imperfections by confronting them
creatively and giving them form. --- The unfolding
of the Issey Miyake website to the rhythm of his
newest collection perfectly reflects the evolution
of this impressive fashion designer by consistently rebuffing the site's technological limits.
In navigating the site, images of Miyake's collection layer over one another, revealing new designs
while never ignoring or concealing the old ones.
The technological restrictions of a single window
are graphically displayed and become the central
theme of the visual presentation. The tools developed to enable this confrontation with the limits
of design are an integral part of contemporary
graphic culture, and Mineur uses them with confidence and skill. --- One of Mineur's more striking
accomplishments was the difficult exercise that
consisted of laying out on paper his colleague John
Maeda's digital installations for a Cartier Foundation catalog. That creation confirmed Mineur's
mediating position between digital and printed
design. While his interactive works are enriched
by his background in more formal design and typography, he also incorporates the approach and imagery of digital domains in his book designs. This
twofold inspirational space—this twofold visual
culture—is what makes Etienne Mineur's projects
exceptional, regardless of the medium. --- Ruedi Baur

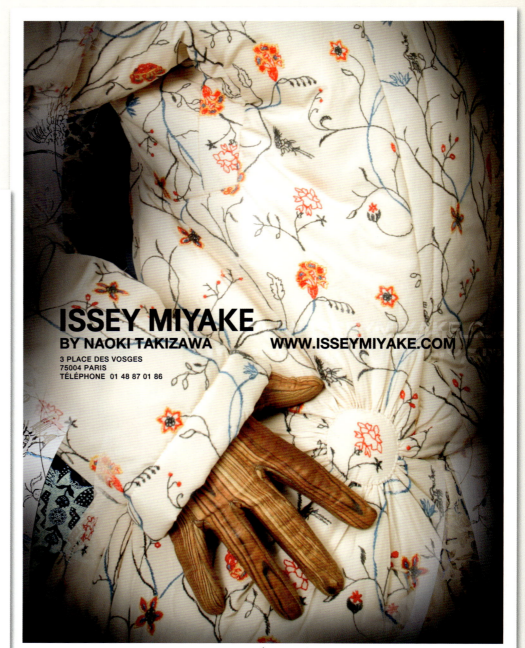

1.   Poster, Issey Miyake, Japan, 2004.
      With Roy Genty

2-3. Website, Issey Miyake, Japan,
      1999-2007. With Roy Genty and Sacha
      Gattino

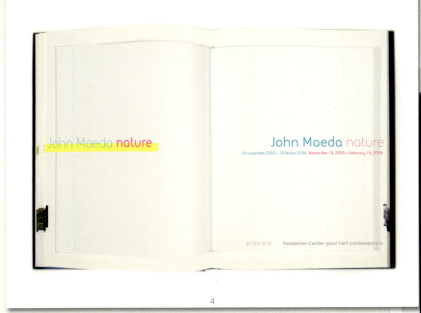

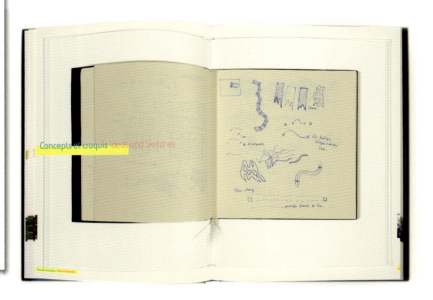

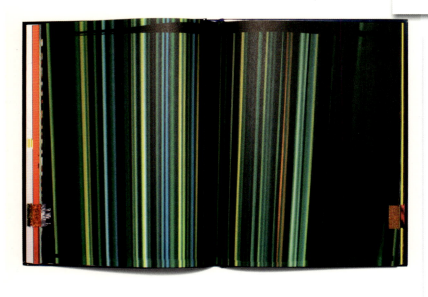

5

4.   Spreads, exhibition catalog, *John Maeda: Nature*, Fondation Cartier pour l'Art Contemporain, Paris, 2005

- -

5.   Typeface. Desktop, self-commissioned, France, 2002

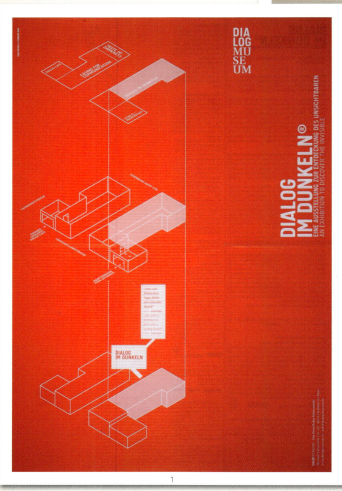

1

2

3

4

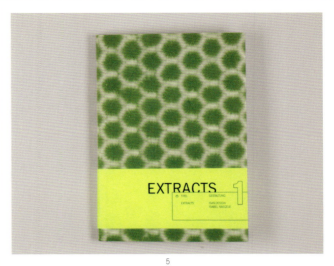

Isabel Naegele (Mainz, Germany). --- I was intro-
duced to Dr. Isabel Naegele through her thesis
project, an interactive installation about food
that invited visitors to share and compare their
eating habits. Naegele was studying medicine at
the time, and this project heralded her second
profession: graphic design. --- Isabel Naegele
has been practicing general medicine for years,
and her training as a doctor manifests itself
in her fascination with complexity. Take the identity she created for the Dialogmuseum, a museum
dedicated to nonvisual experience. The typography
and images she chose carefully manipulated and
complicated different systems of communication,
inviting the visitor to engage in multisensory
experiences inside the darkened exhibition spaces.
--- Collaborating with Naegele was a remarkable
experience for me. The long process of turning
our individual collections of images, small signs,
and urban objects into the book *Scents of the City*
allowed me to fully appreciate her competence and
talent. --- Ruedi Baur

1.   Flyer, Dialogmuseum Frankfurt,
        Germany, 2005-7. With standard.rad

2-3.   Wayfinding signage, Dialogmuseum
        Frankfurt, Germany, 2005-6. The exhi-
        bitions at the Dialogmuseum are kept
        in complete darkness, and sighted
        visitors are led through the rooms
        by blind or visually impaired guides.
        Naegele's design employs tactile
        fonts and maps.
        ----
4.   Catalog cover, Dialogmuseum Frank-
        furt, Germany, 2005-7
        ----
5.   Catalog, *Extracts*, self-commissioned,
        Germany, 2002

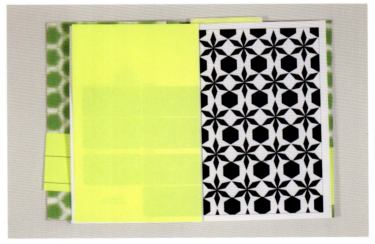

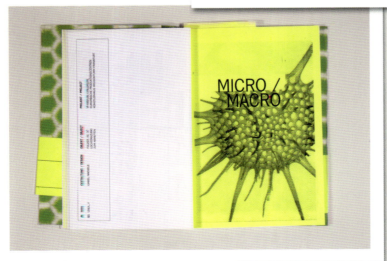

6

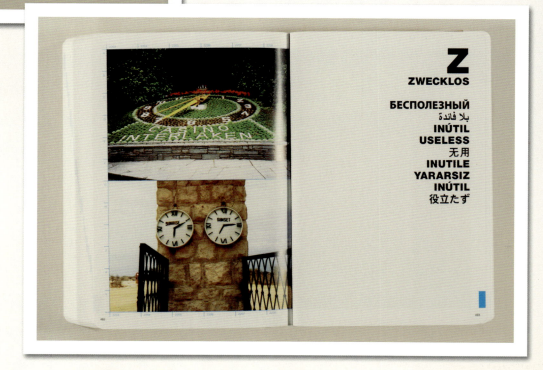

6.   Book cover and spreads, *Scents of the City*, Lars Müller Publishers, Switzerland, 2004. With Ruedi Baur
----
7.   Wayfinding signage, Swiss Re insurance company, Swiss Re, Germany, 2001. With Ruedi Baur and Peter Eckhert

7

Namaiki (Tokyo). --- Japanese society, with all its peculiar rules, can be hard on foreigners, and Namaiki's David D. Smith and Michael Frank were no exceptions. Instead of being humbled by the cultural barrier, though, they embraced it, giving their firm the same name that one of their bosses often called them: namaiki, meaning naughty. --- After Namaiki's founding ten years ago, it didn't take long for the firm's distinctively fanciful style to stand out in Tokyo. The group has worked with such major clients as Nike, and at the same time has made experimental films, designed sets for the Strange Kinoko Dance Company, and produced a local beer, Tokyo Ale. Namaiki's most notable project, though, is SuperDeluxe, a performance space the group opened in 2002. Since then, it has been one of the favorite locations for event planners in Tokyo and was selected by *Time* for the magazine's "Best of Asia" list. For Namaiki, SuperDeluxe is a social hub; the firm often works with the artists who gather there. In a sense, this kind of open collaboration is at the core of Namaiki's creative approach. --- Cheap, colorful plastic has been Namaiki's trademark material for years, but the firm has recently switched to plants, and its latest theme is "agriculture in the city." For *Kinky Muff Land*, Namaiki's latest exhibition, the group built a huge garden playground on the top floor of a building. It is this lighthearted attitude toward creativity and interaction that the firm has brought to Tokyo, and it is the common thread that runs through all of Namaiki's work. --- Keiichi Tanaami

The Good Clients vs. the Bad Designer . at Superdeluxe
2004.10.06(水) - 10(日)

1

2

1.   Event poster, The Good Clients vs. the Bad Designer, Tokyo Designers Block, Japan, 2004
----
2.   Illustration, "Genetic Manipulation with a View to Getting Bigger," self-commissioned, Japan, 2005

3-4.   Magazine poster and cover, *Root Culture*, Root Culture NPO, Japan, 2007
----
5.   Magazine poster series, *Dictionary*, Dictionary, Japan, 2007

AIR CONDITIONER(s) 2007

3

ROOT CULTURE

創刊号　ルートカルチャー

4

http://www.ultradeluxe.tv/333.1/index.htm

5

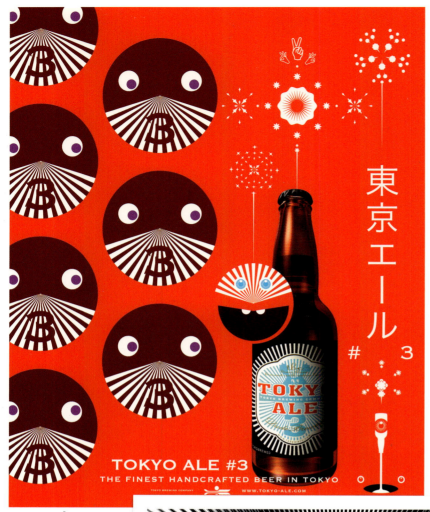

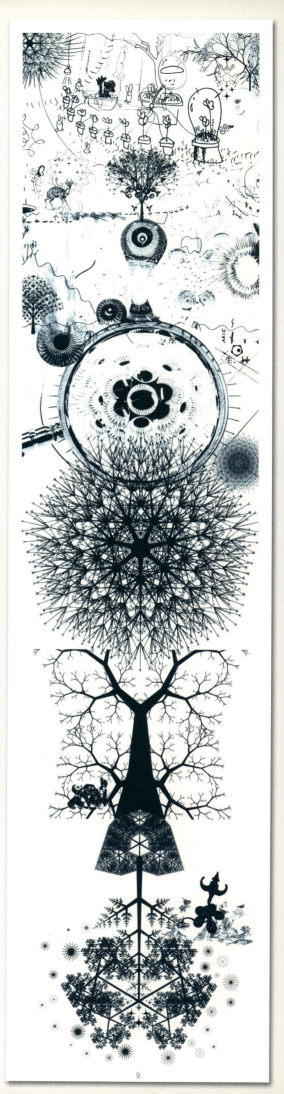

6. Poster, Tokyo Ale, Tokyo Brewing
    Company, Japan, 2007
    ----
7. Installation, "Enormous Propaganda
    Series no.12: Office of the Rising
    Sun," Ginza Graphic Gallery,
    Japan, 2004
    ----
8. Logo, Tokyo Hemp Connection, Tokyo
    Hemp Connection, Japan, 2004
    ----
9. Invitation, Hoya Crystal, Japan, 2007

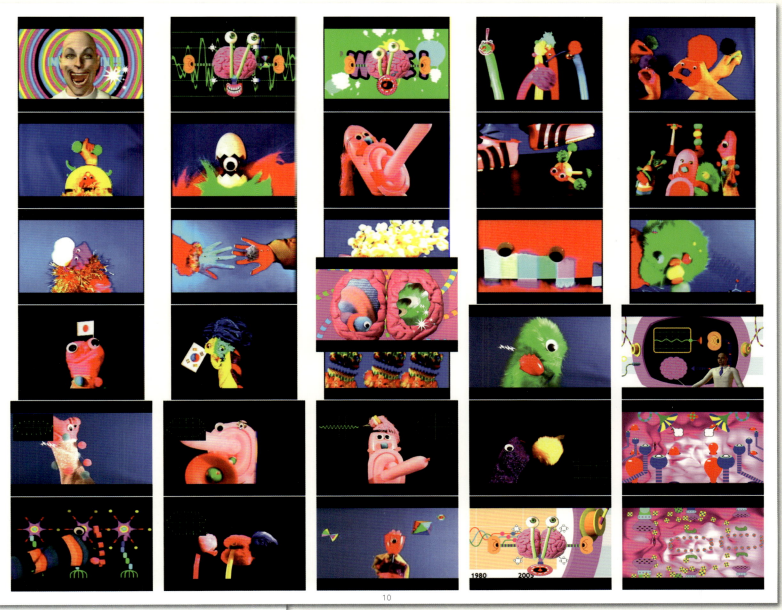

10

11

12

10. Graphics and video stills, MTV Japan
    Video Music Awards, MTV Japan, 2005

----

11. Graffiti on Korean restaraunt menus,
    self-commissioned, Japan, 2005

----

12. Poster, Agricultural Research Super
    Extraordinary (ARSE), ARSE, Japan, 2006

Non-Format (London). --- What do you get when you cross an Englishman, a Norwegian, and a stack of expressive typography? Why, Non-Format, of course! Non-Format is a two-man creative-direction and design team started by Kjell Ekhorn and Jon Forss. Ekhorn is Norwegian (from the far north of the country), and Forss, British (from the west of England). Even though their respective cultures may be oceans apart, their work is coherent, seductive, and beautifully crafted. Their work doesn't shout at you; it doesn't have to. It simply draws you in, intrigues you, and invites you to sit down for a drink and ask a million questions. So I did. --- Both Ekhorn and Forss spent some time working in advertising and the publishing industry before hooking up to work on music packaging projects. Within a year or so of their first collaboration, they were approached to design the independent music monthly *The Wire*. That commission gave them the confidence to strike out on their own under the name EkhornForss Limited, which subsequently became known as Non-Format. --- Forss believes they have always been modernists to some extent, but admits that Non-Format has a reputation for producing decorative work as well, born out of the illustrative typography they have created over the years for *The Wire*. "We were experimenting with ways to add expression to typography," Forss told me, "and that coincided with the move toward very decorative elements used in the compositions. We have since made a conscious effort to move away from this 'faux-baroque' aesthetic, toward a harder-edged approach to typography."
--- Forss was quick to clarify that Non-Format has a much broader attitude toward design than a simple obsession with decorative typographic elements: "We approach each project by establishing exactly what it is a client wants to communicate and then we attempt to find an effective but contemporary method of communicating that message. Our work is often a balance between a desire for very simple and direct communication and a passion for contemporary image-making and typography."
--- It may be this kind of thinking that explains the pair's interest in Japanese design; while their work doesn't overtly reference this visual language, one senses their respect for its formality and rigorous simplicity. In many ways, Japanese design has taught them to trust their emotions and not to be afraid to express them within their own work. --- Brett Phillips

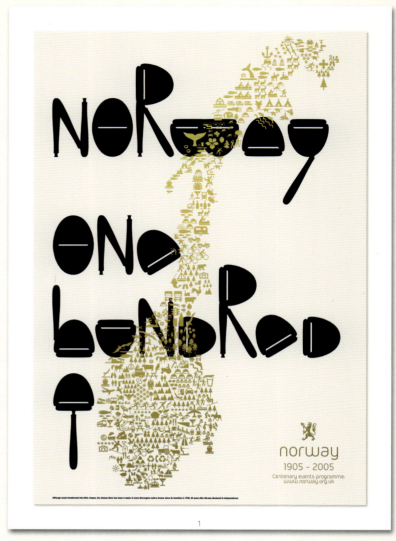

1

2

1. Poster commemorating the 100th anniversary of Norway's independence, Royal Norwegian Embassy, London, UK, 2005
   ----
2. Vinyl packaging, *Back to Black*, Rich Mix and Whitechapel Art Gallery, London, UK, 2005
   ----
3. CD packaging, albums for LOAF Music, Lo Recordings and LOAF, UK, 2006

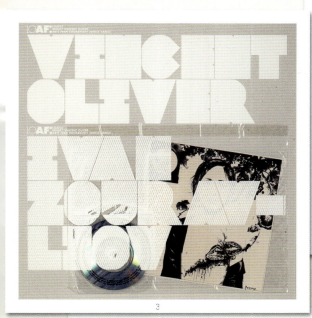
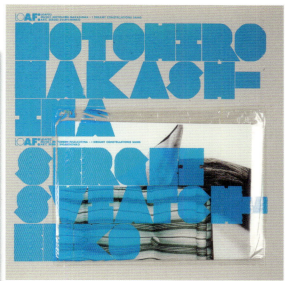

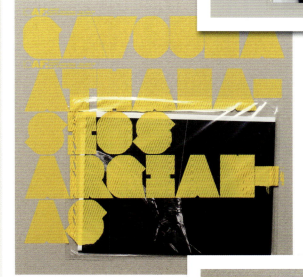
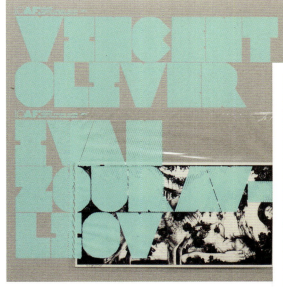
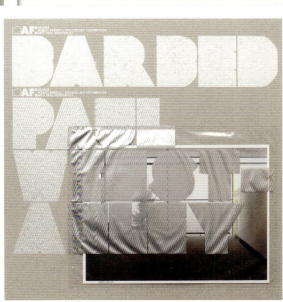
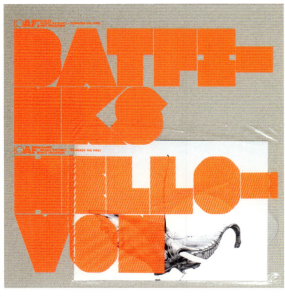

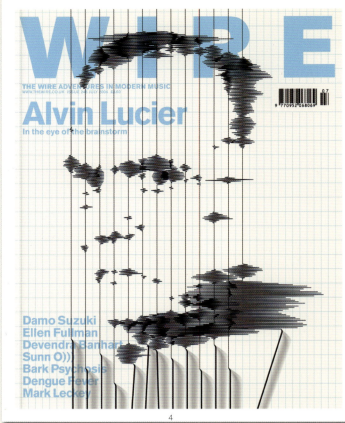

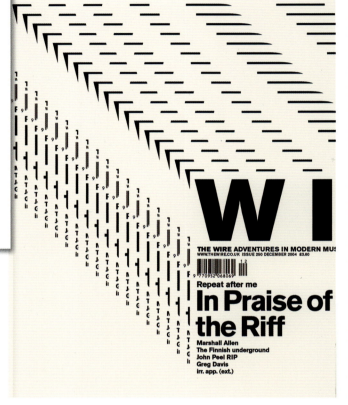

4.   Magazine covers, *The Wire*, The Wire,
      UK, 2001–5
      ----
5.   Festival poster and catalog, Pompei:
      Il romanzo della cenere, Venice
      Biennale, Italy, 2005
      ----
6.   Magazine covers, *Varoom*, Association
      of Illustrators, UK, 2006–7
      ----
7.   CD posters, *Danceflaw* by Cursor
      Miner, Lo Recordings, UK, 2006

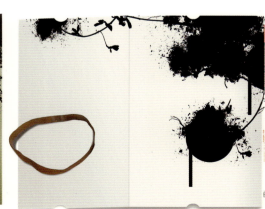

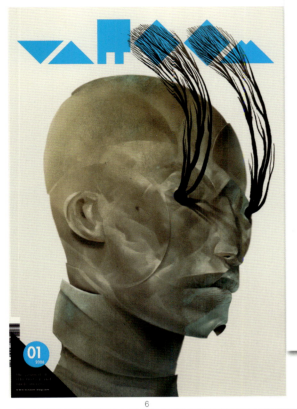

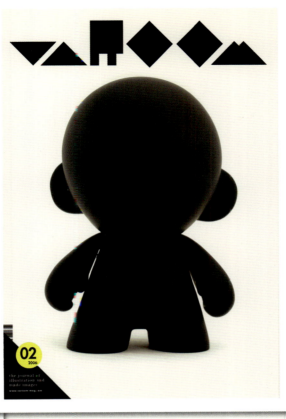

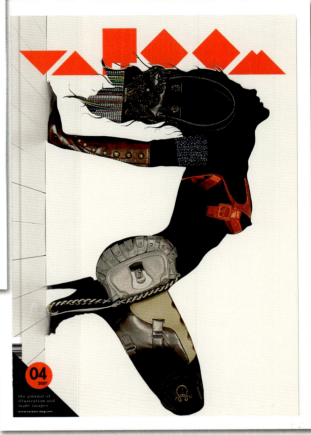

6

7

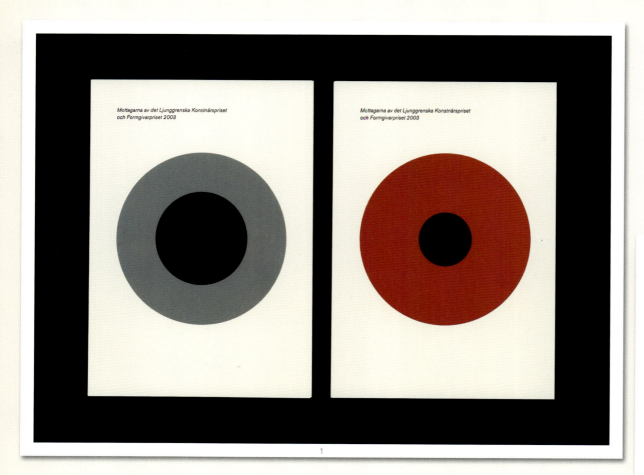

1

2

3

Henrik Nygren (Stockholm). --- You can find Henrik Nygren in a spacious two-floor studio in a beautiful old brewery building in Stockholm. There, he designs books, identities, and other printed matter for national and international clients, mainly in the cultural field. --- After an education of "learning by doing" (he worked at an advertising agency for years instead of studying design in school), Nygren found his calling when he opened his own studio seventeen years ago. Since then, he has developed his own very defined language in which you can see his love for Paul Rand, Olle Eksell, Max Bill, Alvar Aalto, Tadao Ando, and the Minimalists. --- Though he is not completely averse to using technology, and can create sophisticated digital work when he has to, Nygren prefers to conceptualize without a computer. He drafts, selects typography, and chooses materials by hand with the help of two design assistants. This strictly analog process gives his work depth and a timeless character. In the visual identity for the Moderna Museet in Stockholm, Nygren immortalizes another analog technique: handwriting–or, more specifically, Robert Rauschenberg's handwriting. As Nygren says, "It's art. It's then, it's now, and it's tomorrow. It could be misused and still work." --- Nygren's aesthetic is characterized by clean art direction, straightforward typography, simple colors, and a great emphasis on the material as a design element. His work communicates naturally and calmly without any tricks, aiming for total purity, for an ideal that looks, in his words, "almost as if it were not designed at all." --- Julia Hasting

4

1. Book covers, Färgfabriken, Sweden, 2001-3.
----
2. Identity and shopping bag, Riksutställningar, Swedish Traveling Exhibitions, Riksutställningar, Sweden, 2003
----
3. Exhibition poster, *Now*, Färgfabriken, Sweden, 1999
----
4. Book cover Moderna Museet, Sweden, 2005. With Björn Kusoffsky and Greger Ulf Nilson
----
5. Book cover, *Sotbrand*, Modernista, Sweden, 2005

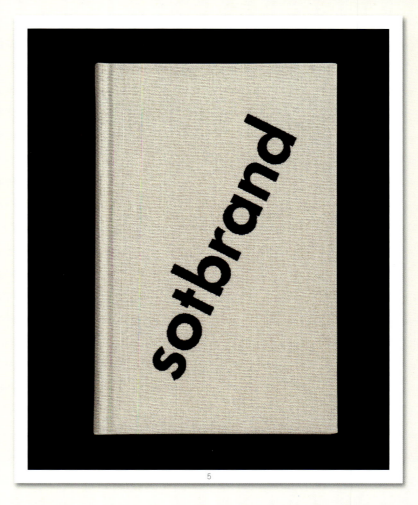

5

6

6.   Cover and spread, exhibition catalog,
        Platser (Places), Statens konstråd,
        Sweden, 1998
----
7.   Book covers and spread, *Vårt
        svenska matarv* (Our Swedish Food
        Heritage), Bokförlaget Arena,
        Sweden, 2002
----
8.   Identity and signage, Baltic Centre
        for Contemporary Art, Baltic Centre
        for Contemporary Art, UK, 1998-2003.
        With Greger Ulf Nilson
----
9.   Identity system, Moderna Museet,
        Moderna Museet, Sweden, 2005. With
        Björn Kusoffsky and Greger Ulf Nilson

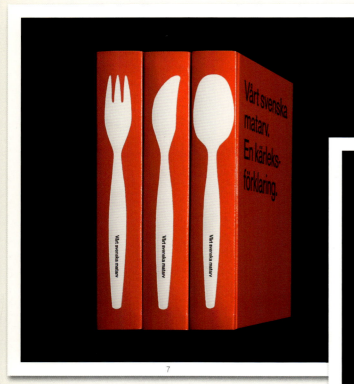

7

8

9

1-2.   Identity, OpTrek artist initiative,
        OpTrek, The Netherlands, 2004

3-7.   Letterhead, ZieZo design foundation,
        ZieZo, The Netherlands, 2003
        ----
8.   Publication design, *Roundaboutproject*
        by Marjan Schoenmakers, Marjan
        Schoenmakers, The Netherlands, 2000
        ----
9.   Exhibition poster, *Graphic Design
        in the White Cube*, curated by Peter
        Bilak, International Biennale of
        Graphic Design in Brno, Czech
        Republic, 2006

Office for Editorial Design (Amsterdam). --- In
the early 1990s, Harmine Louwé was a designer at
Gert Dumbar's Studio Dumbar. Even in those days
she was very much her own master, quietly finding
ways to do her thing within the larger office
structure. Since opening her own studio with
Andrew Breitenberg in 2006, she has fine-tuned her
approach, finding clients who allow her to control
every step of the process. Although she keeps a
firm eye on the client's needs, she usually manages a certain level of autonomy. "Design should
be a research process—not the shortest route to
a finished product," she says. "Each project can
be given a personal twist. In that sense, there
aren't many jobs that are intrinsically boring or
shallow." --- Louwé's work is relatively low-key
and often looks deceptively simple. Only at second
glance does it reveal its complexity: layered
grids, superimposed texts and lines, visual
rhymes, boxes, and frames that suggest ironic
references to information design and bureaucratic
standardization. --- Most of Louwé's designs are
produced for print. Her level of technical expertise is impressive, both in manipulating shapes
on the computer screen and in working with special
materials, such as thin paper stocks and mixed
spot colors. This has allowed her to explore an
aspect of printed matter that is often overlooked
by graphic designers: the third dimension. Many
of the grids, lines, and abstract schemes that pop-
ulate her work suggest depth, bending or snapping
into the endless space of the page or toward the
reader. Sometimes she even uses thin, semitrans-
parent paper that allows the reader to see both
sides of the sheet at once, or to look ahead,
watching the printing on subsequent pages blend.
Applying this treatment to booklets for the
Sterrenwachtlezingen lecture series at Rotterdam
University turned simple handouts into complex
visual adventures. A similar interplay between
back and front was used for design critic Carel
Kuitenbrouwer's stationery, to dazzling effect.
--- Not all of Louwé's projects take place in
the relatively safe realm of science and culture.
She is flexible enough to invent variants of her
visual language for such commercial clients as
Nike, Microsoft, and the cell-phone provider Ben.
"What counts," Louwé says, "is that the idiom
chosen for each job is just right."
--- Jan Middendorp

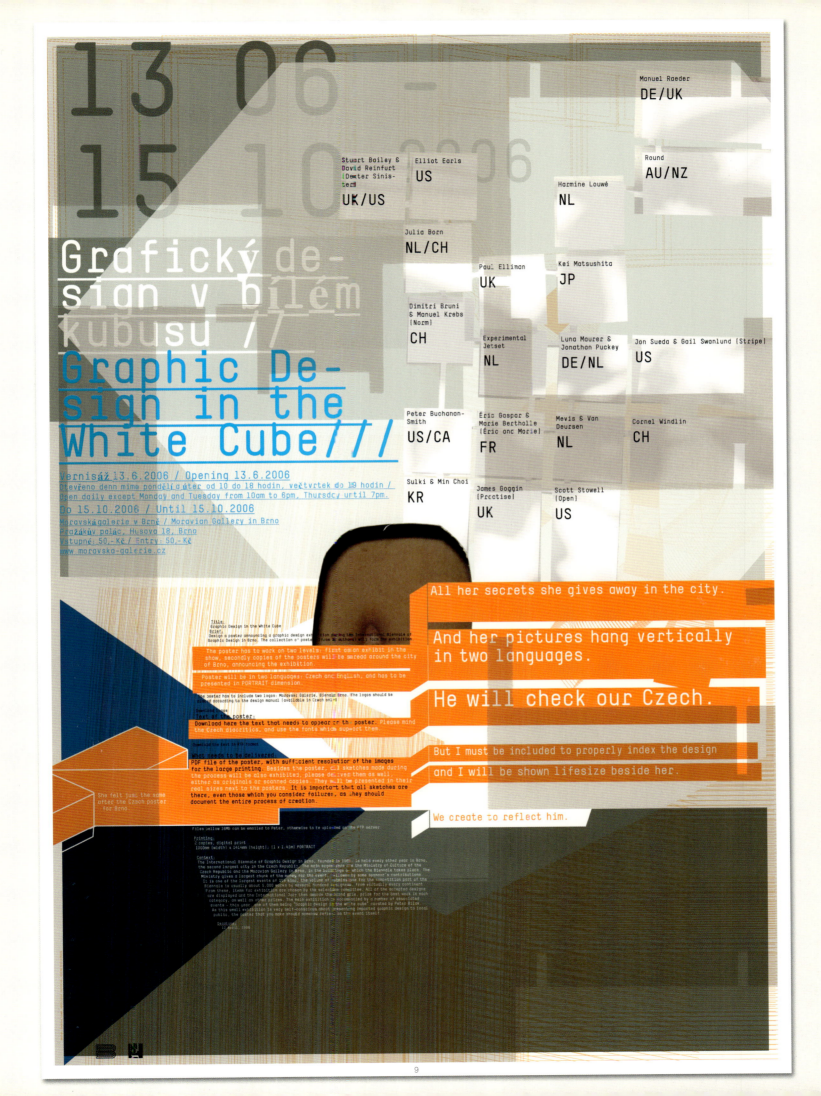

10. Booklet cover and spreads, lecture
by Dutch writer Gerrit Krol on
Ludwig Wittgenstein's theory of
color, Rotterdam University, The
Netherlands, 1996
----
11. Booklet cover and spreads, lecture
by Dutch logician Henk Barendregt
on mathematics and art, Rotterdam
University, The Netherlands, 1997

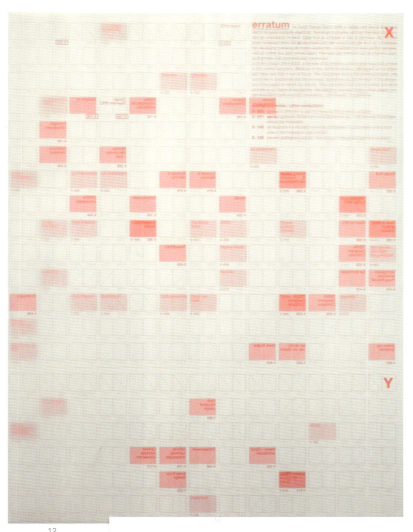

13

12.   Book spreads and errata insert,
    Dutch Design 2004/2005, William Stout
    Architectural Books, USA, 2004.
    Illustrated by Raoul Deleo
----
13.   Identity system, Stalking Muses
    production company, Stalking Muses,
    USA, 2007

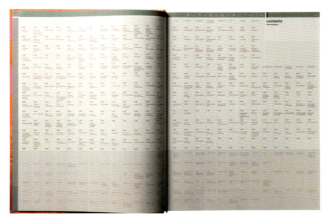

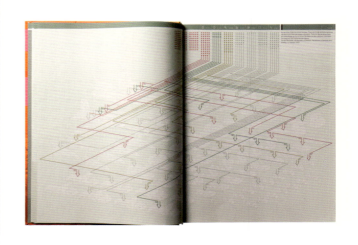

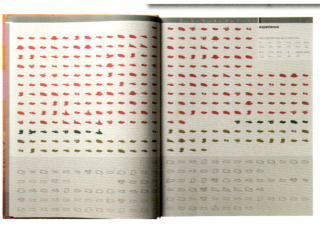

Omnivore (New York). --- Omnivore is a New York-based two-woman studio founded by Alice Chung and Karen Hsu, formerly of the firm 2x4. Their bustling graphics house specializes in experiential design for books, retail spaces, and websites. Equally at home working in any of the mediums available to designers, the studio is relentlessly inventive, utilizing a full range of imagist and typographic vocabularies that encompass everything from vector graphics to nineteenth-century woodblock type. The pair is, as their moniker indicates, hungry for anything, and all the better for it. --- Projects such as the design for the 2004 *Whitney Biennial* have defined the studio's aesthetic. Having created both a book and a box to hold projects by each artist in the show, Omnivore served the dual functions necessary for the museum and the artists—a precise record for the former and a new platform for the latter—much like the exhibition itself. The studio's baroque wallpapered environments for Target show an appetite for glorious excess, proving that omnivores can also be gluttons, to deliriously beautiful effect. --- Chung and Hsu are not restrained designers—they are bold, sometimes loud, and always effective. They are, if anything, a fundamentally New York studio, their various interests and outrageously inventive concepts reflective of the inclusive chaos of the city itself. We should all have such appetites. --- Dan Nadel

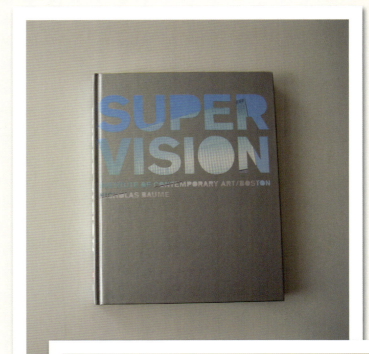

1.   Book cover and spreads, *Supervision*,
      Institute of Contemporary Art and MIT
      Press, USA, 2006
      ----
2.   Identity and catalogs, *Metamorph*
      architecture exhibition, Venice Bien-
      nale, Italy, 2004. With Asymptote
      Architecture
      ----
3.   Catalog cover and spread, Princeton
      University School of Architecture
      Graduate Program in Architecture,
      Princeton University School of Archi-
      tecture, USA, 2004

2

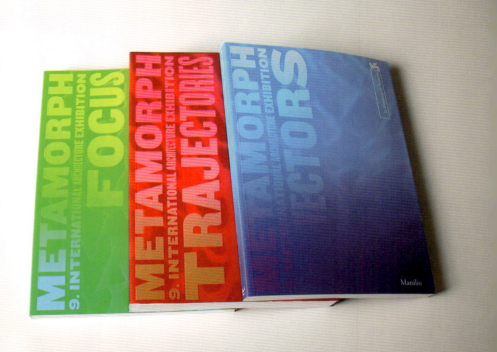

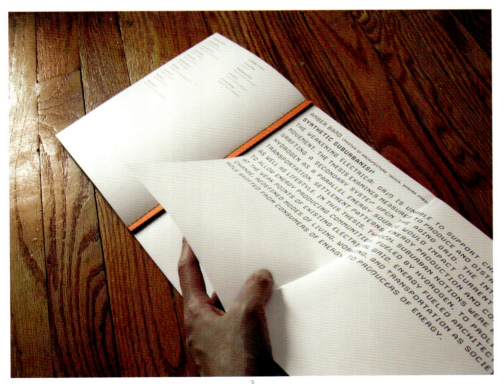

3

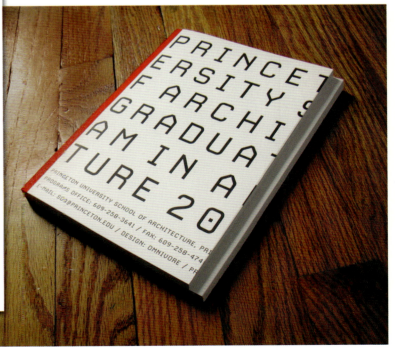

4

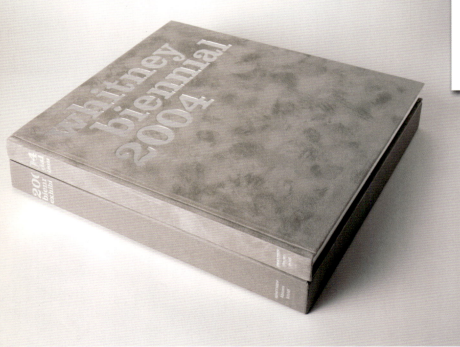

5

4. Wallpaper, Target Inn temporary store, Avi Adler, USA, 2004. With David Stark
----
5. Identity and catalog, *Whitney Biennial*, Whitney Museum of American Art, USA, 2004. Includes a box of artworks specifically created for the catalog by the 107 artists featured in the Biennial

7

6.   Identity and website, Mary Ryan Gal-
      lery, Mary Ryan Gallery, USA, 2007
- -
7.   Textile design, fashion designer
      Keryn Dizon, USA, 2007
- -
8.   Identity and website, David Stark
      Design and Production, David Stark
      Design and Production, USA, 2005.
      With David Stark

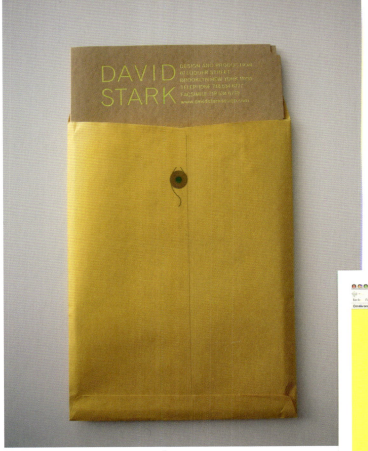

8

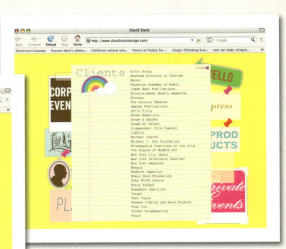

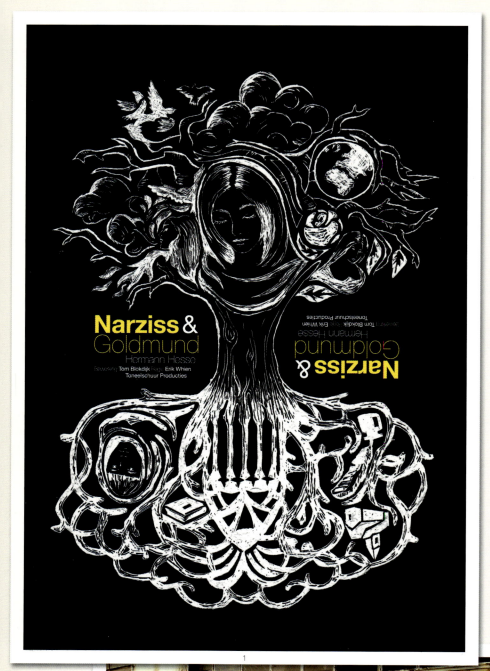

1

178 aardige ontwerpers (Amsterdam). --- *Aardige ontwerpers* can be translated as "friendly designers" or "nice designers." One might wonder why the studio chose this name, when too much kindness can be a problem in the design industry—it might lead someone to do everything the client asks! But 178 aardige ontwerpers knows this. They have learned not to be *too* nice, and to make clearer who they are and where they want to go. Saying no to a client is sometimes more important than saying yes. --- The designers at 178 work in a different field than I do, and I was drawn to them out of curiosity. The studio specializes in communication design for organizations; 178 combines an advertising company with a design firm. The eight designers there believe in the power of the image and in stylistic diversity, collaborating with each other as much as they can. When one designer comes up with an idea, it first receives the critical attention of four or five others in the group before it is presented to the client. The studio, then, is its own most critical client. --- The 178 team loves to experiment. A project always starts with a theme—a word, a thought, a concept, or a framework in which the commission is solved. A human touch and a sense of craft are always visible—it's what the studio is known for. They love large projects in which they combine analog and digital media, but this makes the production process time consuming. The 178 designers work with passion, but at 7 p.m. they leave the office—there are other things in the world to do! --- One of their most successful projects was the redesign for the Dutch music television station TMF. They wanted to bring a looser and more spontaneous character to the company. They wanted freedom and joy. The project accomplished all this with a decidly lo-fi aesthetic. It looks a little old-fashioned, but this is because it's so well crafted, a skill many designers these days seem to lack. --- Irma Boom

2

1.   Poster, "Narziss and Goldmund," a play by Herman Hesse, Toneelschuur Haarlem, The Netherlands, 2006
     ----
2.   Event flyer, Tracing Undercurrents, Melkweg Media, The Netherlands, 2005
     ----
3.   Event posters, 11_restaurant_bar_club, 11_restaurant_bar_club, The Netherlands, 2007

Kiki (Infamous Mudclub, 2 feb)
Redshape & Fabrice Lig (Planet Delsin, 3 feb)
Tobi Neumann (Ratio?, 10 feb)
Christopher Just (Rauw, 9 feb)
Tiefschwarz (Ali) & Sandrien (16 feb)
Sasse (360, 23 feb)
Charles Webster (Teleskope, 17 feb)
Karotte & Julien Chaptal (Static, 24 feb)

11|restaurant_bar_club   www.i11.NL

3

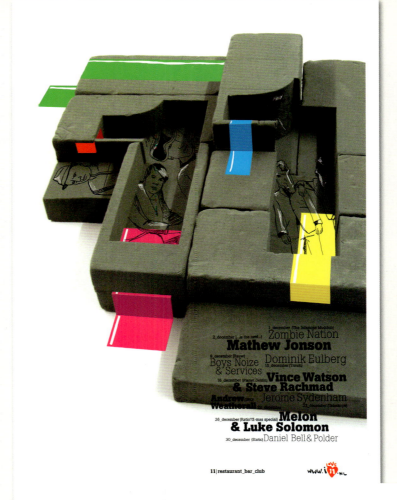

1_december (The Infamous Mudclub)
3_december (...is the next...)   Zombie Nation
Mathew Jonson
8_december (Rauw)   Dominik Eulberg
Boys Noize & Services   15_december (Tzeun)
16_december (Planet Delsin)   Vince Watson & Steve Rachmad
Andrew Weatherall   Jerome Sydenham
23_december (Teleskope)
26_december (Ratio7X-mas special)   Melon & Luke Solomon
30_december (Static) Daniel Bell & Polder

11|restaurant_bar_club   www.i11.NL

[T]ékël (The Infamous Mudclub, 2 maart)
Digitalism & Cajuan Ada (Pixel, 3 maart)
(Rauw, 9 maart)
(Ratio", 10 maart) Marcus Worgull
Superpitcher (Kompakt, 16 maart)
Lawrence & Gui Boratto
& Nuno dos Santos (360, 23 maart)
Marco Passarani, Dexter & Serge (Clone We Are, 30 maart)
(Static, 31 maart)
Exercise One & Jay Haze

11|restaurant_bar_club   www.i11.NL

11.3jaar met (The Infamous Mudclub, 4 mei)
Schaeben & Voss
Cobblestone Jazz, Melon & Bart Skils (11.3, 5 mei)
Headman & Yuksek (Rauw, 11 mei)
Octave One (Planet Delsin, 12 mei)
DJ Yellow & Darko Esser (Mood Elevator, 18 mei)
Mark August (Teleskope, 19 mei) Petter (360, 25 mei)
Serafin & Agnes (Static, 26 mei)

11|restaurant_bar_club   www.i11.NL

4

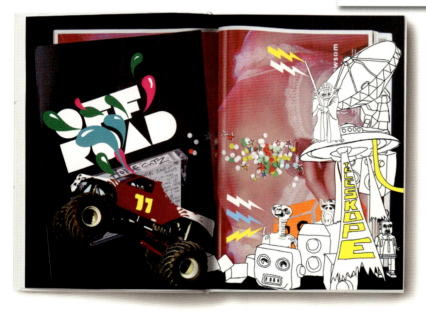

4.   Menu book cover and spreads, 11_
      restaurant_bar_club, 11_restaurant_
      bar_club, The Netherlands, 2007

5-6. Advertising campaign, Utrecht School
      of the Arts, Utrecht School of the
      Arts, The Netherlands, 2006

5

6

Eddie Opara (New York). --- Eddie Opara came to America by way of the London College of Printing to study for his MFA in graphic design at the Yale School of Art. Blessed with a brilliant mind and unbridled talent, he wasted no time before exploring certain theories he had only imagined before. Yale's multidisciplinary curriculum and Opara's cerebral classmates provided the stimulation necessary for him to develop these theories. He also became quite proficient in computer programming and developing code, which opened up new vistas in the then-emerging multimedia juggernaut. --- Opara dreamed of a career in architecture, but he ended up preferring the practice of graphic design. However, he still finds architecture alluring—especially the ideas around the dynamic flow of form and the concept of mapping, which he describes as "a great way to visualize content, especially through layering." These perspectives have filtered into his design work. A friendship with Mikon van Gastel led him to a job at Imaginary Forces in New York, where he worked on the monumental graphic skin for the Morgan Stanley building in Times Square. After that, he joined the New York design firm 2x4 where he switched gears to work in print, rekindling his love for typography. --- Today Opara is creating incredibly beautiful and smart work for an impressive, ever-growing clientele as a partner in the New York branch of The Map Office; Yale classmate and best friend George Plesko runs the Boston office. Their projects include designing and developing large-scale electronic motion-graphics installations, innovative interfaces for software and Internet applications, print packaging, and interior graphics. --- Most of us designers from Africa are constantly grappling with the issue of whether we can create work that is distinctly "African." "If you think about it," Opara explains, "a lot of abstract forms in art originated in Africa. It's a subconscious thing...it just comes out because it's part of who I am. If you've ever seen the amazing way Nigerian women tie wrappers around their waists to get the right flow of form in order to walk properly, it is something else! I love the resultant juxtaposition of forms, and I reference that in my work. Architecture is doing the same thing." --- *Brilliant, exceptional, visionary*—these words do not begin to adequately describe the design phenom that is Eddie Opara. I think his place among the world's great designers is assured. --- Saki Mafundikwa

1.   Promotional flyers, The Map Office, USA, 2007-present. With Salvador Orara
----
2.   Identity system, Brooklyn Museum, Brooklyn Museum, USA, 2004. With 2x4

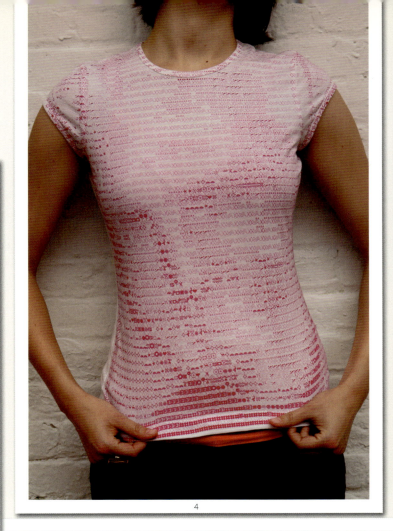

3.   Catalog spreads, Vitra's Antonio
      Citterio line of office furniture,
      Vitra, USA, 2003. With 2x4
      ----
4.   T-shirt, Armani Exchange, USA, 2006
      ----
5.   Bag design, Milan Design Show and
      Orgatec, Vitra, Italy and Germany,
      2004-5. With 2x4
      ----
6.   Promotional booklet, Prada, USA,
      2003. With 2x4

6

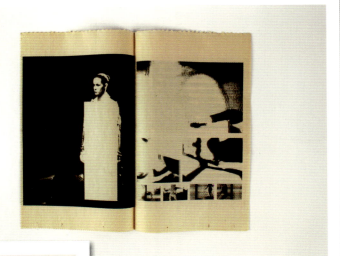

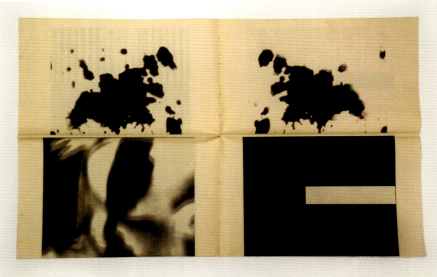

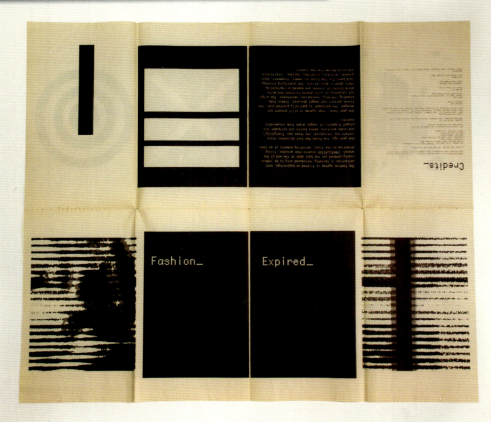

Mark Owens (Los Angeles). --- Mark Owens and I have known each other for a while now, through a variety of connections in academia and the graphic design industry in the United States and the United Kingdom. Similarly, his work occupies disparate spheres, from moving images to print, curating to writing. After graduating from Yale, Owens initially concentrated on motion graphics work notable for its incorporation of a print-based aesthetic. Although still involved in video work for the likes of MTV and VH1, he is simultaneously producing an increasing body of print work and exploratory critical writing. --- An inherent dichotomy between popular culture and critical thinking lies at the heart of Owens's practice. His design work is deceptively pop; closer investigation reveals multiple layers of commentary and reference. Conversely, his critical writing for the design and culture magazine *Dot Dot Dot* and the recent *Forms of Inquiry* exhibition at London's Architectural Association appears deceptively academic, but it deals with distinctly pop subjects. On a T-shirt for the Japanese label 2K, a skate park utopia is augmented by a Buckminster Fuller geodesic dome. An essay on abstraction invokes not only the Bauhaus and De Stijl but also Los Angeles hardcore bands The Germs and Black Flag. The pop angle is emphasized by the media within which Mark operates: the T-shirt, the magazine, the postcard. --- In "Group Theory," another contribution to *Dot Dot Dot*, Owens and fellow designer-writer David Reinfurt investigated the aesthetics of the archetypal design studio portrait. They deconstructed moody black-and-white group photos into a typology of studio dynamics: "the firm," "the workshop," and "the free association." This reading of graphic-design relations was in a way made manifest in Owens's touring exhibition *The Free Library*. Inspired by Jean-Luc Godard's 1967 political-pop student critique *La Chinoise*, the show combined vaguely didactic, site-specific projects created by an international group of like-minded designers in a reading-room environment set up first in a Brooklyn gallery and later in Philadelphia and London. --- While the apparently easygoing colors and shapes visible in Owens's work seem to echo his current Los Angeles location, his work more closely mirrors architecture critic Reyner Banham's vision of the city, where the surface of sea and sun belies a complex relationship to urbanism, modernism, and the American vernacular.---James Goggin

1.   Exhibition identity, *The Free Library*, M+R Gallery, UK, 2005
----
2.   Postcard portrait as Bryan Ferry, self-commissioned, USA, 2007
----
3.   Magazine illustrations, *Färgfabriken*, Färgfabriken, Sweden, 2006

4-5. Magazine spreads, *Dot Dot Dot*, Dot Dot Dot, The Netherlands, 2003-6

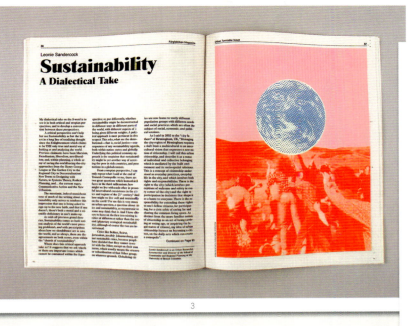

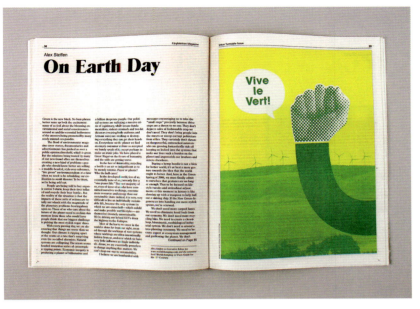

3

4

5

6

6-7.   T-shirt designs, 2X4 T-shirts,
       Australia, 2007

8-10. T-shirts, Gingham, Japan and USA,
       2006-7
       ----
11.   T-shirt, Commonwealth Stacks,
       USA, 2006

7

8

9

11

10

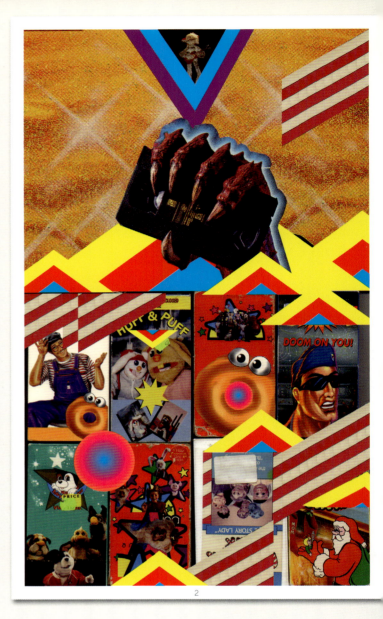

Paper Rad (Providence). --- Paper Rad is an art/comic/design/animation collective based in Providence, Rhode Island. Jessica Ciocci, her brother Jacob, and their friend Ben Jones met in Boston and began working together in 2000. They are resilient pop conceptualists, operating in a non-ironic visual mode that uses the language, if not the substance, of 1970s and '80s visual and technological culture. As Jacob Ciocci writes, "In the '70s and '80s, cartoons and consumer electronics were bigger and trashier than ever, and freaked kids out. Now these kids are getting older and are freaking everybody else out by using this same throw-away trash." --- For much of the early part of this decade, the group produced zines at a rapid pace. These pamphlets combined hand-cut neon letterforms with exuberant cartoon drawings. Their appropriated images of Bart Simpson, the California Raisins, and their own invented characters—Alfe, Roba, and Tux Dog, among them—are drawn in the stark, curvaceous language of 1980s cartoons—simple, rounded shapes stuck onto one another. Their limited-motion flash animations further this aesthetic with hilarious narratives on the nature of friendship, sitting around, or going to the store. These mundane actions are given a coating of neon absurdity that throws each film's message into stark relief. This is, ultimately, the world as Paper Rad sees it, or at least their way of thinking about the world on a D.I.Y. level. Stencils, flash animation, zines, art installations, books, and DVDs are all made entirely on their own, without any help from a fully staffed studio. --- Paper Rad has performed or exhibited at the Museum of Contemporary Art, Chicago, Tate Britain, and the Contemporary Museum, Honolulu, among other venues. They truly are cross-platform creatives, fully functioning in every arena, from print work for XLR8R to music videos for Islands and M.I.A., in which their angular design style flourishes, and surreally satirical imagery and a flashbulb sense of timing give a jumpy, often very funny edge to the music. Paper Rad is constantly innovative, and we will have to keep our eyes wide open to see where the group will wind up next. --- Dan Nadel

1. Promotional poster, *Trash Talking* DVD, Load Records, USA, 2006
   ----
2. Illustration, self-commissioned, USA, 2006
   ----
3. Wallpaper, self-commissioned, USA, 2005
   ----
4. Magazine illustrations, *Todd P.*, Todd P., USA, 2007
   ----
5. DVD cover, *Trash Talking*, Load Records, USA, 2006
   ----
6. Promotional video graphic, *Alfe*, self-commissioned, USA, 2006

4

5

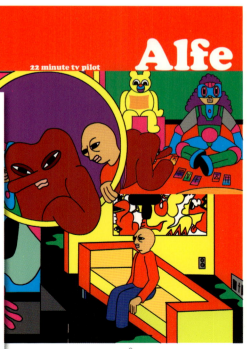

6

7

8

7. CD cover illustration, *Dr. Doo 7"*,
    self-commissioned, USA, 2006
    ----
8. T-shirt design, self-commissioned,
    USA, 2007
    ----
9. Installation, Green on Red Gallery,
    self-commissioned, USA, 2006
    ----
10. Book cover, *Cartoon Workshop*, Pic-
    tureBox, USA, 2006
    ----
11. Book cover, *Paper Rad, BJ and da
    Dogs*, PictureBox, USA, 2005

12-13. Illustrations, self-commissioned,
    USA, 2006-7

9

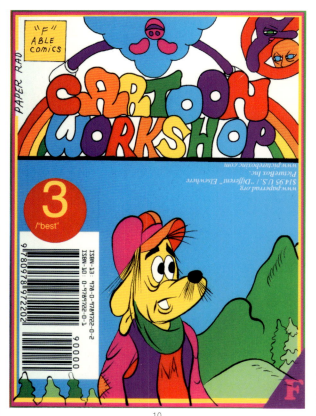

10

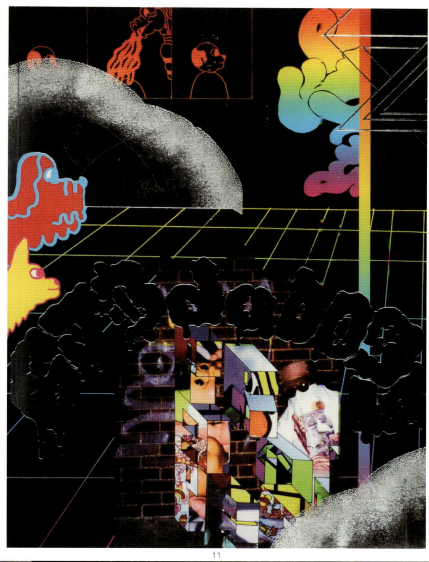

11

12

13

1. Illustration, "Sol vs. Dot Dot Dot,"
    Dot Dot Dot magazine no.9, Dot Dot
    Dot, USA, 2004
----
2. Typeface, Boijmans, Museum Boijmans
    van Beuningen, The Netherlands,
    2006. Art direction by Mevis and
    Van Deursen

3-4. Identity, envelopes, and poster,
    International Biennale of Graphic
    Design in Brno, Moravian Gallery and
    International Biennale of Graphic
    Design in Brno, Czech Republic, 2006

PONIC IS   IF MEMO
THE   RIES COULD
BEGIN   BE CANNED
NING OF   WOULD
ALL ART   THEY HAVE
           EXPIRY
           DATES

62   63

1

THE IDEA OF AN EPOCH ALWAYS FINDS ITS ADEQUATE AND APPROPRIATE FORM.

2

Radim Peško (Amsterdam). *Independent* is probably the best way to describe Radim Peško and his work. After studying at the Art Academy in Prague, Peško worked for a year until he earned enough money to move to Arnhem, The Netherlands, where he studied under his role model Karel Martens at the Werkplaats Typografie postgraduate program. Upon graduating from the program, Peško set his mind to creating things that interested him, and to staying autonomous, both artistically and financially. He works alone in order to maintain total control over all aspects of the design process. Even when designing for clients, Peško works with an independent spirit and has a great personal stake in each project. He explains why many of his fonts are not commercially available by saying that it's impossible for him to sell something so specifically tailored to its client. --- Still, Peško isn't secretive about his work, nor is he a loner. His identity for the 2006 International Biennale of Graphic Design in Brno was deliberately transparent, using brilliantly simple typefaces like his fifty-fifty hybrid of Helvetica and Arial. In his 2006 exhibition *Work from Mars*, Peško celebrated his fellow independent designers by displaying a selection of posters, magazines, typefaces, and interactive projects, initiated and commissioned entirely by the designers themselves. The exhibition title came from Peško's feeling that in an age when so much of what designers do is dictated by clients, self-commissioned work is a downright alien endeavor. If the work of Radim Peško is any indication, though, Mars is exactly where some of the best graphic design can be found. --- Julia Hasting

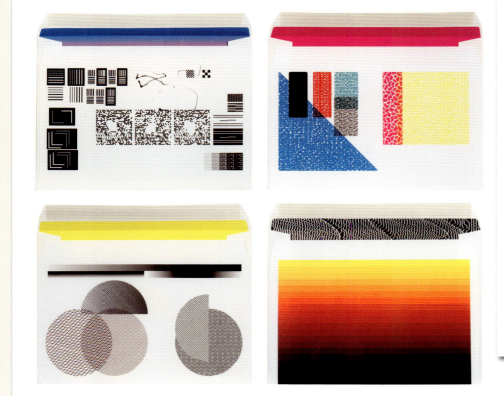

3

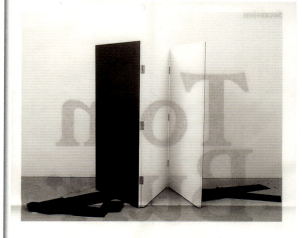

5.   Identity and invitations, Vienna
       Secession, Vienna Secession, Austria,
       2007. With Willi Schmid

----

6.   Exhibition poster, *Music for the
       Artist,* Veemvloer, The Netherlands,
       2005

----

7.   Exhibition catalog cover and spreads,
       Flourish, Moravian Gallery, Czech
       Republic, 2004

----

8.   Typeface, Mitim, printed in *Dot Dot
       Dot* magazine, self-commissioned,
       USA, 2005

Post Typography (Baltimore). --- Post Typography, founded in 2001 by Nolen Strals and Bruce Willen, is not just another rock-poster outfit. Yes, they design rock posters. And their own band, Double Dagger, addresses topics such as "CMYK" and "Punk Rock vs. Swiss Modernism" in their aptly titled songs, described as "designcore." Strals and Willen also design concert posters and music packaging for independent bands and labels around the country. Often screen-printed by hand in their studio, their work embraces a vibrant D.I.Y. approach, flush with raw, funny illustrations and rough-and-ready lettering. --- But what sets Strals and Willen apart from other artists intent on producing handmade, hard-hitting poster art is that they have a philosophy about what they do. Despite their bad-boy attitudes, an intellectual current underlies their work. Their field of practice includes not only graphic design, custom lettering, and illustration, but also "art, apparel, music, curatorial work, design theory, and vandalism." Strals and Willen are part of a new generation of designers that is contributing to the discourse of the profession while refusing to be hindered by its traditional limits. (Paul Carlos, a designer and professor at Parsons The New School for Design, has described their practice as "Wayne and Garth meet Chermayeff & Geismar.") A serious interest in typography and lettering stands behind their in-your-face screen prints, and their work takes an explicitly theoretical turn in experimental projects such as the Conjoined Font and Negative Font. Strals and Willen curated the international exhibition *Alphabet*, which has been touring college campuses around the USA and is accompanied by an original publication. --- No urban posers, Strals and Willen live and work in Baltimore, and many of their projects reflect the city's tough but vibrant urban culture (one poster incorporates a shooting target used in police training). The team's ongoing work for the Johns Hopkins Film Festival shows Baltimore's sophisticated side as well—and proves Post Typography's ability to create professional print campaigns and identity systems. Both designers studied at Maryland Institute College of Art (MICA), where they now teach courses in advanced typography. --- Archived on their website is the manifesto that launched their post-typographic enterprise, back when they were undergraduates at MICA. Ranting against the elitist "typocratic slaughterhouse," they proclaim: "We each will carve our own visage from the faceless screen, and let the ink from our pens bleed into our hands and paper. We will cast off the shackles of Photoshop to return to the freedom of letters without rules. We are the Times New Romans! We are the Franklin Gothics!" --- Ellen Lupton

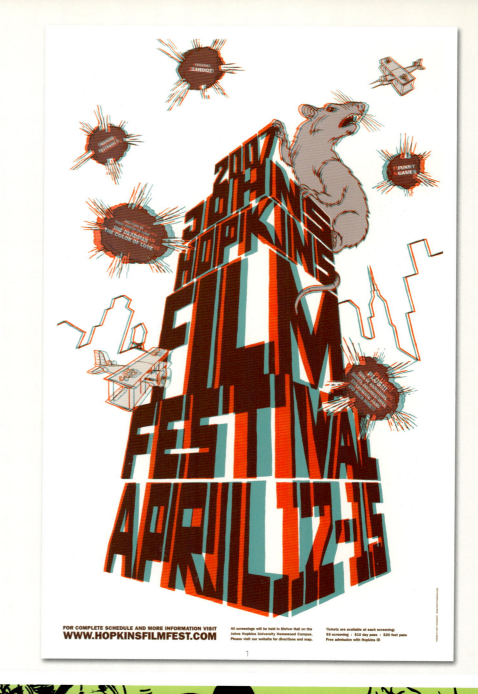

1.   Poster, 2007 Johns Hopkins Film Fes-
    tival, Johns Hopkins Film Festival,
    USA, 2007. Each poster was distrib-
    uted with a pair of 3-D glasses.

----

2.   Poster, concert by Guitar Wolf, The
    Ottobar, USA, 2005. Printed in glow-
    in-the-dark ink

----

3.   Poster and program, 2003 Johns Hop-
    kins Film Festival, Johns Hopkins
    Film Festival, USA, 2003. Each poster
    folds up into a Super 8 camera and
    film cartridge.

----

4.   Poster, 2004 Johns Hopkins Film
    Festival, Johns Hopkins Film Festi-
    val, USA, 2004. The poster is perfo-
    rated and can be made into a 32-page
    flip book.

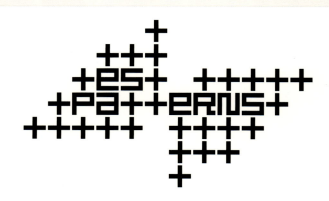

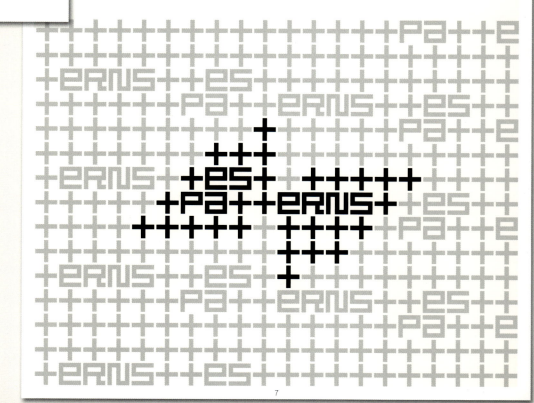

5. Illustration, *New York Times*, New York Times, USA, 2006

----

6. Typeface, Conjoined Font, self-commissioned, USA, 2006

----

7. Exhibition identity, *Test Patterns*, a public exhibition of pattern-based art, Artscape, USA, 2006

----

8. Magazine illustration, *The McKinsey Quarterly*, The McKinsey Quarterly, USA, 2007

----

9. Poster, concert by Against Me!, The Ottobar, USA, 2004

----

10. Poster, lecture by Post Typography, Susquehanna University, USA, 2005

8

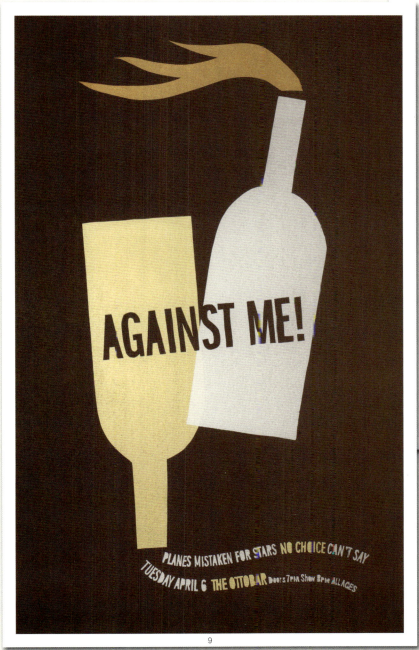

9

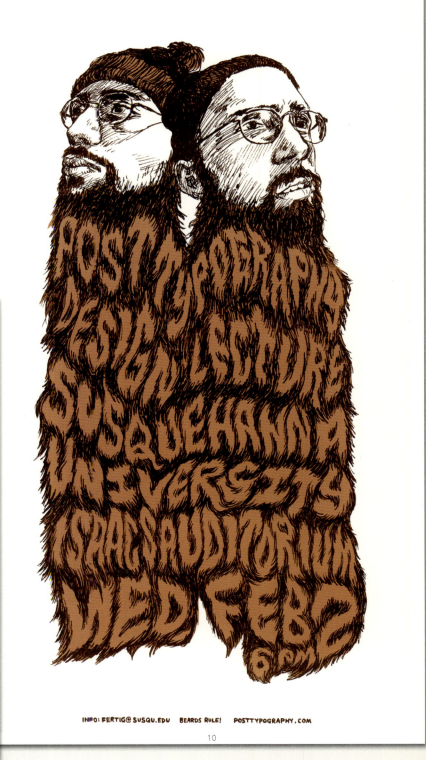

10

1.   Conference poster, Design and Its
      Publics: Curators, Critics, and His-
      torians, The Design Institute at the
      University of Minnesota, USA, 2007
----
2.   Identity system, architecture firm
      WORKac, WORKac, USA, 2007
----
3.   Exhibition identity and catalog,
      *The Good Life: New Public Spaces
      for Recreation*, Van Alen Institute,
      USA, 2006

Project Projects (New York). --- I have this strange feeling that if I were to meet Adam Michaels and Prem Krishnamurthy at a party, they probably wouldn't like me very much. I say this not because I believe they are unsociable beings (not having met them personally, I imagine them to be quite the opposite), but because I have a tendency to ask simple questions in the hope of eliciting complex answers. I fear this conversational tactic would bore the pair instantly. --- Project Projects is a design studio founded in Brooklyn in January 2004. Michaels and Krishnamurthy are passionate and intelligent, and while their work encompasses a considerable range of formal vocabularies and mediums, they consistently place an emphasis on strong ideas, rigorous typography (both in terms of signification and craft), and a careful use of imagery (with a particular emphasis on photography, often generated by the studio). --- Unlike me, with my pithy party questions, Michaels and Krishnamurthy privilege criticality, complexity, and sensitivity toward context, and when choosing projects they look for genuinely engaging subject matter, as well as the potential for collaboration. Not surprisingly, they are also interested in tracing how the field of graphic design has evolved over its relatively brief existence: "We see our profession as an outgrowth of Modernism, and we are inspired by investigating the latent, unexpected potentials to be found." That said, the office seems committed to learning the kinds of lessons that can be gleaned only by crossing disciplinary borders. Their work is the purest kind of graphic design: a direct reflection of intellect, rigor, and discipline. --- Brett Phillips

3

4.   Identity system and printed material,
    D'Amelio Terras gallery, D'Amelio
    Terras, USA, 2006
----
5.   Exhibition identity and catalog,
    Re-Shuffle: Notions of an Itinerant
    Museum, Center for Curatorial Studies
    (CCS), Bard College, USA, 2006. Visi-
    tors assembled their own portable ex-
    hibitions from screen-printed boxes,
    stacks of cards, and mailing labels.
    With CCS graduate students
----
6.   Exhibition identity, signage, and
    catalog, *The Plain of Heaven*,
    Creative Time, USA, 2005
----
7.   Book cover, *Drosscape: Wasting*
    Land in Urban America by Alan Berger,
    Princeton Architectural Press,
    USA, 2006

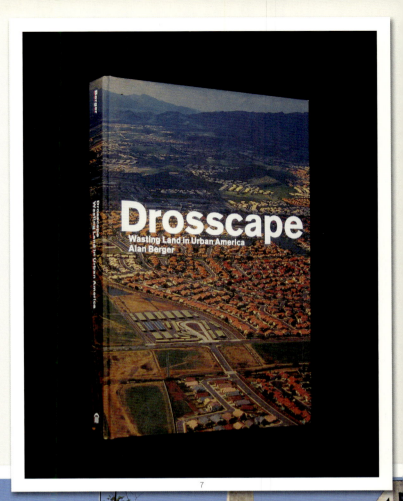

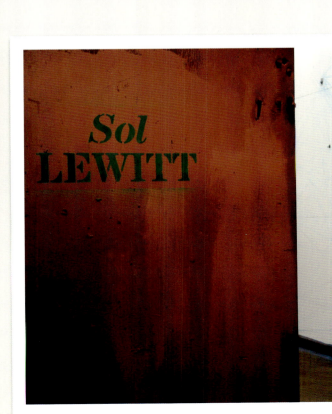

Michael Punchman (Hong Kong). --- Many designers in Hong Kong, as in Japan, are also artists.
In the Chinese city, however, the boundary between the two roles is much more defined: There,
a graphic designer is simply called an "advertising man." Michael Cheung, a.k.a. Punchman, felt
this division restricted his creativity, and so
after working at major advertising agencies for
such clients as Nike, Coca-Cola, and Puma, he
launched his own group, Institute of Matter, in
2000. --- In 2002 he began work on "NO PEACE NO
BOOM," a series of colorful, polished fiberglass
sculptures. He hoped this garish and slightly
nihilistic project, exhibited in the wake of SARS,
9/11, and an economic depression, would cheer up
Hong Kong. He explains that "BOOM" is "not the
explosive sound of destruction, but the rich
reward for making a difference—a call for action."
For him, "'BOOM' represents a belief that there's
always a positive, colorful side to life. As long
as there's peace, there will always be 'BOOM.'"
The series was exhibited at Colette in Paris before
traveling to Milk Gallery in Hong Kong and Gallery
SpeakFor in Tokyo. --- In keeping with his optimistic message, Cheung recently unveiled a character called Punchman, who punches people's despair
with his drooping arms. Thanks to the popularity
of this character, Cheung (who changed his name to
Michael Punchman after its release) has attracted
a wide audience of both children and adults. In
2006 he participated in the Singapore Biennale as
"Vivo Punch," and Punchman (the character) will
be the official drink mascot of the Beijing Olym-
pics in 2008. By changing his name, Punchman was
able to cross the border that divides designer
from artist, and he can now bring his creativity
to both roles. Straddling that line can be a challenge, and Michael Punchman is one of only a few
designers who can do it with both agility and
success. --- Keiichi Tanaami

1.   Mixed-media works, exhibition at
        Fabrica, Benetton, Hong Kong, 2005
        ----
2.   Sculpture series, "Vivo Punch,"
        Singapore Biennale, VivoCity, 2006

2

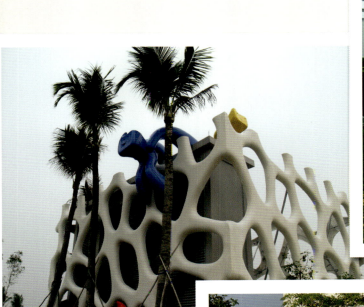

306 --- <u>Michael Punchman</u>

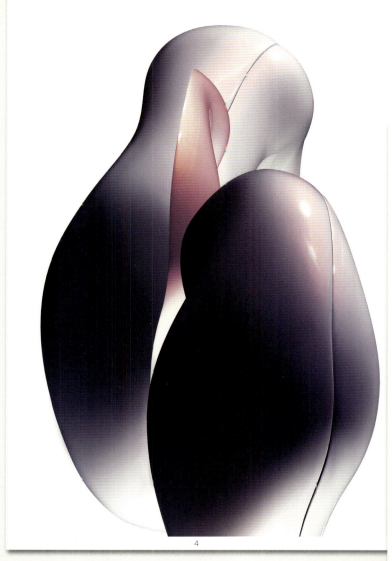

4

5

3. Poster, "NO PEACE NO BOOM," Gallery
    SpeakFor, Japan, 2002
    ----
4. Poster series, "Bloom," *Imajuku Art
    Book Exhibition*, Japan, 2003
    ----
5. Sculpture, "No China No Boom," Over-
    head Gallery and Milk magazine, Hong
    Kong, 2003

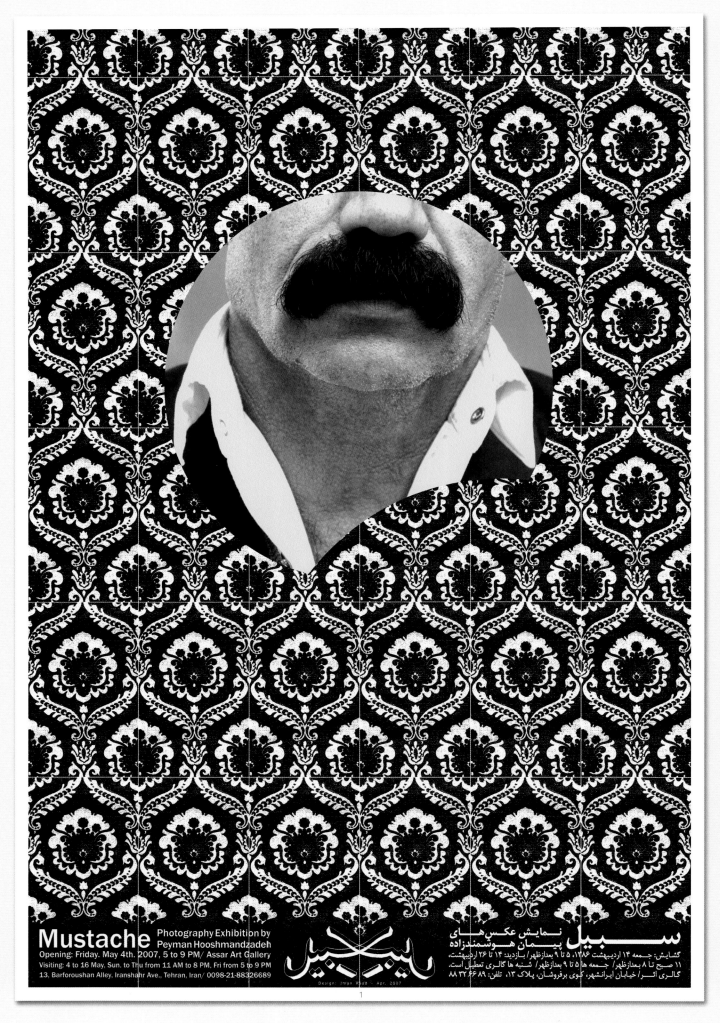

Mustache Photography Exhibition by Peyman Hooshmandzadeh
Opening: Friday. May 4th. 2007, 5 to 9 PM/ Assar Art Gallery
Visiting: 4 to 16 May, Sun. to Thu from 11 AM to 8 PM, Fri from 5 to 9 PM
13, Barforoushan Alley, Iranshahr Ave., Tehran, Iran/ 0098-21-88326689

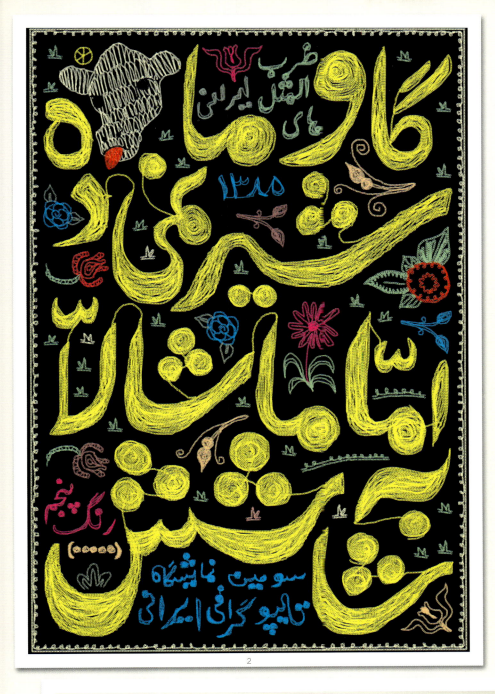

2

1. Exhibition poster, *Mustache*, photographs by Peyman Hooshmandzadeh, Asar Art Gallery, Iran, 2007
    ----
2. Poster, Iman Raad Studio, self-commissioned, Iran, 2006
    ----
3. Book covers, PC and online pocket guides, IACERC Publications, Iran, 2005

Iman Raad (Tehran). --- My first brush with Iranian design was the book *New Visual Culture of Modern Iran* by Reza Abedini and Hans Wolbers. I had fallen in love with Arabic script a few years before, while teaching a typography class at The Cooper Union in New York. Its flowing calligraphic strokes evoked a beauty I had never witnessed in any other script, and I regarded it as an ancient method with little or no possibility for modern adaptation. Yet here was a book that eloquently challenged my ignorance with its raw energy, easily convincing me that this was the edgiest and most boundary-pushing work I had seen in a long while. I took the book with me to the 2006 Tasmeem Conference in Doha, Qatar, where I was a speaker, and I was thrilled to meet four Iranian designers whose work was not only included in the book but was also on display in the gallery at the Virginia Commonwealth University in Qatar. One of them was Iman Raad. --- Iman Raad's work, as the artist explains, comes from such traditional crafts as calligraphy, pottery, weaving, architecture, talismans, religious flags, and posters. He cites a desire by contemporary Iranian designers to create a Persian aesthetic by connecting the ancient world with today—a feat made easier by the amicable coexistence of the traditional and the modern, and the ready acceptance of this hybrid culture by Iranian youths. Furthermore, his decorative "style" is driven by his admiration for functional art, especially the tradition of making tools and ordinary objects more beautiful. --- "I try to explore the language of myths in the modern world," Raad says. "I like my work to have an enigmatic theme. By looking and wandering in ancient sources and discovering what makes them charming, I learn to create modern myths I like to make posters as dignified, magnificent, and charming as an inscription. I should also add that my attention to the myths is somewhat satiric." --- The impressive and innovative work coming out of Iran today is unfortunately lost in the din of political news. With the voice of designers like Iman Raad often drowned out, the ultimate victim of this indifference is the field of graphic design itself. --- Saki Mafundikwa

3

309

BITA FAYYAZI

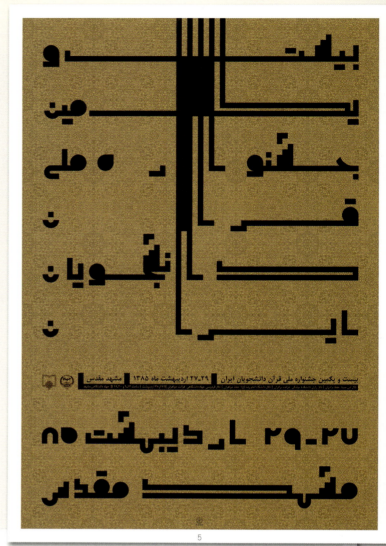

Mandana Moghaddam
and Bita Fayyazi

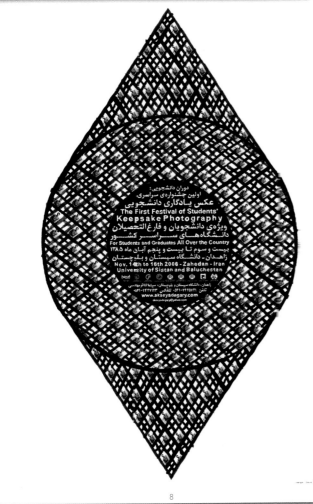

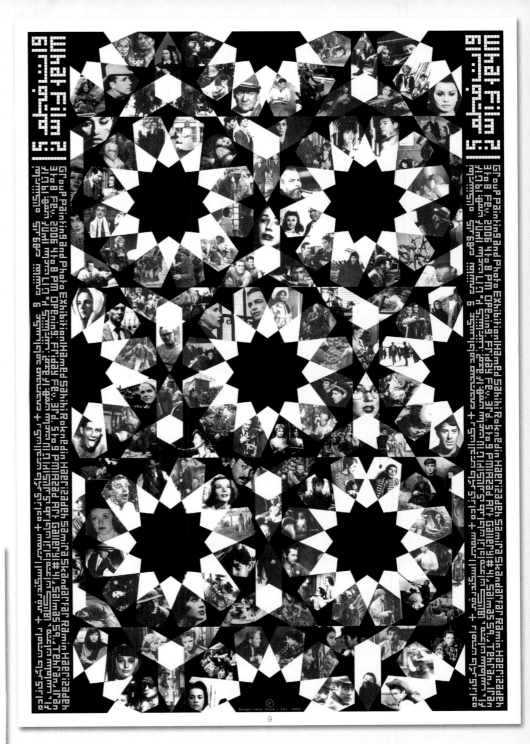

4.   Identity, Iran Pavilion at the 51st
     Venice Eiennale, Tehran Museum of
     Contemporary Art, Iran, 2005
     -
5.   Poster, 21st Quran Festival for
     Students, IACERC, Iran, 2006
     -
6.   Exhibition poster, *DOLME-HA*, paint-
     ings by Rckn-ed-din Haerizadeh,
     Golestan Gallery, Iran, 2007
     -
7.   Exhibition poster, *Concealed and
     Exposed*, photographs by Amirali
     Ghasemi, Parkingallery, Iran, 2005
     -
8.   Poster, The First Festival of Stu-
     dents' Keepsake Photography, Univer-
     sity of Sistan and Baluchestan,
     Iran, 2006
     -
9.   Exhibition poster, *What Film?*, Azad
     Art Gallery, Iran, 2006

1

2

Manuel Raeder (Berlin). --- I have been aware of Berlin-based designer Manuel Raeder's work for quite some time, but have mostly seen only disparate elements in photos or online. I visited the 2006 retrospective exhibition of the Berlin fashion collective Bless in Rotterdam, and although Raeder was heavily involved, I couldn't exactly pinpoint how. This seems to be precisely the point: His projects with friends and clients are so intensely collaborative that it is difficult to see where his input stops and theirs begins. --- When he is not creating self-commissioned projects, Raeder works mostly with arts organizations and fashion designers, designing everything from books and typefaces to exhibition spaces and furniture. Many of his projects are as much about spaces as they are about tangible design objects: They preempt, respond to, and align with a project's given contexts. His poster for an exhibition of works from the art collection of Alexander Schröder employs the collector's inventory of flyers and correspondence rather than showing the artworks themselves, thereby revealing the undocumented aspects of art collections: the homes and storage units in which they usually reside. --- For a publication launch, Raeder designed what he calls an "inverted signage system" of white-striped stickers applied in and around Berlin's Mulackstrasse. Visitors came to understand the signs only after they had arrived at the launch and found the publications in large, striped transparent bags tied to a fence along the street. Looking at the project photography now, it seems difficult to understand, but on that day, in the actual surroundings of the launch, its site-specific nature made complete sense. --- In his regular collaborations with Bless, Raeder plays with the conventions of seasonal fashion look books. Instead of continuing with the established fashion industry practice of sending small-run editions of each new collection to buyers and press contacts, Raeder utilizes the ready-made distribution systems of international fashion magazines. By working with a new publication each season to publish the look book as an exclusive feature, Bless's collections are made more accessible to a much wider and seasonally varied audience. --- Raeder's graphic design is exciting because it defines our practice not as a separate layer of decoration, but as an intrinsic and crucial component of any project, creating meaning from content, format, distribution, and context, just as it does with color, shape, words, and pictures. --- James Goggin

1.   Book cover, *Optik Schröder*, Kunstverein Braunschweig and Verlag der Buchhandlung Walther König, Germany, 2006
----
2.   Signage, "Happy Believers," Werkleitz Biennale, Germany, 2006

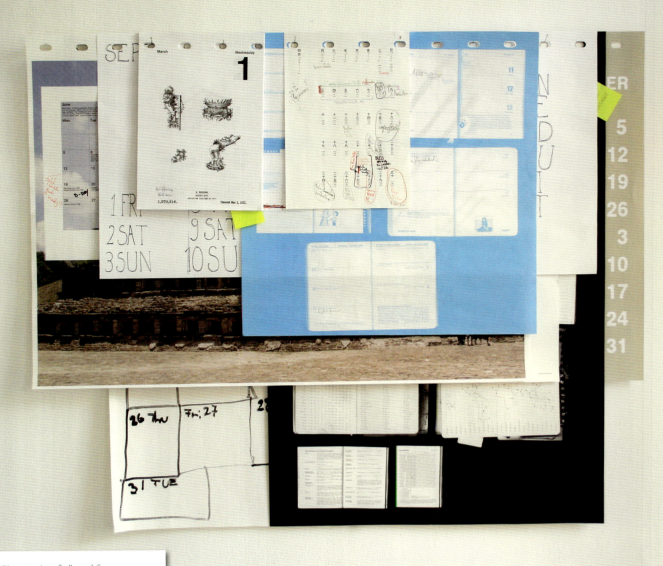

3

3. Calendar, "Loose Leaf," self-commissioned, 2006

4. Agenda, "Popurri," Sternberg Press, Germany, 2007

5. Installation, "Doorstopper," Marres Gallery, The Netherlands, 2003. One month's worth of art and culture magazines, all bound together

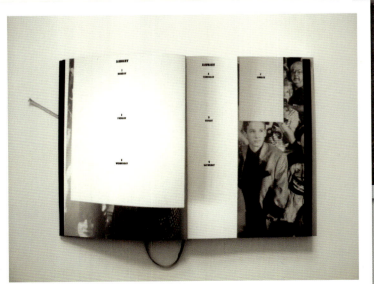

4

5

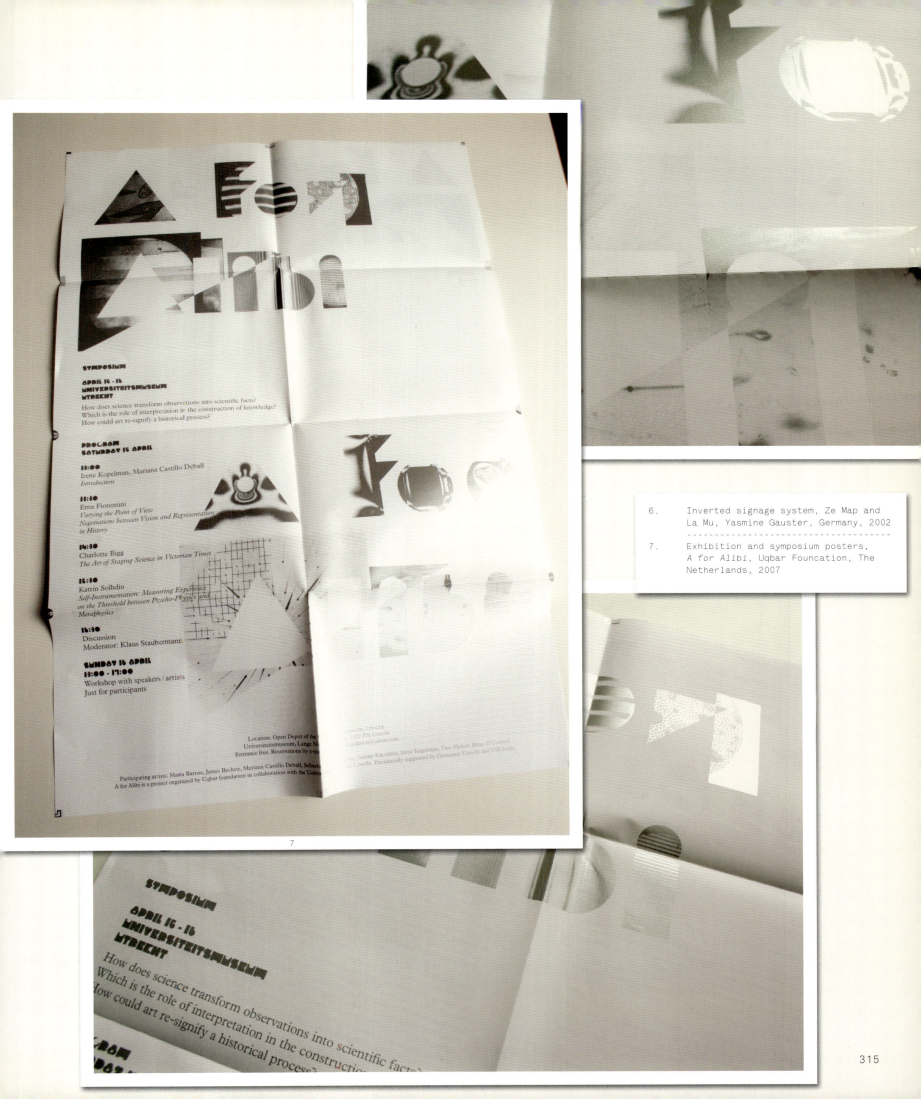

6.   Inverted signage system, Ze Map and
      La Mu, Yasmine Gauster, Germany, 2002
----
7.   Exhibition and symposium posters,
      A for Alibi, Uqbar Founcation, The
      Netherlands, 2007

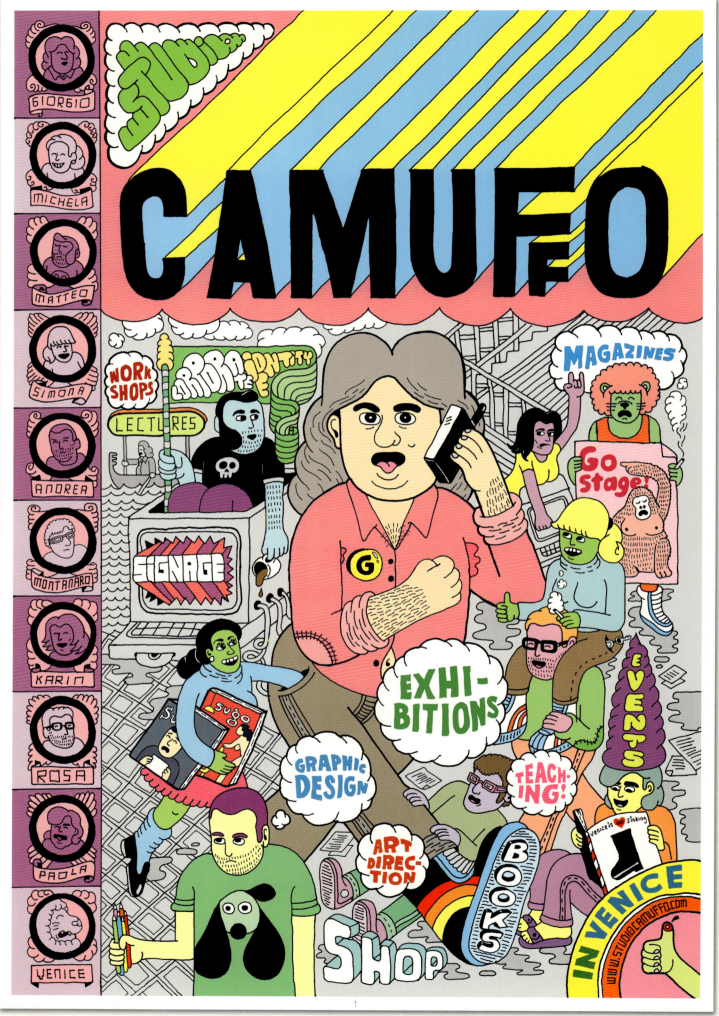

Andy Rementer (Philadelphia). --- Andy Rementer is an American currently living and working in Philadelphia. He earned a graphic design degree from the University of the Arts in Philadelphia and has worked for graphic- and web-design firms in New York. I heard about him from Omar Vulpinari, head of Visual Communication at Fabrica (where Andy is on the Visual Communication staff). Situated just outside Treviso, Italy, Fabrica is Benetton's communication research center, where students handpicked from around the world collaborate on projects that draw strength from the cultural plurality of the designers. It seems like a perfect fit for the eccentric Rementer, whose trademarks are his merciless mirth and zany humor. (He cites "politics and the media, weird sex, nose bleeds, and leg hair" as inspirations.) A master of the deadpan response in interviews, he talks seriously about only one thing: He is happiest creating comics. The medium gives him the freedom to do as he pleases, without a pesky art director hovering over him. And boy, does he utilize that freedom! --- When I first saw his work, I was struck by his exceptional drawing talent and unapologetic humor. His characters poke fun at society with scant regard for political correctness, which pleases Rementer to no end. "The more offensive the better," he gleefully quips. His comic style and palette remind me of work I've seen somewhere before, but I'm hardly a comic aficionado, and I had to read up on him to discover that he considers 1960s counterculture hero R. Crumb a major influence. "Crumb's work is probably the reason I still draw," he admits. --- Zany, biting, offbeat, wacky, witty, wry, dry, paranoid, off the wall: This is the world Andy Rementer inhabits. It's a world where nothing is sacred, where all is fair game and observed with a sharp, if not downright offensive, eye. --- Saki Mafundikwa

1.   Promotional poster, Studio Camuffo, Italy, 2006
        ----
2.   Illustration, "Who Are You?," self-commissioned, USA, 2006
        ----
3.   Comic "Dating 2.0," technotuesday.com, USA, 2007

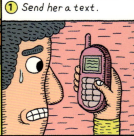

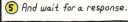

ANDY REMENTER

Andy and I have never met, but I frequent many of his former haunts. It is a delight to be taking a pee in the smelly bathroom at Odessa Cafe in the East Village or at Sweet Ups in Williamsburg and look up to see one of Andy's stickers featuring some sort of grotesque figure glowing in highlighter. His work instantly brings a smile to my face. Andy is currently slapping stickers in the stalls of Fabrica in Italy.

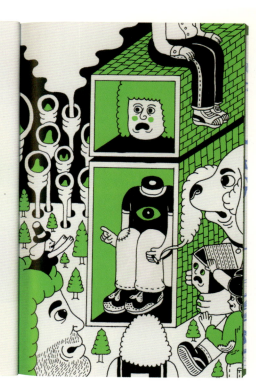

4.   Spreads, *The Artist's Guide*, The Artist's Guide, USA, 2006
----
5.   Comic, "Terror Tech," technotuesday.com, USA, 2007
----
6.   Book illustration, *If You Could Do Anything Tomorrow...*, If You Could, UK, 2007
----
7.   Magazine cover, *Clark* no. 23, Clark, France, 2006

5

7

6

Claudio Rocha (São Paulo). --- "For a guy from
São Paulo, you're cool!" This line from *City of
God*, one of my all-time favorite movies, aptly
describes Claudio Rocha and his friends Tony and
Caio de Marco, who gave an impressive presentation
of their work at TypeCon2004 in San Francisco.
It was, however, the multimedia unveiling of the
de Marco brothers' typeface Samba that stole
the show. The font seemed to draw itself on the
screen, its sexy curves undulating like the hips
of a samba dancer urged on by the frenetic percus-
sive beat of the music. The typeface reminded me
of Shumom, the "alphabet" invented by Sultan Njoya
of Cameroon in 1896, which I always felt was never
meant to be static. I commissioned two of my best
motion-graphics students to animate Shumom, and
now I think I'm "way cool" for a guy from Harare!
--- Our paths crossed again in 2005 at Typo Berlin,
where Rocha's body of work in Brazilian typography
impressed everyone. He is copublisher (with Tony
de Marco) of *Tupigrafia*, an annual magazine that
covers all things typographical with great passion
and humor. The name *Tupigrafia* is a play on words:
tipografia is Portuguese for typography, and
Tupi is the language spoken by native Brazilians.
"There's no set design for our magazine, and we
use a different logo for each issue. Our contribu-
tors have the freedom to art direct and lay out
each issue. This leads to nice surprises and freshness," Rocha explains. --- In Berlin, his presentation included the work of some old typographers,
mavericks who, were it not for *Tupigrafia*, would
have remained unknown. Profeta Gentileza, or
"Prophet Kindness" (a street artist), and Millôr
Fernandes (a cartoonist)—both in their eighties—
have each inspired typefaces and had their work
published in the magazine. Rocha and his partners
belong to a younger generation that, through
the magazine, not only charts new and unexplored
waters, but also ensures that the old masters are
not forgotten. --- *Tupigrafia* is the perfect vehicle for Rocha to showcase his numerous typefaces
and the output of his experimental letterpress
printshop Oficina Tipografica São Paulo. The magazine is a successful marriage of the old, the
new, and the cutting-edge. --- Saki Mafundikwa

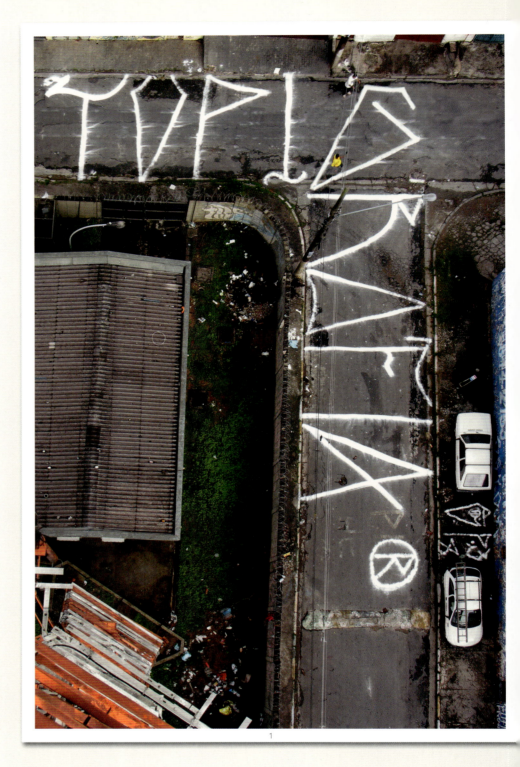

1

1.   Magazine cover, *Tupigrafia* no. 7,
     Tupigrafia, Brazil, 2007
     ----
2.   Promotional poster, *Tupigrafia* no. 2,
     Tupigrafia, Brazil, 2002
     ----
3.   Promotional poster, *Tupigrafia* no. 1,
     Tupigrafia, Brazil, 2002
     ----
4.   Promotional poster, *Tupigrafia* no. 5,
     Tupigrafia, Brazil, 2004

2

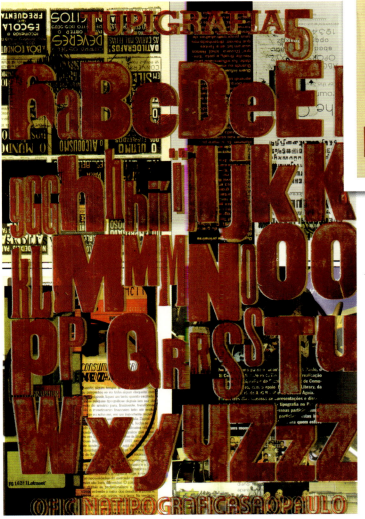

4

TUPIGRAFIA

ABCÇEFGHI
ABCDEFGHLMNXYZ
ABCDEFGHIJKLMNOPQRSTUV
ABCDKM

Revista de Tipografia & Caligrafia

3

6

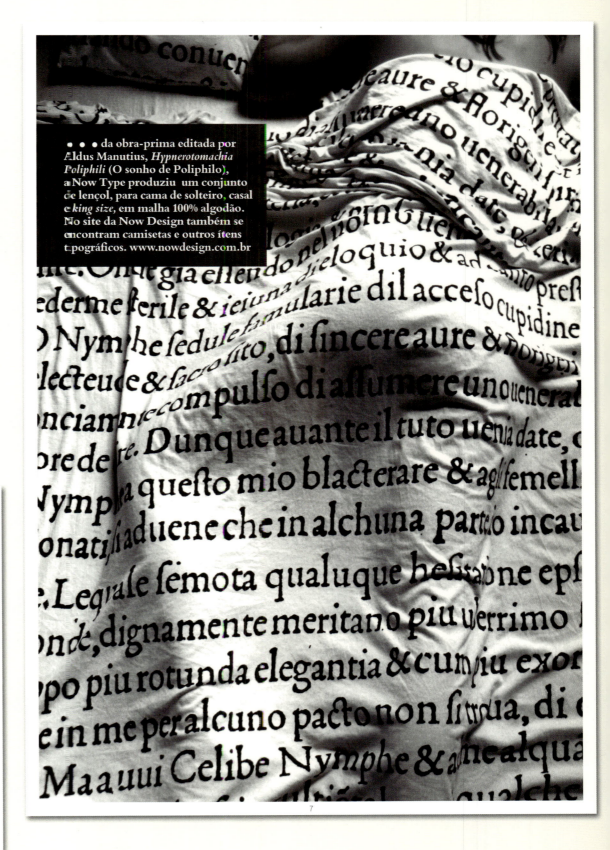

● ● ● da obra-prima editada por Aldus Manutius, *Hypnerotomachia Poliphili* (O sonho de Poliphilo), a Now Type produziu um conjunto de lençol, para cama de solteiro, casal e *king size,* em malha 100% algodão. No site da Now Design também se encontram camisetas e outros ítens tipográficos. www.nowdesign.com.br

7

5.   Poster, "BondoniCaslon," Now Type, Brazil, 2005

---

6.   Exhibition mannequin, "Body Type," Calligraphia Gallery, Brazil, 2007

---

7.   Now Type magazine advertisment, *Tupigrafia* no. 7, Now Design, Brazil, 2007

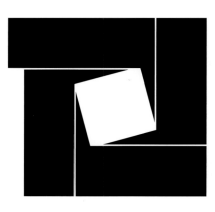

מוזיאון תל אביב לאמנות
TEL AVIV MUSEUM OF ART

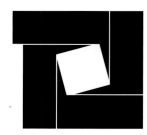

1

2

<u>Michal Sahar</u> (Tel Aviv).
--- Every time I visit
Tel Aviv, it seems like I need a special skill to
find a parking space. I go around the block endlessly, and just when I think I've spotted one,
someone else is already there. It's a small city,
and everyone around is cruising the same cir-
cles. Just like its license plates, Tel Aviv's
graphic design scene is multiplying by the minute.
With the growth of corporate business, publishing
houses, and digital media, the market is getting
rather packed, but the Tel Aviv-based graphic
designer Michal Sahar found a nice spot in the
center of the Israeli cultural parking lot. With
clients like the Tel Aviv Museum and Haifa Museum,
book and catalog commissions from Israel's lead-
ing contemporary artists, and work for various
book publishers, she somehow found the time to
set up today's most attractive Hebrew type foundry,
Hagilda, and to design a long list of best-selling
fonts that are almost a default in every Hebrew-
typing design studio. --- Each one of Sahar's artist's books is like a harmonious conversation
between designer and artist. Sahar's unique design
solutions bring out the essence of their subjects.
The horizontally bound book *Bon Voyage*, for the
artist Irit Hemmo, opens with eight blank pages
of different carbon papers, suggesting the artist's
technique. The process magenta and yellow inks on
the cover of Karen Russo's *Encyclopedia Thermica*
were replaced with phosphorescent pink and yellow,
resulting in a quite distinctive palette. For a
special edition of the same book, Sahar overprint-
ed in black ink on the entire cover, which made
the phosphorescent inks glow when exposed to light.
"The challenges are in every way different," says
Sahar, referring to book design and type design.
"Book design needs a wide range of visual approaches, and a dialog with the artist/writer, while
designing typefaces comes as a response to what's
missing and needs to be created." --- Hagilda's
objective was to change the face of Hebrew typography. It's a bold statement, but Sahar's typefaces deliver. Her fonts, among them Alenbi and
Darom, give a clean, contemporary punch to traditional forms. They're the kind of typefaces that
in time turn into classics. --- Julia Hasting

1-2.   Identity system, Tel Aviv Museum
        of Art, Tel Aviv Museum of Art,
        Israel, 2006
        ----
3.   Book cover and spreads, *Bon Voyage*
        by Irit Hemmo, Omanut La'am Press,
        Israel, 2005. Photographs by
        Oded Löbl

3

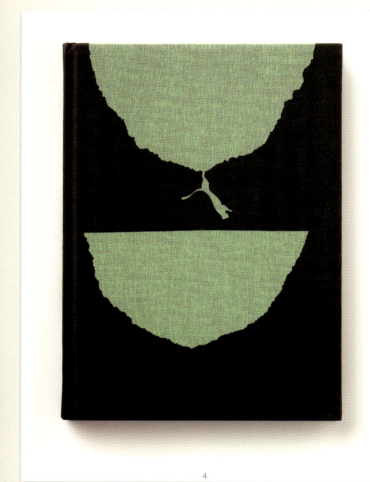

4

5

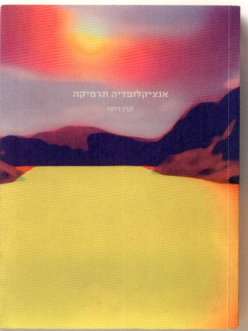

6

Arbel Hagilda / ארבל הגילדה
Hebrew–English typeface

אבגדהוזחטיכלמנסעפצקר
שתרסוףץש*1234567890;
abcdefghijklmnopqr
stuvwxyz&[@]:‹"–?!,.'›
ABCDEFGHIJ£$€(%)®©™
KLMNOPQRSTUVWXYZ

a|א|A|*

We wish to express our gratitude to the donors to the museum's exhibition fund whose generosity has made this exhibition and accompanying publication possible. we also acknowledge the...

הביתן, אותה "קובייה לבנה" שמזמינה אמנים צעירים
להתכנסות בתוכה ולאחר מכן מציגה את עבודותיהם,
שימש בארבעת העשורים האחרונים אכסניה לכמה יוזמות
פורצות דרך בזירת האמנות הישראלית. בתערוכת-היחיד
הראשונה שלה אצלנו, היא הצליחה לשנות את...

Maccabi Block / מכבי בלוק
Hebrew–English typeface

אבגדהוזחטיכלמנסעפצקר
שתרסוףץש*1234567890;
abcdefghijklmnopqr
stuvwxyz&(@):‹"–?!,.'›
ABCDEFGHIJ£$€/%®©™
KLMNOPQRSTUVWXYZ

g|ס|G|*

We wish to express our gratitude to the donors to the museum's exhibition fund whose generosity has made this exhibition and accompanying publication possible. we also acknowledge the initiative and dedicate...

הביתן, אותה "קובייה לבנה" שמזמינה אמנים צעירים
להתכנסות בתוכה ולאחר מכן מציגה את עבודותיהם,
שימש בארבעת העשורים האחרונים אכסניה לכמה יוזמות
פורצות דרך בזירת האמנות הישראלית. בתערוכת-היחיד
הראשונה שלה אצלנו, היא הצליחה לשנות...

4.   Cover, exhibition catalog, work by Doron Rabina at the 2004 São Paulo Biennial, The Israeli Ministry of Education, Culture, and Sport, and Ministry of Foreign Affairs, Israel, 2004. Photograph by Oded Löbl

----

5.   Cover, exhibition catalog, *The Endless Solution*, work by Sigalit Landau, Tel Aviv Museum of Art, Israel, 2005. Photograph by Oded Löbl

----

6.   Book cover, *Encyclopedia Thermica* by Karen Russo, Omanut La'am Press, Israel, 2005. Photograph by Oded Löbl

----

7.   Typeface project, "Fonts Showcase," self-commissioned, Israel, 2002–7

----

8.   Typeface, Arbel Hagilda, self-commissioned, Israel, 2007. Part of a project to revive old Hebrew typefaces that are out of use or digitally distorted

----

9.   Typeface, Maccabi Block, self-commissioned, Israel, 2006

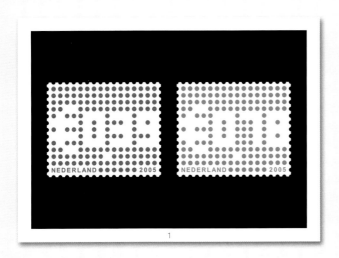

1

2

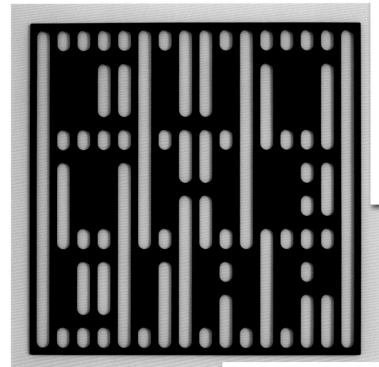

3

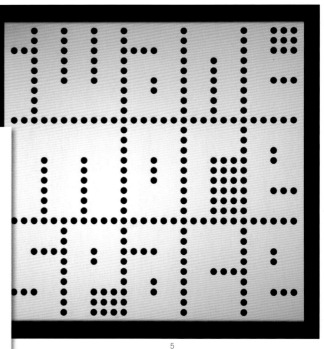

5

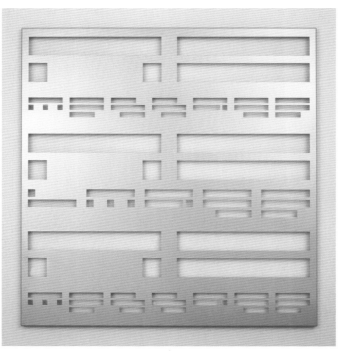

4

Martijn Sandberg (Amsterdam). --- Martijn Sandberg
is sort of an enigma. When I asked him where he
works, he said, "In an ivory tower." When I asked
about his process, he said, "That's classified
information." When I asked about his philosophy,
he said, "Image is message is image," which he
later clarified to "No image no message no image."
So who is Martijn Sandberg, really? I think his
work speaks for itself. --- His installation "We're
Only in It for the Money," of one thousand self-
designed coins embedded in the floor of the Social
Insurance Bank of The Netherlands, combines the
spaces of art and the market. Are the coins money
that serves as art, or art that looks like money?
His laser-cut typography is beautiful simply as
an abstract image, and all the more so when, after
you look at it for a while, letters and meaning
take shape and emerge almost like an optical illusion that challenges the hierarchy of negative and
positive space. You think the holes in the metal
form the letters, but the letters frame the holes.
His design work, then, is just as cryptic as his
answers to my questions. --- It takes a unique
kind of client to appreciate Sandberg's style, but
I'm sure the clients he does attract don't go away
unhappy. The Royal TNT Post took a risk with his
thirty-nine- and seventy-eight-cent stamps—knowing
the challenging typography and conceptual scale
he likes—but the result is nothing short of stun-
ning, so elegant you almost don't want to use them.
Sandberg's very personal style is not instantly
accessible, and perhaps because of this, his work
is always fascinating. --- Irma Boom

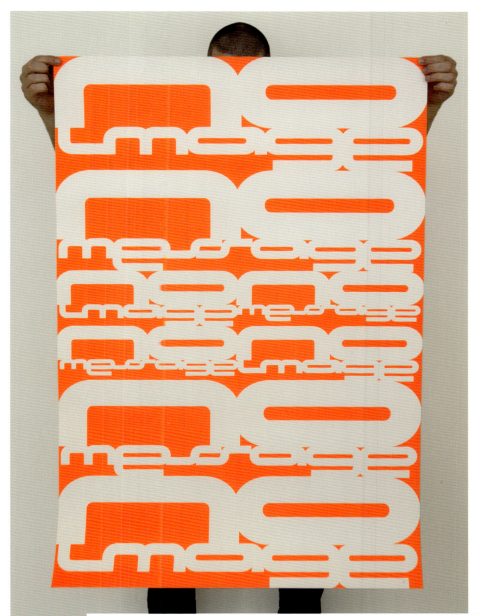

1.   Postage stamps, Royal TNT Post,
      The Netherlands, 2005
      ----
2.   Laser cut, "I Am Still Alive," self-
      commissioned, The Netherlands, 2005
      ----
3.   Laser cut, "Cut the Crap," from the
      Black Series, self-commissioned,
      The Netherlands, 2006
      ----
4.   Laser cut, "No Image No Message,"
      self-commissioned, The Netherlands,
      2001
      ----
5.   Laser cut, "I Want More Space,"
      Zuiderkerkprijs 2004, Ontwikkelings-
      bedrijf Gemeente Amsterdam, The
      Netherlands, 2004
      ----
6.   Posters, "No Image No Message," self-
      commissioned, The Netherlands, 2005

6

7

7. Installation, "If These Walls Could Speak," in an elevator shaft at the Amsterdam Public Library, Amsterdam Municipality, The Netherlands, 2007. Each line of text is a title from the library's collection.
----
8. TNT Parcel Post Boxes, Royal TNT Post, The Netherlands, 2006
----
9. Aluminum sign, "Kill the Pics," self-commissioned, The Netherlands, 2000

8

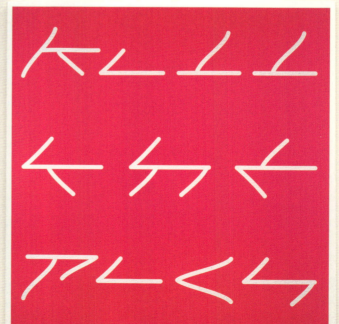

9

10. Reception office, OSG Singelland College in Drachten, OSG Singelland, The Netherlands, 2005

----

11. Steel partitions, "Hallo, is daar Iemand?" (Hello, Is Anybody out There?), Bouwfonds MAB, The Netherlands, 2006

----

12. Installation, "We're Only in It for the Money," Social Insurance Bank of The Netherlands in Zaandam, Social Insurance Bank of The Netherlands, The Netherlands, 2000

----

13. Installation, "Power to the People," Hoofddorpplein transformer station in Amsterdam, Amsterdams Fonds voor de Kunst, The Netherlands, 2000

11

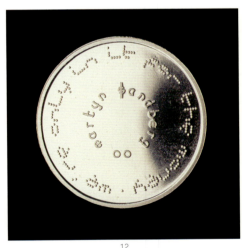

12

13

75B (Rotterdam). --- 75B is run by Robert Beckand, Pieter Vos, and Rens Muis. They work from 9:30 to 5:30 each day. They have lunch from 1:00 to 2:00 every afternoon. The studio is closed on Fridays. It seems as though they lead a pretty regular life, but don't be fooled! 75B is one of the oddest design studios you're likely to come across. I sat down with them to discuss their work and their studio, and here is a sample of our conversation: --- *Is the process more important than the end result?* No, the process does not matter at all; we're all about results. --- *How do you know if something is good?* We don't know. That's the best thing about our work. --- *How stubborn are you?* We're very flexible. It's not our stuff, it's the client's, so we don't really care. --- *What is the most successful project you have done so far?* We're not proud of one particular project We like to look back at failed projects a lot; it's much more fun. --- To be fair, 75B has had its share of duds—the identity for the Designprijs Rotterdam 2007, for example—so I'm glad the boys can take them in stride. When their work is good, though, it's *really* good. Take the Westblaak Skatepark, or their projects for Fonds BKVB. Beckand, Vos, and Muis act cool, but I think at heart they are true designers, so take what they say with a grain of salt: "We don't think designing is a very serious or important profession. Design is overrated." --- Irma Boom

1.   Identity system and posters, Rotterdam 2007: City of Architecture, Rotterdam Marketing, The Netherlands, 2006
- -
2-5. Identity and advertising campaign, Now & Wow nightclub, Now & Wow, The Netherlands, 2002-6

2

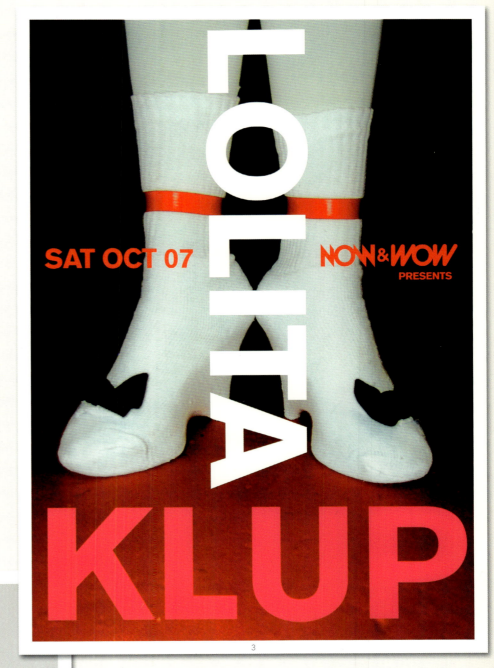

3

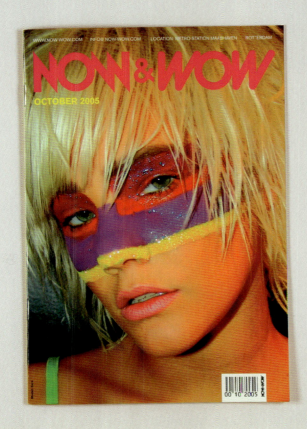

4

5

6

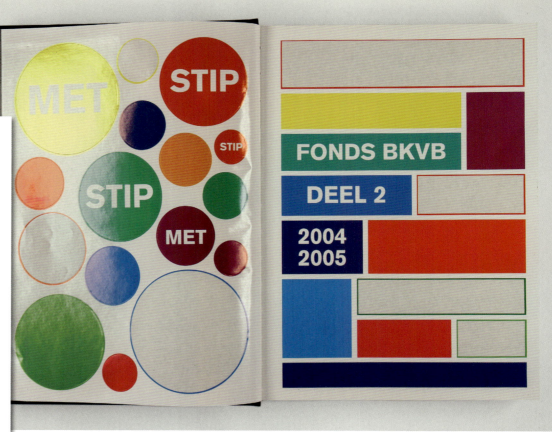

6.   Identity and catalog, The Netherlands
    Foundation for Visual Arts, Design,
    and Architecture (Fonds BKVB), Fonds
    BKVB, The Netherlands, 2001-7
----
7.   Identity and advertising, "Anno" cam-
    paign, Historisch Museum Rotterdam,
    The Netherlands, 2007
----
8.   Design, Westblaak Skatepark, City
    of Rotterdam, The Netherlands, 2000
----
9.   Identity, Designprijs Rotterdam
    2007, Designprijs Rotterdam, The
    Netherlands, 2007

7

8

9

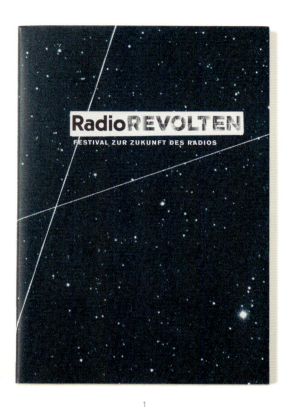

1

Claudia Siegel (Leipzig). --- The two best examples of this young, Leipzig-based designer's work are both about birds. The first, *Die entenrepublik gamsenteich* (The Duck Republic), is the fruit of Claudia Siegel's collaboration with two artists who created an installation about a democratic society of ducks in a pond. Siegel reinterpreted this idea and expanded it into a book. In it, Citizen Duck is serious: The illustrations are scientifically sound, and the quality of the text and graphics removes any doubt as to the veracity of the democratic ducks' story. --- The second work echoes the first. The illustrated essay "The Birds Society" is a very personal attempt to symbolize the difficult return to peace in the former Yugoslavia. In order to illustrate the daily life of neighboring populations that still find dialog impossible, Siegel met with a local homing-pigeon club. Again using a bird to consider the weaknesses inherent in human behavior, Siegel tells of her encounter with the individuals who teach the pigeons to send messages across impenetrable borders. --- The two books illustrate Siegel's personalized and moving approach. Full of sensibility and restraint, her design makes its presence felt not through stylistic features but through the elegant visual interpretation of its subjects. --- Ruedi Baur

1. Catalog cover, festival flyer, and poster, RadioRevolten, Radio Corax, Germany, 2006. With Nicola Reiter
    ----
2. Book cover, spreads, and fold-out map, *Halle-neustadt führer*, Mitteldeutscher Verlag, Germany, 2006. With Daniel Hermann and Markus Bader

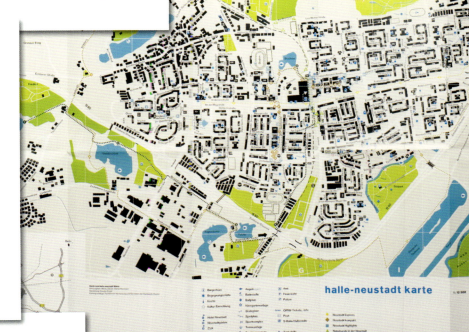

3

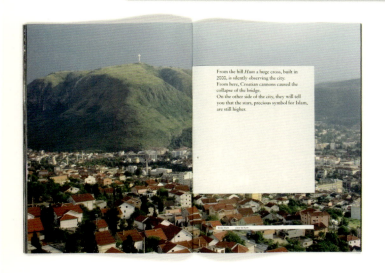

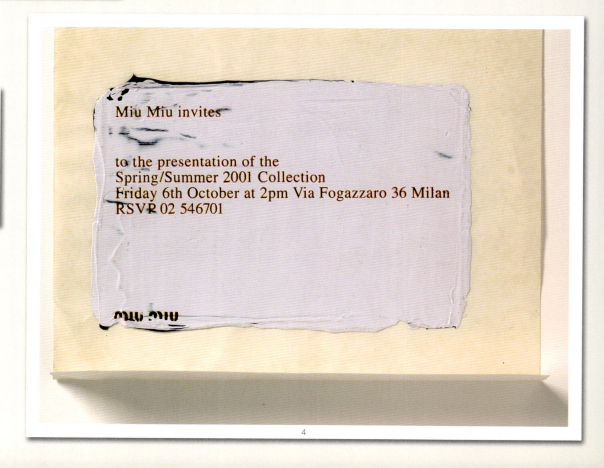

In Mostar Catholic Croats, Orthodox Serbs,
Jews and Muslim Bosnians lived for
more than four centuries together. The city
has grown following the course
of the river Neretva, separated into two
majority groups:
The East bank lies between the river, the Prej
mountains and the slope of the Velez
mountain. It is a confined and uneven space.
The majority of the Muslim community
lives here. The West bank, where the majority
of the Croatian community lives, is broader
and flat.

3.   Photo essay, "The Birds Society,"
     Mostar Files magazine, Mostar, Bosnia
     and Herzegovina, 2006
     ----
4.   Invitation, Miu Miu, Italy, 2001
     ----
5.   Book spreads, *Die entenrepublik gam-
     senteich* (The Duck Republic), Bertram
     Haude, Germany, 2006. With Jens Volz

Miu Miu invites

to the presentation of the
Spring/Summer 2001 Collection
Friday 6th October at 2pm Via Fogazzaro 36 Milan
RSVP 02 546701

miu miu

4

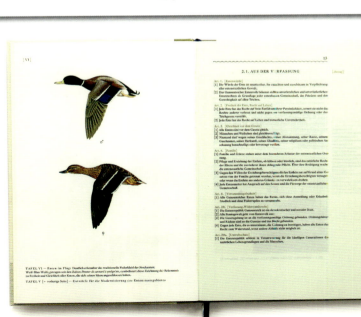

1.   Catalog cover and printed material,
        Interior Design Program, California
        College of Arts and Crafts, USA, 2003
        ----
2.   Catalog cover and exhibition signage,
        2004 SECA Art Award, San Francisco
        Museum of Modern Art (SFMOMA), USA,
        2004. With Simon Evans

Jennifer Sonderby (San Francisco). --- In the
spring of 2001, while she was a graduate student
at the California College of Arts and Crafts (now
California College of the Arts), Jennifer Sonderby
sent me an e-mail offering to come and teach at
my design school, the ZIVA, that summer. She
arrived in Harare with loads of energy and spent
an incredible six weeks teaching and designing.
(She volunteered to design our very first catalog,
which was brilliant but was never printed, due to
lack of funds.) During that summer, we developed
a mutual professional admiration for each other,
fueled in no small way by her prodigious talent,
meticulous attention to detail, and ability to
listen. --- It came as no surprise, then, that
Sonderby was hired as creative director by the
San Francisco Museum of Modern Art (SFMOMA) a few
years ago. It is also no surprise that she and her
team are producing award-winning design work for
this prestigious institution. The breadth of projects she oversees is a perfect fit for her multi-
tasking personality and workaholic ethic: She and
her team of designers sculpt the visual identity
of the museum through the direction of more than
five hundred projects and twenty exhibitions each
year. Having spent several years managing identities for clients in the technology sector, she
strives to create a brand for the museum that communicates clearly yet remains flexible and fluid.
She has also successfully forged a synergy with
the local design and art communities by collaborating on numerous creative projects. --- Sonderby's
thesis project, *Fastphoric*, is a fiction-based
codex dealing with the ways that Western society's
obsession with the acronym, the abridged, and the
"quick-read" have influenced the structure of the
English language. By juxtaposing a traditional
display of text with two other "faster" methods
on each page, the book functions as a hybrid of
reading technologies, both present and future.
It is included in the permanent collection of
Architecture and Design at SFMOMA. --- "Most
important in all of my work is to believe in what
I am creating or doing," Sonderby says. "Whether
teaching in Zimbabwe or contemplating the typeface
for an exhibition catalog, maintaining integrity
both professionally and personally is paramount."
I know of very few people, let alone designers,
who cite integrity as the most important princi-
ple guiding their work, and Sonderby has an abun-
dance of it. --- Saki Mafundikwa

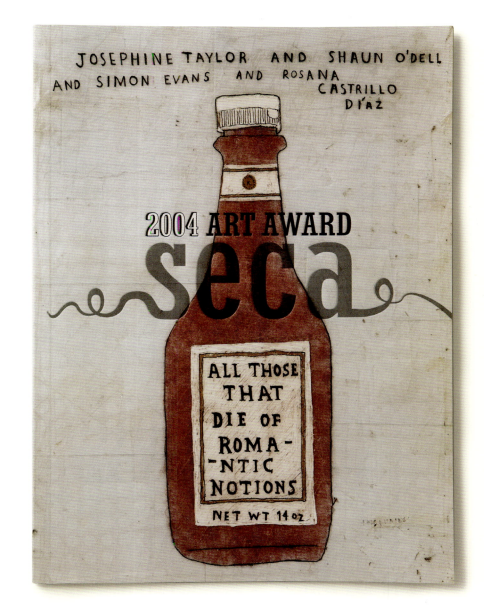

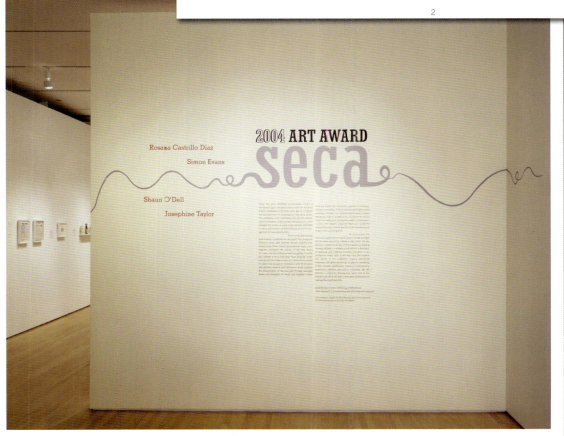

3

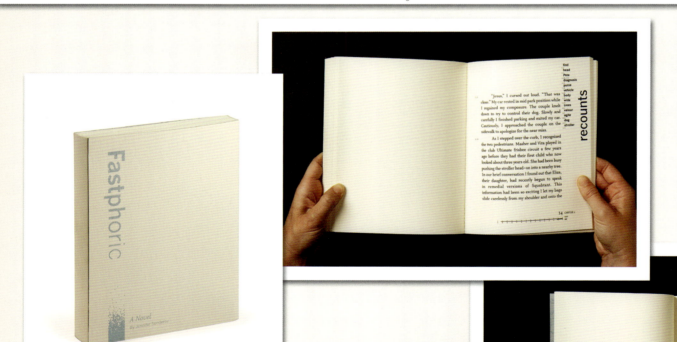

4

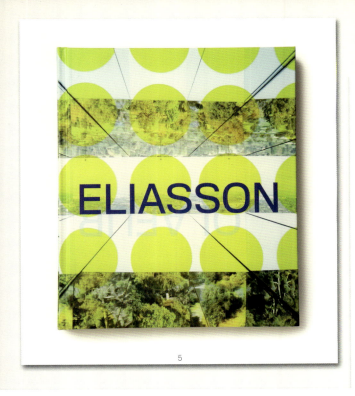

3.   Covers, SFMOMA members' publication,
     SFMOMA, USA, 2005-6. With Public
     Design, Martin Venezky, Geoff Kaplan,
     Jill Bliss, and Lux Design
     ----
4.   Book cover and spreads, *Fastphoric:
     A Novel*, Laliolog Press, USA, 2004
     ----
5.   Cover and spreads, exhibition cata-
     log, *Take Your Time: Olafur Eliasson*,
     SFMOMA, USA, 2007

1.   Exhibition posters, *Zeitgenössische kunst in Essen*, Museum Folkwang, Germany, 2007
---
2.   Poster, "Illegaler," Giroton Germany, 2003
---
3.   Catalog cover and spreads, *Sammeln*, Galerie für Zeitgenössische Kunst, Leipzig, Germany, 2007. With Kay Bachmann and Philipp Paulsen

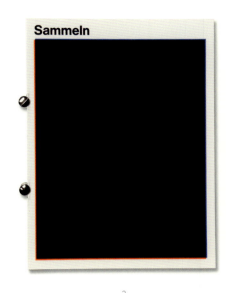

3

<u>Spector</u> (Leipzig). --- A former student at the famous Hochschule für Grafik und Buchkunst in Leipzig, where he now teaches, Markus Dressen knows how to profit from the school's extraordinary typographical tradition without closing himself off to more contemporary graphic and artistic styles. This has allowed him to develop his own unique aesthetic, which runs through every page of his books, from the typography to the texture of the paper. Dressen's works are objects to unfold, touch, handle, and see, as well as to read. --- Let's talk about what the images represented here cannot really show: the choice of paper stock, the subtle folding, the importance of format, the visual narration between one page and the next, the small typographical details—in short, the magic of a high-quality book. His work is not merely a product of his knowledge of books or his intensive confrontation with detail, but rather is the result of a fully developed conceptual framework. Dressen's projects are meaningful—they grow out of important anticipatory work. Despite this extensive planning, his systems do not remain rigid, and the rules that govern his designs adapt to new contexts, keeping his objects interesting even after countless viewings. --- Ruedi Baur

4

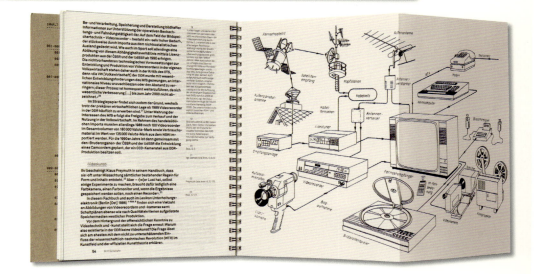

5

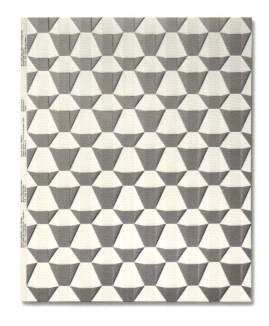

6

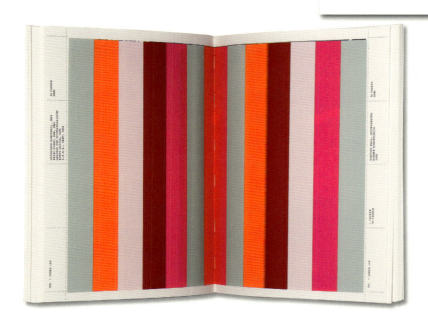

4.   Book cover and spreads, *Grauzone 8mm:*
    Materialien zum autonomen künstler-
    film in der DDR, Hatje Cantz Verlag,
    Germany, 2007. With Pascal Storz

5.   Cover and spread, exhibition catalog,
    Nur hier? Die Galerie der Hochschule
    für Grafik und Buchkunst in Leipzig
    1980-2005, Die Galerie der Hochschule
    für Grafik und Buchkunst, Germany,
    2005. With Pascal Storz

6.   Book cover and spreads, *Rewind*
    Forward by Olaf Nicolai, Hatje Cantz
    Verlag and Ostfildern-Ruit, Germany,
    2003. With Kristina Brusa

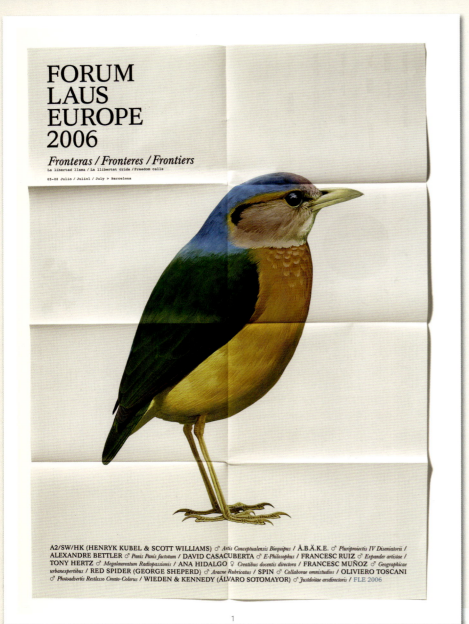

Astrid Stavro (Barcelona). --- Before Astrid Stavro decided to become a graphic designer, she studied philosophy and literature. Initially she wanted to be a journalist. She had always been fascinated by the written word, but it took her a while to become interested in its shape. In the 1980s and '90s she fell in love with Fabien Baron's *Interview* magazine and discovered that thing we call "graphic design." *Interview* opened her mind to a totally new world, and she became a designer shortly thereafter. --- My favorite work of hers is the "Grid-It!" notepad series, something I wish I could have created myself. In her words, this project is "a series of notepads based on the layout grids of famous publications that played a historic role in the development of classic and contemporary design systems. By divorcing the grids from their content, the invisible becomes visible." I think this is an ingenious concept that speaks worlds about book design. The shelving units she built to display the series in stores are 3-D versions of the notepads themselves. The units efficiently organize the notepads according to their grids, providing a thematic look at design history. --- Stavro creates designs that are relevant and appropriate but that challenge the client's brief, often taking a project into unexpected territory. Everything she designs displays passion and a love for detail. Like the "Grid-It!" series, all her work pays homage to the great masters, but with a distinctly personal touch. --- Irma Boom

1. Identity system and poster, Forum Laus Europe, ADG-FAD, Spain, 2006
----
2. Book cover series, Arcadia, Spain, 2006-8

Marc Fumaroli
Educación de la libertad
Prólogo de Juan Goytisolo

Rob Riemen
Nobleza de espíritu
Tres ensayos sobre una idea olvidada
Prólogo de George Steiner

Zygmunt Bauman
Confianza y temor en la ciudad
Vivir con extranjeros

Ramin Jahanbegloo
Elogio de la diversidad
Prólogo de Juan Goytisolo

Ilana Shmueli
Fragmentos de una época
Una carta
Prólogo de Rob Riemen

"La búsqueda de orientación
y el empuje hacia la reflexión
constituyen la verdadera huella
de mi herencia europea."

Ilana Shmueli

ARCADIA

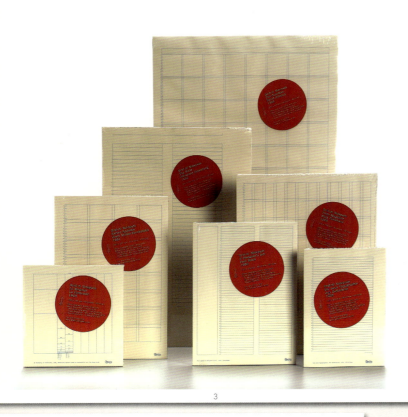

3

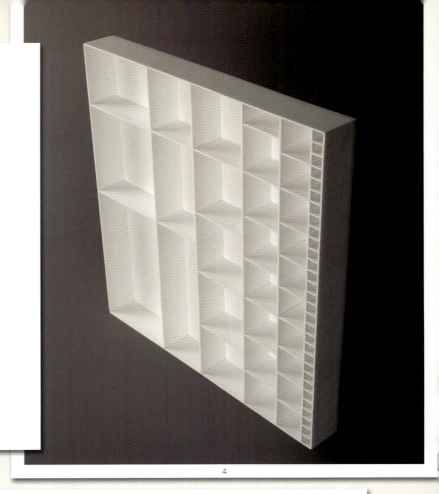

4

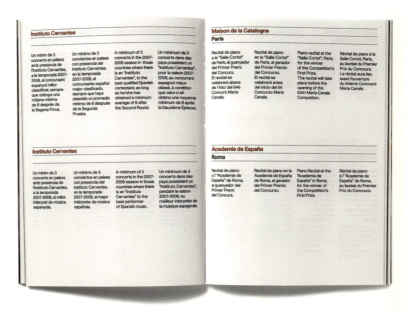

6

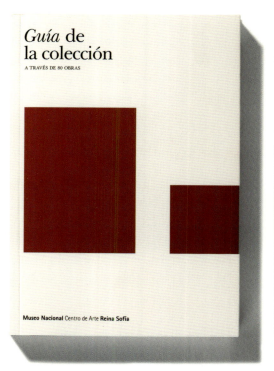

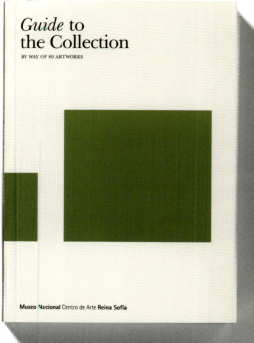

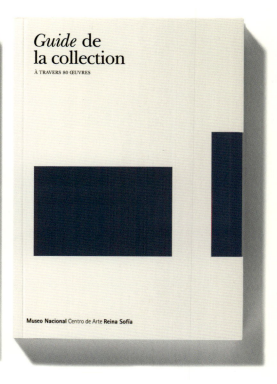

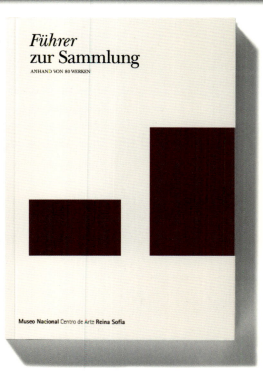

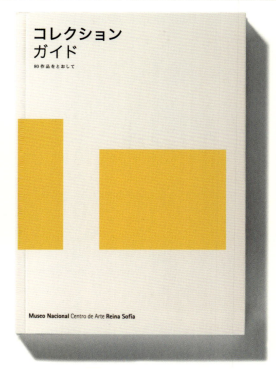

3-4.   Notepad series and shelving unit,
        "Gric-it!," The Royal College of Art,
        UK, 2005-7

- -

5-6.   Poster and program, Maria Canals In-
        ternational Piano Competition, Maria
        Canals International Piano Competi-
        tion and Palau de la Música Catalana,
        Spain, 2007

- -

7.   Guidebook series, Museo Nacional
        Centro de Arte Reina Sofia, Museo
        Nacional Centro de Arte Reina Sofia,
        Spain, 2007

John Tchicai with Strings

1

John Coxon/Wadada Leo Smith
Brooklyn Duos

J Spaceman Guitar Loops

Coxon/Prevost/Wales Acoustic Trio

Frauke Stegmann (Cape Town).--- Frauke Stegmann's work may not look like graphic design at first glance, but she adamantly defines herself as a graphic designer. Her works on paper, ceramics, glass, and textiles are all treated as media for communicating ideas. --- Stegmann left her home country of Namibia in the late 1990s to study first at the Fachhochschule für Gestaltung in Mainz and then at London's Royal College of Art, which is where I met her. After practicing independently in London, Frauke is now based in Cape Town—or, more specifically, in the kitchen of her family-run café, the Birds Boutique. --- Birds Boutique operates as an experimental stage for Stegmann's work. The projects she designs in her corner studio may be available in London or, on a super-local level, on shelves in the café. Not just a gallery, the café is an ongoing project in itself. Stegmann designs the signage, arranges the interior, and creates the glassware and ceramics, in addition to ensuring that the turntable has bird songs on heavy rotation. --- Several materials and motifs are recurring components of Stegmann's work: flora, fauna (particularly the eponymous birds of the café), gold foil, and patterns. In list form these may sound overly decorative, even cute, but Stegmann manages to use what we might think of as celebratory elements in a hearteningly humble and commonplace way. Her liberal use of gold foil parallels the uniform use of CMYK by other graphic designers: For her, the "special" is something for everyday use. All these motifs come together in a captivating CD series for London's improv jazz label Treader. Beauty and humility coexist in immaculately rendered gold-foil animals stamped on cheap, colored office manila. --- Stegmann's calm, low-key model of graphic-design practice points to new possibilities for other independent designers in its diverse palette of materials and the broad scope of its D.I.Y. philosophy. --- James Goggin

PARIS IS BURNING

Sean Landers
Daria Martin
João Onofre
Oliver Payne and
Nick Relph
Andy Warhol

Private View:
Friday 6th June 2003
6pm – 8pm

7th June – 2nd August 2003

Entwistle
6 Cork Street
London, W1S 3EE
+44 (0)20 7734 6440
info@entwistlegallery.com
www.entwistlegallery.com

ENTWISTLE

1.   CD covers, Treader Records, UK,
      2004-7

2-3. Exhibition invitation, *Paris Is
      Burning*, Entwistle Gallery, UK, 2003
----
4.   Exhibition invitation envelope, Rosa
      Loy, Entwistle Gallery, UK, 2004

5

6

Michelangelo Pistoletto
Franz West

Reflection Part I

13 January - 7 February 2004

Sutton Lane
1 Sutton Lane, London EC1M 5PU
Entrance: 25/27 Great Sutton Street
Telephone 020 7253 8580
info@suttonlane.com
www.suttonlane.com

SUTTON LANE

7

5.   Wedding invitation, Jarvis Cocker and
     Camille Bidault-Waddington, UK, 2001.
     With Peter Saville and åbäke
     ----
6.   Vinyl sleeve, *AMPM*, Dreck Records,
     UK, 2003
     ----
7.   Invitation, Sutton Lane Gallery,
     Sutton Lane Gallery, UK, 2004
     ----
8.   Exhibition invitation, *Zest for Life:
     Fernando and Humberto Campana*, Design
     Museum, UK, 2004

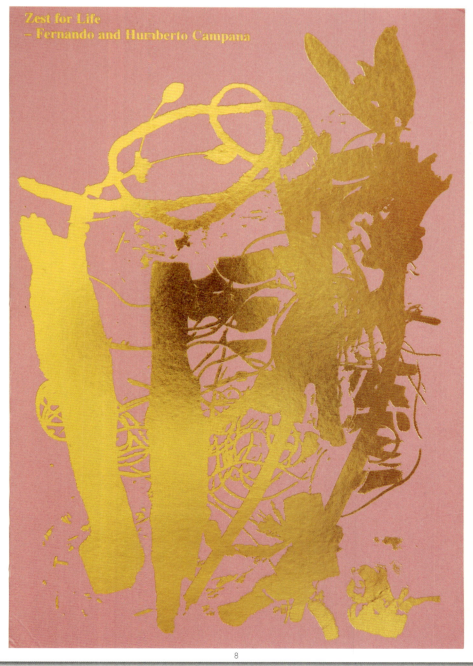

8

Stiletto (New York/Milan).--- Stilettos are heels with an edge and a feminine touch. In Italian the word translates to "knife," and you need two of them to get going. Stefanie Barth and Julie Hirschfeld became a pair of designers in order to experiment and explore across a variety of media and to find clients who share their passion for typography and visual expression in both print and the moving image. --- Stiletto's philosophy is to approach projects from an unexpected angle and to find simple solutions—conceptual ideas with a twist—that surprise themselves and keep passion in the projects. The duo likes the idea of teamwork and sometimes even passes files back and forth, giving them the opportunity to stay flexible while pushing themselves further. Their starting point is always a long brainstorming session: first a dialog and then the concept. --- Although Barth and Hirschfeld design and art direct all projects themselves, collaboration with other artists, designers, typographers, animators, composers, sound designers, and architects happens on many levels and is crucial to the production and fine-tuning of their multidisciplinary work. --- Stiletto's projects reflect a wide range of interests; Barth and Hirschfeld have successfully explored everything from film titles to environmental design, television spots to show packaging, music covers to corporate identities. Watch the credit sequence the pair created for the short film *Balloon Animals* and you will see how a very simple idea, conceptualized, directed, and realized by Stiletto, lifts you up into a light, beautiful, passionate sphere. It's the perfect example of Stiletto's work: timeless, but with an edge—just like the studio's namesake. --- Julia Hasting

1.   Film titles, *Balloon Animals* by
      Michael Karbelnikoff, Michael
      Karbelnikoff and HKM Films, USA, 2006
      ----
2.   Carpet, wallpaper, and website,
      Cenere GB clothing store, Andrea
      Tognon Architecture, Italy, 2006

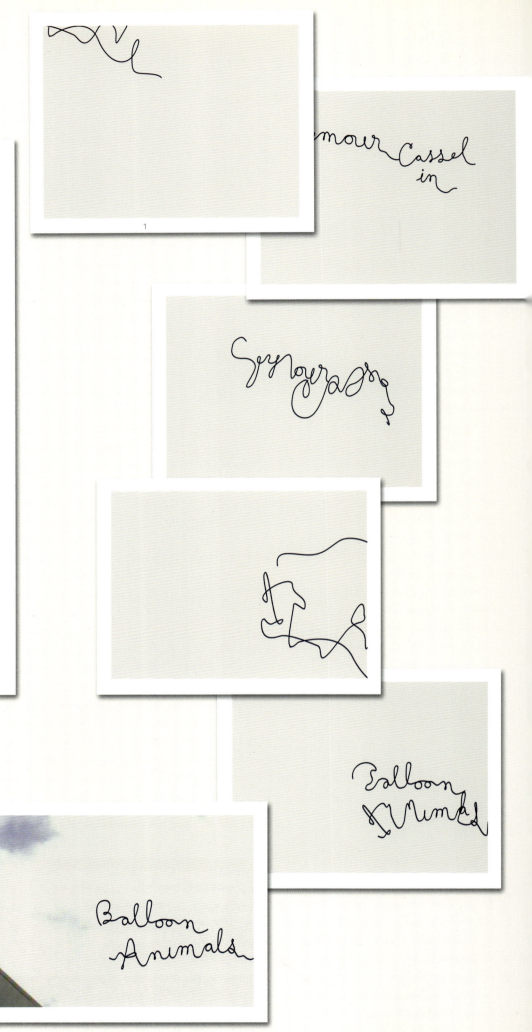

2

g.b.cenere: negozio;
novita: informazioni;
collezioni

RES MAGAZINE
FILM | MUSIC | ART
DESIGN | CULTURE

WHO'S NOW/
WHO'S NEXT

res

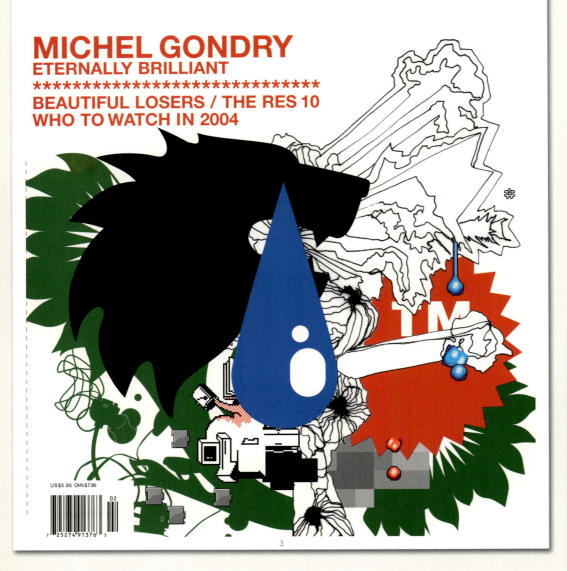

MICHEL GONDRY
ETERNALLY BRILLIANT
****
BEAUTIFUL LOSERS / THE RES 10
WHO TO WATCH IN 2004

US$5.95 CAN $7.95

3

4

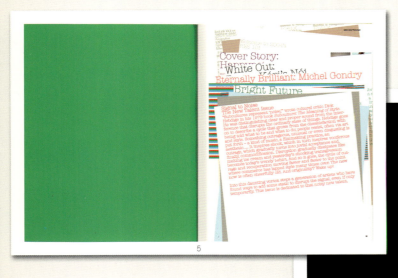

5

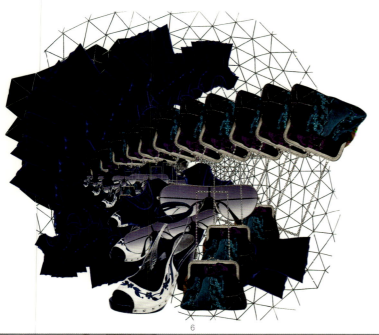

6

7

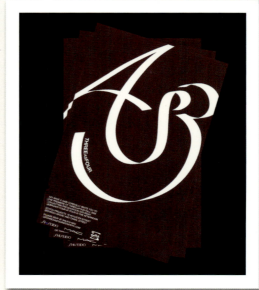

3-5.   Magazine covers and spreads, *Res*,
        Res Media Group, USA, 2003-5
----
6.   Video stills, *Shop Culture*, Condé
        Nast, USA, 2006. Part of a series of
        five video clips about *Lucky* magazine
        and consumer culture
----
7.   Identity, As Four fashion designers,
        As Four, USA, 2004-present

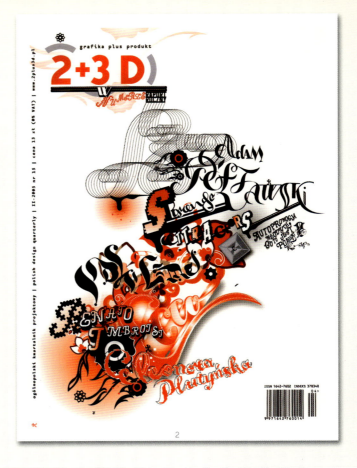

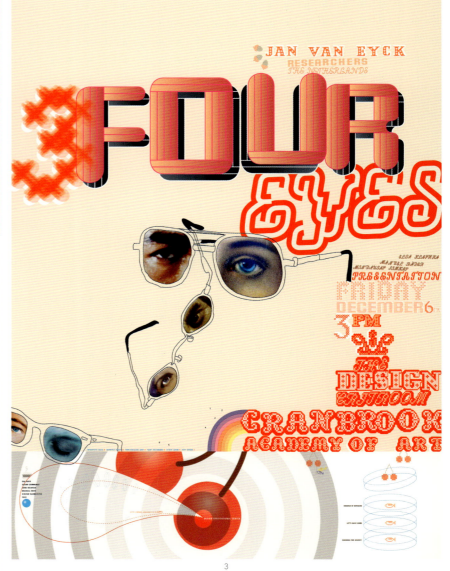

1. Identity and poster, "The Phoenix," architectural renovation project in Birmingham, Alabama, Metropolitan LLC, USA, 2004

----

2. Magazine cover, *2+3 D*, 2+3 D, Poland, 2005

----

3. Poster, self-commissioned typographic experiment, "3 Four Eyes," USA, 2003

----

4. Typeface, Once Upon, self-commissioned, The Netherlands, 2004

----

5. CD and vinyl packaging, *Rotten Cocktails* by Boy Robot, City Centre Offices, Germany, 2005

4

5

<u>Strange Attractors</u> (The Hague/New York).--- With
a deadline fast approaching, the curators of
FiFFteen—a traveling exhibition about the FontFont
type library—wanted something dynamic: an animated
type specimen that would showcase as many FontFonts
as possible. Now, there aren't many studios willing to touch so many different typefaces at once,
let alone able to come up with something that isn't
obvious or boring, so the curators called Strange
Attractors. The result was *Little Yellow Writing
Hood*, a weird and wonderful animated typographic
fairytale that subsequently won the studio several
awards. --- Unlike many other designers interested in conceptual experimentation, Catelijne van
Middelkoop and Ryan Pescatore Frisk are positively
in love with type. They met at the Cranbrook Academy of Art, a school to which they were both
attracted because of its reputation for celebrat-
ing originality, research, and self-expression.
Working together as Strange Attractors, the two
designers seamlessly blend their different styles:
van Middelkoop's meticulously drawn lettering that
combines historical letterforms with newly invented ornament; and Frisk's theoretically informed,
layered design. It's an unusual and multifaceted
combination. In their work they seem to switch
effortlessly between theory and pure play, hand-
drawing and digital wizardry, historical research
and explorations of the ever-changing vernacular
of the postmodern metropolis. --- The outcome of
these restless investigations is diverse, and often
surprisingly functional. Strange Attractors has
created animations for all kinds of clients, from
a Japanese DJ duo to an American real-estate company. The studio has designed websites, posters,
and books for design-related clients, as well as
identities for a health center and an art gallery.
Van Middelkoop and Frisk also enjoy self-initiated
projects that combine design, language, art, and
education. One of these is "Broadcasting Tongues,"
a series of events that examines local graphic
vernacular. Their most impressive self-imposed
project is "Big Type Says More," a spectacular,
seventeen-meter-long installation of letterforms
hard-cut from cardboard, made for an exhibition
at the Museum Boijmans Van Beuningen in Rotterdam
and subsequently acquired for its renowned permanent collection. Is it art? Is it design? It is
one of those instances when the question doesn't
really need to be asked. --- Jan Middendorp

6

7

6. Installation, "Big Type Says More," *Cut for Purpose* exhibition, Museum Boijmans van Beuningen, The Netherlands, 2006. Built by hand over the course of five weeks using industrial hand-held jigsaws, paint, and LEDs
----
7. Film stills, *Little Yellow Writing Hood*, FSI FontShop International, Germany, 2005

Studio Pip and Co. (Melbourne). --- Andrew Ashton, the Australian behind Studio Pip and Co., doesn't sound like a graphic designer. When I asked him about his studies at the Randwick School of Design (now the Design Center Enmore) and about the influences on his work, he talked about Winston Churchill, Drew Barrymore, David Bowie, and Italian cooking. He says he doesn't read books about graphic design, preferring instead to study what he calls "design in action," or, in other words, real-world success stories about problem solving through communication. I guess that's where Bowie comes in. --- Ashton also says he doesn't like to think of himself as a creative person. "I think the notion of being categorized as a 'creative' is a liability," he told me. "People with this ability can often be singled out in curious ways, and after a while they can start believing and living in their own hype." Ashton is smart. He knows that the best design is often the most surprising design, and that surprises rarely come to those who look for them. Perhaps this is why the work coming out of Studio Pip is so impressive. Shunning the restrictions of a creative manifesto, Ashton looks for inspiration in often unconventional, always unexpected places (Drew Barrymore? Really?), constantly pursuing the elusive element of chance and the perfect idea that comes, surprisingly, out of nowhere. Ashton's unique brilliance comes from the fact that, again and again, he finds it. So believe the hype. Maybe *Charlie's Angels* isn't so bad after all. --- Brett Phillips

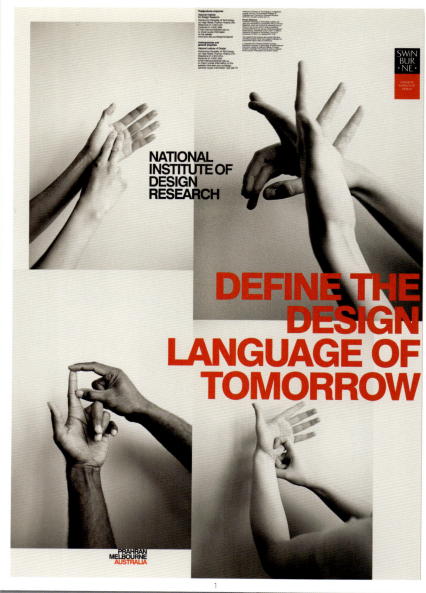

1. Publication, National Institute of Design Research, Swinburne University of Technology, Swinburne University of Technology, Australia, 2004

----

2. Poster, Australian Graphic Design Association National Awards, Australian Graphic Design Association, Autralia, 2002

----

3. Poster, National Institute of Design Research, Swinburne University of Technology, Swinburne University of Technology, Australia, 2004

----

4. Catalog cover and spreads, Australian Graphic Design Association National Awards, Australian Graphic Design Association, Australia, 2002. With David Pidgeon and Darren Ledwich

3

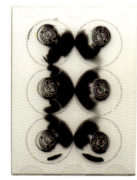

Welcome to the Australian Graphic Design Association National Awards, 2002. It's been ten years since we rolled out the red carpet, and trod the boards in the name of grapic design in Melbourne Victoria.

4

5.   Identity, Saxton Scholars design
        scholarship, Australian Paper,
        Australia, 2003
----

6.   Postcard series, "Sunday Again,"
        self-commissioned, Australia, 2004
----

7.   Color guide cover, *A Paper
        Called Stephen*, Spicers Paper,
        Australia, 2006
----

8.   Identity, Saxton Scholars design
        scholarship, Australian Paper,
        Australia, 2003
----

9.   Cover and spreads, *The Design
        Papers*, National Design Centre,
        Australia, 2006
----

10.   Publication cover and spreads, Na-
        tional Institute of Design Research,
        Swinburne University of Technology,
        Swinburne University of Technology,
        Australia, 2004

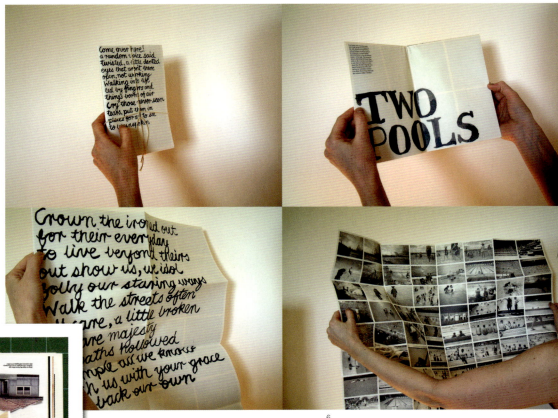

6

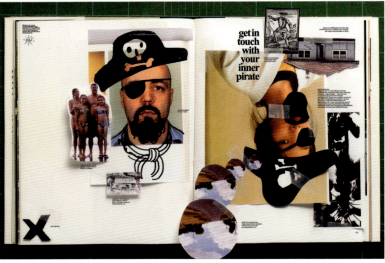

5

7

8

9

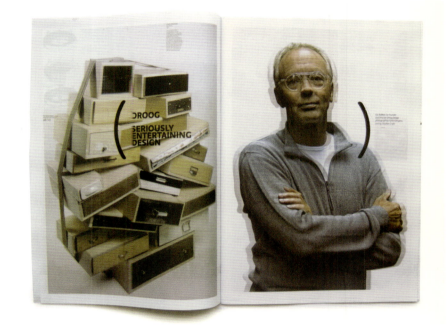

10

1

2

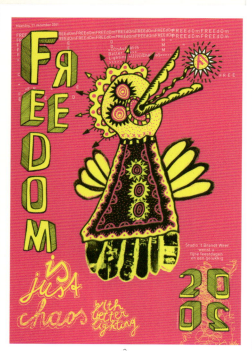

3

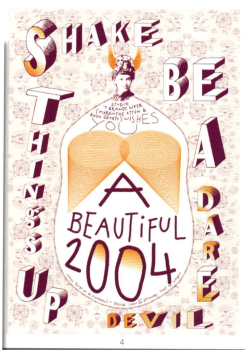

4

Studio 't Brandt Weer (The Hague). --- While preparing a book about graphic design in The Hague, I chanced upon the two-person studio that is 't Brandt Weer. Koen Geurts and Marenthe Otten had recently arrived in the city, fresh out of art school in Genk, Belgium. Their flamboyant style seemed at odds with the institutional atmosphere that dominates The Hague's design scene, and I found their work fascinating. However, I did not include them in my book, because I felt they might be just passing through. Seven years later, they're still there, and although they have worked for local and national administrations, they haven't given up any of their individuality and idiosyncrasy. --- 't Brandt Weer is a Dutch phrase that resembles the word for "fire guard" but literally means "it's burning again." As Geurts has emphatically stated, the pair's ambition was and is to stir things up, to add spice and passion to the Dutch graphic design scene. (A handmade poster reproduced in their 2005 studio book reads "11th Commandment—Thou shalt play with fire!") They do this by proposing layered solutions that avoid the obvious, juxtaposing factual information with striking symbols and metaphors. They make a case for imagination and surprise even when working on jobs that would normally be associated with a less-is-more approach. They take risks. --- This kind of mentality requires willing clients, and Geurts and Otten have been lucky—and smart—enough to find them. One of the most unlikely concepts ever seen in the editorial world was Beau!, a gossip magazine with an edge, packed in 't Brandt Weer's irreverent layout. It worked surprisingly well, lending a quirky, camp appeal to the genre. However, Geurts and Otten seem more at ease with clients such as a children's theater company and a performing arts festival, for which they have designed posters and programs that mix in-your-face illustrations and photomontage with exuberant type. When given carte blanche by the Flemish design magazine Kwintessens (which hires a different designer for each issue), they came up with the loudest, grungiest, most whimsical design the magazine had ever seen, winning them a merit nomination from the New York Type Directors Club. --- The studio's output is unorthodox, but it works—a Belgian colleague called the designs "functional anarchism." 't Brandt Weer was delighted. --- Jan Middendorp

1-4.   New Year's posters, self-commissioned, The Netherlands, 2002-5. The 2002 poster was an official selection at the 2003 Dutch Design Awards.
----
5.   Poster, "Schoonblaffer," Schoon of Schijn, The Netherlands, 2007

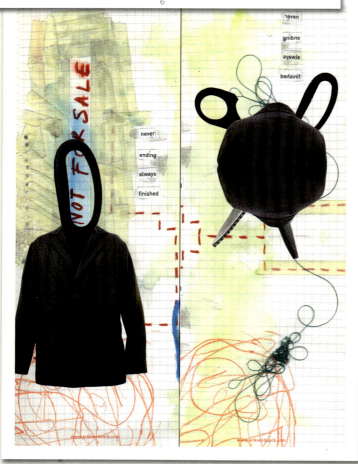

Jakken en hemdrokken | Women's jackets and men's shirts

jak (katoen, linnen) Tholen, ca. 1850, going local 2007 ▶ ▲
women's jacket (cotton, linen) Tholen, c. 1850, going local 2007 ▶ ▲

Schorten | Aprons

Sarah Preckler, schort (katoen) Gent, 2005 ▲ ▶
Sarah Preckler, apron (cotton) Gent, 2005 ▲ ▶

8

6.   Identity, Not for Sale 2006
      fashion collection by Erik Verdonck,
      Erik Verdonck, Belgium, 2006.
      Official selection at the 2007
      Dutch Design Awards
      ----
7.   Book cover and spreads, *Zeelander
      Collectie*, Zeeuws Museum, The
      Netherlands, 2007
      ----
8.   Magazine cover and spreads,
      Kwintessens, Design Flanders,
      Belgium, 2003
      ----
9.   Festival poster, Theater in de
      Living, Villa Basta, Belgium, 2007

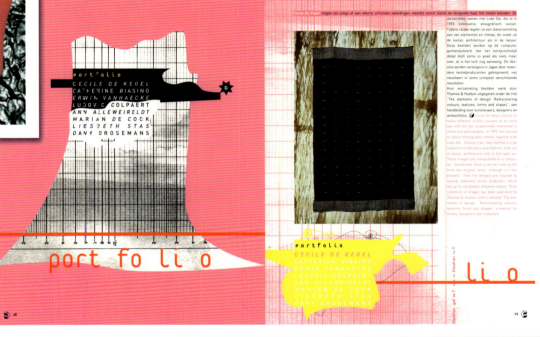

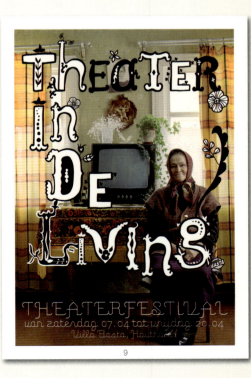

9

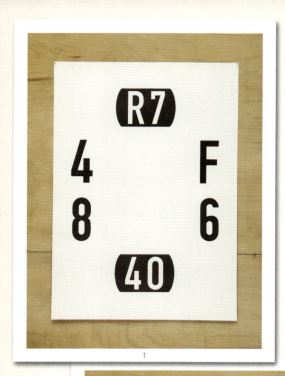

Sulki & Min (Seoul). --- Sulki and Min Choi are truly global designers: literally, from their education in the United States (Yale University) and The Netherlands (Jan van Eyck Academie) to their current base in Seoul, but also conceptually, in the way they think and the references they make. They also move in multiple realms within the design community itself, doing their own work while holding positions in publishing and education. Sulki runs Specter Press, the art and design publishing unit she founded with Min, and Min is an assistant professor in the University of Seoul's graphic design department. --- I have followed Sulki & Min with admiration for many years, and can draw a line from some of their postgraduate projects to the work they do today. While at Yale, Min published the "fugitive magazine" *Specter*, a screen-based publication distributed only by sporadic projection in public spaces. The name, which came from a Korean reading of "illegal publisher" as "ghost publisher," now finds a home with the low-key Specter Press. The multisectional website they designed for the Jan van Eyck Academie offers a neat analogy of their European-Korean links: It eschews three-course-meal website design conventions for a Korean all-dishes-on-the-table-at-once model. --- Key elements of Sulki & Min's work are recontextualization and reappropriation—the latter even shows up as a navigable keyword on their own website, itself a blogging system reappropriated as a functional portfolio. In their "Functional Typography" prints, they highlight the unexpected beauty of usually overlooked serial numbers and packing codes from cosmetics and electronic equipment by scaling them up to poster size. Common pictograms lose their original function and become decorative patterns for a dance festival, or are customized and printed as stickers to accompany a Feminist Artist Network poster about public toilets (usually plastered with stickers, in Seoul) as gendered space. --- In Sulki & Min's projects, borrowed systems are not only given new contexts, but become entirely new languages. In a poster for a Korean musical performance, for example, the designers established a set of symbol, scale, and color variables based on the twelve strings of a gayageum (a traditional Korean instrument), the eight players in a gayageum octet, and the seven pieces constituting the concert. It sounds complex but looks amazing. This is perhaps where the real beauty of Sulki & Min's approach lies. You can be unaware of the intricate underlying system and still be captivated by the work. --- James Goggin

1. Prints, "Functional Typography," self-commissioned, South Korea, 2006. Details from Crabtree & Evelyn body mist, Bic Mini lighter, Apple Power-Book G3 power adapter, and Christian Dior perfume
---
2. Book, *A Revised Inventory of the Curating Degree Zero Archive*, Insa Art Institute, South Korea, 2007
---
3. Exhibition poster, *Toilet Swapping*, Feminist Artist Network, South Korea, 2006
---
4. Poster, gayageum concert by Kho Ji-yeon, Mul Productions, South Korea, 2007
---
5. Festival poster, MODAFE 2005, Ganesa Productions, South Korea, 2005

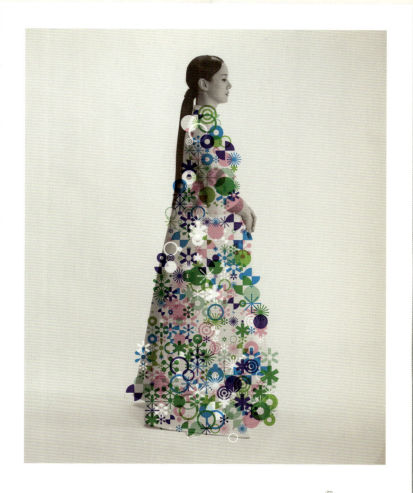

{기포}

4

5

6.	Book cover and spreads, *Our Spot New York* by the artist Sasa, Specter Press, South Korea, 2006. The book appropriates the design of the *Time Out New York* guide that Sasa used during his stay in New York.

7.	Installation, "Office for Archival Reproduction," *Frame Builders* exhibition, Insa Art space, South Korea, 2006. Visitors to the exhibition could make copies of anything in the gallery archives using equipment provided by Sulki & Min.

8.	Magazine cover and spreads, *1/4 Oriëntatie* no. 1, Kunsthuis SYB Gallery, The Netherlands, 2005. Sulki & Min asked members of Kunsthuis to describe buildings in The Netherlands and then identified and photographed buildings in Seoul that matched the descriptions.

9.	Cover and spreads, *Perspecta 35: Building Codes*, Yale School of Architecture, USA, 2004. With Albert Lee

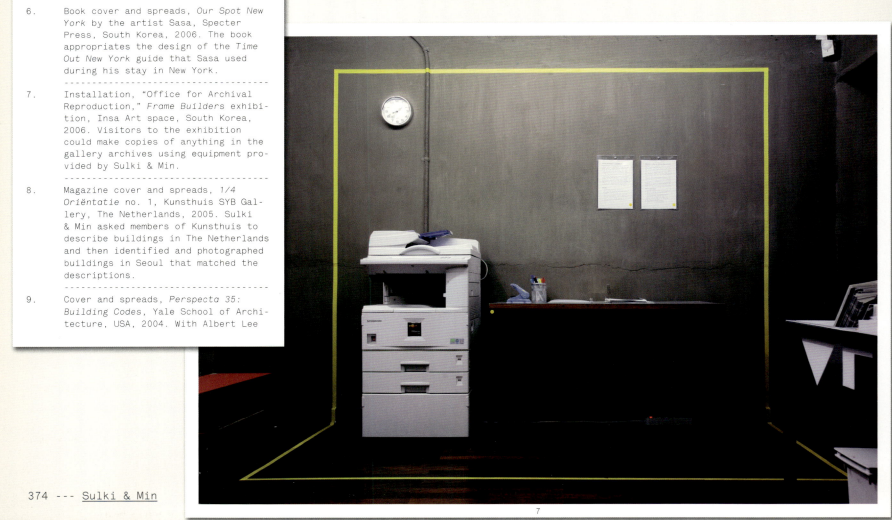

8

9

1.   CD cover, *Wir sind hier* by März,
     März, Germany, 2006
     ----
2.   Poster, *Disko partizani* by Shantel,
     Essay Recordings, Germany, 2007. With
     Maike Truschkowski and Tim Heiler
     ----
3.   Exhibition posters, *Oil* by Isa Gen-
     zken at the German Pavilion in the
     Venice Biennale 2007, German Pavil-
     ion, Germany and Italy, 2007

<u>Surface</u> (Frankfurt).--- Markus Weisbeck, head of
the design studio Surface, belongs in this book,
but I want to make clear that for him, graphic
design is a secondary interest. Although he is
fundamentally a graphic designer, and although his
talent has been evident for years, Weisbeck fig-
ured out early on how to shatter the traditional
boundaries of graphic design by developing a trans-
disciplinary attitude in which music, electronic
media, art, architecture, politics, and graphic
design continually intersect. Editor, collaborator,
and initiator of genre-bending projects, Weisbeck
engages with the content—not just the look—of the
themes he treats. The result is a coherent oeuvre
that has played a major role in the European cultural scene since the 1990s.--- In his posters for
the German Pavilion at the 2007 Venice Biennale,
Weisbeck surpassed the conventional framework
of graphic design by modeling his work completely
on another artist's. The identity he created for
the pavilion added to the power of Isa Genzken's
installation and left the entire city smelling
like oil from the moment the display opened. Markus
Weisbeck's works are multisensory interpretations
of image and typography. They make us stop, listen,
and experience the world anew. --- Ruedi Baur

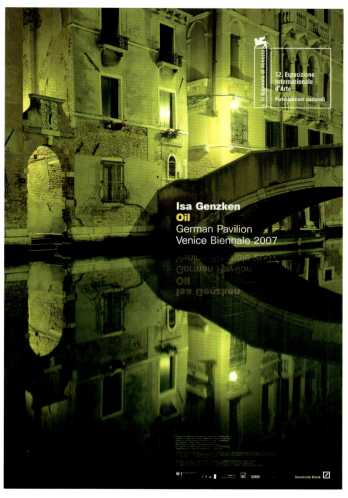

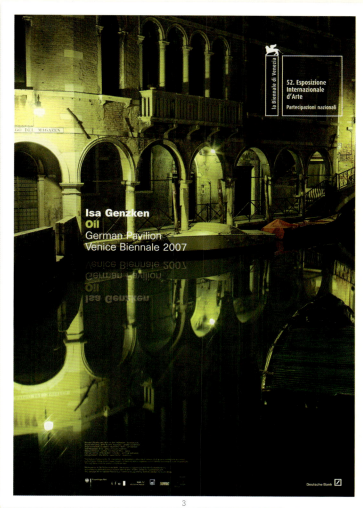

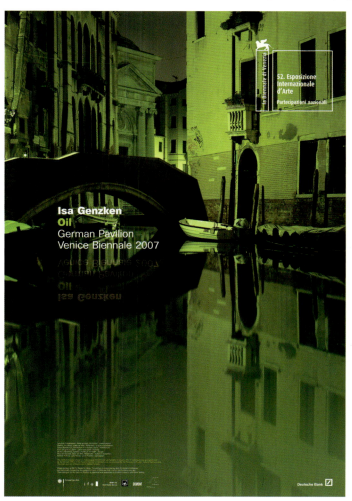

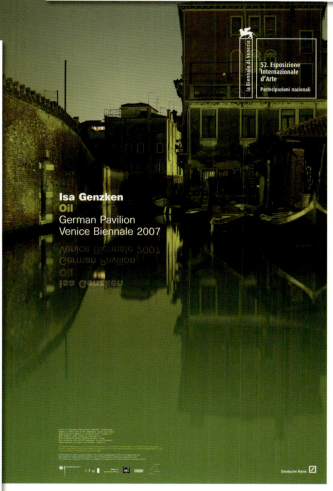

4

4.   Poster, The Forsythe Company 2005-6
       season, The Forsythe Company,
       Germany, 2005

5.   Book, *Adolf Hitler: Reden zur kunst-
       und kulturpolitik 1933-1939* (Adolf
       Hitler: Speeches on Art and Cultural
       Policy 1933-1939), Revolver, Germany,
       2005. Part of Revolver's "Art Propa-
       ganda Documents" series

6.   Book cover, *Daniel Birnbaum: Chronol-
       ogy*, Sternberg Press, Germany, 2007.
       With Indra Häussler

7.   Graphics, "Football/Footfall,"
       William Forsythe, Germany, 2005.

8.   Advertising, Galerie Johann König,
       Galerie Johann König, Germany, 2006

9.   Poem, "Glasball," *Form* magazine,
       Form, Germany, 2007

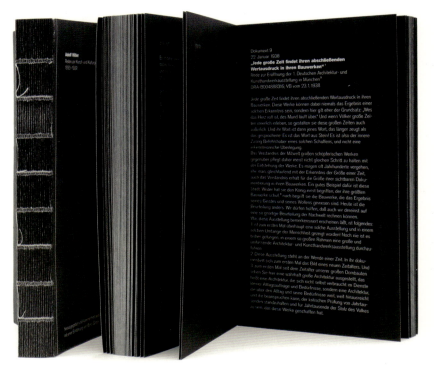

5

Daniel Birnbaum
Chronology

Sternberg Press

6

7

Tue Greenfort, Jeppe Hein, Michaela Meise, Natascha Sadr Haghighian, Johannes Wohnseifer, David Zink Yi, Andreas Zybach, Tue Greenfort, Jeppe Hein, Michaela Meise, Natascha Sadr Haghighian, Johannes Wohnseifer, David Zink Yi, Andreas Zybach, Tue Greenfort, Jeppe Hein, Michaela Meise, Natascha Sadr Haghighian, Johannes Wohnseifer, David Zink Yi, Andreas Zybach, Tue Greenfort, Jeppe Hein, Michaela Meise, Natascha Sadr Haghighian, Johannes Wohnseifer, David Zink Yi, Andreas Zybach, Tue Greenfort, Jeppe Hein, Michaela Meise, Natascha Sadr Haghighian, Johannes Wohnseifer, David Zink Yi, Andreas Zybach, Tue Greenfort, Jeppe Hein, Michaela Meise, Natascha Sadr Haghighian, Johannes Wohnseifer, David Zink Yi, Andreas Zybach, Tue Greenfort, Jeppe Hein, Michaela Meise, Natascha Sadr Haghighian, Johannes Wohnseifer, David Zink Yi, Andreas Zybach, Tue Greenfort, Jeppe Hein, Michaela Meise, Natascha Sadr Haghighian, Johannes Wohnseifer, David Zink Yi, Andreas Zybach, Tue Greenfort, Jeppe Hein, Michaela Meise, Natascha Sadr Haghighian, Johannes Wohnseifer, David Zink Yi, Andreas Zybach, Tue Greenfort, Jeppe Hein, Michaela Meise, Natascha Sadr Haghighian, Johannes Wohnseifer, David Zink Yi, Andreas Zybach, Tue Greenfort, Jeppe Hein, Michaela Meise, Natascha Sadr Haghighian, Johannes Wohnseifer, David Zink Yi, Andreas Zybach, Tue Greenfort, Jeppe Hein, Michaela Meise, Natascha Sadr Haghighian, Johannes Wohnseifer, David Zink Yi, Andreas Zybach, Tue Greenfort, Jeppe Hein, Michaela Meise, Natascha Sadr Haghighian, Johannes Wohnseifer, David Zink Yi, Andreas Zybach, Tue Greenfort, Jeppe Hein, Michaela Meise, Natascha Sadr Haghighian, Johannes Wohnseifer, David Zink Yi, Andreas Zybach, Tue Greenfort, Jeppe Hein, Michaela Meise, Natascha Sadr Haghighian, Johannes Wohnseifer, David Zink Yi, Andreas Zybach, Tue Greenfort, Jeppe Hein, Michaela Meise, Natascha Sadr Haghighian, Johannes Wohnseifer, David Zink Yi, Andreas Zybach, Tue Greenfort, Jeppe Hein, Michaela Meise, Natascha Sadr Haghighian, Johannes Wohnseifer, David Zink Yi, Andreas Zybach, Tue Greenfort, Jeppe Hein, Michaela Meise, Natascha Sadr Haghighian, Johannes Wohnseifer, David Zink Yi, Andreas Zybach, Tue Greenfort, Jeppe Hein, Michaela Meise, Natascha Sadr Haghighian, Johannes Wohnseifer, David Zink Yi, Andreas Zybach, Tue Greenfort, Jeppe Hein, Michaela Meise, Natascha Sadr Haghighian, Johannes Wohnseifer, David Zink Yi, Andreas Zybach

Johann König
Weydingerstrasse 10, 10178 Berlin, Fon 030 / 30 88 26 88
Fax 030 / 30 88 26 90, info@johannkoenig.de, www.johannkoenig.de

8

Ein Glaskörper, kreisrund und in der Größe eines Balles für Kinder, welcher durch seine matte Oberfläche tastungs an wirkt, in seinem Inneren gefüllt mit einem Gas, welches das eigene Gewicht der aus einer italienischen Manufaktur stammenden Arbeit praktisch aufhebt, und es überhaupt möglich macht, wenige Millimeter über dem Boden zu schweben.

9

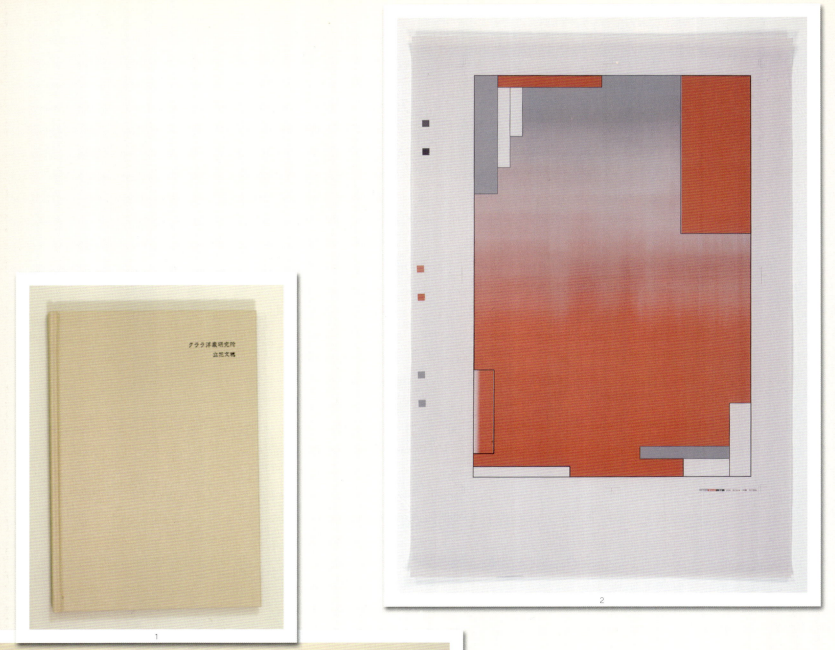

1

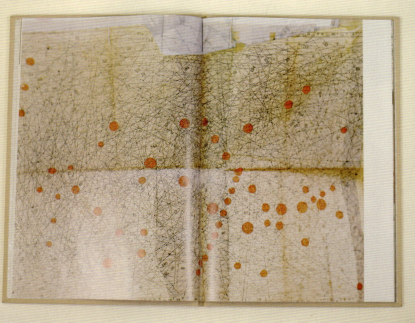

Fumio Tachibana (Tokyo). --- Fumio Tachibana
is unique among his designer contemporaries
because, instead of a computer, he uses a letterpress. Known for his typography and book design,
Tachibana was exposed to the now-archaic art of
letterpress at a young age, while growing up surrounded by paper and ink in a small bookbinding
shop in Hiroshima. --- A love of printing is apparent in Tachibana's early works—mostly jumbled collages of used paper. At first he was interested
in the pieces of paper as mere materials, but
he began to explore each scrap's history and soon
developed a more conceptual understanding of books
and paper. This led to his work in fashion design.
Tachibana found that book covers function similarly to clothing, and he noticed that the Japanese
kanji character for *body* is made up of the characters for *human* and *book*. Tachibana exhibited
these ideas in 2005 in the traveling show *On Conceptual Clothing*. Tachibana's clothes, made out
of book covers, were inspired by a type of paper
made from cloth that he found at a factory in
India. --- Tachibana's later work is subtler and
more minimalist. His solo exhibition at Shiseido
la Beauté in Paris, "L'arbre qui cachait une
incroyable forêt" (I Can See Forests in a Tree),
included a single giant tree made up of many
smaller pieces, each shaped like the kanji character for *tree*. The entire project was a riff on the
character for *forest*, which combines three *tree*
kanji. "SMTWTFS" is a poster series for the exhibition of the same name that repeats a line of
seven letters. The line, which grows looser each
time it is printed, seems to abstract both the
repetitive motion of the printing press itself
and the routine quality of our everyday lives.
--- Tachibana won the Grand Prize at the 21st
International Biennale of Graphic Design in Brno,
and has received awards from both the Member's
Division of the Tokyo Type Directors Club and
the New York Art Directors Club. It is recognition
well deserved for a man who has elevated printing
to the realm of poetry. --- Keiichi Tanaami

1. Book cover and spreads, *Clara/Fumio
    Tachibana*, Burner Bros., Japan, 1999
    ----
2. Poster, self-commissioned, Japan, 2005
    ----
3. Exhibition poster, *Karada* (Body),
    Nadiff, Japan, 1999
    ----
4. Untitled installation, self-commis-
    sioned, Japan, 2000

3

4

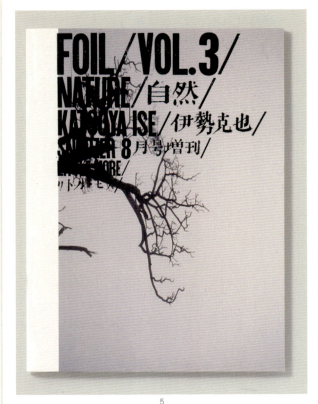

5

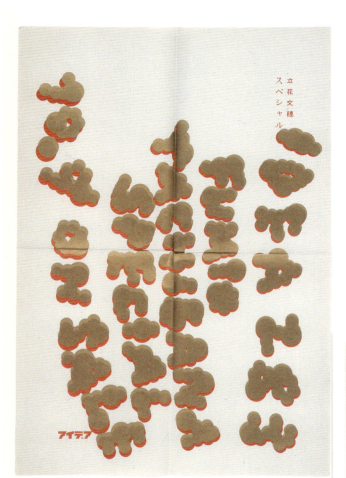

6

5.   Magazine cover and promotional
       poster, *Foil* vol. 3, Little More,
       Japan, 2003
----
6.   Magazine pages and promotional post-
       er, *Idea* no. 283, Seibundo Shinkosha
       Publishing Co., Japan, 2000
----
7.   Exhibition poster, *SMTWTFS*, Azmaya,
       Japan, 2004
----
8.   Installation, "L'arbre qui cachait
       une incroyable forêt" (I Can See
       Forests in a Tree), Shiseido,
       Japan, 2005
----
9.   Calendar, "SMTWTFS06," Azmaya,
       Japan, 2005

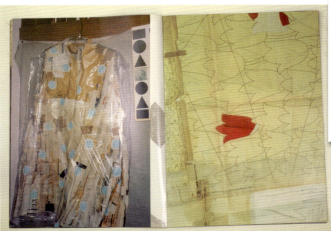

7

8

9

AM RANDE DER ZEIT
MÄNNERWELTEN IM KAUKASUS

Regie: Stefan Tolz
D // 2001 // Farbe // 90 min
Production: Apfelsus Film // SWR / WDR / MDR

DURCH DEN WILDEN KAUKASUS
ERSTER TEIL

Regie: Fritz Pleitgen
D // 2000 // Farbe // 85 min

FILMREIHE BERLIN

DIE LEGENDE DER FESTUNG SURAMI
AMBAWI SURAMIS ZIXISA

Regie: Sergei Paradschanow
UdSSR // 1984 // gOdU // 87 min
IFF Rotterdam 1988, Regisseur der Zukunft

DIE REUE
MONANIEBA

Regie: Tengis Abuladse
UdSSR // 1984 (uraufgeführt 1987) // Farbe // gU // 153 min
Cannes 1987, Großer Spezialpreis der Jury

DIE REISE DES JUNGEN KOMPONISTEN
AXALGASRDA KOMPOSITORIS MOGSAUROBA

Regie: Giorgi Schengelaja
UdSSR // 1984 // Farbe // gOdU // 104 min
Berlinale 1996, Silberner Bär für die beste Regie

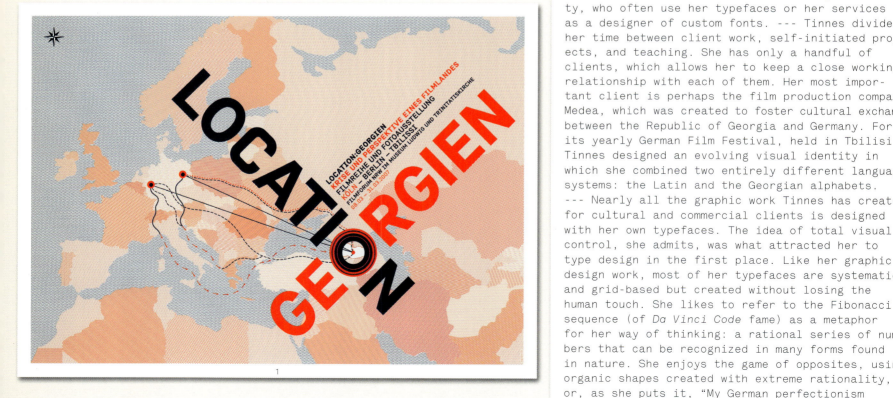

LOCATION GEORGIEN

LOCATION GEORGIEN
KRISE UND PERSPEKTIVE EINES FILMLANDES
FILMREIHE UND FOTOAUSSTELLUNG
KÖLN – BERLIN – TBILISSI
FILMFORUM NRW IM MUSEUM LUDWIG UND TRINITATSKIRCHE
08.03 – 31.03.2007

1

<u>Andrea Tinnes</u> (Berlin).
--- Andrea Tinnes might have become a very efficient designer of corporate identities if she had stayed in Germany. But being a mere problem solver did not satisfy her, and she decided to apply for a scholarship to study at the California Institute of the Arts (CalArts) outside Los Angeles. Some of the things she learned there: There is more to design than problem solving; it is okay to be critical and inquisitive; and designing type is fascinating and fun. Her type-design teacher was Jeffery Keedy, and after graduation she became his assistant. --- Having moved to Berlin in 2000 to found her own one-woman studio, Tinnes is still grateful for what she learned in L.A. "CalArts still informs my definition of design: to combine critical thinking with joyful form-making, to develop an individual voice and style, to reflect history while exploring new ideas, to work independently and cherish spontaneity and effectiveness." She has kept in touch with many people from the CalArts design community, who often use her typefaces or her services as a designer of custom fonts. --- Tinnes divides her time between client work, self-initiated projects, and teaching. She has only a handful of clients, which allows her to keep a close working relationship with each of them. Her most important client is perhaps the film production company Medea, which was created to foster cultural exchange between the Republic of Georgia and Germany. For its yearly German Film Festival, held in Tbilisi, Tinnes designed an evolving visual identity in which she combined two entirely different language systems: the Latin and the Georgian alphabets. --- Nearly all the graphic work Tinnes has created for cultural and commercial clients is designed with her own typefaces. The idea of total visual control, she admits, was what attracted her to type design in the first place. Like her graphic design work, most of her typefaces are systematic and grid-based but created without losing the human touch. She likes to refer to the Fibonacci sequence (of *Da Vinci Code* fame) as a metaphor for her way of thinking: a rational series of numbers that can be recognized in many forms found in nature. She enjoys the game of opposites, using organic shapes created with extreme rationality, or, as she puts it, "My German perfectionism versus the playfulness I picked up in the USA." --- Jan Middendorp

2

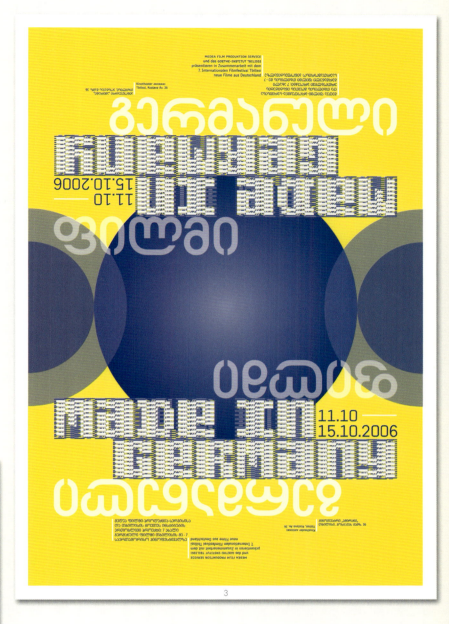

3

1.   Double-sided exhibition poster, *Location: Georgien*, Medea, Germany, 2007
   ----

2.   Posters, Tage des Deutschen films in Tbilisi, Medea, Georgia and Germany, 2002 and 2004
   ----

3.   Poster, Tage des Deutschen films in Tbilisi, Medea, Georgia and Germany, 2006. Received TDC53 Certificate of Typographic Excellence and was exhibited at the 18th International Festival of Posters and Graphic Arts in Chaumont, France, 2007

4

4.   Identity and signage, Merz art and
       design store, Merz, Germany, 2004-5
       ----

5.   Typeface, "TJType Jockey," The Play-
       ground Project, Germany, 2005
       ----

6.   Typeface, Volvox, self-commissioned,
       Germany, 2001. System of five fonts
       that superimpose on one another to
       create ornamental composites
       ----

7.   Poster, Tage des Deutschen films
       in Tbilisi, Medea, Georgia and
       Germany, 2005

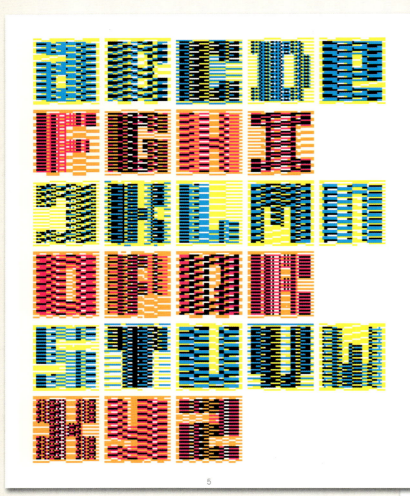

5

6

Toko (Sydney). --- I'd like to start this review by making the rather contentious assumption that although you can take the designer out of The Netherlands, there's no way to take The Netherlands out of the designer. And one has to ask, why would you want to? I mean, the Dutch have it all worked out. Clear, confident, and playful, their contemporary design sensibility seems perfectly balanced against the formalism and structure of a weighty design tradition. For a designer, this combination provides a springboard for very exciting possibilities. I think the Dutch-born, Australia-based design duo Toko is a case in point. --- Michael Lugmayr and Eva Dijkstra met at the St. Joost Academy of Art in Breda, The Netherlands, from which they graduated in 1997 and 1999, respectively. After spending what they refer to as "some quality design time" at Studio Dumbar in The Hague, they made their first big move and relocated to Chicago in 1998. Since officially rubber-stamping their studio with the title Toko in 2003 (the name means "shop" in Dutch slang), the pair has gone on to create work characterized by a strong conceptual approach to the individual demands of each assignment. Toko executes each project with bespoke typography and with eclectic and vibrant color palettes. --- In many ways, Toko's work is a direct reflection of the manner in which Lugmayr and Dijkstra approach life. "We try to stay like a kid," they told me, "not afraid of hurting yourself, free of boundaries and restrictions, and always taking new roads of discovery." When asked what good design signifies for them, their answer was, of course, acutely Dutch: "Good design is the right balance between a good idea and a strong execution." If that's the case, then *eenvoudigweg prachtig werk*, Toko. --- Brett Phillips

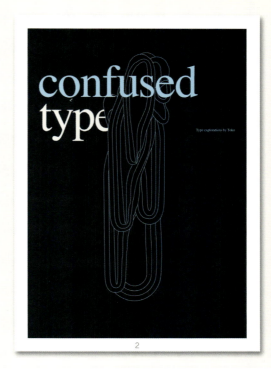

2

1. Poster and card series, "Designed," self-commissioned, Australia, 2007
    ----
2. Book cover and spreads, *Confused Type*, self-commissioned, Australia, 2007

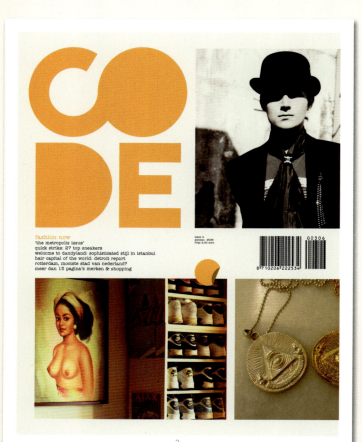

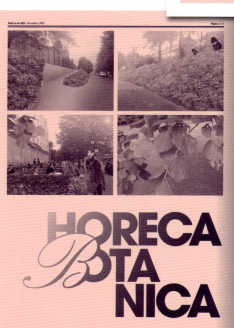

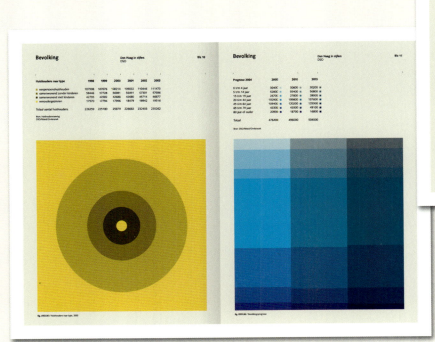

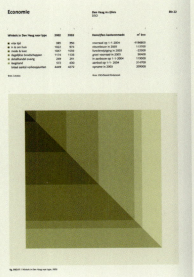

3.   Magazine covers, *Code* nos. 4 and 6,
        Bold Publishing, The Netherlands, 2006

4.   Newspaper, *Duik in de dijk* (Dive
        into the Dike), Stichting BLIKsum,
        The Netherlands, 2005. *Dijk* refers
        to a Rotterdam neighborhood called
        Oostzeedijk.

5.   Publication cover and spreads, *Den
        Haag in cijfers* (The Hague in Facts
        and Figures), DSO, City of The Hague,
        The Netherlands, 2004

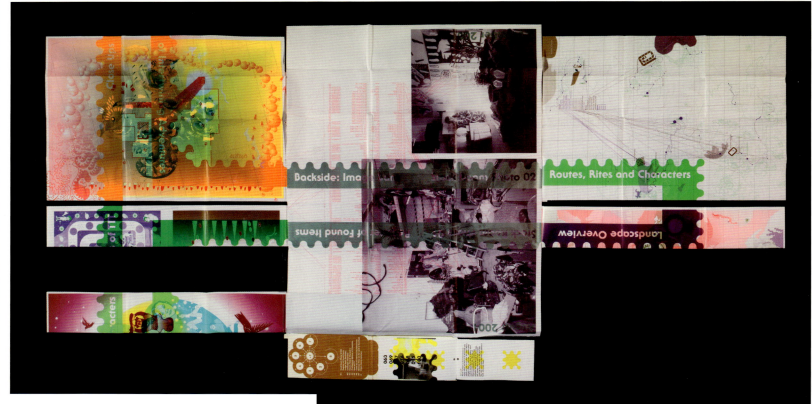

1

2

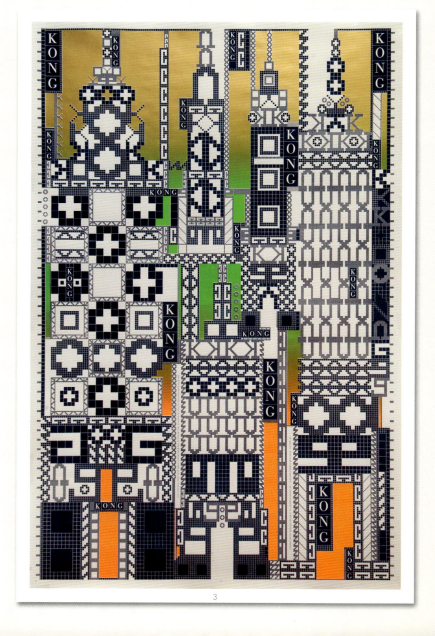

3

1.   Fold-out catalog, "TTT," Jennifer
      Tee, The Netherlands, 2001. With
      Harmen Liemburg
      ----
2.   Promotional poster, CD by Jonus,
      Jonus, The Netherlands, 1999
      ----
3.   Poster, KONG design store, KONG,
      Mexico, 2006
      ----
4.   Promotional poster, Letras Latinas
      Bienal, Mexico, 2006

Typographic Masonry (Amsterdam). --- When Richard
Niessen and Harmen Liemburg started their joint
venture Golden Masters (GM) in 1999, nobody in The
Netherlands was doing what they did. Few designers
were as passionate about form and color, no one
made graphic constructions as dazzling as theirs,
and nobody matched their skills in silk-screening.
The design events they organized were pretty
cool, too (and had the best invitation leaflets).
--- Three years later, when the partnership had
run its course, Niessen and Liemburg embarked on
successful solo careers. While Liemburg's visual
language remained as eclectic as GM's had been,
layering found imagery with exuberant type and
ornament, Niessen's became purer and simpler. He
focused on modular constructions, usually printed
in just two or three colors, emphatically two-
dimensional. After seeing an exhibition dedicated
to Hendrik Th. Wijdeveld, a master of Dutch Art
Deco, Niessen began referring to his own work as
Typographic Masonry. --- An architect by training,
Wijdeveld, who is most famous for editing and
designing the magazine *Wendingen*, used to produce
type and ornament by constructing shapes with
typesetters' brass rules, making the type on
the page look like brick architectural ornaments.
Wijdeveld was an early representative of that
lesser-known Dutch design tradition that revels
in construction, formal complexity, and play, and
that comprises such diverse designers and artists
as M.C. Escher, Jurriaan Schrofer, and Marcel
Wanders. Niessen proudly follows in their foot-
steps. --- Among his most successful works is
an annual report for the Stedelijk Museum in
Amsterdam, for which Niessen designed special patterns to designate each department. He frequently
works with the artist Jennifer Tee, and their
joint projects include an artwork in the council
hall of Amsterdam's South East District and a
communication space for the occupants of a care
center for the elderly, conceived as a post office
with specially designed letterheads, cards, and
envelopes. Niessen's most spectacuar work so far
is "TM-city," an installation he produced in 2007
for the Jesuit Chapel in Chaumont, France, with
his wife, Esther de Vries, and the architect
Raf Snippe. "TM-city" is a modular exhibition
of Niessen's work in the shape of an urban landscape. After Chaumont, "TM-city" will be ready
to travel, while its maker will keep on building.
--- Jan Middendorp

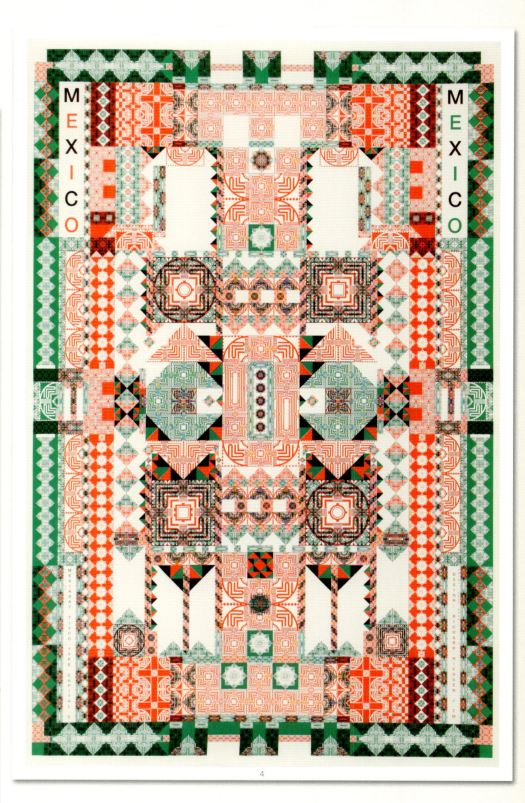

4

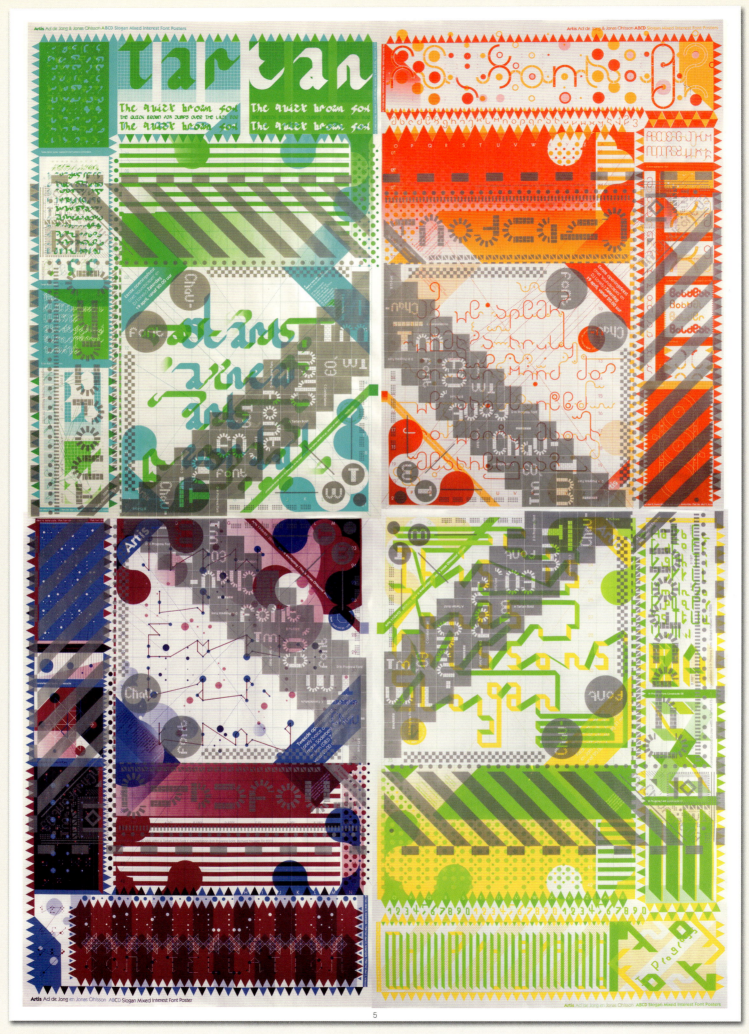

5

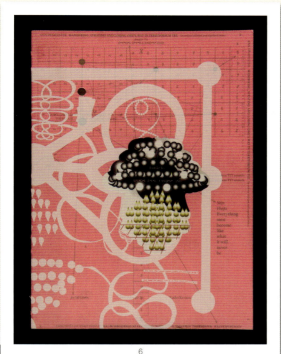

5.   Promotional poster, Jonus, TM, The
     Netherlands, 2003
     ----
6.   Book cover and pages, *Evol Eye
     Lands End*, Jennifer Tee and Artimo,
     The Netherlands, 2004. The book con-
     sists of eight individual booklets,
     randomly bound.
     ----
7.   Poster, Post Office Beatrix, Beatrix
     Care Center, SKOR, The Netherlands,
     2005. The post office is a library
     and social space where residents can
     write and send letters to each other
     and their families. With Gabriel
     Lester and Jennifer Tee

1

Naohiro Ukawa (Tokyo). --- They say a jack of all trades is a master of none, but Naohiro Ukawa is a rare exception. Ukawa is self-taught; he emerged from the first generation of Macintosh users in the late 1980s and is now among the most popular VJs, MCs, record-label owners, event organizers, writers, professors, and contemporary artists in Japan. I call him a creative, all-around designer. He calls himself a "media rapist." --- Never subtle, Ukawa's work reflects the music he loves. His art combines the sensuality of deep house, the regulated experimentation of techno, the chaos of noise, and the stylish cool of punk. As a writer, he is just as provocative. In the statement for his latest solo exhibition, *A Series of Interpreted Catharsis episode2: earthquake*, Ukawa writes, "An earthquake is an explosion, harsh noise without prelude or rehearsal!!!!!" It can be risky to write about earthquakes in a country as prone to them as Japan, especially in a style as outrageous as Ukawa's, but this designer is completely serious. He is even a member of the Japan Society for Natural Disaster Science. --- This sort of lighthearted facade that belies thought-provoking ideas within is common in all of Ukawa's art. "Dr. Toilet's Rapt-Up Clinic" is an installation composed of a block of toilets, surveillance cameras, one-way mirrors, disco lights, and sunglasses. But the work is really a toilet panopticon that examines the boundary between public and private space. --- As his last name, meaning "cosmic river" in Japanese kanji, implies, Ukawa's energy and creativity seem unlimited. He VJs almost every weekend and spends his workweeks meeting deadline after deadline, all the while navigating the whims of the notoriously trendy and fickle Japanese public. Still, Ukawa always manages to create something unexpected, reminding me of my contemporaries in the 1960s performance-art scene. I look forward to the time when Ukawa is finally "discovered" by the world outside Japan, and to seeing what he will have in store for his new audience. --- Keiichi Tanaami

2

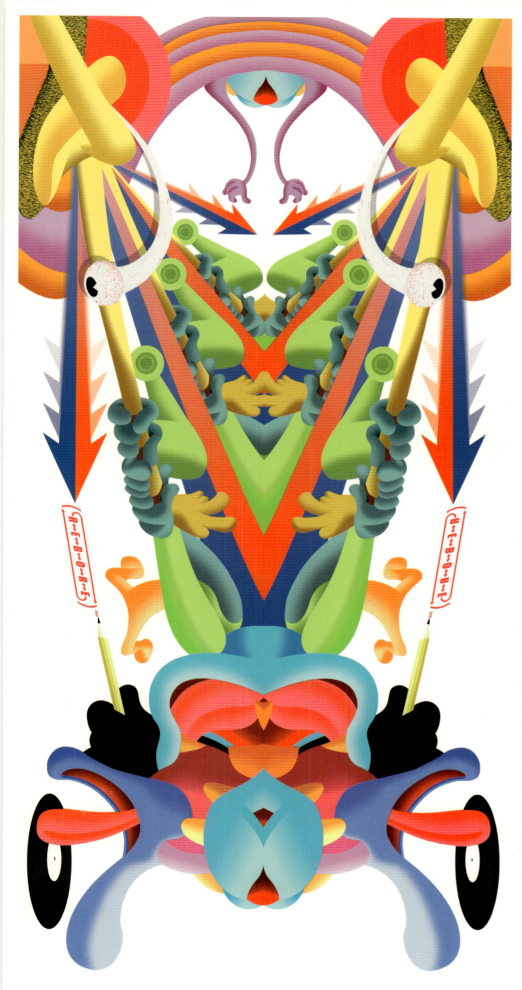

1.   CD covers, Mom/N/Dad Records,
      Japan, 2002-3
      ----
2.   Promotional graphic, Turbosonic
      Boom-Box store, Japan, 2003
      ----
3.   Promotional poster, *Rebore* by Bore-
      doms, Warner Music, Japan, 2004
      ----
4.   Illustration, "Super Ego Burger,"
      self-commissioned, Japan, 2002

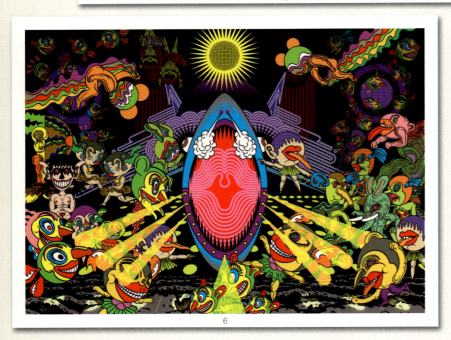

5.   Illustration, "Dani and Mari," VHS,
Japan, 2005
----
6.   Party poster, "Terror Jaws," self-
commissioned, 2004
----
7.   Illustration, "Gundam," self-
commissioned, 2005

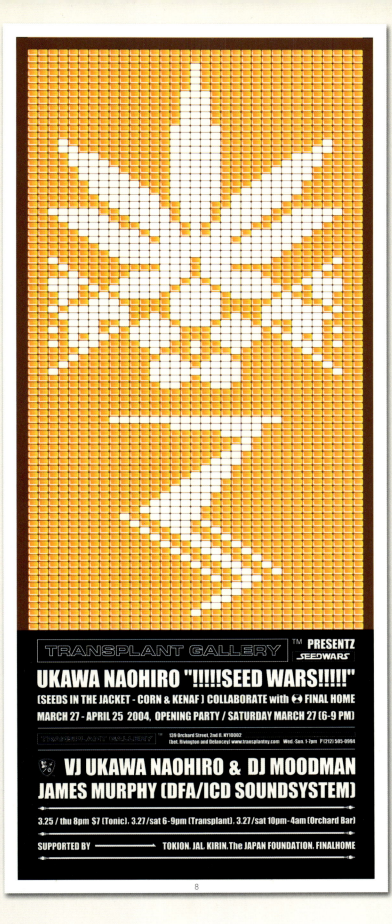

8. Exhibition poster, *!!!!!SEED WARS!!!!!*, Transplant Gallery, USA, 2004

----

9. CD cover, *Party People*, Mom/N/Dad Records, Japan, 2006

----

10. Illustration, "Project Gothic," VHS, Japan, 2004

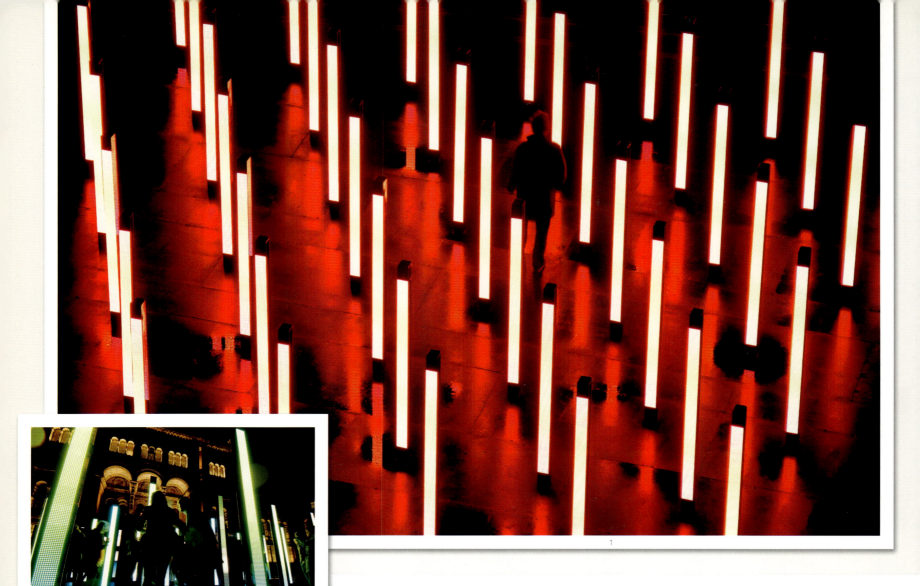

1

1.   Installation, "Volume" at the Victoria and Albert Museum, Sony Playstation and the Victoria and Albert Museum, UK, 2006-7

----

2.   Music video, "To the Music" by Colder, Output Recordings, UK, 2006

United Visual Artists (London). --- While the
phrase *fiat lux* provided the name for an obscure
British band (similar to Depeche Mode) swanning
around in the 1980s, and was later hijacked by
a controversial cult of some five hundred members
based in Switzerland, its typical meaning (translated from Latin) is "let there be light." Let
there be light, United Visual Artists (UVA), and
plenty of it! --- I stumbled upon UVA with a combination of sheer paranoia and a desire to search
out everything new and inspiring in this world,
and seeing the group's work for the first time
made me feel sick and useless. I mean, what have
we graphic designers been *doing* all these years?
Pursuing movement and seduction by pushing around
Pantone color chips—or even worse, concerning ourselves with static baseline grids in hopes that
they will deliver salvation? Could it be that the
modes of communication we have rallied behind so
fiercely fail to compare to the sheer romance of
electromagnetic radiation and frequencies of light?
If so, UVA is in a very good position to take over
the new world of design with little resistance.
--- UVA blends art direction, software engineering, and set design to create what they call
"real-time, immersive, and responsive experiences." The group builds its surprising work out of
existing technologies, treating LEDs, traditional
lighting, and projection systems as sculptural
elements. To me, however, UVA's work is much more
than the sum of its parts. In it, I see the possibilities for graphic design. I see the potential
to inform the methods and modes by which design
practice and process evolve. One only has to look
at "Echo," their installation in Tate Modern's
Turbine Hall, to find a new collaborative design
language already under development. UVA's work
is seductive, textured, layered, and well crafted,
and the elusive romance of movement that "traditional" graphic design pursues through other means
seeps effortlessly through every photon and wave-
length. --- Perhaps a great practice, in time,
is defined by the audience's desire for more,
its need to see where and how far things can go.
If indeed this is the case, then *fiat lux*, UVA.
--- Brett Phillips

2

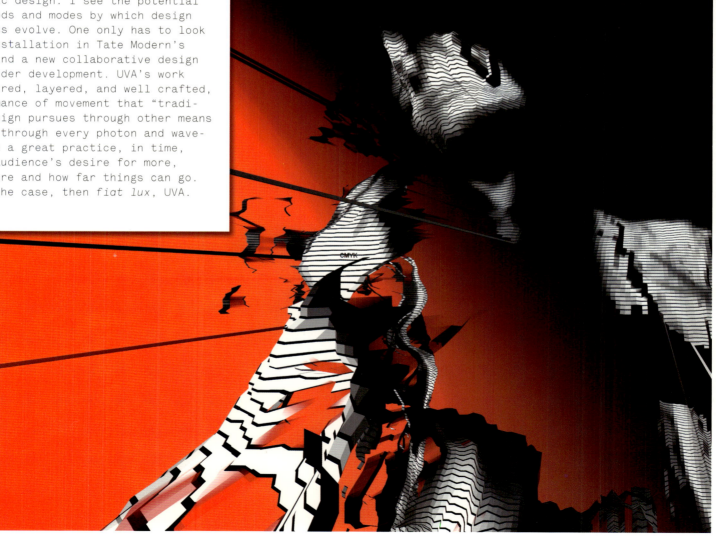

3

4

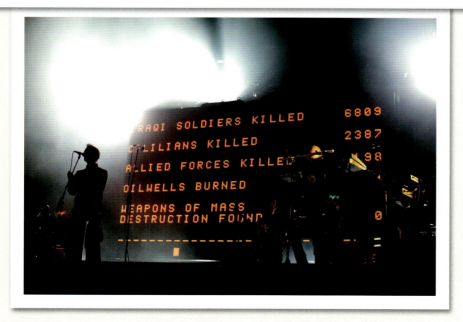

3.   Installation prototype, Storeage
       design agency, The Netherlands, 2006
----
4.   Installation, Kabaret's Prophecy
       nightclub, UK, 2004-7
----
5.   Stage design, Massive Attack's "100th
       Window World Tour," Massive Attack,
       international, 2002-3

1

2

3

Yokoland (Oslo). --- When I first visited
Yokoland, I liked it there. The name sounded
intriguing and reminded me of places I loved from
childhood literature: Astrid Lindgren's world in
Mio my Mio, Michael Ende's *Lummerland*, and Nordic
fairytales. --- Yokoland fulfilled my expecta-
tions. The studio's world is a colorful contemporary graphic fairytale. You're surrounded by hand-
cut cardboard shapes collaged with type and photographs, while darting Lego pieces carry numbers
and messages. Computer keys jump from the keyboard
and go walking through the woods at night; hand-
drawn characters mix with cutouts of photographs;
and when you look sideways, balloons and diamonds
fall from the sky. --- Mixing Pop art with surre-
alistic collages, illustrations, toys, and lettering, Yokoland's handcrafted mixed-media approach
counters today's predominantly digital works of
graphic design. --- When Espen Friberg and Aslak
Gurholt Rønsen started working together under the
name *Yokoland* in high school, they had no intention of founding a design studio; they just
"started collaborating on a few projects." At the
time they did not use the computer much, but they
painted, drew, and collaged together. Later on,
when incorporating the use of the computer in
their work, they maintained the same technique
of working "on top of each other." --- Aslak and
Espen designed the first covers for a friend's
record label, Metronomicon Audio, before going
to college. While at the National Academy of the
Arts in Oslo, they began working at the label,
and it remains an important project for them even
today. --- Yokoland was influenced by Norwegian
musician, illustrator, graphic designer, and
artist Kim Hiorthøy. Aslak and Espen also credit
the *Sampler* books and the writings of Adrian
Shaughnessy for introducing them to graphic
design, and—as alternative music was their starting point—they admire the work of Robert Pollard.
--- It is a bit fairytale-like to have a monograph
published before your professional career begins,
so maybe it's fitting that a group as unconven-
tionally creative as Yokoland has just that. Their
self-titled book is filled with personal projects,
covers, and posters for Metronomicon Audio, in
addition to several projects for friends. Since
the book's release, the pair has gradually grown
to become a real studio: Thomas Nordby joined as
a third partner, and new, client-based projects
continue to push their work in all kinds of direc-
tions. I'm eager to visit Yokoland again and see
what's new there. --- Julia Hasting

1.   Illustration, *Fabrik* magazine,
        Fabrik, Sweden, 2006

2-3.   Exhibition posters, *Under the Bushes,
        Under the Stars*, Reg Vardy Gallery,
        UK, 2007
        ----
4.   CD poster, *When the Clouds Clear* by
        Charlie Alex March, Lo Recordings/
        LOAF, 2006. With Non-Format

5

5. CD packaging, *Did You Order a Radar?*
    by Magnus Moriarty vs. Center of the
    Universe and *Sky-Fi Beatitude* by
    Magnus Moriarty, Metronomicon Audio,
    Norway, 2005
    -
6. CD packaging, *3.0 compilation*,
    Metronomicon Audio, Norway, 2006.
    Photography by Morten Spaberg
    -
7. CD packaging, *My Fashion Statement Is
    Scrambled Eggs* by Koppen, Metronomi-
    con Audio, Norway, 2005

6

7

8

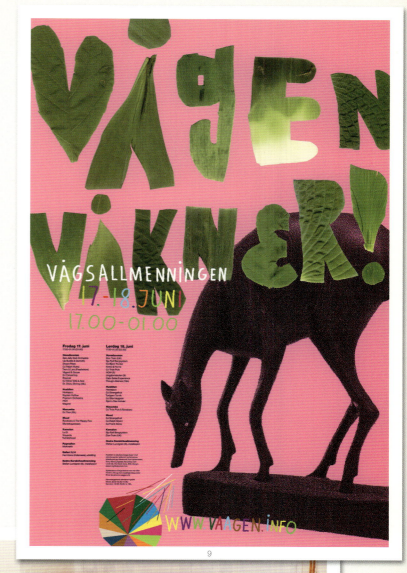

9

10

11

8.   CD cover, *The Great American Brain-killer* by Täppas Strepens, Metronomi-con Audio, Norway, 2005

---

9.   Festival poster, *Vågen Våkner!*, Vågen Våkner, Norway, 2005

---

10. Exhibition poster, *The Remix Project*, Sørlandet Art Museum, Norway, 2006

---

11. CD cover, *Staying Up All Night with the Center of the Universe* by Center of the Universe, Metronomicon Audio, Norway, 2003

10 Design Classics
----
410 --- *De Unie* by J.J.P. Oud
411 --- *Turks Fruit* by Jan Vermeulen
412 --- *Formosa* by Enzo Mari
413 --- *Nella nebbia di Milano* by Bruno Munari
414 --- *La lutte continue* by Jan van Toorn
415 --- *Mask* by Bradbury Thompson
416 --- *Posters* by Alexander Rodchenko
417 --- *Is It In* by Peter Palombi
418 --- *Het Nederlandse affiche* by Wim Crouwel
419 --- *Akarui ankoku* by Tsunehisa Kimura

De Unie (J.J.P. Oud). --- De Unie restaurant, built in Rotterdam in 1925, embodies my own attitude toward design. There is a joy of experimentation evident in this project—an expression of the time when the avant-garde was not yet governed by universal models or constrained by global visual uniformity. --- De Unie stands out in its precision. It is marked by its relationship to its surroundings, by the harmony that it achieves between intention and reality, and by the freedom of its form. Above all, De Unie remains exceptional and unique, rather than a stock solution to be imitated and reproduced. --- The restaurant is remarkable in part because it was born out of the chaotic interdisciplinary exchanges that symbolized the early-twentieth-century avant-garde movement. The plan for the De Unie dealt simultaneously with questions of art, architecture, and design. This approach required the work of a unified team that refused to accommodate the weaker notions put forth by the kind of cautious and unimaginative strategists who try to regulate the visual world. With this process built into its design, De Unie is nothing short of an ode to the steadfast individualism that is so often replaced by standardized, interchangeable, and frequently less interesting design. --- Ruedi Baur

Turks Fruit (Jan Vermeulen).---When I had to read literature in high school, I always chose books by Jan Wolkers. I didn't know a thing about the author; I picked the books solely because of their covers. --- In the 1960s new things were happening in art and pop culture, but book design was still dusty and old-fashioned. Jan Vermeulen's covers for Wolkers, designed between 1961 and 1983, were revolutionary. They are all striking, but the cover for *Turks Fruit*, from 1969, is the most famous. It has heavy, condensed type in green and red with a drop shadow, centered on a black background. For me, though, it means much more. This cover marks my first acquaintance with both graphic design and avant-garde literature. With its contrasting fluorescent colors, a cover like this is hard to hide, and my parents were not amused that I was reading what they called a "vulgar" book. --- Besides being a typographer, Jan Vermeulen was also a publisher, teacher, and poet. A true man of letters, he thoroughly understood the *content* of the books he designed and was able to translate that content into graphics. Wolkers's success depended in large part on these expressive covers, and it's not surprising that he had Vermeulen design all of his books. --- Irma Boom

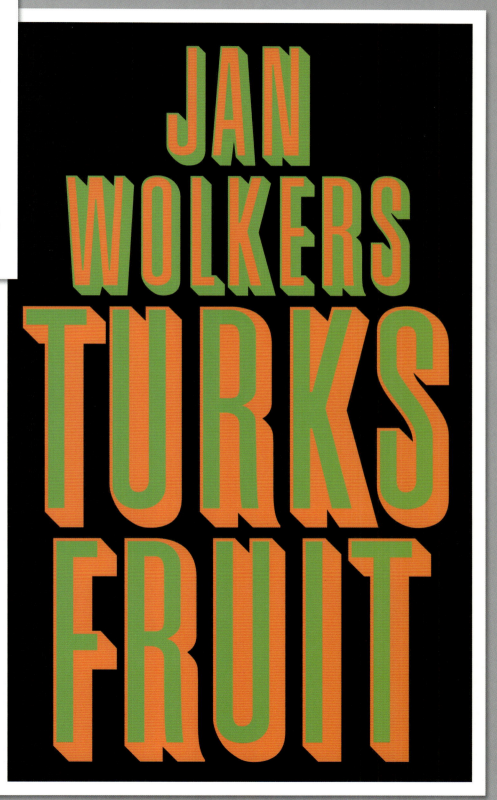

Formosa (Enzo Mari). --- The Italian artist and designer Enzo Mari is known for his products and furniture. But like many of his contemporaries, such as Bruno Munari, Robin Day, and Charles and Ray Eames, he was also accomplished in related fields, particularly graphic design. Mari defined visual communication as "the elimination of the superfluous," and he aimed at conveying a maximum amount of information with a minimum of elements. --- His 1962 Formosa perpetual calendar is both his best-known product and his best piece of graphic design. Where many graphic designers succumb to superfluous decoration, Mari is tied to objectivity and function, and this calendar is elegant in its economy. It is made of black anodized aluminum and white PVC cards lithographed with bright red Helvetica letters and numbers. Timeless both in design and function, the PVC cards are endlessly configurable by the user, year after year. --- When the Formosa was released, Mari participated in a group show of technical art in Milan. Umberto Eco called the work there "programmed art," and this might be the perfect description of the Formosa: a piece of programmed art that functions only by engaging its user in a daily physical experience of the perpetual march of time. --- James Goggin

Nella nebbia di Milano (Bruno Munari). --- We all love using tracing paper to elevate type or imagery to a different level, to overlay one piece of information with another, or to collage two elements with a filter. In his book *Nella nebbia di Milano*, Bruno Munari uses the material in a unique way: as an illustrative element. The tracing paper itself becomes the medium—it is the "mist" in his story. --- This intuitive idea communicates in a poetic way the short, magical journey through the misty streets of a city. In turning the pages of fragile tracing paper, the reader encounters black silhouettes of city traffic, signage, people, and a bird. The pages turn slowly, and we explore surprising little details and events in this calm setting. Step by step we approach the circus, as colors and lights become more and more apparent and the mist rises. On arrival, a very colorful, thicker paper stock juxtaposes with the previously calm setting and underlines the loud, joyful dynamic of the faster-paced performances in the circus. Abstract die-cut shapes change in meaning and link one level of information to the next. On the way home, tracing paper again sets the mood for a beautiful misty park at night. Silence— we hear only the night bird sing. --- Munari's choice of materials, drawings, and typography is spontaneous, light, unquestionable, natural, poetic, and sensational. Applause! --- Julia Hasting

La lutte continue (Jan van Toorn). --- Born in
Tiel, The Netherlands, in 1932, Jan van Toorn is
a designer who mobilizes visual form in ways both
personal and public. Through his roles as a prac-
titioner, educator, writer, and design leader, he
has sharpened the intelligence of our collective
visual discourse. --- In "La lutte continue" (The
Fight Continues), his ideas converge. Published
in 1989 to commemorate the bicentennial of the
French Declaration of Human Rights, this poster
employs diverse design strategies to convey both
the universality and the particularity of human
experience. Van Toorn mixes hand-drawn imagery
with photographs textured by the video grain of
mass media. Scraps of paper radiate like energy
from the central handshake. The layers of type
and image seem casual and thrown together at first
glance, but this is an illusion. Each juxtaposition
has been crafted to build the overall visual concept and political message of the piece. --- Using
cut-and-paste techniques and photomechanical processes, van Toorn makes his own hand present in
his work, not to assert his ego but to emphasize
the manufactured character of human expression.
Jan van Toorn will not let us forget that there
is no neutral typography, no neutral media, and
no neutral voice. --- Ellen Lupton

Quick as a wink,
a typeface can express the
creative mood and spirit of a
photographic idea printed
on fine paper.

Printed by letterpress
on Sterling Letterpress Enamel,
25 x 38 - 80.

4184

WESTVACO

Mask (Bradbury Thompson). --- Bradbury Thompson
taught graphic design at the Yale School of Art,
where I got my MFA in 1985. I studied under such
design luminaries as Paul Rand, Armin Hoffmann,
and Alvin Eisenman, but of all these great designers and teachers, Thompson made the greatest
impact—not only on my work, but on my life in
general. Devoid of any ego whatsoever, Bradbury
Thompson was the gentle giant of graphic design—a
true American original. --- "Mask," printed in *Look*
magazine in 1958, was number 210 in the Westvaco
"Inspiration" ad series. I can safely say that this
is the piece that opened my eyes to the illustrative possibilities of type and led me to choose
typography as my area of specialization. Thompson
was a father figure to all his students, and so
it is no surprise that the idea for this piece
came from a drawing by his six-year-old daughter
of a large face, with her first printed words in
its mouth. --- In 1984 my classmates and I bought
autographed copies of Thompson's *Washburn College
Bible* (a limited-edition publication—fewer than
four hundred copies were printed). I looked at
it again the other day and shed a tear of joy.
It dawned on me that I am indeed very fortunate
to have studied under such a legend, and to own
this masterpiece. --- Saki Mafundikwa

Posters (Alexander Rodchenko). --- The story of
my appreciation for Alexander Rodchenko is a very
personal one. In 1982, while living in Italy, I
saw a performance by the Swedish theater company
Shahrazad. Full of vivid images and fast action,
it told the story of the revolutionary Russian
theater director Vsevolod Meyerhold and his fall
from grace following Stalin's rise to power. Many
scenes in the play referred directly to Constructivist imagery, such as the shouting young woman
on Rodchenko's famous poster advertising "Lengiz—
Books in All Branches of Knowledge." Not only did
I end up organizing the production's tour of The
Netherlands, but I was also alerted to a body of
graphic work—an entire genre—about which I had known
little up to then. --- My favorite of Rodchenko's
posters is the one advertising rubber teats, probably because it's so bizarre. The poet Vladimir
Mayakovsky wrote the text: "Our pacifiers are
the best. They remain so soft and flexible that
you can keep sucking on them until you reach old
age." Rodchenko and Mayakovsky collaborated on
dozens, maybe hundreds, of projects. They invented
a new and direct form of advertising for the young
nation's state-owned companies, creating agitprop
posters and book covers. I often wonder if their
passionate, over-the-top slogans were pure expressions of revolutionary enthusiasm, or if there
was a hint of irony about them—and, if so, whether
the proletariat got it. Curiously, this particular
poster was originally produced by hand, as a single
copy, to be displayed in a shop window. It wasn't
printed until 1961, after having been restored by
Rodchenko's daughter. --- Graphic design as we know
it today can be traced back to a few specific places
where it was first defined. Rodchenko's work is
certainly one of those places. --- Jan Middendorp

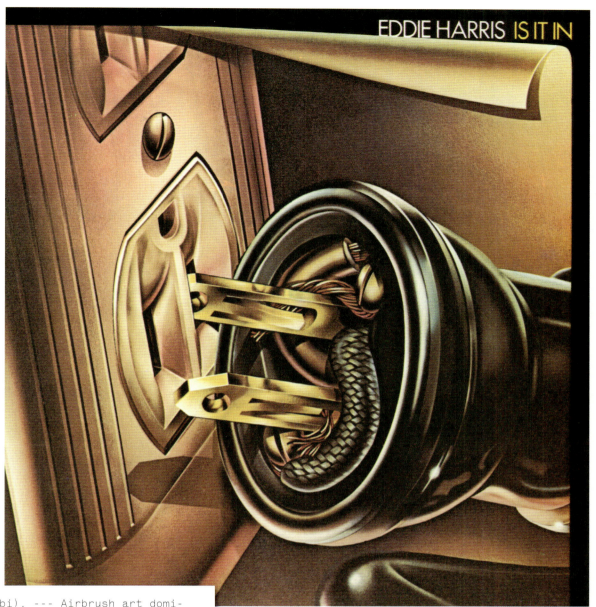

Is It In (Peter Palombi). --- Airbrush art domi-
nated the visual landscape of 1970s America. Its
high-sheen surfaces and curvaceous, oversexed
forms reflected the coked-out, sexed-up '70s
(and signaled the end of the gentler '60s and that
decade's "big idea" design boom). The '70s were
all image, all surface, all the time. No piece
of design is more representative of the era than
airbrush giant Peter Palombi's cover for elec-
tric saxophonist Eddie Harris's record Is It In.
--- The album's title came out of a conversation
the two men had about sex, and Palombi's nervous
question of his first partner, "Is it in?" Palombi,
following the mode of easy metaphor often used
in airbrush art (and commercial illustration in
general), created the image of a plug being insert-
ed into an electrical outlet, its mechanics drawn
to look as organic as possible and its destination
purposefully colored to resemble female genitalia.
The plug and the outlet are hyperrealistic (as all
airbrush art is), as if seen in a dream or on a
cocaine binge. And so, in one fell swoop, Palombi
combines the "electricity" of Harris's music,
the sex and sex appeal of a honking and crooning
saxophone, and, of course, the visceral, stop-you-
in-your-tracks power of a brilliantly perverse and
meticulously rendered image. --- Dan Nadel

het nederlandse affiche 1890-1968

museum fodor amsterdam
keizersgracht 609
12 oktober t m 10 november 1968
zonnehof amersfoort
16 november t m 15 december 1968

Het Nederlandse affiche (Wim Crouwel). --- I sat and thought for weeks about what I could possibly write about Wim Crouwel that could have any impact on you in the context of the work shown here, or more rightly in the context of all he has done since graduating from Academie Minerva in 1949. I scribbled note after note on his unwavering commitment to experimentation, typographic innovation, and research—that is, until I reread his 1977 book *Typography* and realized that my hope of summing up Crouwel was in vain. In it, Crouwel writes, "The designer, with his awareness of and appreciation for the contemporary cultural atmosphere, is inclined to use overstatement to emphasize his findings." --- It would not be an overstatement to recall Crouwel's enormous contributions or to speak about the nuances of his work, but the reality is that you have to take time to study it in the flesh, to engage with it, and to understand its context to truly appreciate its power. Crouwel has contributed as much to the world of design outside his Dutch borders as he has within them. His work is simply timeless—if not from the future—and it is for this reason that our generation of designers should be humbled and grateful. --- Brett Phillips

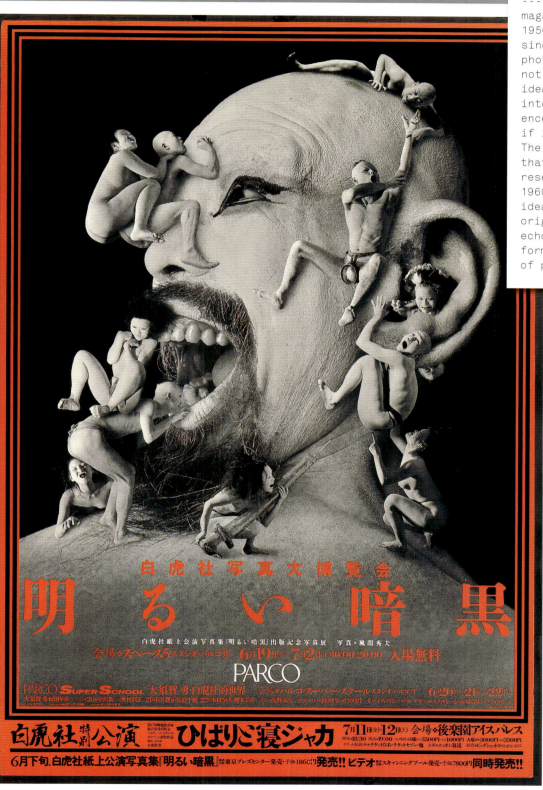

Akarui ankoku (Tsunehisa Kimura). --- A man, laughing out loud, his face in profile and painted white, swarmed by dancers from Ankoku Butoh (the Dance of Utter Darkness). No one needs a deeper explanation to appreciate this work, but it may come as a surprise that it was created in 1985 using entirely analog techniques. Whereas Dadaists and Surrealists used photomontage as a tool for criticism, Tsunehisa Kimura's work has a pure visual intensity that makes an imprint on the viewer's mind as powerfully as any "real" image. --- Inspired as a teenager by avant-garde design magazines, Kimura became a graphic designer in the 1950s and has consistently worked in photomontage since the 1960s. He is the only master of Japanese photomontage in the postwar era, and though he may not have any direct successors, the techniques and ideas of photomontage itself have percolated down into Japanese digital culture. --- Kimura's influence on younger generations is undeniable, even if it takes place on a mostly subconscious level. The images of the collapse of urban civilization that are seen today in films and comics clearly resemble ideas that Kimura first expressed in the 1960s. But, like Japan's appropriation of Kimura's ideas, the practice of photomontage nullifies the original's dominant position over its copies. This echoes what Kimura himself explained about the art form: It is an activity that asks for the approval of pluralism from monists. --- Keiichi Tanaami

100 Graphic Designers
- -
Biographies

Index
- -

A Practice For Everyday Life Kristy Carter, Emma Thomas, Stephen Osman. Live and work in London education Royal College of Art, London; Nagoya University of Arts, Nagoya; University of Brighton (KC) --- Royal College of Art, London; Camberwell College of Arts, London (ET) --- 2003-6 Central Saint Martins College of Art and Design, London (SO) practice 2003-present APFEL; 2003-present lecturer, Ruskin School of Fine Art, Oxford, and Camberwell College of Arts, London (KC) --- 2003-present APFEL; 2003-present lecturer, London College of Communication and Camberwell College of Arts, London (ET) --- 2007-present APFEL; 2007-present lecturer, Camberwell College of Arts, London (SO) selected projects 2004-7 exhibitions and publications, Institute of Contemporary Art, London --- 2005 redesign, Architects' Journal --- 2007 identity, Performa Art Biennial, New York selected bibliography 2007 "European Design Annual 2007," Print magazine --- 2006 "The Graphics Gurus," Wallpaper magazine --- 2006 "Design Profile," Grafik magazine --- 2005 "Showcase," Creative Review --- 2004 "Show Talent," Design Week --- 2001 "The Revolution Will Be Homogenised," I.D. magazine selected exhibitions 2007 Print-Run, Kemistry Gallery, London --- 2006 Work from Mars, Moravian Gallery, Brno --- 2005 The Village Fête, Victoria and Albert Museum, London --- 2003 Creative Futures, Selfridges Window Display and Menier Chocolate Factory, London awards 2006 Best Magazine and Newspaper Redesign nomination, D&AD

Antoine+Manuel Antoine Audiau and Manuel Warosz. Live and work in Paris education Atelier Letellier, Paris (AA) --- École Nationale Supérieure des Arts Décoratifs, Paris (MW) practice 1993-present Antoine+Manuel (AA, MW) selected projects 2007 furniture collection, Edith --- 2005-7 posters, Centre National de Danse Contemporaine --- 2002-7 catalogs, Christian Lacroix --- 2003-6 wall stickers, Domestic --- 2000-6 posters, Collection Lambert selected bibliography 2006 Wallpaper, Laurence King, London --- 2006 Serialize, Die Gestalten Verlag, Berlin --- 2006 "Antoine+Manuel," Ppaper magazine --- 2006 "Graphic Dreamers," Form magazine --- 2005 Antoine+Manuel, Pyramyd, Paris selected exhibitions 2007 Paysage, Galeries Lafayette Maison, Paris --- 2007 Happy Living, Museum of Tomorrow, Taipei --- 2007 Impressions Françaises, International Festival of Posters and Graphic Arts, Chaumont --- 2006 Domestic, Colette, Paris --- 2006 100 Affiches Contemporaines Françaises, Festival d'Échirolles, Grenoble, France

Tarek Atrissi born Beirut. Lives and works in Hilversum, The Netherlands education School of Visual Arts, New York --- Utrecht School of the Arts --- American University of Beirut practice Tarek Atrissi Design --- arabictypography.com selected projects typeface, Asian Games --- identity, nation of Qatar --- identity, Al-Ghad newspaper --- typeface, Jordan Satellite Television awards 2005 Twenty under Thirty, Print magazine --- 2003 Aquent Design Award --- 2003 Type Directors Club Award --- 2002 Adobe Design Achievement Award

Marian Bantjes born 1963, Edmonton, Alberta, Canada. Lives and works on Bowen Island, British Columbia practice 2003-present freelance design --- 1993-2003 owner, Digitopolis Media, Vancouver --- 1983-93 Hartley & Marks Publishers/Typeworks selected projects 2007-8 fabric design, Anni Kuan --- 2007 identity, "Want It!" campaign, Saks Fifth Avenue --- 2007 book cover, Bruce Mau Design selected bibliography 2007 Becoming a Digital Designer, Wiley, New York --- 2007 "Creativity Column," Communication Arts magazine --- 2007 New Village Type, Watson-Guptill, New York --- 2006 Look at This, Laurence King, London --- 2005 Eye magazine selected exhibitions 2006 Global Edit, Salon del Mobile, Milan --- 2006 Spoken with Eyes, Sacramento Art Directors and Artists Club, UC Davis Design Museum, Sacramento, California memberships 2001 Society of Graphic Designers of Canada

Barbara Says António Silveira Gomes, born 1971, South Africa. Lives and works in Lisbon education 1992-97 Faculdade de Belas Artes da Universidade de Lisboa --- 1991-92 Witwatersrand Technikon, Johannesburg --- 1990-91 Joubert Park Technical College, Johannesburg selected projects 2006-7 advertising, Cinema Portugal, Instituto do Cinema Audiovisual e Multimedia --- 2005-7 advertising, Zé dos Bois Gallery, Lisbon --- 2005 exhibition catalog, Portuguese Architecture, Venice Architecture Biennale, Instituto das Artes, Lisbon --- 2004 conference poster, Portuguese Architects Guild, Lisbon selected bibliography 2006 What Is Graphic Design For?, RotoVision, London --- 2006 Barbara Says, Pyramyd, Paris --- 2006 "Barbara Says pour un Graphisme Portugais," Étapes 137, Pyramyd, Paris selected exhibitions 2007 Lahti International Poster Biennial, Lahti Poster Museum, Lahti, Finland --- 2007 Tehran International Poster Biennial, Tehran Museum of Contemporary Art, Tehran --- 2006 175X120: Uma Exposição de Catazes de Rua, Silo Espaço Cultural, Oporto, Portugal --- 2005 China International Poster Biennial, China Academy of Art, Hangzhou --- 2005 International Festival of Posters and Graphic Arts, Chaumont

Big Active Gerard Saint, Mat Maitland, Richard Andrews, Markus Karlsson. Live and work in London selected bibliography 2005 Head, Heart and Hips: The Seductive World of Big Active, Die Gestalten Verlag, Berlin --- 2002 Big Active, Design Exchange/GAS Books, London awards 2007 Yellow Pencil, D&AD

Peter Bilak lives and works in The Hague
education Jan van Eyck Academie, Maastricht
--- Atelier National de Création Typographique,
Paris --- Academy of Fine Arts and Design,
Bratislava practice editorial board, *Deleatur*
and *DeSignUm* magazines --- Studio Dumbar, The
Hague --- art director, BBDO Bratislava, Bratislava
--- lecturer, Royal Academy of Art, The Hague, and
Art Academy Arnhem selected projects type design,
FontShop International --- art direction, *Dot Dot
Dot* magazine --- 2001 poster, Split Summer Festival,
Croatia --- 2000-1 posters, Pulchri Studio, The
Hague selected bibliography 2004 *Dutch Type*,
010 Publishers, Rotterdam --- 2003 *Deep Sites:
Intelligent Innovation in Contemporary Web Design*,
Thames & Hudson, London and New York --- 2003 *Type
Design*, Collins Design, New York --- 2003 "New
Visual Artist Review," *Print* magazine --- 2002
"Peter Bilak: The Patron of Free-Spirited Design,"
Design magazine --- 2000 "The I.D. Forty," *I.D.*
magazine selected exhibitions 2002 *postscript:
zur Form von Schrift heute*, Vienna --- 2001 Seoul
Typography Biennale, Seoul --- 2000 International
Biennale of Graphic Design, Brno awards 2000
Deutscher Preis für Kommunikationdesign --- 1999
Best Book Design, The Netherlands --- 1998 National
Design Award, Slovak Design Center --- 1996
Winner, Adobe International Design Competition
memberships Art Directors Club, The Netherlands

Laurenz Brunner born 1980, Zurich. Lives and works
in Amsterdam and Zurich education 2004-5 Gerrit
Rietveld Academie, Amsterdam --- 2003-4 Central
Saint Martins College of Art and Design, London
selected projects 2007 art direction, Kunst Halle
Sankt Gallen, St. Gallen, Switzerland --- 2007
book, *Casco Issues X: The Great Method*, Casco,
Office for Art, Design and Theory, Utrecht
--- 2005-present art direction, Casco, Office for
Art, Design and Theory, Utrecht --- 2005-present
design, *Tate ETC.* magazine --- 2006 exhibition
design, *Translated Works: Barbara Visser*, Museum
De Paviljoens, Almere, The Netherlands --- 2006
exhibition catalog, *Le Nouveau Siècle*, Museum Van
Loon, Amsterdam selected bibliography 2006 *Swiss
Federal Design Awards*, Birkhäuser, Basel --- 2005
Type One: Discipline and Progress in Typography,
Die Gestalten Verlag, Berlin --- "Graphic Design
Today," *Idea* magazine selected exhibitions
2007 *It's OK to Make Mistakes*, Riviera Gallery,
New York --- 2007 *Juriert Prämiert*, Museum fur
Gestaltung, Zurich --- 2005 *Start*, Gallery Fons
Welters, Amsterdam awards 2006 Swiss Federal
Design Award --- 2005 Albert Klijn Prize, Gerrit
Rietveld Academie memberships 2004 Lineto

Julia Born born 1975, Zurich. Lives and works
in Amsterdam education 1996-2000 Gerrit Rietveld
Academie, Amsterdam selected projects 2007 book,
Casco Issues X: The Great Method, Casco, Office
for Art, Design and Theory, Utrecht --- 2005-pres-
ent art direction, *Metropolis M* magazine --- 2006
exhibition catalog, *Le Nouveau Siècle*, Museum
Van Loon, Amsterdam --- 2006 exhibition identity,
Kunstszene 2004, Zurich --- 2003 exhibition cata-
log, *Link: Municipal Acquisitions 2003*, Stedelijk
Museum, Amsterdam selected bibliography 2007
"Travail du livre," *Étapes* magazine --- 2006
"The Conditions of Graphic Design," *Idea* magazine
--- 2005 *Dutch Resource: Collaborative Exercises
in Graphic Design*, Valiz, Amsterdam --- 2004
Mark: Municipal Art Acquisitions, Stedelijk Museum,
Amsterdam --- 2003 *Swiss Design 2003*, Birkhäuser,
Basel selected exhibitions 2007 *Forms of Inquiry:
The Architecture of Critical Graphic Design*,
Architectural Association, London --- 2006 *Graphic
Design in the White Cube*, International Biennale
of Graphic Design in Brno --- 2005 *Dutch Resource*,
International Festival of Posters and Graphic
Arts, Chaumont --- 2004 *Mark: Municipal Art
Acquisitions*, Stedelijk Museum, Amsterdam awards
2007 Swiss Federal Design Award --- 2005 De Best
Verzorgde Boeken, The Netherlands --- 2004 Die
Schönsten Schweizer Bücher, Switzerland --- 2003
Swiss Federal Design Award --- 2000 Frans de Jong
Pris, The Hague

Build Michael C. Place, born 1969, North
Yorkshire, UK. Lives and works in London education
Newcastle College --- York College practice
2001-present Build --- 1992-2000 The Designers
Republic, Sheffield --- 1990-92 Bite IT, London
selected projects 2007 exhibition identity,
50, Blanka and Candy, London --- 2007 CD covers,
Simple Records, London --- 2006 book, *Promo One*,
Timothy Saccenti, New York --- 2005 CD covers,
London Electrics, London --- T-shirt series,
"Time'Code," Blanka selected bibliography 2007
"A Month in the Life of...a Graphic Designer,"
Creative Review --- 2007 "Fifteen Degrees of
Separation," *IdN* magazine --- 2007 "Build: Brain
Aided Design," *Cyclic Defrost* magazine --- 2006
"Build It and They Will Come," *SOMA* magazine
--- 2004 "Consultancy Profile," *Grafik* magazine
selected exhibitions 2007 *On/Off*, 5 Cromwell
Place, London --- 2007 *Two Faced: The Changing
Face of Portraiture*, COSH Gallery, London --- 2007
Refill 07, MTV Gallery, Sydney --- 2006 *1: An
Exhibition in Mono*, SEA Gallery, London --- 2006
A Nice Set, IdN Space, Hong Kong --- 2004 *Building
Print With Love*, Magma Books, Manchester --- 2003
Offline Computerlove, Maison du Spectacle-la
Bellone, Brussels

Büro Uebele Andreas Uebele, born 1960, Faurndau, Kreis Göppingen, Germany; Rebecca Benz, born 1978, Friedrichshafen, Germany; Katrin Dittmann, born 1975, Heilbronn, Germany; Beate Gerner, born 1978, Heilbronn, Germany; Gerd Häußler, born 1974, Ulm; Katrin Häfner, born 1980, Stuttgart; Silke Sabow, born 1978, Köln. Live and work in Stuttgart practice 1996-present, Büro Uebele; 1998-present professor, Düsseldorf University of Applied Sciences; 1991-95 designer, Behnisch & Partner Architects, Stuttgart; 1987-90 designer, HG Merz Architekten und Museums-Gestalter, Stuttgart (AU) --- 2006-present Büro Uebele; 2005-6 Schwarz-Gruppe, Stuttgart (RB) --- 2002-present Büro Uebele; 2005-7 professor, Mittweida University of Applied Sciences (KD) --- 2003-present Büro Uebele; 2002 designer, Breuninger, Ludwigsburg; 2000 Projektgruppe Informationsarchitektur und Visuelle Kommunikation, Ludwigsburg (BG) --- 2002-present Büro Uebele; 1999 designer, Jean-Benoit Levy and Trafic Grafic, Basel (GH) --- 2007-present Büro Uebele; 2006 Medienformer gmbh, Stuttgart; 2005 Daimler Chrysler AG, Stuttgart (KH) --- 2007-present, Büro Uebele (SS) selected projects 2007 catalog, Bree, Isernhagen, Germany --- 2007 signage, Projektgesellschaft Neue Messe, Stuttgart --- 2006 identity, Evangelischen Stiftung Alsterdorf, Hamburg --- 2006 signage, Pappas car dealership, Salzburg, Germany --- 2004 signage, Osnabrück University of Applied Sciences, Osnabrück --- 2002 signage, DGF Stoess AG, Eberbach, Germany selected bibliography 2006 Orientierungssysteme un Signaletik, Hermann Schmidt Mainz, Mainz; 2003 Weg Zeichen: My Type of Place, Hermann Schmidt Mainz, Mainz; 1999 Schrift im Raum: Visuelle Kommunikation und Architektur, Hermann Schmidt Mainz, Mainz (AU) selected exhibitions 2006 Ball im Kopf/Kult ums Kicken, Museum fur Kunst und Gewerbe, Hamburg --- 2006 Type Zero, Design Center, Stuttgart --- 2005 Briefhüllen, Galerie Spektrum, Goppingen, Germany awards Annual Award, Tokyo Type Directors Club --- Certificate of Typographic Excellence, New York Type Directors Club --- Silver Award, D&AD --- Red Dot Award for Communications Design memberships 2005 German Design Council; 2002 New York Art Directors Club; 2002 Tokyo Type Directors Club; 2002 Art Directors Club Deutschland (AU)

Catalogtree Daniel Gross, born 1973, Hamburg; Joris Maltha, born 1974, Nijmegen, The Netherlands. Live and work in Arnhem education Werkplaats Typografie, Arnhem, The Netherlands (DG, JM) selected projects 2007 infographics, New York Times Magazine --- 2007 infographics, Architect magazine --- 2006 website, Museum Kurhaus Kleve --- 2006 website, VMX Architects selected bibliography 2006 "I.D. Forty," I.D. magazine --- 2006 "Conditions of Graphic Design," Idea magazine --- 2006 Serialize, Die Gestalten Verlag, Berlin --- 2006 "Figures on Speed," Form magazine

Theseus Chan born 1961. Lives and works in Singapore education 1986 Nannyang Academy of Fine Arts, Singapore practice 1996-present WORK, Singapore selected projects 2007 identity, Pedder Red, Pedder Group, Hong Kong --- 2007 design, Pedderzine magazine, Pedder Group, Hong Kong --- 2007 exhibition design, Adidas Original Black and White Collection, Adidas Originals --- 2007 exhibition design, WERK, Ginza Graphic Gallery, Tokyo --- 2007 design, Guerrillazine magazine selected bibliography 2006 "Showcase: Pick of the Year 2006," Grafik magazine --- 2007 "Kraft-werker of the Perfect Imperfect," Special Effects --- 2006 "Creator's Work and Soul," AXIS magazine selected exhibitions 2006 Megazine, Visionaire Gallery, New York --- 2002 WERK: Exhibition, Clun 21 Gallery, Singapore awards 2007 HKDA Award, Hong Kong Designers Association --- 2004-7 British Design and Art Direction Award, D&DA --- 2006 Designer of the Year, President's Design Award, Singapore --- 2000-6 The Gong Show, Singapore Creative Circle Award --- 2005 LAUS award, ADG-FAD, Spanish Art Directors and Graphic Designers Association --- 2001 Art Directors Club Award, New York Art Directors Club --- 2001 British Design and Art Direction award, D&AD

Thomas Buxó lives and works in Amsterdam practice lecturer, Willem de Kooning Academie, Rotterdam selected projects 2004 installation, "Jane," Dutch Foundation for Art and Public Space, with Martine Stig --- 2002-4 performance series, "La Cinca," The Netherlands --- book, De Eroev van Jeruzalem by Sophie Calle, Uitgeverij 1001, Amsterdam --- book, Material World 2, Birkhäuser, Basel, with Sarah Infanger --- book, Open, SKOR, Amsterdam, with Klaartje van Eijk

Change Is Good Rik Bas Backer, born 1967, Amsterdam; José Albergaria, born 1970, the Azores. Live and work in Paris education Art School of Arnhem, The Netherlands (RBB) --- Art School of Lisbon (JA) practice 2001-present Change Is Good (RBB, JA) --- 1995-2000 freelance design (RBB) --- designer, Barbara Says (JA) selected projects 2004 poster, International Festival of Posters and Graphic Arts, Chaumont selected exhibitions 2007 X-Change Is Good: Nogent/More-gens, Bernard Anthonioz Art House, Nogent-sur-Marne --- 2006 Ideas Strasbourg, Chaufferie, Strasbourg

Deanne Cheuk born Perth, Australia. Lives and works in New York education 1992-94 Curtin University, Perth, Australia selected projects 2007 identity, American Rag Cie, Tokyo --- 2006-7 identity, Sue Stemp --- 2006, illustrations, *Fader* magazine --- 2006 illustrations, *Nippon Vogue* --- 2004 book, *Mushroom Girls Virus* selected bibliography 2006 *Neighborhood*, Rinzen, New Farm, Australia --- 2006 *Zoom In Zoom Out*, Viction:ary, Hong Kong --- 2006 *Blk/Mrkt One*, Blk/Mrkt, Los Angeles --- 2006 *The Picture Book*, Laurence King, London --- 2006 *Remastered*, Die Gestalten Verlag, Berlin selected exhibitions 2007 *Leaf Pirate Girls*, American Rag Cie, Tokyo --- 2006 *Felt Tip*, SEA Gallery, London --- 2006 *Enfant Terrible*, Monster Children Gallery, Sydney --- 2006 *BMG Artists Annual*, Blk/Mrkt Gallery, Los Angeles --- 2005 *Carry On*, Feigen Contemporary, New York awards 2004 Young Guns, New York Art Directors Club memberships 2000 New York Art Directors Club --- 2005 Society of Print Desigrers

Cristina Chiappini born 1967, Rome. Lives and works in Rome and Treviso education 1986-91 Instituto Europeo di Design, Rome practice 1989-present freelance design --- 2004-6 professor, University of Rome --- 2003-6 lecturer, University of Treviso selected projects book chapter, "Roses of Flesh, Spines of Light," *Red, Wine, and Green* --- 2002 calendar, Texao --- website, maxdesign.it --- website, Toomotion Group --- website, Stefania Carrera --- website, AIDOS selected bibliography 2006 *The Anatomy of Design*, Rockport, Beverly, Massachusetts --- 2005 "10th European Annual," *Print* magazine --- 2004 *Red, Wine, and Green*, Venice --- 2003 "Design Index," *ADI* magazine selected exhibitions 2004 *The Forms of the Digital*, MiArt Milano, Italy --- 2002 *New Italian Graphic Designers*, Galleria Contemporaneo, Mestre, Italy --- 1998 *Percorsi*, Raddolta Gallery, Rome awards 2004 Certificate of Excellence, Canadian Web Awards --- 2004 Certificate of Excellence, Italian Ministry for Innovation and Technology

Brian Chippendale born 1973. Lives and works in Providence education Rhode Island School of Design practice 1994-present drummer, Lightning Bolt --- 1995 founder, Fort Thunder, Providence selected projects 2007 *Maggots*, PictureBox, New York --- 2006 *Ninja*, PictureBox, New York --- 1995-present posters, Fort Thunder, Providence

Peter Cho born 1976, Pennsylvania. Lives and works in Los Angeles education 2003-5 University of California, Los Angeles --- 1997-99 Media Laboratory, Massachusetts Institute of Technology, Cambridge, Massachusetts practice 2000-present Peter Cho Studio, Los Angeles --- 2006-7 Agency:Collective, San Francisco --- 1999-2000 Imaginary Forces, Los Angeles selected projects 2006-7 exhibition signage, Santa Monica Museum of Art --- 2006-7 identity, Massachusetts Institute of Technology's Committee on Campus Race Relations --- 2005 identity, University of California, San Diego Visual Arts Department --- 2004 design, Samsung Cyber Brand Showcase, Samsung, Time Warner Center, New York --- 2001 exhibition design, Asia Society, New York selected bibliography 2004 "Dynamic Typography: Past, Present, and Future," *Creative Code: Aesthetics + Computation*, Thames & Hudson, London and New York --- 1998 "Digital Typography," *Formdiskurs* journal selected exhibitions 2006 *Object Lessons*, Gigantic Art Space, New York --- 2005 *Takeluma*, Telic Gallery, Los Angeles --- 2002 *Tokyo Type Directors Club Exhibition*, Ginza Graphic Gallery, Tokyo --- 2000 *TypoJanchi*, Seoul Typography Biennale, Seoul Arts Center Design Gallery, Seoul --- 2000 *Print on Screen*, ARS Electronica, Linz, Austria awards 2004 Honorable Mention in Net Art, Prix ARS Electronica --- 2002 Interactive Design Award, Tokyo Type Directors Club ---2002 Silver Medal, New York Art Directors Club --- 2000 "New Visual Artists Review," *Print* Magazine --- 1998 Gold Award, *I.D.* magazine Interactive Media Review

Cobbenhagen & Hendriksen Marijke Cobbenhagen, born 1978, Amsterdam; Chantal Hendriksen, born 1978, Deft, The Netherlands. Live and work in Amsterdam education 2003-5 Werkplaats Typografie, Arnhem, The Netherlands; 1998-2002 Gerrit Rietveld Academy, Amsterdam (CH) --- 2002-4 Werkplaats Typografie, Arnhem, The Netherlands; 1997-2001 School of the Arts Utrecht (MC)

Paul Cox born 1959, Paris. Lives and works in Paris selected projects 2006 stage design, "Amoveo" ballet, Opéra Garnier, France --- 2005 stage and costume design, "Nutcracker," Grand Théâtre de Genève, Geneva --- book, *Cependant...: le livre le plus court du monde (Nevertheless...: the shortest book in the world)*, Le Seuil, Paris selected exhibitions 2007 *Méthode*, Lux, Scène nationale de Valence --- 2006 *Picture Elements*, Centre de création pour l'enfance, Tinqueux --- 2006 *Jeu de construction*, Casina di Raffaello, Villa Borghese, Rome --- 2006 *La force de l'art*, Grand Palais, Paris --- 2006 *Open 20*, Artothèque de Caen --- 2005 *Paul Cox*, Gallery G8, Tokyo --- 2005 *Voyage en Zigzag (Hommage à Rodolphe Töpffer)*, Bâtiment des Forces Motrices, Geneva --- 2005 *Projection*, Galerie District, Marseille --- 2004 *1 mur, 9 tables & 53416 objets*, Musée de l'Objet-École d'art, Blois --- 2003 *The Ganzfeld (unbound)*, Adam Baumgold Gallery, New York --- 1999 *Le Langage des Fleurs*, Le salon d'Art, Bruxelles --- 1999 *Carte du Tendre Perpétuel*, Galerie Franck Bordas, Paris awards 2003 Bourse de Création du Centre National du Livre memberships 2003 Alliance Graphique Internationale

Vanessa van Dam born 1971, Amsterdam. Lives
and works in Amsterdam education 1991-96 Gerrit
Rietveld Academie, Amsterdam practice 1996-
present freelance design selected projects 2007
catalog, De Nederlandsche Bank art collection,
De Nederlandsche Bank --- 2006 book, *Any Resem-
blance to Existing Persons Is Purely Coincidental*,
Revolver, Frankfurt, with Martine Stig --- 2005
book, *Getting the Picture*, Museum Jan Cunen
--- 2005 book, *Dat Museum is een Mijnheer: de
Geschiedenis van het Van Abbemuseum 1936-2003*,
Artimo --- 2004 poster series, Hedah Center for
Contemporary Art Maastricht selected bibliography
2007 "Any Resemblance to Existing Persons Is
Purely Coincidental," *FOAM* magazine --- 2004 *False
Flat: Why Dutch Design Is So Good*, Phaidon Press,
London and New York --- 2002 "Vanessa van Dam:
ruimte voor ruis," *Items* magazine --- 2001 *New
Design Amsterdam*, Rockport, Beverly, Massachusetts
--- 2001 *Apples and Oranges: Best Dutch Graphic
Design*, BIS, Amsterdam selected exhibitions 2007
En Passant, Center for Visual Art, Dordrecht, The
Netherlands --- 2006 *Any Resemblance to Existing
Persons Is Purely Coincidental*, Motive Gallery,
Amsterdam --- 2002 *Roadshow Dutch Graphic Design*,
American Institute of Graphic Arts and Design
Center Stuttgart, New York and Stuttgart --- 1999
Mode(s) d'Emploi, Fonds BKVB, Amsterdam awards
2006 Best Book Design

Sara De Bondt born 1977, Leuven, Belgium. Lives
and works in London education Hogeschool Sint-
Lukas, Brussels --- Jan van Eyck Academie,
Maastricht --- Universidad de Bellas Artes,
Granada, Spain practice Foundation 33, London
selected projects 2006-present identity, Wiels
Contemporary Art Center, Brussels --- 2007 exhibi-
tion catalog and graphics, Victoria and Albert
Museum, London --- 2007 catalog, *Book Works*,
London --- 2007 exhibition identity, *Contour
2007, The Biennial for Video Art*, Mechelen,
Belgium --- 2004-present exhibition guides,
Camden Arts Centre, London selected bibliography
2007 *Wiels: The Birth of a Visual Identity*,
Wiels, Brussels --- 2007 *Grafik* magazine
--- 2006 *Serialize*, Die Gestalten Verlag, Berlin
--- 2007 *Design 360* magazine --- 2006 *Idea* maga-
zine selected exhibitions 2007 *150 Years of the
Victoria and Albert Museum*, Victoria and Albert
Museum, London --- 2007 *The House Number Project*,
The Martin Frostner Foundation, Stockholm
--- 2007 *My Favorite Game*, Ithaca Public Art
Gallery, Athens and Ithaca, Greece --- 2006 *A
Visual Identity for Wiels*, Wiels Contemporary Art
Center, Brussels --- 2005 *The Free Library*, Riviera
Gallery, New York, and Space 1026, Philadelphia

Dexter Sinister David Reinfurt and Stuart
Bailey. Live and work in New York education
Yale University, New Haven; University of North
Carolina (DR) --- Werkplaats Typographie, Arnhem;
University of Reading (SB) practice 2006-present
Dexter Sinister, New York, founder, O-R-G design
studio, New York; professor, Columbia University,
New York, and Rhode Island School of Design (DR)
--- 2006-present Dexter Sinister, New York; 2000
founder, *Dot Dot Dot* magazine; professor, Parsons
The New School for Design, New York, and Pasadena
Arts Center, Pasadena (SB) selected projects
2006-present Just-In-Time Workshop and Occasional
Bookstore, New York selected exhibitions 2007
*Forms of Inquiry: The Architecture of Critical
Graphic Design*, Architectural Association, London
--- 2007 *Hektor Meets Dexter Sinister*, Swiss
Institute, New York --- 2007 *On the Future of
Art School*, STORE Gallery, London

Bob van Dijk born 1967, The Hague education Royal
Academy of Art, The Hague practice 2001-present
NLXL --- 2000-present Bob van Dijk Studio
--- 1992-2000 Studio Dumbar selected projects
advertising, Coke Side of Life campaign, Coca-Cola
--- 2002 advertising, Hewlett-Packard --- posters,
JetLag nightclub --- 1996 design, Dutch Euro coin
awards 1996 Dutch Design Prize memberships
Alliance Graphique Internationale

Arem Duplessis lives and works in New York
education 1994-96 Pratt Institute, New York
--- 1989-93 Hampton University, Hampton, Virginia
practice 2004-present art director, *New York Times
Magazine* --- 2002-4 design director, *Spin* magazine --- 1999-2001 design director, *GQ* magazine
--- 1998-99 art director, *Blaze* magazine selected
projects 2005-6 catalogs, Anthropologie --- 2002-3
design consultant, *Essence* magazine --- 2002
design consultant, Tishman Speyer/Rockefeller
Center --- 2000-1 redesign, *Honey* magazine and
Heart & Soul magazine selected bibliography
2007 *The Art Directors Annual*, RotoVision, London
--- 2007 *SPD 42*, Society of Publication Designers,
Gloucester, Massachusetts --- 2007 *AIGA 27*, AIGA
Annual Design Competition, New York --- 2005
Becoming a Graphic Designer, John Wiley & Sons,
Hoboken, New Jersey --- 2001 *Magazine Design That
Works: Secrets for Successful Magazine Design*,
Rockport, Beverly, Massachusetts awards 2007
Gold Medal, The Society of Publication Designers
--- 2007 Typography 28, The Annual of the Type
Directors Club --- 2007 Distinctive Merit,
The Art Directors Annual --- 2007 Gold Medal,
Society of Newspaper Designers memberships
American Institute of Graphic Arts --- Society
of Publication Designers --- New York Type
Directors Club --- New York Art Directors Club

<u>Enlightenment</u> Hiro Sugiyama, born 1962, Tokyo; Akiyoshi Mishima, born 1978, Osaka; Shigeru Suzuki, born 1979, Saitama, Japan; Kaname Yamaguchi, born 1979, Iwate, Japan. Live and work in Tokyo <u>education</u> 1982-86 Toyo Institute of Art and Design (HS) --- 1997-2000 Osaka Communication Arts School (AM) --- 1998-2002 Toyo Institute of Art and Design (SS) --- 2002-4 Toyo Institute of Art and Design (KY) <u>practice</u> 1997-present founder, Enlightenment; 1990-97 Flamingo Studio (HS) <u>selected projects</u> 2007 VJ, m-flo tour, Avex, Japan <u>selected bibliography</u> 2005 *Lie of Mirror*, self-published --- 2005 *Complete Display Box Set*, self-published --- 2003 *Both Sides*, self-published --- 2000 *2-Delight*, self-published <u>selected exhibitions</u> 2007 *The Borderline*, Hiromi Yoshii Gallery, Tokyo --- 2007 *The Armory Show*, New York --- 2006 *Entrance to Another World*, Diage, Shanghai --- 2006 *After the Reality*, Deitch Projects, New York --- 2006 *Organized by 163*, AAA Gallery, Paris

<u>EYE</u> EYE Yamataka, born 1964. Lives and works in Nara, Japan <u>practice</u> 1996-present singer, Boredoms <u>selected projects</u> 2007 CD cover, *Super Roots*, Shock City --- 2007 T-shirts, Boredoms --- 2006 vinyl sleeve, *OOIOO*, Jetset Records --- 2005 poster, Boredoms <u>selected bibliography</u> 2006 *Ongaloo*, Little More, Tokyo --- 2005 *Weoem*, Pam Books, Tokyo --- 1986 *Nanoo*, Little More, Tokyo <u>selected exhibitions</u> 2006 *Magical Art Room*, Tokyo --- 2005 *Ongaloo*, Kyoto and New York --- 1996 *Nanoo*, Parco Gallery, Tokyo

<u>Stephen Farell</u> born 1968. Lives and works in Chicago <u>education</u> 1987-91 Ohio State University <u>practice</u> 1991-present, principal and creative director, slipstudios --- 1993-present contributor, Digital Type Foundry --- 1999-present chair and associate professor, School of the Art Institute of Chicago <u>selected bibliography</u> 2004 *VAS: An Opera in Flatland*, University of Chicago Press, Chicago --- 2003 "Evolutionary Tales," *Eye* magazine --- 2003 "VAS Review," *Rain Taxi* magazine --- 2001 *Typographics*, Rockport, Beverly, Massachusetts --- 2000 "Classical Handwriting Meets Digital Design," *Design* magazine --- 1999 "Visible Citizens," *Émigré* journal --- 1996 "TOC," *Émigré* journal <u>selected exhibitions</u> 2004 *AIGA 25*, National Design Center, New York --- 2004 *50th Type Directors Club Exhibition*, Parsons The New School for Design, New York --- 2001-4 *Adversary*, USA --- 2002 *The Manuscript Illuminated*, Art Directors Club Gallery, New York --- 2000 *Design Culture Now*, Cooper-Hewitt, National Design Museum, New York <u>awards</u> 2004 Silver Medal, D&AD --- 2003 and 1996 50 Books/50 Covers, AIGA --- 2000 National Design Award in Communications Nomination, Smithsonian --- 1997 three Pushcart Prize nominations --- 1995 Tsujinaka Fiction Award of Kyoto, James Joyce Foundation

<u>FLAG Aubrey/Broquard</u> Bastien Aubry, born 1974; Dimitri Broquard, born 1969. Live and work in Zurich <u>education</u> School for Design, Biel (BA, DB) <u>practice</u> 2002-present FLAG (BA, DB) <u>selected projects</u> book illustrations, *Armpit of the Mole* by Michael Quistrebert, Fundació Trenta Quilòmetres Per Segon, Barcelona --- book, *Daniele Buetti*, Hatje Cantz Verlag, Stuttgart --- posters, Seedamm Kulturzentrum, Switzerland --- book, *And There Will Be Light*, self-commissioned, JRP Ringier, Zurich --- exhibition catalog, *Fuerchte Dich*, Helmhaus Zurich, Zurich --- zine, *La Mort C'Est Pop* --- Vinyl sleeve, *Demotape* by Fettes Brot, Yomama Recordings

<u>Flamingo Studio</u> Teruhiko Yumura, born 1942 <u>education</u> Tama Art University, Tokyo <u>practice</u> founder, Flamingo Studio --- founder, Tokyo Funky Stuff <u>selected bibliography</u> 2007 *Japanada: The Ganzfeld* no. 5, PictureBox, New York <u>awards</u> Art Directors Club award, Tokyo Art Directors Club --- Rookie Award, Tokyo Illustrators Club

<u>Friends With You</u> Sam Borkson, born 1979, Plantation, Florida; Arturo Sandoval, born 1976, Havana, Cuba. Live and work in Miami <u>practice</u> 2002-present Friends With You (SB, AS) <u>selected projects</u> 2006 installation, "Skywalkers," Art Basel Miami Beach, Miami --- 2006 installation, "Garden of Friendship," Diesel Denim Gallery, New York --- 2006 toy series, "Good Wood Gang," Giant Robot, New York, and Kidrobot, Los Angeles --- 2004 installation, "Get Lucky," Merry Karnowsky Gallery, Los Angeles, and Box Space, Miami <u>selected exhibitions</u> 2006 *The Official Friends With You Bootleg Show*, Helium Cowboy, Hamburg --- 2006 *Pictoplasma 2*, Berlin --- 2006 *MTV Underground Toys*, The Showroom, New York --- 2005 *Optic Nerve*, MOCA, Miami --- 2004 *Aqui Uzumaki*, HPGRP Hanna, Tokyo --- 2004 *Characters by Design*, Gray Matters Gallery, Dallas --- 2004 *Plushtastrophe*, Toronto, San Francisco, and Portland, Oregon --- 2003 SHIFT MOV Animation Festival, Tokyo

<u>Martin Frostner</u> born 1975, Stockholm. Lives and works in Stockholm <u>education</u> Konstfack University of Art, Crafts, and Design, Stockholm <u>selected projects</u> 2006 magazine, Färgfabriken Center for Contemporary Art and Architecture, Stockholm --- 2005 exhibition design, Moderna Museet, Stockholm --- 2005 book design, Walter König Verlag and Färgfabriken --- 2004 exhibition design, Interactive Institute and Swedish Traveling Exhibitions <u>selected bibliography</u> 2006 *Étapes* magazine --- 2005 *Creative Review* --- 2003 "Swedish Design," *IdN* magazine --- 2002 *Super: Welcome to the Graphic Wonderland*, Die Gestalten Verlag, Berlin <u>selected exhibitions</u> 2003 *Konst! Zvecia Extra Ordinaria*, Maniero Associazione Culturali, Rome --- 2003 *Invisible Wealth*, Färgfabriken, Stockholm --- 2002 *Young Swedish Design*, Designers Block, London --- 2001 *Peace, Vaccination, and Potatoes*, Galleri Konstfack, Stockholm --- 2000 *Young Swedish Design*, Kulturhuset, Stockholm <u>awards</u> 2004 The Arts Grant --- 2002 Stawonowska Award, Konstfack University of Arts, Crafts, and Design --- 2002 The Rector's Grant, St. Johanneslogen

Mieke Gerritzen born 1962, Amsterdam. Lives and works in Amsterdam education 1982-87 Gerrit Rietveld Academy, Amsterdam practice 1987-present NL Design/All Media, Amsterdam selected projects 2007 design, Masters Diploma, Sandberg Institute Amsterdam --- 2007 exhibition catalog, *Style First*, All Media and Musée de Design et d'Arts Appliqués Contemporains, Lausanne --- 2006 poster, Visual Power Show, Essen selected bibliography 2006 *Creativity for All*, BIS, Amsterdam --- 2006 *Eye* magazine --- 2003 *Deep Sites: Intelligent Innovation in Contemporary Web Design*, Thames & Hudson, London and New York --- 2002 *Form* magazine awards 2005 IF Award --- 1997 Best Book Design in the World Award, Leipzig --- 1996 Best Dutch Book Design Award

Good Design Company Manabu Mizuno, born 1972, Tokyo. Lives and works in Tokyo education 1991-95 Tama Art University, Tokyo practice 1996-97 Draft, Tokyo --- 1995-96 Pablo Production, Tokyo selected projects 2007 exhibition poster, *Le Corbusier*, Mori Art Museum, Tokyo --- 2007 art, Takeo Paper Show, Tokyo --- 2006 book, *School of Design*, Seibundo Shinkosha, Tokyo --- 2006 identity, NTT, DoCoMo --- 2006 catalog, *Visual Book for Skyline Coupe*, Nissan and *Esquire* magazine selected exhibitions 2006 *School of Design*, Ginza Graphic Gallery, Tokyo awards 2006 Show Gold, The One Club --- 2006 Silver Medal, The Tokyo Art Directors Club --- 2005 Runner-up, Asahi Advertising Award --- 2003 New Designer Awards, Japan Graphic Designers Association Award memberships Japan Graphic Designers Association

Arjan Groot born 1972. Lives and works in Amsterdam education Gerrit Rietveld Academie, Amsterdam practice editor, *A10* magazine --- designer, 020 nultwintig, Amsterdam

Michelle Gubser born 1973, Zurich. Lives and works in Paris education 1992-97 École Cantonale d'Art de Lausanne, Lausanne practice 2006-present founder, Aer, Paris --- 2006-present lecturer, Institut d'Arts Visuals, Orléans --- 2006 and 2007 workshop leader, Académie Royale des Beaux-Arts de Bruxelles, Brussels --- 2002-6 freelance design, Paris --- 1997-2002 designer, Integral Ruedi Baur, Paris selected projects 2007 store identity, 107RIVOLI --- 2005-7 exhibition design, *Now! Design à Vivre*, Designer's Days, SAFI --- 2006-7 poster and exhibition catalog, *La rue est à nous...tous!*, IVM, Paris --- 2006 signage, Municipalité de Bussigny, Switzerland --- 2005 exhibition catalog, Centre Pompidou, Paris selected bibliography 2007 *Vu d'ici*, ArBA ESA, Brussels --- 2006 "Bruxelles 10 fois," *Étapes* magazine --- 2004 "Histoire sans parole," *Étapes* magazine

Hanjse van Halem born 1978, Enschede, The Netherlands. Lives and works in Amsterdam education 2000-3 Gerrit Rietveld Academie, Amsterdam --- 1998-2000 Royal Academy of Art, The Hague practice 2003-present Hansje van Halem Graphic Design, The Netherlands selected projects 2007 postage stamps, TNT Post, The Hague --- 2004 exhibition catalog, *Mark: Municipal Art Acquisitions*, Stedelijk Museum, Amsterdam --- 2004-5 invitations, ROOM Artist Initiative, Rotterdam --- 2003 annual report, UPRO, Dutch BroArt Directors Clubasting Company selected exhibitions 2004 *Mark: Municipal Art Acquisitions*, Stedelijk Museum, Amsterdam --- 2006 *Inside Out*, Fonds BKVB, Amsterdam awards 2005 Most Beautiful Books Award, Grafische Cultuurstichting --- 2004 Most Beautiful Annual Report Award, Grafische Cultuurstichting

George Hardie born Chichester, UK. Lives and works in Chichester education 1967-70 Royal College of Art, London --- 1964-67 St. Martin's School of Art, London practice 1990-present professor, University of Brighton --- 1973-92 NTA Studios, London --- 1970-73 Nicholas Thirkell Associates, London selected projects 2006 symposium posters, Illustration Today, Parsons The New School for Design, New York --- 2005 postage stamps, Royal Mail, UK --- 2004 book, *Manual*, Broken Books, Chichester, UK --- 1999 stamp, Royal Mail, UK selected bibliography 2007 "Good Graphic Design Is the Poetry of Art," *Open Manifesto*, Sydney --- 2005 "*Manual: A Book about Hands*, A Review" and "The Rules of the Game," *Eye* magazine --- 2002 "George Hardie fabbricante di segni," *Abitare* --- 1996 *A Smile in the Mind*, Phaidon Press, London and New York selected exhibitions 2006 *Manual*, Nagoya University of Arts, Nagoya --- 2006 *Rules and Conventions: Hardie's Collection of Rulers*, Vitsoe Showroom, London --- 1999 *Post Impressions: The Art of the Stamp*, British Library, London awards 2003 Silver award, Swiss Art Directors Club --- 1994-99 Silver award, Design and Art Directors of Great Britain --- 1997 Pentagram Prize, Images 22, Association of Illustrators memberships 2005 Royal Designer for Industry --- 1996 Double Crown Club --- 1994 Alliance Graphique Internationale --- 1972 Design and Art Directors of Great Britain

Jonathan Hares born 1975, Bristol. Lives and works in London and Lausanne education 1998-2000 Royal College of Art, London --- 1995-98 University of Brighton selected projects typeface, Superstudio, Lineto --- 2006 book, *Design Products Year Review*, RCA, London --- 2006 exhibition design, *Design for Daily Life*, Design Museum, London --- 2005 book, *Colour Glass Destroys All Hate* by Helen Maurer --- 2004 exhibition design, *Pain*, Science Museum, London --- 2003 exhibition design, *Sigmar Polke*, Tate Modern, London --- 2002 exhibition design, *SuperStudio*, Design Museum, London selected bibliography 2006 *Grafik* magazine --- 2006 *Gas Book*, GAS As Interface Co., Ltd., Tokyo --- 2005 *Eye* magazine selected exhibitions 2006 *Marcel et Richard*, Basta Gallery, Lausanne --- 2006 *The Free Library*, M+R Gallery, London --- 2005 *Shots on a Brave New World*, DESIGNMAI2005, Berlin --- 2005 *Extra Ordinary*, Kulturhuset, Stockholm

Kazunari Hattori born 1964, Tokyo. Lives and works in Tokyo education 1984-88 Tokyo National University of Fine Arts and Music practice 1988-2001 Light Publicity Ltd., Tokyo selected pro-jects 1995-present book covers, Obunsha --- 1997-present advertising, Kewpie Half mayon-naise, Q.P. Corporation --- 2001-present art direction, *Here and There* magazine --- 2006-pres-ent art direction, Uniqlo --- 2002-4 art direc-tion, *Ryuko Tsushin* magazine selected bibliography 2006 "Kazunari Hattori: 100 Pages," *Idea* magazine --- 2005 *Seven*, Amazing Angle Design Consultants --- 2004 "Graphic," *Ryuko Tsushin* magazine --- 2003 *Graphic Wave*, TransArt Inc. --- 2002 *Between A and B*, self-published selected exhibi-tions 2007 *Graphic Trial*, Printing Museum, Tokyo --- 2005 *Seven*, Pao Galleries, Hong Kong --- 2004 *Kazunari Hattori*, Creation Gallery, Tokyo --- 2003 *Graphic Wave 8*, Ginza Graphic Gallery, Tokyo --- 2002 *Between A and B*, Apel Gallery, Tokyo awards 2004, 2006, 2007 awards, Tokyo Type Directors Club --- 1999-2001, 2003-6 awards, Tokyo Art Directors Club --- 2004 Yusaku Kamekura Design Award, Japan Graphic Designers Association memberships 2002 Tokyo Art Directors Club --- 1997 Japan Graphic Designers Association --- 1996 Tokyo Type Directors Club

Will Holder lives and works in London education 1990-94 Royal Academy for the Arts, The Netherlands practice 2005-7 Tomorrow Book Studio, Jan van Eyck Academy, Maastricht --- 2005-7 editor, *F.R. DAVID*, De Appel Foundation, Amsterdam --- 2000-6 profes-sor, Gerrit Rietveld Academie, Amsterdam selected projects 2007 book, *Intellectual Colours: Ryan Gander*, Silvana Editoriale, Paris --- 2007 book, *Magnetic Promenade and Other Sculpture Parks*, Studio Voltaire, London --- 2007 exhibition publi-cations, *Between Thought and Sound: Graphic Notation in Contemporary Music*, The Kitchen, New York --- 2005-7 identity, De Appel, Amsterdam

Homework Joanna Górska, born 1976, Gdynia, Poland; Jerzy Skakun, born 1973, Olsztyn, Poland. Live and work in Warsaw education 1996-2001 Fine Art Academy, Gdansk; 2000-1 ESAG Peninnghen, Paris (JG) --- 1994-99 Fine Art Academy, Gdansk; 1997 Hochschule fur Gestaltung St. Gallen, Switzerland (JS) practice 2001-2 graphic designer, Pracownia Studio, Gdansk (JG) --- 1998-2000 graphic designer, Pracownia Studio, Gdansk; 2001-3 art director, Icon advertising, Warsaw (JS) selected projects 2006-7 postage stamps, Polish Post --- 2002-7 posters, Dramatyczny Theater, Warsaw --- 2005-7 posters, Vivarto, Poland --- 2003-7 festival poster, Mañana --- 2005-7 posters, Pulaski Museum, Poland --- 2007 posters, Polish Theater in Bydgoszcs selected bibliography 2007 "Pen," 2/1 no. 191 --- 2006 *9 Femmes Graphistes*, Centre du Graphisme et de la Communication Visuelle d'Échirolles, France selected exhibitions 2006 International Poster Biennale, Warsaw --- 2006 *Golden Bee*, Moscow --- 2006 International Poster Biennale, Mexico --- 2004 International Poster Biennale, Hong Kong --- 2004 Triennial of the Stage Poster, Sofia awards 2005 Statuette, Poster Festival, Krakow --- 2004 Silver Medal, International Poster Biennale, Mexico --- 2002 Grand Prix, Polish Calendar Competitions Vidical, Warsaw memberships 2005 Polish Graphic Design Association

Mario Hugo born 1982. Lives and works in New York education 2000-3 Boston College, Massachusetts --- 2003-5 Pratt Institute, New York practice 2006-present freelance design --- 2005-6 Syrup, New York selected projects 2006 illustrations, Dolce & Gabbana 10th anniversary book --- 2007 cover, *Flaunt* magazine --- 2007 glass and textile design, Rockwell selected bibliography 2007 "Canny Naturalism," *Flaunt* magazine --- 2007 "Black and White," *IdN* magazine --- 2007 *Fashion Unfolding*, Viction:ary, Hong Kong --- 2007 *New Geo*, Die Gestalten Verlag, Berlin --- 2007 *Kelvin*, Die Gestalten Verlag, Berlin selected exhibitions 2007 *I've Got Something I'd Like to Show You*, Vallery Gallery, Barcelona --- 2007 *If You Could*, Exposure Gallery, London --- 2006 *Resist*, Who's Next, Paris --- 2006 *Cavalier*, Nog Gallery, London

Keiko Itakura born 1973. Lives and works in Tokyo education Tama Art University, Tokyo selected bibliography 2005 "Profile," *TOKION* magazine --- 2004 *AXIS* magazine --- 2004 *+81* magazine --- 2003 *Brain* no. 43 selected exhibitions 2006 Bangkok International Art Festival --- 2006 *Hello Kitty Secret House*, Hong Kong --- 2005 *FOREST*, Diesel Denim Gallery, New York --- 2004 *K*, Transplant Gallery, New York awards 2005 Design Merit Award, New York Art Directors Club --- 2004 Certificate of Typographic Excellence, New York Type Directors Club --- 2003 Non-Members' Prize, Tokyo Type Directors Club

Keiji Ito born 1958, Tokyo. Lives and works in Tokyo practice founder, Unidentified Flying Graphics --- professor, Kyoto University of Art and Design --- lecturer, Sokei Academy of Fine Arts and Design selected projects covers, *SWITCH*, *BRUTUS*, *Ryuko Tsushin*, and *Relax* magazines, Japan --- CD covers, Towa Tei, Buffalo Daughter, Kirinji, Maki Nomiya, Yo Hitoto, Bonnie Pink, Orange Pekoe, ELT, Inoue Yosui Okuda Tamio, and Yutaka Fukuoka --- books, *Motorway* and *Future Days*, Seishin-sha, Japan --- book, *Room-Grass-Forest*, Kyoto University of Art and Design, Japan selected exhibitions 2005 *Sunshine Girl Meets Gravity Boy*, Gallery 360, Tokyo --- 2005 *Psionic Distortion*, Plum Blossoms Gallery, New York --- 2004 *24 Jazz Funk Greats*, Bukowskis Gallery, Stockholm --- 2003 *Future Days*, Harajuku Rocket, Tokyo --- 2002 *Tokyo Art Jungle*, Tokyo International Forum, Tokyo --- 2001 *Active Wire*, Haja Center, Korea --- 1999 *Motorway*, Gallery 360, Tokyo --- 1993 *Tel Aviv International Poster Exhibition*, Tel Aviv Art Museum, Tel Aviv awards 2001 Tokyo Art Directors Club --- 1999 Gold Award, New York Art Directors Club

James Jarvis born 1970, London. Lives and works in London education Royal College of Art, London --- University of Brighton practice 2003-present, Amos Toys company selected projects 2003 toy series, "In-Crowd," Amos Toys, London --- comic book, *Vortigern's Machine*, Amos Toys, London, with Russell Waterman --- 1998-2003 toy series, "Silas," London selected exhibitions 2000 *World of Pain*, Parco Galleries, Tokyo, Nagoya, and Hiroshima

Körner Union Sami Benhadj, born 1977, Algiers; Tarik Hayward, born 1979, Ibiza, Spain; Guy Meldem, born 1979, Switzerland. Live and work in Lausanne education ÉCAL (SB, TH, GM) practice 2002-present Körner Union (SB, TH, GM) selected projects 2007 photography, Herman Miller --- 2005-7 photography, Swiss Department of Culture --- 2005-7 photography and illustrations, Vitra --- 2006 illustrations, Aprilia --- 2005 advertising, LICRA selected bibliography 2006 *Cneai = Neuf Ans*, Hyx, Orléans --- 2006 *Alfredo Häberli Design Live*, Birkhäuser, Basel --- 2006 *Real Fantasies*, CMV --- 2005 *Regeneration*, Thames & Hudson, London --- 2004 *Future Breed Machine*, Nieves, Zurich selected exhibitions 2007 *Diagonale de bras*, Galerie J, Geneva --- 2007 *Eau Savage 2*, Fieldgate Gallery, London --- 2006 *I Know You But You Don't Know Me*, Fette's Gallery, Los Angeles --- 2005 *We Do Wie Du*, Kunstmuseum, Thun, Switzerland --- 2003 *Les Meilleurs de Suisse*, La Station, Nice awards 2004, 2006, 2007 Swiss Federal Prize, Swiss Department of Culture --- 2006 Most Beautiful Swiss Book, Swiss Department of Culture --- 2005 Leenaards Grant, Leenaards Foundation --- 2004 BFF Promotion Award

Laboratoires CCCP = Dr. Pêche + Melle Rose live and work in Orléans, France practice 1998-present Laboratoires CCCP (DP, MR) selected projects 1999-2007 poster series, CDN Orléans, France --- schizoide.org selected bibliography 2007 *Laboratoires CCCP = Dr. Pêche + Melle Rose*, Hesign and Page One, Germany --- 2006 *All Men Are Brothers*, Hesign, Germany --- 2006 *Type Image Message*, Rockport, Beverly, Massachusetts, --- 2006 "Design's Philosophy," *360* magazine selected exhibitions 2007 *Colorado International Invitational Poster Exhibition*, Fort Collins, Colorado --- 2007 *Lahti International Poster Biennial*, Lahti, Finland --- 2005 *Pre-Partem/Post-Mortem*, DDD Gallery, Osaka, and Ginza Graphic Gallery, Tokyo awards 2003 Grand Prize, International Poster Biennial, Toyama, Japan --- 2003 Honor Award, Yusaku Kamekura Design Awards, Toyama, Japan

Jürg Lehni born 1978. Lives and works in Zurich and New York education 1999–2004 ÉCAL --- 1998–99 Swiss Federal Institute of Technology practice 2006 Sony SET Studio, Tokyo --- 2003–4 Cornel Windlin, Zurich selected projects 2007 website, Konstantin Grcic, with Alex Rich --- 2006 design proposal, Swiss banknote, Norm --- 2005–6 posters, Philippe Decrauzat --- 2003–4 website, Lineto selected bibliography 2008 *Design and the Elastic Mind*, Museum of Modern Art, New York --- 2007 "Tools Make the Designer," *Eye* magazine --- 2007 *Processing*, MIT Press, Cambridge, Massachusetts --- 2007 *Contemporary Graphic Design*, Taschen, Cologne --- 2004 "Emerging Designers Make Their Mark," *I.D.* magazine selected exhibitions 2007 *Hektor Meets Dexter Sinister*, Swiss Institute, New York --- 2006 *Landscape/Portrait*, Information Gallery, Tokyo --- 2005 *Rita + Hektor*, Tensta Konsthall, Stockholm --- 2004 *Fresh Type*, Museum für Gestaltung, Zurich --- 2003 *Tourette's II*, Gallery W139, Amsterdam awards 2003 and 2006 Swiss Federal Competition of Design, Swiss Federal Department of Culture --- 2005 Grant, sitemapping.ch --- 2001 New Talent Competition, Milia --- 2000 Grant, City and Canton of Lucerne

Lehni-Trüb Urs Lehni, born 1974; Lex Trüb, born 1971. Live and work in Zurich education School of Art and Design, Lucerne (UL) --- School of Art and Design, Zurich (LT) practice 1999–2000 Cornel Windlin, Zurich (UL) selected projects 2006–present exhibition identity, *Reihe:Ordnung*, Kunstverein Hamburger Bahnhof, Hamburg --- 2007 exhibition catalog, *Switzerland Federal Office of Culture*, Venice Biennale --- 2007 *Our* magazine --- 2006–7 exhibition catalog, Migros Museum, Zurich selected bibliography 2006 *Look at This*, Laurence King, London --- 2005 *Swiss Federal Design Grants*, Birkhäuser, Basel --- 2004 *Fresh Type*, Edition Museum für Gestaltung, Zurich --- 2002 *Young Swiss Graphic Design*, Lars Müller, Zurich --- 2001 "Nova Helvetica," *Idea* magazine selected exhibitions 2005 Swiss Design Prize, Musée de Design et d'Arts Appliqués Contemporains, Lausanne --- 2005 *Cool School*, Gallery of Academy of Arts, Architecture, and Design, Prague --- 2005 *Signes Quotidien*, Centre Culturel Suisse, Paris --- 2004 International Biennale of Graphic Design in Brno --- 2004 *Fresh Type*, Museum für Gestaltung, Zurich awards 2006 Third Place, International Poster Competition, Chaumont --- 2006 The Minister of Culture of the Czech Republic Award, International Biennale of Graphic Design in Brno --- 2002–4 and 2006 Most Beautiful Swiss Book --- 2003 First Place, Swiss Poster Award

Ghariokwu Lemi born 1955, Lagos, Nigeria. Lives and works in Lagos education 1968–73 Yaba College of Technology, Lagos practice 1976–present Ghariokwu Lemi Ltd. --- 1976 Promark International Advertising --- 1975 Pal Advertising --- 1974 Image Makers Advertising

LUST Thomas Castro, born 1967, The Phillipines; Jeroen Barendse, born 1973, The Netherlands; Dimitri Nieuwenhuizen, born 1971, The Netherlands. Live and work in The Hague practice 2002–present professor, Arnhem Academy of Art and Design; 2003–4 class advisor, Willem de Kooning Academy, Rotterdam (TC) --- 2001–present professor, Arnhem Academy of Art and Design (JB) --- 2002–present professor, Utrecht School of the Arts (DN) selected bibliography 2007 *Emergence: Young Graphic Designers*, Pyramyd, Paris --- 2007 *The Layout Look Book*, Collins Design, New York --- 2006 *What Is Graphic Design For?*, RotoVision, London --- *Dutch Resource*, International Festival of Posters and Graphic Arts, Chaumont --- 2004 *False Flat: Why Dutch Design Is So Good*, Phaidon Press, London and New York selected exhibitions 2007 *Generation Random*, Gallery TAG, The Hague --- 2007 *Faith in Exposure*, Nederlands Instituut voor Mediakunst, Montevideo --- 2007 *Post More Bills*, Pasadena, California --- 2005 *Halte Brussel*, Atelier HSL, Belgium awards 2005 Best Annual Report Design --- 2004 Designprijzen, Digital Depot --- 2004 Award of Excellence, *Communication Arts* --- 2003 Best Dutch Book Designs

MadeThought Ben Parker and Paul Austin. Live and work in London practice 2000–present MadeThought (BP, PA) selected projects identity, 25th Anniversary of the Air Force 1, Nike --- identity, Design Miami 2006 --- identity, Viaduct furniture dealer --- identity, Isarn restaurant, London --- identity, Reiss fashion retailer, London --- identity, Established & Sons furniture design, London selected exhibitions 2006 *My 2007*, Colette, Paris awards 2004 Graphic Designers of the Year, *Blueprint*

Eduardo Marín born 1965, Havana. Lives and works in Havana education 1986–88 Instituto Politénico de Diseño Industrial selected exhibitions 2007 *Posters*, Cuban Art Space, New York --- 2007 *Carteles de Relevo*, ICAIC, Havana --- 2006 *Oficios 362: El Diseño dentro del Cine*, Centro Provincial de Artes Plásticas y Diseño, Havana --- 2006 *SPARK 06*, International Festival of Media Arts and Design, New Zealand --- 2005 *La Cubanidad! Cuban Posters 1940–2004*, MAK, Vienna --- 2003 *Cuban Posters 1937–2003*, Ogaki Poster Museum, Ogaki, Japan --- 2001 *Diseño del Fin de Siglo*, Centro Wifredo Lam, Havana awards 2001 Premio de Curaduría, Diseño del Fin de Siglo, Centro Wifredo Lam, Havana --- 1998 Premio Juan David, Galería Juan David, Havana

Gabriel Martínez Meave born 1972, Mexico City. Lives and works in Mexico City education Universidad Iberoamericana practice 1994–present founder, Kimera Design Studio selected projects typefaces, Arcana and Organica, Adobe awards 2002 and 2003, First Prize, Premio Diseño, Mexico --- 2001 First Prize, National Biennial of Design, Mexico --- New York Type Directors Club awards

Luna Maurer born 1972, Stuttgart. Lives and
works in Amsterdam education 1999-2001 Sandberg
Institute --- 1997-99 Gerrit Rietveld Academie,
Amsterdam --- 1995-99 Fachhochschule für Gestaltung
Pforzheim practice 2001-present Luna Maurer Studio
--- professor, Gerrit Rietveld Academie, Amsterdam
--- 2004 jury member, Municipal Art Acquisitions,
Graphic Design, Stedelijk Museum, Amsterdam
selected projects 2007 catalog, *Drawing Typologies:
Municipal Art Acquisitions*, Stedelijk Museum,
Amsterdam --- 2007 website, Sandberg Institute
--- 2007 "City-Walk," The Hague, with LUST
--- 2005-7 website, print materials, and films,
Skycatcher, De Balie Centre for Culture and
Politics, Amsterdam selected bibliography 2007
"e-culture," *Amsterdam Index*, BIS, Amsterdam
--- 2006 *Graphic Design in the White Cube*, 22nd
International Biennale of Graphic Design in
Brno --- 2006 "Follow Me," *Amsterdam Index*, BIS,
Amsterdam --- 2006 "Regels en ruimte," *Items* maga-
zine --- 2003 *Deep Sites: Intelligent Innovation
in Contemporary Web Design*, Thames & Hudson,
London and New York selected exhibitions 2006
Graphic Design in the White Cube, 22nd Interna-
tional Biennale of Graphic Design, Brno --- 2006
Inside Out, Netherlands Foundation for Visual
Arts, Design, and Architecture, Amsterdam
--- 2005 *Grote kunst voor kleine mensen*, Museum
De Paviljoens, Almere, The Netherlands --- 2005
Recent Graphic Design, Stedelijk Museum, Amsterdam
--- 2003 *European Design Biennial*, London Design
Museum --- *Rotterdam Designprijs*, Museum Boijmans
van Beuningen, Rotterdam awards 2005 Best Dutch
Books award --- 2004 Europrix --- 2004 Prix
Europa for interactive fiction --- 2003 Rotterdam
Designprijs --- 2002 Kunstaanmoedigingsprijs
Amstelveen

Thomas Mayfried born 1966, Karlsruhe, Germany.
Lives and works in Munich education 1994-99
State University for Design, Karlsruhe, Germany
--- 1986-88 Bavarian State College for Photography,
Munich practice 1999-present founder, Thomas
Mayfried Visual Communication --- 1996-99 designer,
Werner Jeker, Lausanne --- 1988-94 freelance
photography selected projects 2007-present iden-
tity, BDA Bayern --- 2007-present identity, Franz
Marc Museum, Kochel am See, Germany --- 2003-pres-
ent identity, Haus der Kunst, Munich selected
bibliography 2006 "The Latest Branding Adventure,"
AXIS magazine

Laura Meseguer born 1968, Barcelona. Lives and
works in Barcelona education 2003-4 Koninklikje
Academie van Beeldende Kunsten, Royal Academy of
Art, The Hague --- 1988-92 Escola d'Arts i Oficis
Aplicats Llotja, Barcelona practice 2005-present
freelance design --- 1992-present designer, Type-
Ø-Tones, Barcelona --- 1996-2005 Cosmic Gráfica,
Barcelona --- 1994-96 Estudi Pati Núñez, Barcelona
--- 1990-93 Bassat, Ogilvy & Mather, Barcelona
--- 1989-90 Dayax Testa, Barcelona --- 1988-89
Team Work, Barcelona selected projects 2007 catalog for exhibition, *Sintopía(s): De la relación
entre arte, ciencia y tecnología*, Cervantes
Institute, Beijing --- 2007 book, *Rolling Paper:
Graphics on Cigarette Rolling Paper*, Index Book,
Barcelona --- 2003-7 typeface, Rumba, Royal Academy
of Art, The Hague --- 2006 book design, *Todas
las muñecas son carnívoras*, Destino, Barcelona
--- 2005 identity, Peralta graphic design studio,
Amsterdam selected bibliography 2007 "Field Guide
to Emerging Typeface Designers," *Step* magazine
--- 2006 "Typography Twenty-Six: tipografía euro-
pea made in USA," *Visual* magazine --- 2005 "Fans
de la Lletra," *El temps d'art* magazine --- 2005
Interrobang 3, Society of Typographic Aficionados,
Alameda, California --- 2004 "Trabajamos aquí"
Cosmic Gráfica magazine selected exhibitions 2006
*Vaya Tipo 3: Segundo Congreso de Tipografía en
España*, Ca revolta, Valencia, Spain --- 2005
Diseñadores para un Libro: Homenaje al Quijote,
Iglesia de El Salvador, Toledo, Spain --- 2005
D'après: Versiones, ironías y divertimientos,
Museu Valencià de la Illustració i la Modernitat,
Valencia, Spain --- 2005 *Lettertypes from The
Hague, Type and Media 2003-5*, Festival DeArt,
Moscow --- 2004 *PraaHaag*, The Academy of Arts,
Architecture and Design, Prague --- 2004 *Type
and Media 2003-4*, Meermano Museum, The Hague
awards 2005 Certificate of Excellence, New York
Type Directors Club --- 2004 Award of Excellence,
Communication Arts --- 1993 Laus Silver Award,
ADG-FAD memberships 2004 Association Typographique
Internationale

mgmt. design Ariel Apte Carter, born 1969, Stanford, California; Alicia Cheng, born 1970, Ann Arbor, Michigan; Sarah Gephart, born 1970, Hanover, New Hampshire. Live and work in New York education 1999 Yale School of Art, New Haven (AAC, AC, SG) --- 1992 Barnard College, New York (AAC) --- 1991 Connecticut College (AC) --- 1992 Oberlin College (SG) practice Doyle Partners; designer, *New York Times Magazine*; designer, 2x4, New York; Chronicle Books; Design MW (AAC) --- Method, New York; Cooper-Hewitt, National Design Museum, New York; Proforma, Rotterdam (AC) --- designer, 2x4, New York; General and Specific, New York; Memo, New York (SG) selected projects 2007 book, *The Yale Building Project: The First Forty Years*, Yale school of Architecture, New Haven --- 2005-7 information graphic, "31 Days in Iraq," *New York Times* --- exhibition design, American Folk Art Museum, New York --- exhibition design, International Center of Photography, New York --- 2006 book, *An Inconvenient Truth* by Al Gore, Melcher Media and Rodale, New York --- 2006 book, *Poetry, Property, and Place*, Yale School of Architecture, New Haven awards 2007 AIGA 365 --- 2007 AIGA 50 Books/50 Covers --- 2005-7 *Print* magazine Design Annual --- 2005 Honor Award, Society of Environmental Graphic Designers --- 2004 Merit Award, Society of Environmental Graphic Designers

Étienne Mineur born 1968. Lives and works in Paris education École Nationale Supérieure des Arts Décoratifs, Paris practice 2000 cofounder, Incandescence --- 1992 cofounder, Index --- independent art director, Hyptique and Nofrontière memberships 2006 Designers Interactive --- 2000 Alliance Graphique Internationale

Isabel Naegele born 1962, Plainfield, New Jersey. Lives and works in Darmstadt, Germany education 1993-99 Johann-Wolfgang von Goethe Universität, Frankfurt --- 1997 HfG Offenbach, Germany practice 1999-present freelance design --- 1999-present professor, Fachhochschule Mainz --- 1998 Studio Dumbar, The Hague --- 1997 Intégral Ruedi Baur, Paris selected projects 2004-present identity, Dialogmuseum, Frankfurt --- 2000-present exhibition design, Andreas Heinecke, Hamburg --- 2000-present orientation and wayfinding for Swiss Re, with Intégral Ruedi Bauer selected exhibitions 2001 *Tensions Contemporaines*, Centre du Graphisme et de la Communication Visuelle, Echirolles, France --- 2000 *Mahlzeit*, Titania, Frankfurt --- 1999 *Werkschau Isabel Naegele*, Theaterhaus Frankfurt, Frankfurt awards --- 1998 New York Type Directors Club, *America: Cult and Culture*, AIGA National Design Center --- 1997, 1995 Die 100 besten Plakate --- 1995 Deutscher Design Preis, Deutscher Design Club --- 1995 Deutscher preis fur Kommunikationsdesign, Design Zentrum Nordrhein Westfalen memberships 2005 Institute Designlabor Gutenberg --- 2000 Allianz Deutscher Designer

Namaiki David Duval-Smith, born 1970, New Zealand; Michael Frank, born 1966, UK. Live and work in Tokyo selected projects 2006-present graphics, Hoya Crystal, Tokyo --- 2006-present Root Culture NPO --- 2003-6 workshop, "Can't Eat the Plastic," Hara Museum of Contemporary Art, Tokyo --- videos, graphics, and stage design, UA, Tokyo selected bibliography 2007 "Namaiki: Let the Plants Design!," *PingMag* magazine --- 2007 "Namaiki's Green Graffiti," *Theme* magazine --- 2004 *Roppongi Crossing*, Mori Art Museum, Tokyo --- 2002 *Japan Graphics*, Actar Publishers, Barcelona and New York selected exhibitions 2008 *Edible Jungle*, Yogyakarta National Museum, Yogyakarta, Indonesia --- 2004 *Tokyo Style in Stockholm*, Stockholm --- 2004 *Fusion: Architecture and Design in Japan*, The Israel Museum Jerusalem, Jerusalem --- 2003 *uLTRAdELUXE oSAKAAAAA!!!*, KPO Kirin Plaza Osaka, Osaka

Non-Format Kjell Ekhorn and Jon Forss. Live and work in London selected projects 2007 posters, Design+Music Seminar, Insomnia Festival, Norway --- canvas bags, *Re-Bag* exhibition, SEA Gallery, London --- CD packaging, Lo Recordings --- Advertising, *The Economist* magazine and AMV --- Advertising, Summer Hoops and LeBron James Zoom III campaigns, Nike --- CD packaging, Propeller Recordings --- Advertising, Coke Side of Life campaign, Coca-Cola --- CD packaging, Rich Mix and Whitechapel Art Gallery selected bibliography 2007 *Non-Format Love Song*, Die Gestalten Verlag, Berlin --- 2006 *Non-Format*, "Design and Designers" series, Pyramyd, Paris --- *+81*, *All Access*, *Cover*, *Creative Review*, *Grafik*, *MdN*, *Neo2*, and *XFUNS* magazines awards 2007 Yellow Pencil Award, D&AD --- 2007 Best in Book, *Creative Review Annual* --- 2007 Nomination, Tokyo Type Directors Club --- 2006 Non-Members Prize, Tokyo Type Directors Club --- 2006 Certificate of Typographic Excellence, New York Type Directors Club --- 2004-5 Award of Excellence, *Communication Arts*

<u>Henrik Nygren</u> born 1963, Uppsala, Sweden. Lives and works in Stockholm <u>education</u> 1995 Yale Summer Program in Graphic Design, Brissage, Switzerland --- 1987-89 Antiqua/CFH Master Class, Stockholm --- 1985-86 Berghs School of Design, Stockholm <u>practice</u> 1991-present Henrik Nygren Design --- 1983-91 freelance design <u>selected projects</u> 2007-present identity, R2 Asset Management Ltd. --- 2007-present identity, Beckmans College of Design, Stockholm <u>selected bibliography</u> 2006 "Baltic: The Centre for Contemporary Art" and "Moderna Museet," *c/id: Visual Identity and Branding for the Artsi*, Laurence King, London --- 2004 "The Order of Pages: Can Graphic Design Reinvigorate the Photographic Monograph?" *Eye* magazine --- 2003 "Nature and Culture," *Scandinavian Style: Classic and Modern Scandinavian Design and Its Influence on the World*, Carlton Books, London --- 2000 "Interview with Henrik Nygren, Art Director and Designer," *+81* magazine --- 1996 "A Discretionary Eye," *Form* magazine <u>selected exhibitions</u> 2006 Form/Design Center, Malmö --- 2003 *Three Little Indians*, Svensk Dorm, The Swedish Society of Crafts and Design, Stockholm --- 2002 *Henrik Nygren*, Form/Design Center, Malmö --- 1999 *Henrik Nygren: Graphic Designer and Art Director*, IDEE, Tokyo <u>awards</u> 2007 The Berling Prize --- 2007 Electrolux Brand Award --- 2007 Silver Egg, The Golden Egg Awards --- 1997 Honorable Mention, Excellent Swedish Design --- 1994 Gold Egg, The Golden Egg Awards --- 1994 Finalist, Art Directors Club, Europe <u>memberships</u> 2000 Stockholm Typographic Guild --- 1990 Svenks Form, The Swedish Society of Crafts and Design

<u>Office for Editorial Design</u> Harmine Louwé, lives and works in Amsterdam <u>education</u> St. Joost Art Academy, Breda, The Netherlands <u>practice</u> 1992-present freelance design --- 1986-92 Studio Dumbar <u>selected bibliography</u> *Eye*, *Idea*, *Items*, and *Experience* magazines --- "Studio Dumbar: Behind the Seen," Grafische Vormgeving, Lier, Belgium --- 2001 *Apples and Oranges: Best Dutch Graphic Design*, BIS, Amsterdam --- 2004 *False Flat: Why Dutch Design Is So Good*, Phaidon Press, London and New York

<u>Omnivore</u> Alice Chung and Karen Hsu <u>practice</u> 2002-present Omnivore (AC, KH) --- 2004-present faculty member, Yale School of Art, New Haven (KH) <u>selected projects</u> 2002-3 identity, Margaret Mead Film and Video Festival, American Museum of Natural History, New York --- exhibition identity, *Commodification of Buddhism*, Bronx Museum of the Arts, New York --- catalog, *Design Studioworks 10*, Harvard School of Design, Cambridge, Massachusetts --- identity, Princeton School of Architecture --- illustrations, *Details* and *Metropolis* magazines <u>selected exhibitions</u> 2004 *Fresh Dialogue*, American Institute of Graphic Arts, New York --- 2004 *50 Books/50 Covers*, American Institute of Graphic Arts, New York

<u>178 aardige ontwerpers</u> Joost Hoekstra, born 1974; Erik Hoogendorp, born 1969; Jos Kluwen, born 1974; Frederik Nysingh, born 1969; Merel Sas, born 1974; Annabelle Scweinbenz, born 1977. Live and work in Amsterdam <u>education</u> Hogeschool voor de Kunsten Utrecht (JH, EH, JK, MS) --- Hochschule fuer Technik und Gestaltung, Mannheim, Germany (AS) <u>selected projects</u> 2007 advertising campaign, HKU <u>selected bibliography</u> 2007 interview, *Volkskrant* newspaper --- 2006 *Grafik* magazine --- 2005 *Items* magazine --- 2004 *False Flat: Why Dutch Design Is So Good*, Phaidon Press, London and New York <u>awards</u> 2007 and 2006, nominations, Art Directors Club, The Netherlands

<u>Eddie Opara</u> lives and works in New York <u>education</u> Yale University, New Haven --- London College of Printing <u>practice</u> The Map Office --- 1997-2004 lecturer, Rhode Island School of Design <u>selected projects</u> publication and typography, *Thank You from the Hilltops* --- 2006 T-shirt, Armani Exhange --- 2004-5 identity, Brooklyn Museum --- 2005 installation, "Prada Guilt," Prada Store, New York --- 2005 identity, Endeavor talent agency --- 2005 bag, Vitra furniture

Radim Peško born 1976, Czech Republic. Lives and works in Amsterdam <u>education</u> 2002-4 Werkplaats Typografie, Arnhem --- 1996-2001 Academy of Art, Architecture, and Design, Prague <u>selected projects</u> 2007-present identity, Vienna Secession --- 2007 type design, Cerruti, Paris --- 2005 type design, *Dot Dot Dot* magazine --- design, Moravian Gallery, Brno <u>selected exhibitions</u> 2007 *Forms of Inquiry: The Architecture of Critical Graphic Design*, Architectural Association, London --- 2007 *Speaking of Which...*, Le Comptoir, Liège, Belgium --- 2006 *Work from Mars*, Moravian Gallery, Brno --- 2005 *DDD/We Shift Gear into Present Tense*, Tallinn, Estonia --- 2004-5 *E-A-T: Experiments and Typography*, Prague, The Hague, and Bratislava

<u>Mark Owens</u> born 1971, Dallas, Texas. Lives and works in Los Angeles <u>education</u> 1998-2000 Yale University, New Haven <u>practice</u> founder, Life of the Mind <u>selected projects</u> 2007 T-shirts, 2x4 --- 2006-7 T-shirts, Commonwealth Stacks --- 2006 illustration, *Färgfabriken* magazine <u>selected bibliography</u> 2007 "Forms of Inquiry: The Architecture of Critical Graphic Design," *New Brutalists / New Romantics*, Architectural Association, London --- 2006 "Graphics Incognito," *Dot Dot Dot* magazine --- 2003 "Group Theory," *Dot Dot Dot* magazine --- 2002 "Soft Modernist: Discovering the Book Covers of Fred Troller," *Dot Dot Dot* magazine --- 2000 "Reading the City," *Visible Language*, Rhode Island School of Design <u>selected exhibitions</u> 2007 *True Believers*, Riviera Gallery, New York --- 2005 *The Free Library*, M+R Gallery, London, Space 1026, Philadelphia, and Riviera Gallery, New York

<u>Post Typography</u> Nolen Strals, born 1978, Blue Ridge, Georgia; Bruce Willen, born 1981, Portales, New Mexico. Live and work in Baltimore <u>education</u> 1997-2001 Maryland Institute College of Art, Baltimore (NS) --- 1998-2002 Maryland Institute College of Art, Baltimore (BW) <u>practice</u> 2001-present Post Typography (NS, BW) --- 2001-7 DMJM+Harris, Baltimore (NS) --- 2004-6 Shaw-Jelveh Design, Baltimore; 2003 House Industries, Hockessin, Delaware (BW) <u>selected projects</u> 2006-present illustrations, *New York Times* --- 2007 conference identity, Greenbuild 2007, USGBC --- 2001-7 posters, Johns Hopkins Film Festival --- 2007 CD packaging, albums by The Hope Diary <u>selected bibliography</u> --- 2007 *Nozone X: Forecast*, Princeton Architectural Press, New York --- 2006 "2006 Field Guide to Emerging Talent," *STEP* magazine --- 2006 *D.I.Y: Design It Yourself*, Princeton Architectural Press, New York --- 2005 "Punk Rock vs. Swiss Modernism," *Metropolis* magazine <u>selected exhibitions</u> 2007 *HOME*, 2219, Baltimore --- 2006 *Punk Rock vs. Swiss Modernism: The Art and Design of Double Dagger*, Millersville University, Millersville, Pennsylvania --- 2005 *Alphabet: An Exhibition of Hand-Drawn Lettering and Experimental Typography*, Artscape, Baltimore --- 2005 *Fresh Ink: An International Network of Contemporary Poster Artists*, Pennsylvania College of Art & Design, Lancaster, Pennsylvania --- 2004 *Daydream Nation: Through the Perilous Night*, Three Rivers Arts Festival Gallery, Pittsburgh <u>awards</u> 2007 Award of Excellence, Society for News Design --- 2004-6 *Print* magazine Regional Design Annual --- 2005 *Communication Arts Design Annual*

<u>Paper Rad</u> Jacob Ciocci, born 1977; Jessica Ciocci, born 1976; Benjamin Jones, born 1977. Live and work in Providence <u>education</u> Carnegie Mellon University, Pittsburgh, Oberlin College (JaC) --- Wellesley College (JeC) --- Massachusetts College of Art (BJ) <u>selected exhibitions</u> 2006 *Cosmic Wonder*, Yerba Buena Center for the Arts, San Francisco --- 2006 *Panic Room*, Deste Foundation Center for Contemporary Art, Athens --- 2005 *Breaking and Entering: Art and the Video Game*, Pace Wildenstein, New York --- 2005 *Shit*, Printed Matter, New York --- 2005 *Mixtape Clubhouse*, Space 1026, Philadelphia --- 2004 *Collage Party*, Bergdorf Goodman, New York --- 2004 *T's 4 Me 2 Wear & U 2 C*, Art Basel Miami --- 2004 *(K-RAA-K)3*, KC Belgie, Hasselt, Belgium --- 2003 *Radical Entertainment*, Institute of Contemporary Art, London --- 2002 *The Bedroom Show*, John Connelly Presents, New York <u>selected bibliography</u> 2005 "Web Works That Insist on Your Full Attention," *New York Times* --- 2005 "Emerging US Artists," *ArtReview* --- "Crazy Cartoons: Paper Rad Scare the Shit out of Cute," *Vice* magazine --- 2004 "Feel the Heat: What's Hot Now?," *Paper* magazine

Project Projects Prem Krishnamurthy, born 1977,
New Brunswick, New Jersey; Adam Michaels, born
1978, Evanston, Illinois. Live and work in New
York education 2000 Technische Universität, Dresden;
2000 Hochschule für Technik und Wirtschaft,
Dresden; 1997 Freie Universität, Berlin; 1995-99
Yale University, New Haven, Connecticut (PK)
--- 1996-2000 Minneapolis College of Art and
Design, Minneapolis (AM) practice 2004-present
Project Projects (PK, AM) --- 2006-present, pro-
fessor, Parsons The New School for Design, New
York; 2004-present professor, University of
Connecticut, Storrs; 2003 New York Times Magazine;
2000-2 Leonardi Wollein Visual Communication,
Berlin (PK) --- 2002-3 AM/GD, New York; 2002 Art
and Auction magazine; 2001-2 Architecture maga-
zine; 2000-1, Love (+$), Minneapolis, Minnesota
(AM) selected projects 2007-present design,
Paper Monument journal --- 2007 exhibition design,
Berlin/New York Dialogues, Center for Architecture,
New York selected bibliography 2007 Materials,
Process, Print, William Stout, San Francisco
--- 2006 "Practice and Process," Eye magazine
--- 2006 "The Conditions of Graphic Design,"
Idea magazine selected exhibitions 2007 Forms
of Inquiry: The Architecture of Critical Graphic
Design, Architectural Association, London --- 2007
The Park at the Center of the World, Center for
Architecture, New York --- 2006-7 Bunch Alliance
and Dissolve, Contemporary Art Center, Cincinnati
--- 2006 Mind the Gap, Smack Mellon, New York
awards 2007 Design Distinction, I.D. Annual Design
Review --- 2006 Young Guns Award, New York Art
Directors Club --- 2002 Second Place, Museuminsel
International Identity and Signage Competition
--- 2001 Merit Awards, Society of Publication
Designers

Michael Punchman born 1967, Hong Kong. Lives and
works in Hong Kong selected projects sculpture
series, "BOOM" selected exhibitions 2006 Heart to
Heart, Hong Kong --- 2005 Flux, Hong Kong --- 2004
Boom Goes East, Hong Kong --- 2003 Imajuku Art
Book Exhibition, Tokyo awards 2003 Final Entry,
Hong Kong Art Biennial --- 2002, 2000, 1998
Certificates of Excellence, HKDA --- 2002 Takaaki
Iwamura Prize, Japan Poster Grandprix --- 1998
Best Single Print, 4AS --- 1995 Best Print Adver-
tisement, Asian Advertising Awards --- 1980
Freshman Art Director Award, 4AS

Iman Raad born 1979, Mashad, Iran. Lives and works
in Tehran selected projects 2007 conference poster,
Iranian Graphic Designers Society --- 2006-7
identity, Mashad International Exhibition Co.
--- 2001-5 posters, IACECR Cultural Center of Mashad
--- 2007 book covers, Ney Publications, Tehran
--- 2004-7 book covers, IACECR Publications, Mashad
selected bibliography 2007 "Pick of the Month,"
IdN magazine --- 2007 Iranian Typography, Nazar
Publications, Iran --- 2006 "Persian Illustration,"
Varoom magazine --- 2006 New Visual Culture
of Modern Iran, Mark Batty Publishers, New York
--- 2005 "Iranian Typography," Novum magazine
selected exhibitions 2007 Iranian Typography,
The Basel School of Design, Basel --- 2006 Warsaw
International Poster Biennale, Warsaw --- 2006
International Biennale of Graphic Design in Brno
--- 2005 Iranian Poster Exhibition, Ogaki Poster
Museum, Ogaki, Japan --- 2005 Bolem van het
Oosten, Moderne Iraanse en Arabische Affiches,
Dutch Poster Museum, Hoorn, The Netherlands awards
2007 Iranian Graphic Designers Society Diploma,
Tehran International Poster Biennial memberships
2003 Iranian Graphic Designers Society

Manuel Raeder lives and works in Berlin education
Jan van Eyck Akademie, Maastricht --- London
College of Printing practice workshop leader,
École Nationale Supérieure des Arts Décoratifs,
Paris; University of Toulouse le Mirail;
Hochschule für bildende Künste, Hamburg

Andy Rementer born 1981. Lives ard works in
Philadelphia education 2000-4 University of the
Arts, Philadelphia practice 2004-7 Fabrica, Italy
--- 2005 Team Heavy, New York --- 2004-5 Vh1,
New York selected projects comic series, "Techno
Tuesday" selected bibliography 2007 Hand Job,
Princeton Architectural Press, New York --- 2007
"Jeremyville Sessions," IdN magazine --- 2007
Street Sketchbooks, Thames & Hudson, London and
New York --- 2007 "Megafaces," Clark magazine
selected exhibitions 2007 I Love Tourism, Bevilaqua
la Masa, Venice --- 2007 Friends of the Endless
Journey, The Grass Hut Gallery, Portland, Oregon
--- 2006 Charming Suicide, ORO Gallery, Göteburg,
Sweden --- 2006 Walter's Daydream, Renowned
Gallery, Portland, Oregon

Claudio Rocha born 1957, São Paulo. Lives and
works in São Paulo

Michal Sahar born 1970, Tel Aviv. Lives and
works in Tel Aviv education 1992-96 Bezalel Academy
of Art and Design, Jerusalem --- 1994 School of
Visual Arts, New York practice 2002-present founder,
Hagilda Independent Type Designers Cooperative,
Tel Aviv --- 1996-2000 Tel Aviv Group, Tel Aviv
selected projects 2007 typeface, Arbel Hagilda
--- 2007 exhibition catalog, Tel Aviv Museum of
Art --- 2007 book design, "Saf" series, Hakibutz
Hameuhad Publishers, Tel Aviv --- 2006-present
identity, Contemporary Art Department, Tel Aviv
Museum of Art --- 2004 exhibition catalog, work
by Doron Rabina, São Paulo Biennale, Israeli
Ministry of Eduation, Culture, and Sport, and
Israeli Ministry of Foreign Affairs selected bib-
liography 2007 "Hagilda Tel Aviv," I.D. magazine
--- "Local Is Unique: Interview with Hagilda,"
Time Out Tel Aviv --- 2002 "The Type Developers,"
The Hebrew Status, Shoken, Ha'aretz awards 2006
First Place, Tel Aviv Museum of Art logo competi-
tion --- 2004 Prize in Art and Design, Israeli
Ministry of Education, Culture, and Sport --- 1996
Sandberg Prize for Graduating Exhibitions, Bezalel
Academy of Art and Design, Jerusalem --- 1996
Student Exchange Scholarship, School of Visual
Arts, New York, and Bezalel Academy of Art and
Design, Jerusalem --- 1995, 1994, 1993 Excellency
Award, Bezalel Academy of Art and Design, Jerusalem

Martijn Sandberg born 1967, Den Helder, The
Netherlands. Lives and works in Amsterdam education
1990-91 Rijksakademie van Beeldende Kunsten,
Amsterdam --- 1986-91 Hogeschool voor de Kunsten
Utrecht selected projects 2007 installation,
"Hallo, Is Daar Lemand?," Floriande, The Netherlands
--- 2007 signage, Karel Appel Center, Amsterdam
--- 2006 design, parcel post boxes, Royal TNT
Post --- installation, "Forever Young," OSG
Singelland Collene, Drachten, The Netherlands
selected bibliography 2006 "Dozen met Dubbele
Bodems", Items magazine --- 2005 "Drawing
Songlines: Martijn Sandberg's Graphic Message,"
DAMn magazine --- 2005 "Simply Pimply," Frame
magazine selected exhibitions 2007 Billboard VI:
Martijn Sandberg, Centrum Beeldende Kunst, Apeldoom,
The Netherlands --- 2006 Kunst per Post, Museum
Escher in het Paleis, The Hague --- 2004 Migrating
Identity, Arti et Amicitiae, Amsterdam --- 2002
Image Message, Galerie Markus Richter, Berlin

75B Robert Beckand, born 1972, The Hague; Pieter
Vos, born 1971, Utrecht; Rens Muis born 1974,
Rotterdam. Live and work in Rotterdam education
1993-97 Graphic Design, Willem de Kooning Academy,
Rotterdam (RB, PV, RM) practice 1997-present 75B
(RB, PV, RM) selected projects 2007 identity,
Kunstgebouw --- 2007 book, Kunst moet je voelen,
Zeeuws Museum, Micdelburg, The Netherlands selected
bibliography 2006 75B: 10x10, Veenman Publishers,
Rotterdam --- 2006 Serialize, Die Gestalten
Verlag, Berlin --- 2004 False Flat: Why Dutch
Design Is So Good, Phaidon Press, London and
New York --- 2001 Apples and Oranges: Best Dutch
Graphic Design, BIS, Amsterdam --- 2001 Holland
Design, Actar, Barcelona selected exhibitions
2007 75B: 10x10, Blaak Gallery, Rotterdam --- 2002
Dutch Graphic Design 1990-2001, American Institute
of Graphic Arts, New York --- 2001 Nuevos Diseñadores
Holadeses Laus Location, Barcelona --- 1998
Do Normal San Francisco Museum of Modern Art,
San Francisco

Claudia Siegel born 1974, Dresden. Lives and works in Leipzig education Academy of Visual Arts, Leipzig --- Bauhaus Kolleg, Dessau awards 2007 Most Beautiful Book Award --- 2004 Art Prize, Sparkhasse Leipzig

Jennifer Sonderby lives and works in San Francisco education California College of the Arts, San Francisco --- University of Kansas practice creative director, San Francisco Museum of Modern Art selected exhibitions 2007 San Francisco Museum of Modern Art, San Francisco --- 2007 Nagoya International Design Center, Nagoya

Spector Markus Dressen, born 1971, Munster, Germany. Lives and works in Leipzig education 1993-99 Hochschule für Grafik und Buchkunst, Leipzig practice 2000-present Spector

Frauke Stegmann born 1973, Windhoek, Namibia. Lives and works in Cape Town education Royal College of Art, London --- Hochschule für Gestaltung, Mainz, Germany practice David James Associates selected projects 2007-present poster series, Jaco Bouwer --- 2006-present hand-cast porcelain, self-commissioned --- 2005-present CD covers, Treader, London --- 2007 logo, PWHOA knitwear --- 2007 invitations, Chiltern Street Studio, London --- 2007 invitation, Bell-Roberts Gallery, Cape Town selected bibliography 2005 "Special Report on Process," Grafik magazine --- 2004 "Iconography 2," IdN magazine --- 2003 "More Is More," Design Week --- 2003 Hand to Eye: Contemporary Illustration, Laurence King, London --- 2002 The Graphics Book, RotoVision, London selected exhibitions 2006 Felt-Tip, SEA Gallery, London --- 2005 European Design Show, Design Museum, London --- 2003 Young Talents, Graphic Europe Conference, Barcelona --- 2002 Creative Futures, Creative Review, London awards 2005 Best Projects, Grafik magazine --- 2003 Shortlist, Arts Foundation Award --- 2002 Future Stars of Fashion, Creative Review --- 2002 Creative Futures, Creative Review

Astrid Stavro born 1972, Trieste, Italy. Lives and works in Barcelona education 2003-5 Royal College of Art, London --- 1997-2000 Central Saint Martins College of Art and Design, London practice 2001-5, Pocko, London --- 1996 Ipsum Planet, Madrid --- 1995 Alfonso Sostre, Madrid --- 1993-95 La Tinta China, Madrid selected projects 2007 identity, Maria Canals Piano Competition, Palau de la Musica, Barcelona --- 2007 museum guide design, Museo Nacional Centro de Arte Reina Sofia, Madrid --- 2006-7 book covers, Arcadia, London --- 2006 identity, Forum Laus Europe, ADG-FAD selected bibliography 2007 100@360: Top 100 New Designers in the World, Laurence King, London --- 2007 Tactile, Die Gestalten Verlag, Berlin --- 2006 D&AD Annual, D&AD, London --- 2006 Buryport Critical Forum, Department of Communication Art and Design, The Royal College of Art, London --- 2006 "Grid Squad," Wallpaper magazine --- 2006 "The Annual," Creative Review selected exhibitions 2006 Art Directors Club of Europe, ADG-FAD, Barcelona --- 2006 Art of the Grid, Books Actually, Singapore --- 2006 Work from Mars, International Biennale of Graphic Design in Brno --- 2004 Inspiration Style Lounge, Victoria and Albert Museum, London --- 2002 GB: Graphics Britain, Magma, London awards 2007 Gold Award, Design Week --- 2007 Platinum and Gold, Graphic Design Awards --- 2007 Distinctive Merit, New York Art Directors Club --- 2007 Honorable Mention, I.D. Design Annual --- 2006 Gold Award, Art Directors Club of Europe --- 2006 Gold, Laus Awards memberships 2006 Asociación de Directores de Arte y Diseñadores Gráficos

Stiletto Stefanie Barth and Julie Hirschfeld, live and work in New York and Milan practice 2000-present Stiletto (SB, JH) selected bibliography Grafik, Idea, Print, Creative Review, The Face, Wallpaper, and I.D. magazines --- Restart: New Systems in Graphic Design, Universe, New York --- New Typographic Design, Laurence King, London --- Fresh Dialogue 3, Princeton Architectural Press, New York awards Two New York Art Directors Club Awards

Strange Attractors Catelijne van Middelkoop, born 1975, Alphen aan den Rijn, The Netherlands; Ryan Pescatore Frisk, born 1977, Rochester, New York. Live and work in The Hague education 2000-2 Cranbrook Academy of Art, Bloomfield Hills, Michigan; 1996-2000 Royal Academy of Art, The Hague; 1994-96 University of Amsterdam, Amsterdam (CM) --- 2004-5 Royal Academy of Art, The Hague; 2000-2 Cranbrook Academy of Art, Bloomfield Hills, Michigan; 1995-99 Savannah College of Art and Design, Savannah, Georgia (RPF) selected projects 2006 video, *TokyoChat*, W+K TokyoLab, Tokyo --- 2006 installation, "Big Type Says More," Museum Boijmans van Beuningen, Rotterdam --- 2005 CD cover, *Rotten Cocktails*, City Center Offices, Berlin --- 2005 book illustration, "The New Typographers," *Visual Communication on Typography*, Sage, London --- 2005 magazine cover, *2+3D* --- 2005 video, *Little Yellow Writing Hood*, FontShop International selected bibliography 2007 *Contemporary Graphic Design*, Taschen, Cologne --- 2007 *Typography 28*, Harper Design, New York --- 2007 "Strange Attractors," Designprijs Rotterdam --- 2007 "Strange Attractors," *Tactile*, Die Gestalten Verlag, Berlin --- 2006 "Strange Attractors: De-Criminalizing Ornament," *I.D.* magazine selected exhibitions 2007 *53rd Annual Exhibition*, New York Type Directors Club --- 2006 *Cut for Purpose*, Museum Boijmans van Beuningen, Rotterdam --- 2004-6 *The Foreign Affairs of Dutch Design*, BNO, Amsterdam, Cape Town, and Dublin --- 2004 *Young Guns 4*, New York Art Directors Club awards 2004 and 2007 Certificate of Typographic Excellence, New York Type Directors Club --- 2006 The I.D. Forty, *I.D.* magazine --- 2005 Red Dot for High Quality in Communication Design memberships 2004 Type Directors Club --- 2003 Association of Dutch Designers

Studio Pip and Co. Andrew Ashton, Shelley Bennet, Sarah Fruzer. Live and work in Melbourne practice 2003-present Studio Pip and Co.; 1994 founder, Precinct Design (AA) selected projects 2007 identity, Melbourne Fringe Festival --- 2007 identity, Melbourne International Chamber Music Competition --- 2005-6 identity, Melbourne Design Festival --- 2004 identity, National Design Centre, Victoria, Australia --- 2002 identity, Australian Graphic Design Association Awards --- 2000 identity, Australian Business Arts Foundation selected bibliography *The Age*, *Australian Art Monthly*, *Design Week*, *Eye*, and *Step* magazines awards AGDA Pinnacle Award --- Silver, Australian Writers and Art Directors Award --- 1998-2006 Australian Graphic Design Biennial Awards --- 2001-4 Melbourne Art Directors Awards memberships Alliance Graphique Internationale, Australian Graphic Design Association

Studio 't Brandt Weer Marenthe Otten, born 1969, Deverne, The Netherlands; Koen Geurts, born 1970, Bilzen, Belgium education 1990-94 Academy of Arts and Visual Communication, Genk, Belgium (MO, KG) selected projects 2007 book, *Zeelander Collectie*, Zeeuws Museum, Middelburg, The Netherlands --- 2007 article illustration, "The Secret," *Elle Holland* --- 2007 identity, Villa Basta cultural center, Belgium --- identity, Dorrith de Roode Fashion Design selected bibliography 2007 *Emergence 6*, Pyramyd, Paris --- 2006 *Experimental Magazine* --- 2005 *Clubspotting*, Happy Books, Rome selected exhibitions 2004 *Fashion Award Sector Showcase*, D&AD, London awards 2006 Certificate of Typographic Excellence, New York Type Directors Club memberships 1999 Association of Dutch Designers

Sulki & Min Sulki Choi, born 1977; Min Choi, born 1971. Live and work in Seoul education Jan van Eyck Academie, Maastricht; Yale University, New Haven (SC, MC) --- Choongang University, Arseong, South Korea (SC) --- Seoul National University (MC) practice Pentagram, New York (SC) --- Imagedrome, Seoul (MC) selected projects 2007 identity, Anyang Public Arts Foundation --- catalog, Korean Pavilion at the Venice Biennale, Arts Council Korea --- 2007 identity, Springwave Festival --- 2006-7 identity, Insa Art Space --- 2006 catalog, Gwangju Biennale Foundation --- 2006 website and book, *Report (Not Announcement)*, BAK selected bibliography 2006 "Sulki and Min Choi," *Idea* magazine --- 2006 "Sulki and Min Choi," *Art in Culture* --- 2005 "Sulki and Min," *IdN* magazine --- 2005 "Sulki and Min," *Art & Design* magazine --- 2004 "Graphic Design in Korea," *Idea* magazine selected exhibitions 2006 *Graphic Design in the White Cube* and *Work from Mars*, Moravian Gallery, Brno --- 2006 *Sulki & Min 060421-060513*, Gallery Factory, Seoul --- 2006 *Frame Builders*, Insa Art Space, Seoul --- 2005 *Parallel Life*, Frankfurter Kunstverein, Frankfurt awards 2006 Art Award of the Year, Arts Council Korea --- 2005 50 Books/50 Covers, AIGA --- 2005 De Best Verzorgde Boeken

Surface Markus Weisbeck, born 1965, Offenburg, Germany. Lives and works in Berlin education HfG Offenbach, Germany selected bibliography 2005 *Surface*, Youth Press, Brussels --- 2000 *Trade*, Scalo, Zurich --- 1999 *Trigger*, Die Gestalten Verlag, Berlin --- 1999 *Whereishere*, Laurence King, London selected exhibitions 2006 *Whitney Biennial*, New York --- *International Poster Exhibition*, Japan

Fumio Tachibana born 1968, Hiroshima. Lives and works in Tokyo education 1992-94 Tokyo National University of Fine Arts and Music --- 1988-92 Musashino Art University selected exhibitions 2005 *D-Tay*, Gallery 360, Tokyo --- 2005 *L'arbre qui cachait une incroyable forêt*, Shiseido, Paris --- 2004 *On Conceptual Clothing*, Museum of Musashino Art University, Tokyo --- 1999 Mattress Factory, Pittsburgh --- 1995 *Made in USA*, Sagacho Exhibit Space, Tokyo awards 2004 Grand Prix, International Biennale of Graphic Design in Brno --- 2001 Gold Prize, New York Art Directors Club --- 1997 Gold Prize, Tokyo Type Directors Club --- 1996 Gold Medal, International Biennale of Graphic Design in Brno memberships 2006 Alliance Graphique Internationale --- 1997 Tokyo Type Directors Club

Andrea Tinnes born 1969, Germany. Lives and works in Berlin education 1996-98 California Institute of the Arts, Valencia, California --- 1989-96 University of Applied Sciences, Mainz, Germany practice 2007-present professor, Burg-Giebichenstein, University of Art and Design, Halle, Germany --- 2004-present founder, Typecuts font studio, Berlin --- 2006-present professor, Bergen National Academy of the Arts, Bergen, Norway selected projects 2002-present identity, German Film Festival, Tbilisi --- 2007 exhibition poster, *Location:Georgien* --- 2007 typeface, Viceroy, ReVerb, with Verena Gerlach and Andreas Eigendorf --- 2006 typeface, PTL Roletta, Primetype selected bibliography 2007 "Typeface/Interface" by Jan Middendorp, *Eye* magazine --- 2007 *Contemporary Graphic Design*, Taschen, Cologne --- 2006 *Influences: A Lexicon of Contemporary Graphic Design*, Die Gestalten Verlag, Berlin --- 2003 *Graphic Design for the 21st Century*, Taschen, Cologne selected exhibitions 2007 *Type Directors Club53*, The One Club, New York --- International Festival of Posters and Graphic Arts, Chaumont --- 2005 *Alter Ego*, California Institute of the Arts, Valencia, California awards 2007 Certificate of Typographic Excellence, New York Type Directors Club --- 2001 Red Dot Award for Communication Design, Design Zentrum Nordrhein Westfalen

Toko Eva Dijkstra, born 1974, Barendrecht, The Netherlands; Michael Lugmayr, born 1970, Krefeld, Germany. Live and work in Sydney education Academy of Fine Arts and Design St. Joost, Breda, The Netherlands (ED, ML) practice Toko; Otherwise Inc.; Studio Dumbar (ED, ML) --- Lava (ED) --- Frost (ML) selected projects 2007-present book, *Confused Type*, self-published --- 2007 identity, *Cut&Paste*, Sydney --- 2005-present art direction, *Code* magazine --- 2006 identity, Het Zuidelijk Toneel theater company selected bibliography 2007 *Empty* magazine --- 2007 *Emergence*, Pyramyd, Paris --- 2006 "The Condition of Graphic Design," *Idea* magazine --- 2006 "Dutch Design," *Experiments* magazine

Typographic Masonry Richard Niessen, born 1972; Esther de Vries, born 1974. Live and work in Amsterdam education Gerrit Rietveld Academie, Amsterdam selected projects 2007 exhibition design, "TM-City" installation, International Festival of Posters and Graphic Arts, Chaumont --- 2007 book, *Start a New Art World*, Die Gestalten Verlag, Berlin, with Ad de Jong --- 2006 mural, Stadsdeel Zuidoost, Amsterdam --- 2006 poster, KONG design store, Mexico City --- 2006 *Annual Report*, Stedelijk Museum, Amsterdam selected bibliography 2007 *TM-City*, Uitgeverij Boek, Amsterdam --- 2007 "Opgeruimde punkmentaliteit in boekvorm," *De Volkskrant*, Amsterdam --- 2006 "Graphic Design, the Remix," *Items*, BIS, Amsterdam --- 2004 "Nieuwe letters Richard Niessen," *Items*, BIS, Amsterdam selected exhibitions 2007 *TM-City*, International Festival of Posters and Graphic Arts, Chaumont --- 2006 *Ogaki International Invitational Poster Exhibition*, Ogaki, Japan --- 2006 *Work from Mars*, International Biennale of Graphic Design in Brno --- 2005 *China Poster Biennale*, China Academy of Art, Hangzhou --- 2004 *Mark*, Stedelijk Museum, Amsterdam --- 2004 *Place*, CCCB, Barcelona awards 2006 Best Verzorge Boeken --- 2006 Ehrendiplom Schönste Bücher aus aller Welt --- 2004 Best Verzorge Boeken

Naohiro Ukawa born 1968, Kagawa, Japan selected exhibitions 2006 *Rapt! Twenty Contemporary Artists from Japan*, Kings ARI, Melbourne --- 2005 *Gundam*, Suntory Museum, Osaka --- 2004 *UZULIVE!!*, Chukyo University, Aichi, Japan --- 2004 *!!!!!SEED WARS!!!!!*, Transplant Gallery, New York --- 2001 *JAM*, Barbican Gallery, London awards 2003 Best Dance Music Video, MTV --- 2003 Best Digital Video, SpaceShower TV

United Visual Artists (UVA) Chris Bird, born 1972, Middlesex, UK; Matt Clark, born 1974, London; Dave Ferner, born 1983, Newcastle, UK; Dave Green, born 1977. Bloxwich, UK; Joel Gethin Lewis, born 1980, London; James Medcraft, born 1982, Essex, UK; Ash Nehru, born 1972, Middlesex, UK; Annika Stark, born 1976, Wuppertal, Germany. Live and work in London education 1988-91 Leeds University, Leeds (CB) --- 1994-97 Camberwell College of Arts, London (MC) --- 2002-5 Ravensbourne College of Design and Communication, Kent (DF) --- 1996-2000 Staffordshire University, Stoke on Trent, UK (DG) --- 2001-3 Royal College of Art, London; 1998-2001 Imperial College, London (JGL) --- 2001-5 London College of Printing, London (JM) --- 1991-94 Trinity College, Cambridge University (AN) --- 1998-2001 University of East London, London (AS) practice 2002-present UVA; 1991-2002 free-lance graphic design (CB) --- 2002-present UVA; 1999-2002 art and design director, BCD, London; 1998-99 freelance graphic design; 1997-98 *Guest List* magazine, London (MC) --- 2005-present UVA; 2003-5 freelance graphic design (DF) --- 2006-present UVA, 2001-3 Firstsight Vision, London (DG) --- 2005-present UVA; 2004 Fabrica, Treviso, Italy; 2000-4 *Dazed&Confused* magazine, London; 2001 AMO, Rotterdam and New York (JGL) --- 2005-present UVA; 2001-5 freelance graphic design (JM) --- 2003-present UVA; 1997-2003 owner, Autopilot, London; 1994-97 Eidos Interactive, London (AN) --- 2004-present UVA; 2002-4 freelance film production; 2001-2 NBC, London; 1996-2001 Grey Advertising, Düsseldorf (AS) selected projects 2006-7 installation, "Volume," Victoria and Albert Museum, London --- 2004-7 installation, Kabaret's Prophecy Nightclub, London --- 2006 music video, Colder, Output Records --- 2006 installation, Storeage design agency --- 2006 installation, "Echo," Tate Modern, London --- 2002-3 stage design, Massive Attack selected bibliography 2007 "All Eyes and Ears," *Frame* magazine --- 2007 "The Beauty of Non-Interacting," *ArtReview* --- 2006 *VJ: Audio-Visual Art and VJ Culture*, Laurence King, London --- 2005 *New Bar and Club Design*, Hali Publications, London --- 2004 *Club Design*, daab, Cologne selected exhibitions 2007 *Picture House*, Belsay Hall, Newcastle --- 2007 *Pixelache*, Museum of Contemporary Art Kiasma, Helsinki, Finland --- 2006 *Estación Futura*, ArtFutura, Barcelona --- 2005 *OneDotZero*, Institute of Contemporary Arts, London --- 2005 *Mirror*, Kemistry Gallery, London awards 2007 Outstanding Achievement award, D&AD

Yokoland Aslak Gurholt Rønsen, Espen Friberg, Thomas Nordby, born Oslo. Live and work in Oslo education 2002-5 National College of the Arts, Oslo; 2001-2 Central Saint Martins College of Art and Design, London (AGR) --- 2001-4 National College of the Arts, Oslo (EF) --- 2004-7 National College of the Arts, Oslo (TN) practice 2001-present Yokoland (AGR, EF) --- 2006-present Yokoland (TN) selected projects 2006-7 illustrations, *Parergon* magazine --- 2006-7 posters, LOAF/Lo Recordings --- 2005-present identity, By Alarm --- 2001-present identity, Metronomicon Audio selected bibliography 2007 Grafik 150, *Grafik* magazine --- 2007 "Grafik Pick of the Year 2006," *Grafik* magazine --- 2007 "European Design Annual," *Print* magazine --- 2006 "A Breath of Fresh Air," *I.D.* magazine --- 2006 *Yokoland: As We Go Up, We Go Down*, Die Gestalten Verlag, Berlin selected exhibitions 2007 *Harry Smith Anthology Remixed*, Alt. Gallery, Newcastle, UK --- 2007 *Under the Bushes, Under the Stars*, Reg Vardy Gallery, Sunderland, Norway --- 2006 *The Remix Project*, Sørlandet Art Museum, Kristiansand, Norway --- 2005 *Fra Det Ene til Det Andre*, Galleri Badet, Oslo awards 2007 nomination, D&AD --- 2007 Prize of Honor, By Alarm --- 2007 Art and Photography Book of the Year, Årets vakreste bøker --- 2007 Gold Award Book of the Year, Editorial Design, and Company Identity, Visueltprisen/Grafill --- 2006 Silver Award, Poster, Visueltprisen/Grafill

- A10, 149
- Abedini, Reza, 309
- Aer, 152
- AIDOS. See Italian Association for Women in Development
- Akkurat, 40
- Albergaria, José, 65
- Amakane, Suzy, 128
- Amos Toys, 193
- Amsterdam
  - Born, Julia, 36-39, 40
  - Brunner, Laurenz, 40-43
  - Buxó, Thomas, 52-55
  - Cobbenhagen & Hendriksen, 84-87
  - van Dam, Vanessa, 92-95
  - Gerritzen, Mieke, 140-143
  - Groot, Arjan, 148-151
  - van Halem, Hansje, 156-159
  - Maurer, Luna, 232-235
  - Office for Editorial Design, 268-271
  - 178 aardige ontwerpers, 276-279
  - Peško, Radim, 292-295
  - Sandberg, Martijn, 328-331
  - Typographic Masonry, 392-395
- APC, 65
- APFEL. See A Practice For Everyday Life
- Aristophanes, 200
- Arnhem
  - Catalogtree, 56-59
- Ashton, Andrew, 364
- Atrissi, Tarek, 16-19
- Aubry, Bastien, 124
- Audiau, Antoine, 12-15
- Austin, Paul, 220

- Bailey, Stuart, 100
- Balloon Animals, 356
- Baltimore
  - Post Typography, 296-299
- Bangkok International Art Festival, 185
- Bantjes, Marian, 20-23
- Barbara Says, 24-27, 65
- Barcelona
  - Meseguer, Laura, 240-243
  - Stavro, Astrid, 348-351
- Barendse, Jeroen, 216
- Baron, Fabien, 348
- Baroocha, Hisham, 76
- Barth, Stefanie, 356

- Bas Baker, Rik, 65
- Baur, Ruedi, curating:
  - Büro Uebele, 48-51
  - Cristina Chiappini, 72-75
  - Étienne Mineur, 248-251
  - Isabel Naegele, 252-255
  - Michelle Gubser, 152-155
  - Paul Cox, 88-91
  - Peter Bilak, 32-35
  - Siegel, Claudia, 336-339
  - Spector, 344-347
  - Surface, 376-379
- Beau!, 368
- Beauty and the Book (Born), 37
- Beck, 29, 117
- Beckand, Robert, 332
- Beirut
  - Atrissi, Tarek, 16-19
- Bell, Pedro, 212
- Benhadj, Sami, 196
- Berlin
  - Raeder, Manuel, 312-315
  - Tinnes, Andrea, 384-387
- Besems, Dinie, 232
- Betsky, Aaron, 52
- Big Active, 28-31
- Bilak, Peter, 32-35
- Birds Boutique, 352
- Bite IT, 45
- Blade Runner, 45
- Blasko, George, 281
- Bless, 312
- Boom, Irma, curating:
  - Arjan Groot, 148-151
  - Astrid Stavro, 348-351
  - Cobbenhagen & Hendriksen, 84-87
  - Hansje van Halem, 156-159
  - Julia Born, 36-39
  - Martijn Sandberg, 328-331
  - 178 aardige ontwerpers, 276-279
  - 75B, 332-335
  - Thomas Buxó, 52-55
  - Vanessa van Dam, 92-95
- Boredoms, 117
- Borkson, Sam, 133
- Born, Julia, 36-39, 40
- Bowie, David, 364
- Brooklyn
  - mgmt. design, 244-247
- Broquard, Dimitri, 124
- Brunner, Laurenz, 40-43
- Build, 44-47
- Buxó, Thomas, 52-55
- Byrne, David, 136

- Cape Town
  - Stegmann, Frauke, 352-355
- Carter, Ariel Apte, 244
- Carter, Kirsty, 8-11
- Cartier Foundation, 248
- Casa Brutus, 144
- Casco, 37
- Castro, Thomas, 216
- Catalogtree, 56-59
- Catalogue, 173
- CDN. See Centre Dramatique National
- Centre Dramatique National (CDN), 200
- Chan, Theseus, 60-63
- Change Is Good, 64-67
- Cheng, Alicia, 244
- Cheuk, Deanne, 68-71
- Chiappini, Cristina, 72-75
- Chicago
  - Farrell, Stephen, 120-123
- Chichester, UK
  - Hardie, George, 160-163
- La Chinoise, 284
- Chippendale, Brian, 76-79
- Cho, Peter, 80-83
- Chung, Alice, 272
- Cinema Portugal film festival, 25
- Ciocci, Jacob, 289
- Ciocci, Jessica, 289
- Cobbenhagen & Hendriksen, 84-87
- Comme des Garçons Guerrilla Store +65, 60
- Cox, Paul, 88-91
- Crazy Ken Band, 128
- Crumb, R., 317
- The Crying of Lot 49 (Pynchon), 100

- van Dam, Vanessa, 92-95
- De Bondt, Sara, 96-99
- Design Miami, 220
- Designer's Republic, 45
- Designprijs Rotterdam 2007, 332
- van Deursen, Linda, 93
- Dexter Sinister, 100-103
- Dialogmuseum, 253
- van Dijk, Bob, 104-107
- Dijkstra, Eva, 389
- Dot Dot Dot, 284
- Double Dagger, 296
- Dressen, Markus, 345
- Duchamp, Marcel, 165
- Duplessis, Arem, 108-111

- ÉCAL. See École Cantonale d'Art de Lausanne
- École Cantonale d'Art de Lausanne (ÉCAL), 196
- Eeuwens, Adam, 52
- Ekhorn, Kjell, 260
- EkhornForss Limited, 260
- Enlightenment, 112-115
- Die Entenrepublik Gamsenteich, 336
- EYE, 116-119

- Fabrica, 317
- Farrell, Stephen, 120-123
- Fedra, 32
- Fernandes, Millôr, 320
- FiFFteen, 361
- FLAG Aubry/Broquard, 124-127
- Flamingo Studio, 128-131
- Flirt, 25, 65
- Forss, Jon, 260
- Fort Thunder, 76
- Foucault, Michel, 52
- Foundation 33, 97
- Frank, Michael, 256
- Frankfurt
  - Surface, 376-379
- Friberg, Espen, 404
- Friends With You, 132-135
- Frisk, Ryan Pescatore, 361
- Frostner, Martin, 136-139
- Fujimoto, Yasushi, 60

- van Gastel, Mikon, 281
- Gephart, Sarah, 244
- Gerritzen, Mieke, 140-143
- Geurts, Koen, 368
- Gibson, Brian, 76
- Gill, Eric, 216
- Girard, Alexander, 240
- Globish, 88
- GM. See Golden Masters
- Godard, Jean-Luc, 284
- Goggin, James, curating:
  - Dexter Sinister, 100-103
  - Frauke Stegmann, 352-355
  - Jonathan Hares, 164-167
  - Kazunari Hattori, 168-171
  - Laurenz Brunner, 40-43
  - Lehni-Trüb, 208-211
  - Manuel Raeder, 312-315
  - Mark Owens, 284-287
  - Sulki & Min, 372-375
  - Will Holder, 172-175
- Golden Masters (GM), 393
- Gomes, António Silveira, 25
- Good Design Company, 144-147
- Gore, Al, 244

- Górska, Joanna, 176
- Groot, Arjan, 148-151
- Gross, Daniel, 56
- Grupo Nudo, 225
- Gubser, Michelle, 152-155
- Guerrillazine, 60

- The Hague
  - Bilak, Peter, 32-35
  - van Dijk, Bob, 104-107
  - LUST, 216-219
  - Strange Attractors, 360-363
  - Studio 't Brandt Weer, 368-371
- van Halem, Hansje, 156-159
- Hardie, George, 160-163
- Hares, Jonathan, 164-167
- Hasting, Julia, curating:
  - Antoine Audiau, 12-15
  - Catalogtree, 56-59
  - Change Is Good, 64-67
  - Henrik Nygren, 264-267
  - Jürg Lehni, 204-207
  - Körner Union, 196-199
  - Manuel Warosz, 12-15
  - Michal Sahar, 324-327
  - Radim Peško, 292-295
  - Stiletto, 356-359
  - Yokoland, 404-407
- Hattori, Kazunari, 168-171
- Haus der Kunst, 236
- Havana
  - Marín, Eduardo, 224-227
- Hayashi, Nakako, 168
- Hayward, Tarik, 196
- "Hektor," 204
- Hemingway, Ernest, 120
- Hemmo, Irit, 324
- Here and There, 168
- heta-uma design movement, 113, 128
- Hiorthøy, Kim, 404
- Hirschfeld, Julie, 356
- Holder, Will, 172-175
- Holland Dance Festival, 104
- Homework, 176-179
- Hong Kong
  - Punchman, Michael, 304-307
- Hsu, Karen, 272
- Hugo, Mario, 180-183

- Ibelings, Hans, 149
- Illustration, 113
- Imaginary Forces, 281
- An Inconvenient Truth (Gore), 244
- Institute Néerlandais, 65
- Institute of Matter, 304
- Interview, 348
- Itakura, Keiko, 184-187
- Italian Association for Women in Development (AIDOS), 73
- Ito, Keiji, 188-191

- Jackson, Trevor, 45
- Japan Society for Natural Disaster Science, 396
- Jarvis, James, 192-195
- JetLag, 104
- Jones, Ben, 289
- Just-In-Time Workshop and Occasional Bookstore, 100

- Keedy, Jeffery, 384
- Kewpie, 168
- Kimera, 229
- Kinky Muff Land, 256
- Körner Union, 196-199
- Krishnamurthy, Prem, 300
- Kuitenbrouwer, Carel, 268
- Kuti, Fela Anikulapo, 212
- Kwintessens, 368

- Laboratoires CCCP = Dr. Pêche + Melle Rose, 200-203
- Lagos, Nigeria
  - Lemi, Ghariokwu, 212-215
- Lambert, Fred, 152
- Landowska, Wanda, 8
- Lausanne
  - Hares, Jonathan, 164-167
  - Körner Union, 196-199
- Lehni, Jürg, 204-207
- Lehni, Urs, 209
- Lehni-Trüb, 208-211
- Leipzig
  - Siegel, Claudia, 336-339
  - Spector, 344-347
- Lemi, Ghariokwu, 212-215
- LeWitt, Sol, 165
- Liemburg, Harmen, 393
- Lightning Bolt, 76
- Lisbon
  - Barbara Says, 24-27, 65
- Little Yellow Writing Hood, 361
- London
  - Big Active, 28-31
  - Build, 44-47
  - Carter, Kirsty, 8-11
  - De Bondt, Sara, 96-99
  - Hares, Jonathan, 164-167
  - Holder, Will, 172-175
  - Jarvis, James, 192-195
  - MadeThought, 220-223
  - Non-Format, 260-263
  - Thomas, Emma, 8-11
  - United Visual Artists, 400-403
- Los Angeles
  - Cho, Peter, 80-83
  - Owens, Mark, 284-287

- Louwé, Harmine, 268
- Lovink, Geert, 140
- Lugmayr, Michael, 389
- Lunenfeld, Peter, 140
- Lupton, Ellen, curating:
  - Deanne Cheuk, 68-71
  - Homework, 176-179
  - Marian Bantjes, 20-23
  - Martin Frostner, 136-139
  - mgmt. design, 244-247
  - Mieke Gerritzen, 140-143
  - Peter Cho, 80-83
  - Post Typography, 296-299
  - Stephen Farrell, 120-123
  - Thomas Mayfried, 236
- LUST, 216-219

- MadeThought, 220-223
- Maeda, John, 81, 248
- Mafundikwa, Saki, curating:
  - Andy Rementer, 316-319
  - Arem Duplessis, 108-111
  - Claudio Rocha, 320-323
  - Eddie Opara, 280-283
  - Gabriel Martínez Meave, 228-229
  - Ghariokwu Lemi, 212-215
  - Iman Raad, 308-311
  - Jennifer Sonderby, 340-343
  - Laura Meseguer, 240-243
  - Tarek Atrissi, 16-19
- Maggots, 76
- Mainz, Germany
  - Naegele, Isabel, 252-255
- Maison d'Art Bernard Anthonioz, 65
- Maltha, Joris, 56
- de Marco, Caio, 320
- de Marco, Tony, 320
- Marín, Eduardo, 224-227
- Martens, Karel, 216, 292
- Martínez Meave, Gabriel, 228-231
- Maurer, Luna, 232-235
- Mayfried, Thomas, 236-239
- Medea, 384
- Melbourne
  - Studio Pip and Co., 364-367
- Meldem, Guy, 196
- Meseguer, Laura, 240-243
- Metronomicon Audio, 404
- Mexico City
  - Martínez Meave, Gabriel, 228-231
- mgmt. design, 244-247
- Miami
  - Friends With You, 132-135
- Michaels, Adam, 300

- Middendorp, Jan, curating:
  - Andrea Tinnes, 384-387
  - Barbara Says, 24-27
  - Bob van Dijk, 104-107
  - Eduardo Marín, 224-227
  - Luna Maurer, 232-235
  - LUST, 216-219
  - Office for Editorial Design, 268-271
  - Strange Attractors, 360-363
  - Studio 't Brandt Weer, 368-371
  - Typographic Masonry, 392-395
- Milan
  - Stiletto, 356-359
- Mineur, Étienne, 248-251
- Mista Gonzo, 128
- Miyake, Issey, 248
- Mizuno, Manabu, 144
- Moderna Museet, 265
- Mroszczak, József, 176
- Mu, 68
- Muis, Rens, 332
- Munich
  - Mayfried, Thomas, 236-239
- Murakami, Takashi, 113
- Mushroom Girls Virus (Cheuk), 68

- Nadel, Dan, curating:
  - Brian Chippendale, 76-79
  - EYE, 116-119
  - FLAG Aubry/Broquard, 124-127
  - Flamingo Studio, 128-131
  - Friends With You, 132-135
  - George Hardie, 160-163
  - James Jarvis, 192-195
  - Omnivore, 272-275
  - Paper Rad, 288-291
  - Sara De Bondt, 96-99
- Naegele, Isabel, 252-255
- Namaiki, 256-259
- Nemoto, Takashi, 128
- New York
  - Cheuk, Deanne, 68-71
  - Dexter Sinister, 100-103
  - Duplessis, Arem, 108-111
  - Hugo, Mario, 180-183
  - Lehni, Jürg, 204-207
  - Omnivore, 272-275
  - Opara, Eddie, 280-283
  - Project Projects, 300-303
  - Stiletto, 356-359
  - Strange Attractors, 360-363
- New York Times Magazine, 108-111
- Niessen, Richard, 393
- Nieuwenhuizen, Dimitri, 216
- Nieves, 209
- Ninja, 76

- Njoya, Sultan, 320
- Non-Format, 260-263
- Nygren, Henrik, 264-267

- Office for Editorial
  Design, 268-271
- Omnivore, 272-275
- 178 aardige ontwerpers,
  276-279
- Opara, Eddie, 280-283
- l'Opéra de Nancy et de
  Lorraine, 88
- Orléans, France
  - Laboratoires CCCP = Dr.
    Pêche + Melle Rose,
    200-203
- Oslo
  - Yokoland, 404-407
- Otten, Marenthe, 368
- Owens, Mark, 284-287

- Panter, Gary, 124
- Paper Rad, 288-291
- Paris
  - Audiau, Antoine, 12-15
  - Change Is Good, 64-67
  - Cox, Paul, 88-91
  - Gubser, Michelle, 152-155
  - Mineur, Étienne, 248-251
  - Warosz, Manuel, 12-15
- Parker, Ben, 220
- People's Republic of Korea
  (RPDC), 225
- Perec, Georges, 136
- Peško, Radim, 292-295
- Philadelphia
  - Rementer, Andy, 316-319
- Phillips, Brett, curating:
  - Big Active, 28-31
  - Build, 44-47
  - Emma Thomas, 8-11
  - Kirsty Carter, 8-11
  - MadeThought, 220-223
  - Mario Hugo, 180-183
  - Non-Format, 260-263
  - Project Projects, 300-303
  - Studio Pip and Co.,
    364-367
  - Toko, 388-391
  - United Visual Artists,
    400-403
- PictureBox, 76
- Place, Michael, 45
- Pollard, Robert, 404
- Post Typography, 296-299
- A Practice For Everyday
  Life (APFEL), 8-11
- Profeta Gentileza, 320
- Project Projects, 300-303
- Providence
  - Chippendale, Brian, 76-79
  - Paper Rad, 288-291
- Punchman, Michael, 304-307
- Pynchon, Thomas, 100

- Raad, Iman, 308-311
- Raeder, Manuel, 312-315
- Rahmens, 144
- Reinfurt, David, 100, 284
- Rementer, Andy, 316-319
- Right About Now lecture
  series, 40
- Rocha, Claudio, 320-323
- Rome
  - Chiappini, Cristina,
    72-75
- Rønsen, Aslak Gurholt, 404
- Rotterdam
  - 75B, 332-335
- RPDC. See People's Republic
  of Korea
- Russo, Karen, 324
- Ryuko Tsushin, 168

- Sahar, Michal, 324-327
- San Francisco
  - Sonderby, Jennifer,
    340-343
- Sandberg, Martijn, 328-331
- Sandoval, Arturo, 133
- São Paulo
  - Rocha, Claudio, 320-323
  - "Schizoide," 200
- Schröder, Alexander, 312
- Scriptographer, 204
- Seoul
  - Sulki & Min, 372-375
- 75B, 332-335
- Shaughnessy, Adrian, 404
- Siegel, Claudia, 336-339
- Silex, 124
- Singapore
  - Chan, Theseus, 60-63
- Skakun, Jerzy, 176
- Smith, David D., 256
- Snippe, Raf, 393
- Sommerhalder, Benjamin, 209
- Sonderby, Jennifer, 340-343
- Specter, 373
- Specter Press, 373
- Spector, 344-347
- Stavro, Astrid, 348-351
- Stegmann, Frauke, 352-355
- Stig, Martine, 93
- Stiletto, 356-359
- Stockholm
  - Frostner, Martin, 136-139
  - Nygren, Henrik, 264-267
- Strals, Nolan, 296

- Strange Attractors, 360-363
- Strange Kinoko Dance
  Company, 256
- Studio Dumbar, 104, 268,
  389
- Studio Pip and Co., 364-367
- Studio 't Brandt Weer,
  368-371
- Stuttgart
  - Uebele, Büro, 48-51
- Subito, 185
- Sugiyama, Hiro, 113
- Sulki & Min, 372-375
- Super Flat, 113
- SuperDeluxe, 256
- Surface, 376-379
- Sydney
- Toko, 388-391

- Tachibana, Fumio, 380-383
- Takeo Paper Show, 144
- Tanaami, Keiichi, curating:
  - Enlightenment, 112-115
  - Fumio Tachibana, 380-383
  - Good Design Company,
    144-147
  - Keiji Ito, 188-191
  - Keiko Itakura, 184-187
  - Laboratoires CCCP = Dr.
    Pêche + Melle Rose,
    200-203
  - Michael Punchman, 304-307
  - Namaiki, 256-259
  - Naohiro Ukawa, 396-399
  - Theseus Chan, 60-63
- Tehran
  - Raad, Iman, 308-311
- Tel Aviv
  - Sahar, Michal, 324-427
- Thomas, Emma, 8-11
- Tinnes, Andrea, 384-387
- Tokion, 68
- Toko, 388-391
- Tokyo
  - Enlightenment, 112-115
  - EYE, 116-119
  - Flamingo Studio, 128-131
  - Good Design Company,
    144-147
  - Hattori, Kazunari,
    168-171
  - Itakura, Keiko, 184-187
  - Ito, Keiji, 188-191
  - Namaiki, 256-259
  - Tachibana, Fumio, 380-383
  - Ukawa, Naohiro, 396-399
- Tomasula, Steve, 120
- Tomaszewski, Henryk, 176
- Tomorrow Book Studio, 173
- Track, 113
- Trüb, Lex, 209
- Tupigrafia, 320

- TypeCon2004, 320
- Type-Ø-Tones, 240
- Typographic Masonry,
  392-395
- typography, Arabic, 16, 309
- Tyrell, Eldon, 45

- Uebele, Büro, 48-51
- Ukawa, Naohiro, 396-399
- United Visual Artists
  (UVA), 400-403
- "urban vinyl," 193
- UVA. See United Visual
  Artists

- van Middelkoop, Catelijne,
  361
- Vancouver
  - Bantjes, Marian, 20-23
- VAS (Tomasula), 120
- Volgare, 120
- Vos, Pieter, 332
- de Vries, Esther, 393
- Vulpinari, Olmar, 317

- Warosz, Manuel, 12-15
- Warsaw
  - Homework, 176-179
- Weisbeck, Markus, 376
- WERK, 60
- Wijdeveld, Hendrik Th., 393
- Willen, Bruce, 296
- Willis, Wesley, 209
- Windingen, 393
- Windlin, Cornel, 40
- The Wire, 260
- Wolbers, Hans, 309
- women's rights, 73
- WORK, 60

- Yokoland, 404-407
- Yumura, Teruhiko, 113, 128

- ZDB. See Zé dos Bois
- Zé dos Bois (ZDB), 25, 65
- Zurich
  - FLAG Aubry/Broquard,
    124-127
  - Lehni, Jürg, 204-207
  - Lehni-Trüb, 208-211